TERTULLIAN
TREATISES ON PENANCE

ON PENITENCE
DE PAENITENTIA

ON PURITY
DE PUDICITIA

ANCIENT CHRISTIAN WRITERS

THE WORKS OF THE FATHERS IN TRANSLATION

EDITED BY

JOHANNES QUASTEN, S.T.D.
Catholic University of America
Washington, D.C.

WALTER J. BURGHARDT, S.J., S.T.D.
Woodstock College
Woodstock, Md.

No. 28

TERTULLIAN

TREATISES ON PENANCE

ON PENITENCE
AND
ON PURITY

TRANSLATED AND ANNOTATED

BY

WILLIAM P. LE SAINT, S.J., S.T.D.

Professor of Theology
West Baden College
West Baden Springs, Indiana

NEWMAN PRESS

New York, N.Y./Ramsey, N.J.

Library of Congress
Catalog Card Number: 58-10746

ISBN: 0-8091-0150-5

PUBLISHED BY PAULIST PRESS
Editorial Office: 1865 Broadway, New York, N.Y. 10023
Business Office: 545 Island Road, Ramsey, N.J. 07446

PRINTED AND BOUND IN THE UNITED STATES OF AMERICA

CONTENTS

PAGE

ON PENITENCE

INTRODUCTION 3

TEXT

PAGAN PENITENCE 14
THE CHRISTIAN CONCEPT 15
SIN AND PENITENCE 16
NATURE AND DIVISIONS OF SINS 17
GOD'S PARDON THE FRUIT OF PENITENCE . . . 20
CONVERSION AND RELAPSE 21
THE PENITENCE OF CATECHUMENS 23
WARNINGS AGAINST PRESUMPTION 24
PENITENCE OF THE BAPTIZED 27
SCRIPTURE PROOFS OF GOD'S MERCY 29
EXOMOLOGESIS 31
PUBLIC PENANCE DIFFICULT BUT SALUTARY . . . 32
VALUE OF BODILY MORTIFICATION 34
EFFICACY OF EXOMOLOGESIS 35

ON PURITY

INTRODUCTION 41

TEXT

IN PRAISE OF PURITY 53
A SHAMEFUL EDICT 54
ENEMIES OF CHASTITY 55
THE APPEAL TO SCRIPTURE 57
REMISSIBLE AND IRREMISSIBLE SINS 59
AN OBJECTION ANSWERED 60
A QUESTION OF TERMINOLOGY 61
GRAVITY OF ADULTERY PROVED BY THE OLD LAW . . 62
INCONSISTENCY OF THE SENSUALISTS 63
THE OLD LAW AND THE NEW 65
BIBLICAL EXAMPLES 66

THE PARABLES OF THE LOST SHEEP AND THE DRACHMA . 68
CORRECT INTERPRETATION OF THE PARABLES . . 70
THE PRODIGAL SON 72
SOME PRINCIPLES OF EXEGESIS 75
THE PRODIGAL A TYPE OF THE PAGAN SINNER . . 76
CONCLUDING COMMENT ON THE PARABLES . . . 79
PENANCE AND PARDON NECESSARY FOR PAGANS . . 80
THE SHEPHERD OF ADULTERERS 82
THE EXAMPLE OF CHRIST 83
THE APOSTOLIC DECREE 83
THE INCESTUOUS CORINTHIAN NOT PARDONED BY PAUL . 85
HYMENAEUS AND ALEXANDER 88
POINTS OF CONTRAST BETWEEN FIRST AND SECOND
    CORINTHIANS 90
FURTHER PROOFS THAT PAUL DID NOT FORGIVE INCEST . 95
CONSISTENCY OF THE APOSTLE 98
PAUL'S ATTITUDE TO MARRIAGE 100
CONDEMNATION OF IMPURITY 102
SCRIPTURE REFUSES PARDON TO ADULTERY . . . 106
ST. JOHN'S TEACHING IN THE APOCALYPSE . . . 109
THE EVIDENCE OF HIS FIRST EPISTLE 111
THE EPISTLE TO THE HEBREWS 115
PRESCRIPTIONS OF LEVITICUS 116
PRIVILEGES PECULIAR TO THE APOSTLES . . . 118
THE POWER OF THE KEYS IS PERSONAL TO PETER . . 120
MARTYRS AND THE FORGIVENESS OF SINS . . . 122
A FINAL WORD 124
LIST OF ABBREVIATIONS 127

NOTES
ON PENITENCE 131
ON PURITY 189

INDEXES 299
REFERENCES
    1. OLD AND NEW TESTAMENT 301
    2. AUTHORS 305
    3. LATIN AND GREEK WORDS 310
    4. GENERAL INDEX 317

ON
PENITENCE

INTRODUCTION

Orthodox Christianity regards the doctrine of the divine forgiveness of sins as an essential article of faith. The nature of this forgiveness, its manner and measure, its causes and its effects, have all been subjects of controversy, but whoever accepts the Apostles' Creed as an expression of elementary Christian doctrine professes his belief in the basic truth that in some sense, in some way and under certain conditions God does pardon the sins of men. This belief has its foundation in Scripture [1] and finds its historical expression in the traditional teaching of the Church. The great interest of Tertullian's treatises on repentance derives from the influence which they exercised on the development of this tradition in the West, and from the contribution which they make to our understanding of the Church's ministerial forgiveness of sins at a period quite close to the apostolic or sub-apostolic age. By common consent of competent critics they are the two most important documents of ancient Christian literature for the study of one of the most difficult questions in the history of dogma: the doctrine and discipline of ecclesiastical penance during the first centuries of our era. Bernhard Poschmann, a writer whose authority in all that concerns the early history of penitential theology is unexcelled, has stated that the judgement which one forms of the theory and practice of penance in Christian antiquity will be determined, in large measure, by the interpretation which one puts upon the *De paenitentia* and *De pudicitia* of Tertullian. [2]

3

The penitential system of the early Church was founded on her belief that she had received from Christ a power to remit and to retain sin.[3] The earliest post-canonical evidence that this power was exercised in the forgiveness of sins committed after Baptism is preserved in the *Pastor Hermae*, an apocryphal apocalyptic tract written, at least in part, to refute the opinions of 'certain teachers' who insisted that there was no ecclesiastical penance but that of Baptism.[4] Further evidence from the same period is furnished by more or less explicit and detailed statements in Irenaeus, Clement of Alexandria and certain Church Orders composed at this time, particularly the Syriac *Didascalia* and the so-called *Apostolic Tradition* of Hippolytus; there are, moreover, pertinent notices in Eusebius on the practice of Dionysius of Corinth (*c.* 171 A.D.) and the penance of Natalius at Rome (*c.* 200 A.D.); the subject is treated more completely by Origen in a number of interesting and instructive passages; the witness of Cyprian at the middle of the third century is, of course, formal and frequent.[5]

It is clear, then, that the teaching of Tertullian on the ecclesiastical forgiveness of sins does not exist in a literary vacuum. The evidence which his writings afford on the doctrine and discipline of the Church *circa* 200 A.D. may be summarized as follows. There is a well-known ritual of penance in the Church called *exomologesis*, established as a means of assisting members of the Church to obtain pardon for sins committed after Baptism. This ritual includes confession of one's sins and the performance of public penance by way of deprecation and satisfaction. It terminates directly in the restoration of the sinner to peace and communion with the Church, and, at least indirectly, in the forgiveness of his sins in the sight of God. The whole process is directed by ecclesiastical authority, and the pardon conceded at its close is granted by the bishop. Tertullian has no interest in ascribing the efficacy of *exomologesis* to any particular act or acts within the whole complexus. He is content that at the end of the process the sinner is reconciled not only to the Church but also to God Himself.[6]

This description of Tertullian's teaching is drawn from both the *De paenitentia* and the *De pudicitia*. As will be seen, they are works quite different in spirit, written for different purposes at different periods of his life, but the picture which they present of the orthodox Christian theory and practice of penance is essentially the same. The *De paenitentia* is a work of Tertullian's Catholic period, a kind of sermon addressed to the faithful on the subject of repentance and forgiveness, largely expository and hortatory in character, tolerant in tone. The *De pudicitia* was composed after Tertullian's lapse into Montanism. It is a violent, argumentative party pamphlet, directed against a particular piece of Church legislation on penance which Tertullian and his faction of rigid fanatics considered intolerably lax. It is significant that, in spite of these divergencies, the only substantial difference between the two treatises in what concerns the nature and administration of *exomologesis* is this: in the *De paenitentia* Tertullian places no restriction of any kind on the Church's power to forgive sins; in the *De pudicitia* he introduces the Montanist distinction between remissible and irremissible sins, conceding a power to the bishop to forgive the former but restricting forgiveness of the latter to God alone.

The interpretation of many passages in both treatises has been and remains controversial. This is true especially of those texts which bear on the existence of private penance in the early Church, the distinction between mortal and venial sins, the effect of episcopal absolution, the role of the faithful, particularly the martyrs, in the forgiveness of sins, the concept of compensatory satisfaction. The problem, however, which has been most discussed and about which the sharpest difference of opinion exists has to do with the crucial question of whether or not the Church granted pardon to the capital sins of apostasy, murder and adultery before the middle of the third century. Many theologians and historians of dogma assert that the *De paenitentia* and *De pudicitia* of Tertullian clearly prove that it was not the practice of the early Church to pardon serious sins; others insist, just as positively, that these treatises prove the exact opposite.[7] These and other controversial questions will be considered in the notes, in connection with the translation and interpretation of passages pertinent to each particular problem. No attempt can be made to settle long-standing disputes in footnotes to a text, but it is hoped that a complete and objective canvassing of the opposing arguments will be of some help to the interested reader in forming his own opinion as to the merits of rival positions.

The extreme difficulty and obscurity of Tertullian's style and language are responsible, in no small measure, for the development of the controversies here referred to. It is indeed unfortunate that subjects of such great interest and importance should be set forth in phrases which often seem designed to conceal rather than to reveal their author's thought. Serious students, however, will find that, in spite of their obscurity, the treatises are invaluable not only as source books for the theology of penance but also for the light which they throw on many other questions relating to the life and faith of the early Church. Tertullian is notoriously the most difficult of all Latin prose writers, yet he always means *something*, and the effort which one makes to pierce through to his meaning can be an enjoyable as well as a rewarding experience. The literary value of the *De paenitentia* and *De pudicitia* may seem negligible, but their theological and historical significance is unsurpassed. They are books to be studied, not merely read. Tertullian was one of the most learned men of his age,[8] and no one who is interested in the study of antiquity, whether secular or religious, will find any of his writings disappointing or dull.

Since the importance of these treatises is theological rather than literary or artistic, it has seemed best to translate them quite literally, even though this results in a version which reflects the distortions of Tertullian's style as well as the ambiguity of his thought, and even though one feels that with Tertullian, as with St. Paul, no literal translation can ever give the full meaning of all that he intends to say. A paraphrase of his thought would be easier to read and understand than a close reproduction of its original expression, but there is always the danger that in a free translation, particularly of controversial matter, the text will be amplified by interpretations and interpolations which are tendentious. In the interest of clarity and intelligibility difficult passages will be discussed in the notes; in the interest of impartiality the text will be translated as literally as possible.

All translators of Tertullian have found it necessary to apologize for the awkward English which is the result of their efforts to produce a faithful version of his vigorous and imaginative but highly irregular prose. His whole habit of thought and manner of expression, even his method of argumentation, are utterly foreign and strange to us. Such expressions as 'to drink the sheep of a second penance' (*De pud.* 10.12), and 'dregs of milk which contain the virus of lust' (*De pud.* 6.15) produce little effect upon the modern reader beyond a desire to emend the text. The ancients themselves found him difficult and obscure. Lactantius says he is *parum facilis, minus comptus, multum obscurus* (*Div. Inst.* 5.1.23) and Jerome describes him as *creber in sententiis sed difficilis in loquendo* (*Epist.* 58.10). Tertullian is a writer of marvelous fertility and inventiveness, yet these very qualities contribute to the incoherence which is so marked a characteristic of his style. His sentences are quite often poorly constructed, a jumble of ideas which pour out in unnatural combinations of words and phrases, strange metaphors, neologisms, cryptic allusions, paradoxes and paralogisms, antitheses, multiple parentheses—a rich but disordered miscellany complicated by asyndeton, ellipsis and the use of every form of brachylogy known to grammarians. Efforts to modernize Tertullian inevitably end in failure. Perhaps the best apology a translator can make for his work is that a polished version would not be faithful to a rough original; if his English does not read smoothly, it may be pleaded in extenuation that the Latin doesn't either.[9]

My thanks are due to the general editors for their understanding and kindness in permitting me to include in this volume all of the notes which I considered necessary for an adequate elucidation of the text. The theological importance of the two treatises and the great obscurity of Tertullian's language and style will explain the number and length of these notes. The *De paenitentia* and *De pudicitia* raise so many questions which have been treated in such detail by so many students that even to give an account of the pertinent literature requires considerable time and space. Then, too, a rather extensive annotation of the treatises seemed desirable in view of the fact that, although they have been studied carefully by philologists and theologians for many years—and with particular zeal during the past fifty years—there is no commentary on them in any language which gathers together into a single volume the results of these various investigations and makes them available to the reader as he puzzles out the meaning of the text.

ON PENITENCE [10]

The *De paenitentia*, as has been said, was written by Tertullian while he was yet a Catholic. It contains a brief explanation of what Christians understand by the virtue of penitence, discourses on the importance of this virtue and shows how it is to be practiced in the Church. It is not, however, and it was not intended to be, a systematic study of the penitential theory and practice of Christian antiquity. The purpose of the treatise is moral and ascetical, not didactic; the emphasis, throughout, is on the importance and necessity of penitence rather than on its nature or external forms. Quite probably it was originally a sermon which Tertullian preached to the people at Carthage; [11] it is direct and personal in its approach, often admonitory, resembling closely a type of composition which ancient rhetoricians described as 'paraenetic.' [12] Most patrologists are of the opinion that it was addressed to catechumens, but there are good reasons for holding with Rauschen that it was also intended as an instruction and exhortation for the baptized. [13]

The work falls naturally into three parts. In the first (cc. 1-4) Tertullian speaks of penance as a virtue. Pagans have no concept of what this virtue means. For them *paenitentia* is no more than an unpleasant emotion caused by a past act; it may even follow upon an act which was good in itself (c. 1). Christians, however, understand that it is sin which makes repentance necessary and gives it meaning. Repentance supposes the reprobation of one's evil deeds and an amendment of life; it is motivated by fear of God; it is required by the divine justice; it effects the forgiveness of sins and, thus, has salvation as its fruit (c. 2). Repentance is demanded for all sins, external and internal alike (c. 3). God Himself commands it and He has also promised to reward it (c. 4).

Chapters 5 and 6 deal more specifically with the penitence of those who have not yet been baptized. Conversion to a new life is essential in repentance, and once this conversion has been signed and sealed by Baptism it must never be 'unsealed' or repudiated by a return to sin (c. 5). The obligation of penitence presses most urgently upon the catechumens. The thought of their future Baptism must not encourage them to sin, rashly confiding in the pardon which they are about to receive. Forgiveness is certainly the effect of Baptism, but we are baptized *because* we have ceased to sin, not *in order that* we may cease to do so. Our freedom from punishment will be bought at the price of the penance we practice; if this penance does not include a sincere conversion, it is false coin and God will reject it (c. 6).

Chapters 7–12 have to do with the important question of post-baptismal penitence. Sins committed by persons who are not yet members of the Church are forgiven by *paenitentia prima*; this includes conversion and the reception of Baptism. If anyone should be so unfortunate as to sin after he has been baptized, God, in His mercy, allows him a *paenitentia secunda* for the forgiveness of his offense. This second penitence must not be neglected—and it may not be repeated (c. 7). The possibility of a second forgiveness is proved by a number of passages in the New Testament, particularly by the parables of the lost drachma, the lost sheep and the prodigal son (c. 8). *Paenitentia secunda* requires the performance of those external penitential acts which constitute the well-known discipline of *exomologesis* (c. 9). The performance of public penance is humiliating and most men try to avoid it, but if they neglect it, they cannot be saved (c. 10). It is proper that one should suffer when one has sinned (c. 11), yet the pain which *exomologesis* causes the sinner is as nothing to the punishment of hell which it enables him to escape (12).

This third section of the treatise has been much discussed and variously interpreted. It poses two principal problems, distinct but closely related: (1) Is the *paenitentia secunda* described here essentially an ecclesiastical process, terminated by ecclesiastical absolution, or is it a private personal matter between the sinner and God, terminated by an absolution [14] granted by God and by Him alone? (2) If it is terminated by an ecclesiastical absolution, does this reconcile the sinner to God or only to the Church? These questions will be treated at some length in notes on the text, but it may be said here, briefly, that the positions which seem to be most easily defended are these: (1) The *paenitentia secunda* of which Tertullian speaks in this treatise is necessarily externalized by *exomologesis*, and *exomologesis* is an ecclesiastical process which ends with ecclesiastical absolution. (2) This absolution reconciles the sinner directly and immediately to the Church but indirectly and mediately to God Himself. These propositions are established with good probability from evidence in the *De paenitentia* itself; they are proved conclusively if this is combined with evidence supplied by the *De pudicitia.* The problem of whether or not the *peccata capitalia* were excluded from ecclesiastical absolution belongs to a discussion of the *De pudicitia* and will be examined in connection with the analysis of that treatise. It may be noted here, however, that there is nothing in the *De paenitentia* which indicates that the Church refused to pardon serious sins, and a number of passages which prove rather conclusively that she granted it.

It seems best to date the *De paenitentia* some time between 200 and 206 A.D. (Monceaux) or 198 and 202/3 A.D. (Harnack). It was certainly written before 207, the year in which Tertullian began to express some sympathy with Montanist ideas. There is not the slightest trace of any such sympathy in this treatise. In fact, as will be seen, Tertullian finds it necessary in the *De pudicitia* to repudiate the earlier tolerance which he showed in dealing with the subject of penitence, presumably tolerance of the sort manifested in the *De paenitentia*. Noeldechen believes that the work was composed early in the year 204 A.D., arguing (1) that the reference in c. 12.2 to recent volcanic disturbances is to be understood as an allusion to the eruption of Vesuvius in 203 A.D., (2) that the death of Plautian in January 204 A.D. occasioned Tertullian's remark on the nature of pagan repentance in c. 1.4, (3) that the special attention given to the ambitious conduct of office seekers, c. 11.4, indicates that Tertullian wrote shortly after the close of the year, the season during which it was customary for politicians to solicit the electorate.[15] The only one of these arguments which can be taken seriously is the first, and even this is rejected by Harnack, who considers it arbitrary to suppose that a reference to Vesuvius is intended when Vesuvius is not mentioned by name or otherwise identified.[16]

✓ ✓ ✓

The translation was made from J. G. Ph. Borleffs's edition of the *De paenitentia* in volume 4 of the series *Scriptores christiani primaevi* (The Hague 1948) 83–113. In his new edition of the *De paenitentia*, published in volume 1 of the *Corpus christianorum* (Turnhout 1955) 321–40, Dr. Borleffs has included the readings of the recently discovered *Codex Ottobonianus*, and these readings have been considered carefully in a reexamination and revision of the translation. It is a pleasure to acknowledge my indebtedness to Dr. Borleffs for his kindness in sending on to me the proofsheets of this new edition some considerable time before its publication. A number of older texts have also been studied in the preparation of this translation. Among these may be mentioned F. Oehler, *Quinti Septimii Florentis Tertulliani quae supersunt omnia* 1 (Leipzig 1853) 643–65; E. Preuschen, *Tertullian. De paenitentia et De pudicitia* (2nd ed. Freiburg 1910); G. Rauschen, *Tertulliani De paenitentia et De pudicitia* (Bonn 1915).

English translations of the *De paenitentia* were made in the last century by C. Dodgson, Tertullian 1 (LF 10, Oxford 1842) 349–69, and S. Thelwall, Tertullian (ANF 4, Amer. repr., New York 1925) 657–66. These are, for the most part, accurate and intelligent versions, but in many difficult places, either because of their antiquated style or their extreme literalness, they are, if not quite meaningless, at least painfully and unnecessarily hard to follow. They are, of course, both based on texts which are no longer critically acceptable, particularly since the discovery of the *Codex Trecensis* in 1916 and the *Codex Ottobonianus* in 1946. Acknowledgement must be made, however, of the help which they have frequently furnished. The translations of P. De Labriolle (French), H. Kellner (German) and C. Mohrmann (Dutch) have also been consulted regularly and with profit.[17]

ON PENITENCE

PAGAN PENITENCE

1. Men who are as we ourselves once were, blind and unenlightened by the Lord,[1] see in repentance[2] nothing more than nature teaches them:[3] a certain affection of the soul caused by a past decision which gives offense.[4] They are, however, as far from a reasoned understanding of it as they are from the author of reason Himself.[5] For reason is a property of God's,[6] since there is nothing which God, the creator of all things, has not foreseen, arranged and determined by reason; moreover, there is nothing which He does not wish to be investigated and understood by reason.[7] Accordingly, all those who are ignorant of God are, of necessity, ignorant also of what is His, for no one's property is ever laid open to strangers.[8] And, therefore, because they traverse the whole course of life without the rudder of reason, they know not how to weather the storm which overhangs the world.[9]

How unreasonably they conduct themselves[10] in the practice of penitence will be sufficiently shown by this single circumstance that they give themselves to it[11] even when their deeds are virtuous. They repent their loyalty, love, straightforwardness, generosity, patience and mercy.[12] When they meet with ingratitude in some affair or other,[13] they reproach themselves because they did what was good, and they fix most deeply in their hearts that repentance which follows upon[14] their best actions, reminding themselves carefully never to do good again in the future. Conversely, they cling less closely to penitence when their deeds are evil. In a word, through one and the selfsame repentance, they do what is wrong more readily than they do what is right.

THE CHRISTIAN CONCEPT

2. But if they conducted themselves like men who possess God and, therefore, reason also, they would, first of all, weigh the merit of penitence, and then they would never use it to make conversion a cause of greater wickedness.[15] In fact, they would restrict their repentance because they would also restrict their sins, checked, as is evident, by their fear of the Lord.[16] But where there is no fear, there, likewise, is no conversion,[17] and where there is no conversion, repentance must needs be vain, since it fails to produce the fruit for which God planted it, that is, the salvation of man.[18]

For after men, in their presumption, had committed so many and such serious sins, beginning with Adam, the head of the human race;[19] and after the condemnation of man and of the world, which is his portion;[20] and after his exile from Paradise and his condemnation to death—then God turned again to His mercy[21] and, in His own person, consecrated repentance from that time on, rescinding the sentence which He had passed before in anger and contracting to pardon His handiwork and image. Therefore, He gathered together His people and favored them with a profusion of bountiful gifts and, although He experienced their ingratitude so often, yet always did He exhort them to repentance, and He inspired all the prophets so that repentance might be preached.[22]

After this,[23] having promised the grace with which in the latter days He intended to illumine the whole world

through His spirit, He commanded that there should first
be a Baptism of penance, so be it He might prepare, in the
pledge of penance, those whom He would call through
grace to the promise determined for the seed of Abraham.[24]
Of this John is not silent, for he says: *Begin to repent.* In
truth, salvation was nearing the nations,[25] because the
Lord was bringing it as God had promised.

His precursor preached repentance as a prerequisite for
the cleansing of souls, so that whatever the filth resulting
from ancient error,[26] whatever the defilement of the
human heart resulting from ignorance, repentance might
sweep it up and scrape it away and throw it out of the
house, making ready the heart as a clean dwelling place
for the coming visitation of the Holy Spirit, in order that,
with His heavenly blessings, He might gladly there take up
His abode.[27] There is just one reason why these blessings
are conferred, and that is the salvation of man—once his
former sins have been effaced. This is the reason for repentance and this its office: to further the work of divine
mercy, a thing advantageous to man and of service to God.

Sin and Penitence

Now the nature of repentance, which we learn when we
come to know the Lord, establishes the definite rule that
no violent hand, so to speak, must ever be laid on any good
deed or design.[28] God, we may be sure, will not sanction
the reprobation of good deeds, for they are His.[29] Since He
initiates and preserves them, so also must He needs approve
them; since He approves them, so also must He reward
them. Therefore it does not matter if the ingratitude of
men leads to repentance even for benefactions; neither
does it matter if a desire for gratitude incites to beneficence.[30]

Both the one and the other are things secular and transitory. Actually, how small your gain if you do good to a grateful man, or your loss if you do good to an ingrate! A good deed has God as its debtor, and a bad deed also, because every judge settles a case on its merits.[31] Now since God presides as judge in order to exact and safeguard justice, something so precious in His sight, and since it is for this that He establishes every single precept of His moral law,[32] can it be doubted that, just as in all of our actions, so, too, in the case of repentance justice must be rendered to God? And this can be done properly only if repentance is restricted to things that are sinful.

Now no deed but an evil one deserves to be called a sin, and no man commits a fault when he does what is good.[33] But if he does not commit a fault, why does he trespass on repentance, the preserve of those who do transgress? Why does he impose on virtue a duty which belongs to vice? Thus it happens that when a thing is practiced where it should be avoided, it is neglected precisely there where it should be practiced.

NATURE AND DIVISIONS OF SINS

3. And now the occasion demands that we specify the things for which penitence seems both proper and necessary, that is to say, things which are to be regarded as sins. To do this, however, may seem superfluous since, when we know the Lord, our soul, in the solicitous care[34] of its creator, rises spontaneously to the knowledge of truth and, having received the commandments of the Lord,[35] learns from them, at once, that whatever is forbidden by God must be regarded as a sin.[36] For it is clear that God is an immensity of goodness;[37] and, certainly, nothing could

displease goodness but evil, since it is between opposites that there is no concord.

It will not be devoid of interest, however, to touch lightly on the fact that some sins are carnal, that is, sins of the body, and others are sins of the spirit; for since man is constituted a composite of these two substances, he does not sin otherwise than through the components of which he is made. But it is not the fact that body and soul are two distinct realities which makes these sins different; rather, for this reason, they are the more alike, since the two make one.[38] A man should not distinguish sins according to the distinction of these substances, so as to suppose, on this account, that one is lighter or graver than the other. The fact of the matter is that both flesh and spirit are the work of God, the one formed by His hand, the other brought to its perfection by His breath.[39] Therefore, since both equally belong to the Lord, the Lord is equally offended whichever one of them sins. How can you make a distinction between acts of the flesh and of the spirit when their association and partnership is so close, in life and death and in the resurrection, that, as a result, both together, at that time, will be raised to life or to damnation,[40] since both together, as we know, either sinned or lived in innocence?

This we have said, by way of preface, so that we may understand that penance[41] is no less necessary to one component than it is to the other, if in anything it should have sinned.[42] Both have a common guilt and a common judge, I mean God; therefore the remedy of penance is also common to them both.

The reason why sins are called 'spiritual' or 'corporeal' is that every sin is either a thought or a deed. Thus a corporeal sin is one of deed, because a deed, like a body, can be seen and touched; a spiritual sin, however, is one of the soul, because, like a spirit, it can neither be seen nor held fast.[43] From this it is evident that not only sins of deed but sins of the will, as well, are to be avoided and to be purged by penance. For even though human shortsightedness considers no sins wrong but those of deed, being incapable of penetrating the coverts of the will, we should not, on this account, ignore its sins as God sees them. God can do everything. Nothing which causes sin in any way escapes His sight. Since He is not ignorant of it, neither does He fail to mark it out for punishment. He does not veil His own clear vision, nor does He fail to act on it.

But what of the will as cause of the deed? We may, of course, prescind from such sins as are imputed to accident, necessity or ignorance.[44] Apart from these, however, there is no sin except in the will. Since, then, it causes the deed, is it not all the more subject to punishment as being more responsible for the fault? And if some obstacle prevent it from accomplishing its intention, it is, even then, not free from blame, for it bears its own guilt and cannot be excused because of that unintended failure of external accomplishment after its own act was complete.

Finally, how does the Lord prove that He *builds an addition upon the Law*,[45] except by prohibiting even sins of the will? For He designates as an adulterer not only the man who violates the marriage of another by intercourse,[46] but that man, also, who contaminates it by a lustful look.[47] Accordingly, it is quite dangerous for the mind to represent to itself[48] something which is prohibited, just as it is rash, through an act of the will, to effect it in deed.

Since the force of this will act is so great that in satisfying us with its own gratification it takes the place of the deed, it follows that it will be punished in place of the deed. It is sheer folly to say, 'I willed, but I did not act.' Rather you should complete the act, since you will it; or you should not will it at all, since you are not going to complete it. Actually, you condemn yourself by the confession of your own conscience,[49] for if you desired a thing that was good you would have tried to carry it through to completion; if, on the other hand, you fail to carry it through to completion because it is evil, you ought not even to desire it. Whatever position you take, guilt holds you fast, for you have either willed what is evil or you have failed to accomplish what is good.[50]

GOD'S PARDON THE FRUIT OF PENITENCE

4. For all sins, therefore, whether they be committed by the flesh or by the spirit, whether in deed or in desire, He who has appointed that chastisement follow upon judgement, has also promised that pardon will follow upon repentance,[51] for He says to the people: *Repent and I will save you.*[52] Again He says: *I live*, saith the Lord, *and I prefer repentance rather than death.*[53] Repentance, then, means life, since it is preferred to death. Do thou, a sinner like myself—yes and a lesser one than I, for I recognize my eminence in evil—lay hold on it and grip it fast, as one who is shipwrecked holds to a plank of salvation.[54] It will buoy you up when you are plunged into a sea of sin and bear you safely to the haven of divine mercy. Seize the blessed and unexpected opportunity which is given you, so that you, a man who once was nothing in the sight of God but a *drop in the bucket*[55] and *dust of the threshing floor*[56] and *a potter's vessel*[57] may become, from now on, that *tree planted by the waters, whose leaf will not wither, which bears fruit in due season*[58] and which will not know the fire or the ax.[59]

Now that you have found the truth, repent your errors; repent that you have loved what God does not love, for not even we ourselves permit our servant lads to love things that displease us, since the essence of obedience consists in a union of wills.[60]

The excellence of repentance is a rich subject and, therefore, it is one which should be treated with great eloquence. We, however, according to the measure of our limited abilities, insist upon but one point: God's command is the best and the greatest good.[61] It is presumptuous, I think, to debate about the goodness of a divine decree, for we ought to obey it, not because it is good, but rather because God has decreed it. The reason for an act of obedience is, first of all, the dignity of the divine majesty. The authority of the one who commands is of greater significance than the advantage of the one who obeys. Why do you keep asking yourself, 'Is repentance good or is it not?' God has commanded it! Rather, He not only commands, He even exhorts! He coaxes us to it by offering salvation as its reward. He yearns to be trusted, even taking His oath, with the words, 'I live.'[62]

O blessed are we for whose sake God binds Himself by oath; most wretched, if we believe not the Lord, even on His oath. Therefore, what God commends so highly, what He even, in human fashion, guarantees under oath, this we should certainly embrace and guard in all earnestness, so that, established in the pledge of divine grace, we may thus be established, also, in its joys and its rewards.[63]

CONVERSION AND RELAPSE

5. A point I now [64] insist upon is this, that the penance which has been revealed to us by the grace of God,[65]

which is required of us and which brings us back to favor with the Lord, must never, once we have known and embraced it, be violated thereafter by a return to sin.[66] In this case, no plea of ignorance excuses you; for you have known the Lord, you have accepted His law and then, after doing penance for your sins,[67] you give yourself over to sin again. Therefore the more you are detached from ignorance, the more you are attached to wilful disobedience;[68] for if you were sorry for your sins because you began to fear the Lord, why did you choose to cancel that which fear inspired, if not for the reason that you have ceased to fear? In truth, it is nothing but wilful disobedience which destroys the fear of God.

But since there is no excusing cause [69] which saves men from punishment even when they know not the Lord— for ignorance of God is not excusable, since He is set plainly before men and can be known through the very gifts we have received from heaven [70]—how much more perilous it is to despise Him once He is known! And that man despises Him who, having received from Him a knowledge of good and evil, insults his own understanding, which is God's gift, by taking up again what he knows he should forswear and what he has already forsworn. He repudiates the giver when he abandons the gift; he rejects the benefactor when he dishonors the benefaction.[71] How can God Himself be pleasing to a man who takes no pleasure in His gift?[72] Clearly, therefore, he is not only wilfully disobedient to the Lord, but he is ungrateful to Him also.

But does he sin venially against the Lord [73] who, in penance, renounces His adversary, the devil,[74] and thus subordinates him to the Lord, but who then, falling back into sin again, exalts him once more and is a cause of his joy, so that the evil one, recovering his booty,[75] laughs in the face of the Lord? Does he not—it is a dangerous thing to say, but for edification I must speak out—prefer the devil to the Lord? For after he has known them both, he seems to have instituted a comparison between them and to have pronounced judgement that he is the better whose possession he has again elected to be. Therefore the man who began to satisfy the Lord by repenting his sin will satisfy the devil by repenting his repentance,[76] and he will be as hateful to the Lord as he is dear to his adversary.

Some say, however, that God is satisfied[77] if He be honored in heart and mind, even though this be not done externally.[78] Thus they sin, yet lose not reverential fear and faith. That is to say, they lose not chastity and commit adultery! They lose not filial piety and poison a parent! So also will they lose not pardon and be cast down into hell, seeing that they sin and lose not reverential fear. A wonderful example of wrongheadedness: because they fear, they sin! I suppose that they would not sin, if they did not fear. On this principle, he who does not wish God to be offended should have no reverence for Him at all, if it is fear which sponsors his offense. But conceptions such as these have always teemed from the seed of those hypocrites whose friendship with the devil is inseparable, whose penance never perseveres.[79]

The Penitence of Catechumens

6. Accordingly, whatever our modest talent has attempted to set forth with a view to exciting a penitence which is undertaken but once and permanently preserved[80] —this is intended for all who have obligations to the Lord,[81] since all are striving for salvation through their efforts to

win the favor of God. It presses most urgently, however, upon those recruits [82] who have just recently begun to give ear to the flow of divine discourse [83] and who, like puppies newly born, creep about uncertainly, with eyes as yet unopened. They say, indeed, that they renounce the past, and they do begin to do penance, yet they fail to bring it to completion. [84] The very termination of desire incites them to embrace something of their old desires, just as fruits which have already begun to turn bitter and sour with age, still flatter themselves, to some extent, upon their charms. [85]

It is a rash confidence in the efficacy of Baptism which leads to all of this culpable delay and hesitancy in the matter of penitence. Since they are certain of an assured pardon for their sins, they steal, meanwhile, the intervening time and make of it an interlude [86] for sinning, rather than for learning not to sin. What folly it is, what perversity, to practice an imperfect penitence and then to expect a pardon for sin! This is to stretch forth one's hand for merchandise and not to pay the price. And the price which the Lord has set on the purchase of pardon is this [87]—He offers impunity to be bought in exchange for penitence. [88] If, then, merchants first examine a coin, which they have stipulated as their price, to see that it be not clipped or plated or counterfeit, [89] do we not believe that the Lord, also, preexamines our penitence, seeing that He is going to give us so great a reward, [90] to wit, life everlasting?

WARNINGS AGAINST PRESUMPTION

'But let us postpone, for a while, our complete conversion. When we are baptized, then, I fancy, will be time enough to be free from fault.' [91] By no means! Rather we should rid ourselves of sin when pardon is in abeyance and punishment in prospect; when we do not yet merit deliverance, so that we may be able to merit it; [92] when God threatens, not when He pardons. For what slave, once his condition is changed for that of freedom, feels shame for his thefts and truancy? What soldier, after his discharge from the army, bothers about his brands? [93] A sinner ought to weep for his faults *before* they are pardoned because the time of penitence is also a time of danger and of dread.

I do not deny that the divine benefaction, I mean the forgiveness of sins, is absolutely assured to those who will enter the water; [94] they must make an effort, however, to succeed in getting there. And who will oblige you, a man so renegade to penitence, with a single dash of any water at all? [95] It is easy, of course, to approach it dishonestly, and to cause the one who is in charge of this affair to be deceived by your protestations, but God guards His treasure and He will not permit the unworthy to take it by surprise. For what does He say? *There is nothing hidden which shall not be revealed.* [96] No matter how dense the darkness in which you shroud your actions, *God is light.* [97]

There are some, however, who are of the opinion that God must needs grant what He has promised, even to those who are not worthy of it, and they make His generosity a matter of obligation. Now if it is of necessity that He grants us the *symbol of death,* [98] then He does it unwillingly; but who can promise himself that what He grants unwillingly will endure? For are there not many who later fall away? Will not that gift be taken away from many? Certainly these are the persons who slip in by stealth and who, after they have obtained by force the security of penitence, [99] build upon sand a house that will fall. [100]

Let no one flatter himself, therefore, that because he is

classed among the auditors in the catechumenate,[101] he is, on this account, still permitted to sin. As soon as you know the Lord you must fear Him; as soon as you have made His acquaintance you must revere Him. But what is the point of knowing Him when you have the same attachments which you had before when you knew Him not? What, then, distinguishes you from the perfect servant of God? Is there one Christ for the baptized and another for the catechumens? Is there a different hope or reward? a different fear of judgement? a different need of repentance? That cleansing water is a seal of faith, and this faith has its beginning and finds its reward in a genuine repentance.[102] We are not baptized so that we may cease committing sin but because we have ceased, since we are already clean of heart.[103] This, surely, is the first Baptism of the catechumen.[104] His fear is perfect[105] because he has been in contact with the Lord; his faith is sound because his conscience has embraced repentance once for all.

But if we cease from sin only after Baptism, then it is of necessity and not of our own free will that we clothe ourselves with innocence.[106] Who is the man of outstanding virtue, he who is not permitted to be wicked or he who does not wish to be so? he who is forced or he who is pleased to be sinless? If no one who is under obligation to the Lord must cease from sin until he is bound by Baptism, then let us not keep our hands from theft unless hard bars imprison us, let us not guard our eyes against concupiscence and lust unless police restrain us. If any one is of such a mind as this, it would be difficult to say whether, after his Baptism, he is not grieved because he has ceased committing sin, instead of happy because he has escaped it.

Accordingly, the catechumens ought to desire Baptism, yet they ought not to receive it presumptuously. He who desires it, honors it; he who receives it presumptuously, despises it. In the former reverence is manifest, in the latter recklessness; the former is careful, the latter negligent; the former wishes to deserve it, the latter promises it to himself as something which is his due; the former receives it, the latter usurps it. Who do you think is worthier of it, if not the man who commits fewer sins? Who commits fewer sins, if not the man who has the greater reverential fear and who, on this account, has undertaken to perform the proper penance?[107] For he has feared to continue sinning, lest he should not deserve to receive it. On the other hand, the man who receives it presumptuously, since he has promised it to himself with perfect assurance, could not have had reverential fear; and thus his penitence was defective because it was without the instrument of penitence, which is fear. Presumption is the part of rash irreverence. It puffs up the petitioner and contemns the donor; thus it is sometimes disappointed, since it promises itself something which is not yet its due and so always offends the one who is expected to grant it.[108]

PENITENCE OF THE BAPTIZED

7. Grant, Lord Christ, that Thy servants may speak of the discipline [109] of penitence, or hear of it, only while the duty of avoiding sin rests on them as catechumens.[110] In other words, may they, thereafter, know nothing of repentance nor have any need of it. I am reluctant to make mention here of a second hope, one which is indeed the very last,[111] for fear that in treating of a resource which yet remains in penitence, I may seem to indicate that there is still time left for sin.[112] God grant that no one come to such a conclusion, as though the road still lay open before

him for sin because it still lies open for penitence, and as though he were free to find in the superabundance of heavenly mercy justification for the excesses of human presumption.[113] Let no one be worse because God is better, sinning just as often as he is forgiven. Otherwise, while there will be no end to his sin, there will be, of a certainty, an end to his immunity.

We have escaped once. Let us not place ourselves in danger again, even though it seems that we shall again escape. Most men who are saved from shipwreck divorce both ship and sea from that time on, and they show their appreciation of the gift of God, that is, their salvation, by remembering their peril. I praise their fear and I appreciate their timidity. They are unwilling, a second time, to burden the mercy of God. They are afraid that they may seem to trample under foot that which they have received. Assuredly it is with a wise solicitude that they avoid chancing a second time something which they have once learned to fear. Thus in checking their presumption they give proof of their fear, and man's fear is God's glory.

But that stubborn enemy of ours never gives his wickedness a rest. Rather he is then most furious when he sees that a man is completely free; then he is most on fire when he is quenched.[114] He must needs grieve and groan that, when pardon is granted for sins, so many works of death[115] in man are mastered, so many titles of his former dominion[116] are erased. He grieves that that sinner, the servant of Christ, is to judge him and his angels.[117] Therefore he watches, he attacks, he lays siege,[118] in the hope that by some means or other he may be able to strike at his eyes with concupiscence of the flesh or entangle his soul in worldly delights or destroy his faith through a fear of the civil authorities or bring him to deviate from the right way by perverted doctrines.[119] Never is he at a loss for stumbling blocks or temptations.

Accordingly, since God foresees this virulence of his, He has permitted the door of forgiveness, although it is closed and locked by the bar of Baptism, still to stand somewhat open.[120] He has placed in the vestibule a second penitence so that it may open the door to those who knock;[121] only once, however, because it is already a second time; never again, however, because the last time was in vain.[122] For is not even this 'once' enough?[123] You have what you no longer deserved, since you lost what you had received.[124] If the indulgence of the Lord favors you with what you need for the restoration of that which you lost, be grateful for His repeated, nay rather, for His increased beneficence.[125] For to give back is a greater thing than to give, since it is worse to have lost than never to have received at all.

But if a man is obliged to a second penitence, his spirit must not be cast down and crushed by despair. Of course, he should be reluctant to sin again, but to repent again he should not be reluctant. He should be ashamed to place himself again in danger, but to be saved again no one should be ashamed.[126] When a disease recurs the medicine must be repeated.[127] You will prove your gratitude to the Lord, if you do not refuse what He offers you anew. You have sinned, yet you can still be reconciled. You have someone to whom you can make satisfaction, yes and one who wills it.[128]

SCRIPTURE PROOFS OF GOD'S MERCY

8. If you doubt that this is true, consider[129] what the Spirit says to the churches. He charges the Ephesians with

having abandoned charity;[130] He reproaches the Thyatirenes with *fornication* and *eating food sacrificed to idols*;[131] He accuses the Sardians of *works that are not complete*;[132] He censures the men of Pergamos for *teaching false doctrines*;[133] He upbraids the Laodiceans for *placing their trust in riches*;[134] and yet He warns them all to repent—even adding threats. But He would not threaten the impenitent, if He failed to pardon the penitent;[135] this would be doubtful only if He had not revealed elsewhere this profusion of His mercy.[136] Has He not said: *He who is fallen shall rise and he who was turned away shall return?*[137] He it is, most assuredly, He it is who *will have mercy rather than sacrifice.*[138] The heavens and the angels who are there rejoice at man's repentance.[139] Look you now, sinner, be of good heart! You see where it is that you are a cause of joy.[140]

What meaning do those lessons of our Lord's parables have for us? Take, for example, the woman who loses a drachma and hunts for it and finds it and calls together her friends to rejoice with her. Is this not the story of the sinner who is saved?[141] And one ewe lamb of the shepherd's strays away, yet the whole flock was no more dear than the one. That one is sought out; that one is desired above all others. But then it is found and carried back on the shoulders of the shepherd himself. And, truly, it had suffered much in straying.[142] Nor shall I neglect to speak of that gentlest of fathers, who takes back home his prodigal son[143] and gladly raises him up in his arms, repentant in his destitution; then, slaying the fatted calf for him, he celebrates his joy with a banquet.[144] And why not? For he had found his son whom he had lost and he held him all the more precious because he had won him back.

Whom are we to understand by that father? God, of

course! No one is so much a father. No one is so devoted. Therefore He will take you back as His son, even though you will have wasted what He gave you.[145] Even though you come back stripped of all things, He will receive you— precisely because you have come back. He will be happier over your return than over another's self-control, but only if you repent from the bottom of your heart, only if you contrast your hunger with the repletion of your father's servants, only if you abandon the filthy herd of swine, only if you seek out your Father, even though He be offended,[146] and say to Him: *Father, I have sinned and I am no longer worthy to be called Thine.*[147] Confession [148] lightens an offense as much as concealment aggravates it, for confession is counseled by satisfaction [149] and concealment by impenitence.

EXOMOLOGESIS

9. Since this second and last penitence is so serious a matter, it must be tested in a way which is proportionately laborious. Therefore it must not be performed solely within one's conscience but it must also be shown forth in some external act.[150] This external act, rather expressively designated by the Greek word for it in common use, is the exomologesis.[151] Herein we confess [152] our sin to the Lord, not as though He were ignorant of it, but because satisfaction receives its proper determination [153] through confession, confession gives birth to penitence and by penitence God is appeased.

Exomologesis, then, is a discipline[154] which leads a man to prostrate and humble himself. It prescribes a way of life which, even in the matter of food and clothing, appeals to pity. It bids him to lie in sackcloth and ashes,[155] to cover his body with filthy rags, to plunge his soul into sorrow, to exchange sin for suffering.[156] Moreover, it demands that you [157] know only such food and drink as is plain; this means it is taken for the sake of your soul, not your belly. It requires that you habitually nourish prayer by fasting, that you sigh and weep and groan day and night to the Lord your God, that you prostrate yourself at the feet of the priests [158] and kneel before the beloved of God,[159] making all the brethren commissioned ambassadors of your prayer for pardon.[160]

Exomologesis does all this in order to render penitence acceptable and in order to honor God through fear of punishment,[161] so that in passing sentence upon the sinner it may itself be a substitute for the wrath of God and, by temporal punishment, I will not say prevent eternal torments but rather cancel them.[162] Therefore, in humbling a man it exalts him. When it defiles him, he is cleansed.[163] In accusing, it excuses. In condemning, it absolves.[164] In proportion as you have had no mercy on yourself, believe me, in just this same measure God will have mercy upon you.

Public Penance Difficult but Salutary

10. Most men, however, shun this duty as involving the public exposure of themselves, or they put it off from day to day, thinking more about their shame, it seems to me, than about their salvation. They are like men who have contracted some disease in the private parts of the body, who conceal this from the knowledge of the physicians [165] and thus preserve their modesty but lose their lives.[166] It is, I suppose, unbearable to shame that it should offer satisfaction [167] to the Lord after He has been offended,

and that it should enter once more into the possession of that salvation which has been wasted.[168]

Oh you are a brave fellow, surely, in your shyness—wearing a bold front for sin, a bashful one for pardon! As for me, I have no room for shame when I profit at its expense and when shame itself exhorts a man, as it were, and says to him: 'Regard me not! For thy sake it is better that I be lost.'[169] If ever the danger to shame is serious, this is certainly the case when it stands in the presence of insult and mockery, when one man is exalted through another's ruin, when one ascends over another who is laid low.[170] But among brethren and fellow-servants, where there is one hope, fear, joy, sorrow and suffering, because there is one Spirit[171] from one Lord and Father, why do you think these men are any different from yourself? Why do you flee, as from scoffers,[172] those who share your misfortunes? The body can not rejoice at the suffering of a single one of its members;[173] the whole body must needs suffer along with it and help in its cure.

Where there are two together, there is the Church[174] —and the Church is Christ.[175] When, therefore, you stretch forth your hands to the knees of the brethren, you are in touch with Christ[176] and you win the favor of Christ by your supplications. In like manner, when they shed tears for you, it is Christ who suffers, Christ who supplicates the Father. And what the Son requests is always easily obtained.[177] Great is the profit, I'm sure, which the concealment of a sin promises to modesty! For it is plain, is it not, that if we withdraw something from the knowledge of men, we shall also hide it from God? Is this the relative importance which we attach to human respect and God's knowledge?[178] Is it better to be condemned in secret than to be absolved in public?[179]

'Oh but it is a painful thing to undertake exomologesis in this way!' I should prefer to say that one suffers pain because one has sinned.[180] Or, rather, when penance is to be performed, there is no longer any question of suffering, since it is become a means of salvation. It is painful to be cut and to be cauterized and to be tortured by some medicinal caustic.[181] Nevertheless, remedies which are unpleasant justify the pain they give by the cure they effect, and they render present suffering agreeable because of the advantage which is to come in the future.

VALUE OF BODILY MORTIFICATION

11. Let us suppose that besides the shame which is their principal concern they are also afraid of the bodily mortification involved, which requires that, unwashed and filthy, they live without joy, in rough sackcloth and frightful ashes, their faces wasted with fasting.[182] Well, is it fitting that we beg pardon for sin in scarlet and purple?[183] Come, then, bring a pin to part the hair and powder to polish the teeth and scissors to trim the nails and, if any meretricious beauty, any artificial bloom may be had, hasten and apply it to the lips or cheeks![184] Yes, and seek out baths of greater luxury, sequestered in garden spots or by the sea. Multiply expenses, search for the rich, gross flesh of fatted fowls, refine old wine and, if anyone should ask you why you make good cheer, then say to him: 'I have sinned against the Lord. I am in danger of perishing forever. Therefore am I now weakened and wasted and tormented, so that I may win for myself the pardon of God whom I have injured by my sin!'[185]

Men who seek public office are neither ashamed nor reluctant to put up with discomforts of body and soul alike in striving for what they want, yes and not only with discomforts but even with humiliating affronts of every kind. What rough garments do they not affect! What homes do they not besiege with visits, late at night and early in the morning! They bow low whenever they meet a person of consequence. They frequent no carousals. They gather at no drinking bouts. Rather, they are exiles from the enjoyment of indulgence and festivity—and all for the fleeting pleasure of a single year![186] Shall we, with eternity at stake, hesitate to bear what they who seek axes and rods[187] are able to endure? Shall we fail to offer to the Lord, when He is offended, that renunciation of food and fine apparel to which the gentiles condemn themselves, when no one at all has been offended? These are they of whom the Scripture makes mention: *Woe to those who bind their sins together, as though with a long rope.*[188]

EFFICACY OF EXOMOLOGESIS

12. If you shrink from exomologesis, then meditate in your heart on hell which exomologesis will extinguish for you.[189] Picture to yourself, first of all, how great this punishment is so that you will not hesitate to use the means which you have to escape it. What shall we think of that great vault of eternal fire when some of its tiny vents shoot out such bursts of flame that nearby cities are either all destroyed or, from day to day, expect this same destruction?[190] The most majestic mountains burst asunder giving birth to their engendered fire and—a fact which proves to us the eternity of damnation—although they do burst asunder, although they are consumed, yet never are they extinct. Meanwhile, who will not see in these tortured mountains exemplary illustrations of the damnation with

which we are threatened? Who will not agree that sparks such as these are, as it were, projectiles and admonitory missiles [191] from some immense and immeasurable fire?

Therefore, since you know that in exomologesis you have a second safeguard against hell which backs up that first line of defense, the Lord's Baptism, [192] why do you abandon the means of salvation which is yours? Why are you slow to take hold of something which will restore you to health? Even dumb, irrational animals recognize, in due season, remedies supplied to them by God. When a stag is transfixed by an arrow, it knows that it must eat dittany in order to expel the arrowhead with its barbs projecting backwards from the wound. [193] If a swallow blinds her young, she has learned to restore their sight with her own peculiar herb, the celandine. [194]

Will the sinner knowingly spurn exomologesis, which has been instituted by God for his restoration? that exomologesis which restored the king of Babylon to his royal throne? Long did he offer to the Lord a sacrifice of penance, performing his exomologesis for seven squalid years, his nails growing wild like the talons of an eagle, his hair unkempt like the shaggy mane of a lion. [195] Oh the blessedness of this harsh treatment! [196] One whom men shunned with horror, God received! The ruler of Egypt, on the contrary, pursuing the people of God, whom he had persecuted for a long time and long kept back from their Lord, fell upon them in battle and, after all the warnings of the plagues, he perished in the parted sea, passable to none but the chosen people, when the waves rolled back upon him. [197] For he had rejected penitence and its instrument, exomologesis. [198]

Why should I say more about these two planks, [199] so to speak, of safety for mankind? Why more concern for the employment of my pen than for the obligations of my own conscience? Since I am a sinner, branded with every mark of infamy [200] and born for nothing else but penance, I cannot easily keep silence about something which Adam himself, the author of the human race and also of sin against the Lord,[201] does not pass over in silence, once he is restored, through exomologesis, to his own particular paradise.[202]

ON
PURITY

INTRODUCTION

The *De pudicitia*[1] is one of Tertullian's most violent Montanist treatises—a passionate, bigoted and yet utterly sincere attack on the doctrine and discipline of the orthodox Church. Tertullian felt and professed a deep love for the Church of Christ. He was convinced that it was not he who had left the Church; rather it was the Church that had left him! This she did, he believed, when she refused to accept the utterances of Montanist prophets as the authentic word of God, and when she refused to impose upon her members the austere moral discipline inculcated by the new 'revelations' of the Paraclete. In his various Montanist writings Tertullian protests against the Church's toleration of second marriage, her attitude towards flight during times of persecution, her relatively mild legislation in the matter of fasting and other external penitential practices. All of his Montanist tracts are characterized by a warped and exaggerated asceticism; in all of them Tertullian's indignation is impressive, even when his position is impossible and his arguments absurd.

The *De pudicitia*, possibly the last of Tertullian's extant works, criticizes the policy which the Church follows in granting pardon to serious sins. In none of his writings does he show a fiercer temper. He is without pity in his condemnation of human frailty, completely unashamed in his demands for harshness and intolerance. From beginning to end he is the true fanatic; he is impatient of all opposition; his mind is closed to every viewpoint but his own; he is convinced that he stands at Armageddon and battles for the Lord. The modern reader can feel nothing but sorrow that so great and devoted a talent should have served so bigoted a cause.

The treatise was occasioned by the peremptory edict of a Catholic bishop decreeing that members of the Church who committed adultery were not to be permanently excluded from the Church but were to be readmitted to communion after the performance of public penance. This decree Tertullian condemns as subversive of that perfect purity which is demanded of the Christian. Any indulgence granted to sins of the flesh he regards as a profanation of the body of Christ and an invitation to further sin. His arguments are almost exclusively scriptural. He insists that the sacred text, rightly understood, clearly proves that the Church must not forgive sins of adultery and fornication. He draws on a bewilderingly large number of texts from both the Old and the New Testament to establish this thesis, revealing throughout the whole treatise a familiarity with the Bible which is truly amazing. One hardly knows which is the more remarkable—his readiness in quoting Scripture or his genius for distorting it.

The argument is developed in chapters 5 to 20. Chapters 1 to 4 are introductory, and chapters 21 and 22 an epilogue. Tertullian begins his treatise with a statement on the excellence of chastity and a complaint that this virtue has suffered harm as the result of a recent episcopal directive allowing pardon to adultery and fornication. Tertullian acknowledges that he himself, before he was enlightened by the new prophecy, found no fault with the practice of forgiving serious sins, but he rejoices that he now has a finer appreciation of purity and is a better and a holier man than he was before (c. 1). If his opponents say that Scripture proves the kindness and mercy of God, he will answer that it also proves His severity and justice. This apparent contradiction is resolved if we remember that sins are of two kinds: some are remissible and others irremissible. Penance is required for all sins; if it is done for remissible sins, the Church grants pardon at its close; if it is done for irremissible sins, no such ecclesiastical pardon is allowed. Thus God shows His mercy in the first instance and His justice in the second (c. 2). When penance is done for irremissible sins it is not done in vain, since pardon will be granted in heaven even though it is not allowed on earth. This conflicts with the opinion of his adversaries, who insist that forgiveness of such sins is the fruit of an absolution which the Church gives here below (c. 3). There is no essential difference between adultery and fornication as far as carnal defilement is concerned. Public penance is required for both these sins, but the Church may not forgive them. If a Christian should be guilty of unnatural vice, he is not only refused absolution but is even excluded from the performance of exomologesis (c. 4).

Tertullian finds his first scriptural argument in the Decalogue. God prohibits idolatry, adultery and murder, in that order. This proves the gravity of adultery, and shows how inconsistent his opponents are when they forgive sins of impurity while refusing to forgive murder and idolatry (c. 5). The law of the Old Testament has not been abrogated but it has been perfected in Christ, who condemns not only external sins of the flesh but even lustful desires. Examples of immorality under the old dispensation are no excuse for laxness under the law of Christ (c. 6). The parables of the lost sheep, the lost drachma and the prodigal son may seem to justify the Church in her practice of forgiving the serious sins of her subjects. This, however, perverts the meaning of the parables since, if we study them carefully, we shall see that Christ is there promising pardon to pagans, not to Christians. Hence the parables of mercy prove that all sins may be forgiven to pagans in the *paenitentia prima* of Baptism, but not to Christians in the *paenitentia secunda* of exomologesis (cc. 7–9). It is incorrect to say, as his opponents do, that Christ's mercy is meant more for Christians than it is for pagans, since pagans sin in ignorance and, therefore, have less need of mercy. This may be consistent with the teaching of Hermas, the shepherd of adulterers, but it is not consistent with the teaching of the Gospels (c. 10). Nor does the fact that Christ personally forgave serious sins prove that the Church may do so (c. 11).

The teaching and example of the apostles may be added to the lessons of the Gospel. When the apostles were assembled in the council at Jerusalem they laid no burdens upon the faithful but the obligation of abstaining from sacrifices, fornications and blood, that is to say, from idolatry, adultery and murder. These, then, are the sins which they consider irremissible (c. 12). The letters of St. Paul, particularly *First* and *Second Corinthians*, are cited by the laxists as proving that pardon may be granted to a Christian guilty of adultery. It can be shown, however, that the sinner whom Paul forgives in his second letter is not the incestuous man whom he condemned in his first. Moreover, the whole tenor of Paul's epistles is inconsistent with the notion that he would ever tolerate the forgiveness of adultery by the Church (cc. 13–17).

Scripture not only condemns adultery but teaches explicitly that it is to be punished by excommunication, and by an excommunication which lasts not just for a short time but for life. If impurity is forgiven, it is forgiven by *paenitentia prima* to those who have not yet become members of the Church. There is also, however, a *paenitentia secunda* for those who sin after Baptism. If they have been guilty of lesser or remissible sins, pardon is granted them by the bishop; if they have been guilty of greater or irremissible sins, pardon is granted by God alone (c. 18). St. John, in the Apocalypse, permits no pardon to Christians guilty of adultery; rather he condemns them to 'the pool of fire,' with no indication that they will be pardoned; and in his (first) epistle he speaks quite clearly of a *sin unto death*, that is to say, an irremissible sin (c. 19). So, too, Barnabas, in his *Epistle to the Hebrews*, teaches that second penance was never promised by the apostles to Christians guilty of adultery or fornication (c. 20).[2]

In conclusion, Tertullian concedes that the Church has a power to forgive sins, but he insists that the exercise of this power is restricted by a new revelation of the Paraclete. His opponents claim that the Church's power to forgive sin derives from the fact that Christ gave to St. Peter the keys of the kingdom of heaven and promised that whatsoever he loosed on earth would be loosed also in heaven. This power, however, belonged to Peter personally, and it now belongs to the church of the Spirit, not to the hierarchical church. Therefore it is possessed by those only who have the Spirit, and it is not possessed *ex officio* by the bishops as successors of the apostles (c. 21). Finally, this power must not be allowed to the martyrs. Martyrdom will efface one's own sins but not the sins of others. If the martyrs are permitted to forgive adultery, they must be allowed to forgive apostates and murderers also, apostates in particular, since apostasy is so much more excusable than adultery (c. 22).

It will be seen from this rapid survey that the distinction between remissible and irremissible sins is essential to the argument of the *De pudicitia*. We must remember that when Tertullian makes this distinction he means 'remissible or irremissible by the Church,' not 'remissible or irremissible by God,' since he states explicitly that sins which the Church may not forgive, God actually does forgive (3.3, 5; 18.18). The distinction is new in Tertullian's penitential theology; at least, it is not mentioned or implied in the *De paenitentia* or any other of his pre-Montanist writings. Its importance is sufficiently indicated by the fact that it is responsible for, or closely identified with, all of the principal controversies which have arisen over the interpretation of this treatise.

The three most crucial questions in dispute are these: (1) Which sins did Tertullian consider to be of such objective gravity that they were excluded from ecclesiastical absolution? (2) Who was the author of the edict which occasioned the composition of the *De pudicitia*? (3) Is there any convincing evidence in this treatise that at the beginning of the third century the Church refused to pardon the sins of murder and apostasy and that she was just beginning to pardon sins of adultery and fornication?

The first of these problems is complicated by a lack of precision in Tertullian's division of sins. He uses a number of different expressions to describe sins which are of greater (*maxima, capitalia, mortalia, exitiosa, maiora, gravia*) or lesser (*mediocria, modica, leviora, peccata cotidianae incursionis*) guilt, and it is not always possible to determine the exact meaning or extension of these terms. Then, too, he does not always clearly indicate which sins are to be subjected to public penance and which may be forgiven without it. Finally, he gives different lists of serious sins in different places, and his attitude towards these sins does not always seem to be completely consistent.

The safest conclusions which emerge from a study of passages pertinent to Tertullian's classification of sins[3] appear to be these. (1) There is some evidence, though it is by no means conclusive, that Tertullian recognized two distinct classes of sins, corresponding roughly to the modern division of mortal and venial sins. It is not certain, however, that he uses *maiora*, *mortalia*, *capitalia*, etc., as synonyms, or that all of the sins which he speaks of as *remissibilia* would be venial in the sense in which we use the word today. In terms of forgiveness, Tertullian says that some sins are *remissibilia* and others are not; in terms of gravity, he says that some sins are of greater and others of lesser guilt. Though he teaches, as a Montanist, that all sins of lesser guilt are remissible, he does not teach that all sins of greater guilt are irremissible. (2) It is not clear from the *De pudicitia* that Tertullian recognized the existence of an intermediate class of sins between the *levia* and the *maxima* which were forgiven by private penance. (3) The catalogue of crimes in 19.25 is intended as a typical and not an exhaustive inventory of serious sins. It corresponds rather closely with other lists given elsewhere in the writings of Tertullian. In all such lists the capital sins of idolatry (apostasy), murder and adultery are conspicuous, but they are not the only sins which Tertullian regards as mortal. The matter may be summed up thus. Both as Catholic and Montanist Tertullian recognized a distinction between sins of greater and those of lesser gravity. It cannot be proved that in his Catholic period he considered *any* grave sin irremissible, nor can it be proved that in his Montanist period he considered *all* grave sins irremissible.

The problem of determining the authorship of the edict which occasioned the composition of the *De pudicitia* has been studied frequently and needs no more than a brief synopsis here. Three principal views have been proposed. Older editors and commentators attributed the decree to Zephyrinus, bishop of Rome from 198 to 217. With the discovery of the *Philosophoumena* of Hippolytus in 1850, scholars all but unanimously accepted Callistus (bishop of Rome 217–222) as the author, since they considered that the charge of laxity in forgiving sins of impurity which Hippolytus makes against Callistus (*Philosoph.* 9.12) must be understood as referring to his issuance of the edict of toleration which Tertullian condemns in *De pud.* 1.6. Other passages in the *De pudicitia* which are thought to prove the Roman provenance of the edict will be found in cc. 13.7 and 21.5, 9. In recent years, however, scholars have been abandoning the idea that the decree was issued by a bishop of Rome. K. Adam, P. Galtier, B. Poschmann and other authorities on the history of penance argue quite convincingly that it was promulgated by an African bishop, probably Agrippinus of Carthage. This view has, at present, a certain ascendancy, although it is not universally received and the decree continues to be referred to in the literature as the 'Edict of Callistus.'[4]

The evidence from the *De pudicitia* that before the year 200 the Church did not grant absolution to the sins of murder and apostasy (idolatry), and that it was only about this time that she began to forgive adultery and fornication may be summarized thus. Tertullian repeatedly insists that his opponents are inconsistent in granting absolution to adultery, while refusing it to murder and apostasy.[5] It is inconceivable that he could have used such an argument if the Church actually did grant pardon to these sins at this time. That adultery was not forgiven before the third century seems clear from the very fact that an edict was issued *circa* 215 decreeing its forgiveness. Then, too, it is difficult to account for the bitterness of Tertullian's language in the *De pudicitia*, if the bishop whose legislation he condemns were simply continuing an earlier tradition of tolerance.

Against this position and these arguments various lines of attack have developed. Some theologians attempt to settle the matter dogmatically, contending that ecclesiastical absolution is a necessary means of salvation for those who have sinned seriously after Baptism, and that, therefore, the Church, at no time in her history, could have withheld absolution from those who were properly disposed to receive it. The argument proceeds *a non posse ad non esse*; if a thing is impossible, it never happened! The Church may not refuse to pardon serious sins; therefore there can be no evidence in the *De pudicitia* that she did refuse to pardon them. There are a number of sound theological objections to this argument, but even apart from them, most students will be unwilling to accept it because of an understandable reluctance to settle historical questions on *a priori* grounds.[6]

Not a few writers concede that the *De pudicitia* proves the existence of a rigid but slowly relaxing penitential discipline *at the time* and *in the place* where the treatise was written. They insist, however, that while it furnishes evidence for the practice of a particular church in Africa, it may not be cited as proving that the universal Church, or even the Church of Rome, refused to pardon serious sins before the beginning of the third century. It will be observed that, according to this interpretation, Tertullian in the *De pudicitia* protests against a practice which was just beginning in the African Church, not one which had always existed but which he thought should be changed because of a new revelation. The author of the peremptory edict is the innovator; Tertullian himself is not. Thus, on the evidence of the *De pudicitia*, it is admitted that the African church did refuse to pardon murder and apostasy and was just beginning to pardon the sin of adultery at the time Tertullian wrote this treatise.

Not all students will admit that this is a correct interpretation of the text of the *De pudicitia*, nor do they see that it comes to grips with a fundamental problem in Tertullian's teaching on ecclesiastical penance. This problem is created by the apparent contradiction between the teaching of the *De paenitentia* and the *De pudicitia* on the forgiveness of serious sins. In the former treatise Tertullian says that all sins may be and are forgiven by the Church; in the latter he insists that adultery *must not* be forgiven and he asserts that murder and apostasy *are not* forgiven by the Church. Various solutions of this problem have been proposed, none of them completely satisfactory. The following explanation, although it admittedly leaves some subordinate questions unanswered, seems to be most consistent with the evidence furnished by both treatises.

In the *De paenitentia* Tertullian taught that all sins, no matter how grave, may be forgiven by *paenitentia secunda*. In the *De pudicitia*, under the influence of Montanist rigorism, he repudiates this teaching when he says that adultery must not be forgiven by the Church. Thus the *De pudicitia* does not prove that the orthodox Church, even the local church in Africa, refused to pardon adultery before the promulgation of the peremptory edict. This edict may well have been issued precisely in order to check the growing rigidism of a party of puritans in some particular locality.[7] Tertullian never protests that the edict is an innovation; rather he admits that he himself has changed his viewpoint on the subject of ecclesiastical absolution after his enlightenment by the new prophecy. The innovator is not the bishop who implements a tradition of tolerance by his formal decree of indulgence, but Tertullian who protests against it.[8]

The evidence of the *De pudicitia* that murder and apostasy were not forgiven by the Church at this time is more difficult to deal with. Some students, as noted above, simply concede that the local church which Tertullian has in mind did refuse forgiveness to these sins. This explanation, however, does not do full justice to the evidence of the *De paenitentia* that the Church grants pardon to all sins, with no distinction made as to their gravity. Others contend that in the *De paenitentia* Tertullian teaches that *God* forgives all sins, not that the *Church* does. This is an easy solution but it, too, seems to ignore the evidence of the *De paenitentia* that it is exomologesis, the ecclesiastical *paenitentia secunda*, which effects the forgiveness of all sins, no matter how serious. B. Poschmann suggests that when Tertullian says that the Church refuses pardon to murderers and apostates, he means that she does not grant them peace and communion during their lifetime, but only at the hour of their death. Thus there is a sense in which it can be said that these sins are not remitted (*De pudicitia*), even though they are remissible (*De paenitentia*).[9] Positive arguments that murder and apostasy were forgiven in the Church before the middle of the third century have been developed by Galtier and others, particularly from evidence in the *Acta Petri*, Cyprian, Dionysius of Alexandria, Hippolytus, *Pastor Hermae*, Clement of Alexandria and early Church councils.[10]

It is impossible to say exactly when the *De pudicitia* was written. The dates 217/22 are frequently given, but they depend on the theory that Callistus was author of the edict against which the *De pudicitia* was a protest and, hence, they have no more certainty than has this theory. Patrologists generally place it, along with the *De monogamia* and the *De ieiunio*, among Tertullian's latest works.[11] The *De monogamia* was composed about 217, and some authorities are of the opinion that it precedes the *De pudicitia*. This sequence, however, can neither be proved nor disproved. In the absence of any more definite evidence we must be content to say, simply, that the treatise was composed some time after 212/13, since it was at this time that Tertullian broke with the Church and allied himself with the Montanist party at Carthage.

⚡   ⚡   ⚡

The text used in the preparation of this translation is that of E. Dekkers, *Corpus christianorum. Series latina* 2.1280–1330. Other editions, however, have also been used and, occasionally, their readings are preferred. Among these are A. Reifferscheid–G. Wissowa, *Corpus scriptorum ecclesiasticorum latinorum* 20 (1890) 219–73, and the texts of Oehler, Preuschen and Rauschen already mentioned.[12] The only English translation is that of S. Thelwall, *Tertullian* (repr. in ANF 4, New York 1925) 75–101. The versions of P. de Labriolle, *De paenitentia, De pudicitia. Texte et traduc.* (Textes et documents, publ. par H. Hemmer et P. Lejay, Paris 1906), and H. Kellner–G. Esser, *Tertullians ausgewählte Schriften* 2 (BKV 24, Kempten-Munich 1915) 375–472, have been particularly helpful in many difficult places.

ON PURITY

1. Purity is the flower of virtue. It does honor to the body and is an ornament of both sexes. It preserves blood untainted and guarantees parentage.[1] It is the foundation stone of sanctity and is universally recognized as a presumptive proof of upright character. Although it is found but infrequently and is with difficulty brought to perfection and hardly ever permanently preserved, yet it will, in some measure, remain in the world,[2] if nature prepare the way for it, if education encourage it and if severity enforce it. For the soul's every virtue is the result of birth, education or compulsion.[3]

But as evil more and more prevails—and this is a characteristic sign of the latter days[4]—good is no longer even permitted to be born, so corrupt is the race; nor may it be fostered, so neglected is education; nor may it be exacted, so enfeebled is the law. In fact, the virtue of which we are beginning to speak is now become so obsolete that purity is thought of as the moderation of lust, not its complete renunciation,[5] and he is considered to be sufficiently chaste who is not too unchaste.[6] Let the purity of the world and the world itself take the responsibility for this.[7] Let its own nature take the responsibility, if it is the result of birth; its education, if it is the result of instruction; its servitude, if it is the result of compulsion.[8] And yet, if it had been preserved,[9] it would have been the more unfortunate, for it would have been fruitless inasmuch as it would have been practiced apart from God. I should prefer no good at all to one which is useless. What is the good of being something which is good for nothing?[10]

A Shameful Edict

But now the condition of our own virtues is in decline. The foundations of Christian purity are shaken, that purity which draws from heaven all that it has—its nature from the laver of regeneration, its schooling from the ministry of preaching, its rigor from verdicts pronounced in both Testaments, firmly sanctioned by the fear of an eternal fire and the desire of an eternal kingdom.[11] I even hear that an Edict has been issued, indeed a peremptory one[12] (nor could I permit it to pass unnoticed) which opposes this rigor.[13] The Pontifex Maximus,[14] forsooth—I mean[15] the 'bishop of bishops!'—issues this pronouncement: *I forgive sins of adultery and fornication to those who have performed penance.*[16] Oh Edict, upon which one cannot write: *Good deed.*[17] And where shall this indulgence be posted? There, I fancy, on the very doors and under the very titles of debauchery.[18] Penitence such as this[19] should be promulgated where the sin itself will be committed. There one should read the pardon where one enters with its hope. But instead of this it is read in Church and it is promulgated in Church—and the Church is a virgin! Far, far from the bride of Christ[20] be such a proclamation! She who is faithful and pure and holy ought to preserve even her hearing from defilement. She has none to whom she can make such a promise,[21] and even if she should have them, she will not make it, for with less difficulty could the temple of God on earth be called by the Lord a *den of thieves*[22] than a den of adulterers and fornicators.

ENEMIES OF CHASTITY

This book, therefore, will also be directed against the Sensualists.[23] It will, moreover, oppose an opinion which I formerly held while in their company.[24] Let them, on this account, upbraid me all the more with the accusation of inconstancy. To break with a group is never an antecedent proof[25] of guilt. As if one were not in greater danger of going astray with the many, since truth is loved in company with the few![26] But inconstancy which is to my advantage will no more disgrace me than inconstancy which is to my disadvantage would do me honor. I am not ashamed that I have abandoned an error. Rather I rejoice that I am quit of it, since I recognize that I am now a better man and one of greater purity. Nobody blushes when he makes progress.

In Christ, also, knowledge has its ages, and through these even the Apostle passed. *When I was a child*, he says, *I spoke as a child, I understood as a child; but now that I am become a man, I have put off the things that belonged to the child.*[27] Thus did he change his earlier views. Nor was he at fault because he became *a zealot* for Christian rather than for *the paternal traditions*[28] and even desired that they be *cut off* who urged that circumcision be retained.[29] Would that this might be done to those also who destroy the true and genuine integrity of the flesh, for they cut away not just a superficial extremity but rather the very essence of decency itself when they promise pardon to adulterers and fornicators in opposition to fundamental Christian discipline.[30] The world itself bears witness to this discipline when, at times, it even goes so far as to strive to do it injury by the carnal defilement of our women rather than by their torture, seeking to wrest from them something which they hold more precious than life itself.[31]

But now this glory is being extinguished, and by the very ones who ought to have refused the more steadfastly to grant pardon to sins of this kind. For they marry as often as they wish precisely for fear of being forced to fall into adultery and fornication—on the plea that *it is better to marry than to burn*![32] No doubt it is for the sake of continence that incontinence is necessary! No doubt a fire will be extinguished by flames! Why, then, under the pretense of penitence, are they subsequently indulgent to crimes whose remedies they supply by the right of multiple marriage? For the remedies are superfluous where the crimes are indulged, and the crimes will continue if the remedies are superfluous.[33]

And so, either way, they make a mockery of both their solicitude and their indifference. Most futilely do they guard against crimes which they pardon, and most foolishly pardon crimes which they guard against. For either there should be no precaution where pardon is granted, or there should be no pardon where precaution is observed. They show caution as if they were unwilling that any such thing should be permitted, but they indulge it as if they were willing it should be permitted. And all the while, if they are unwilling it should be permitted, they ought not to indulge it; if they wish to indulge it, they ought not to take precautions against it.[34] For adultery and fornication may not be thought of as sins which are at once both little and great,[35] so that they may be regarded with a solicitude which guards against them and, at the same time, with an indifference which indulges them. But since they are at the very summit of iniquity, they may not be treated with tolerance as trifling and also with caution as capital.

We also, however, take precautions against serious or

capital sins. So much so that, after Baptism,[36] we are not even permitted to enter upon a second marriage, since it is nothing but nuptial and dotal contracts which, mayhap, distinguish it from adultery and fornication. And for this reason, with the greatest severity, we excommunicate digamists as persons who bring disgrace upon the Paraclete by their irregular discipline.[37] We set the same liminal limit [38] for adulterers and fornicators also. They will shed tears barren of peace and receive from the Church nothing more than the publication of their shame.[39]

THE APPEAL TO SCRIPTURE

2. 'But God,' they say, 'is good and most kind. He is *merciful* and *compassionate* [40] and *rich in mercy,*[41] which *He prefers to every sacrifice.*[42] *He desires not so much the death as the repentance of the sinner.*[43] He is *the savior of all men, and especially of the faithful.*[44] Therefore the children of God must also be *merciful* and *peacemakers,*[45] *forgiving each other as Christ also forgave us,* [46] *not judging, lest we be judged.*[47] For *to his master a man stands or falls; who are you to judge the servant of another?* [48] *Forgive and you will be forgiven.*' [49] Many such things as these they bandy about, unmanning rather than strengthening discipline, flattering God and pandering to themselves.

We are able to adduce, in rebuttal, just as much contrary testimony,[50] which shows forth the threat of God's severity and calls forth our own constancy.[51] For although God is by nature good, yet He is also just and, as the case requires, He knows how *to heal* but also how *to strike.*[52] He *brings peace,* but He also *creates evil.*[53] He desires repentance, yet He commands Jeremias not to intercede for the sinful people, since, He says, *even if they fast I will not hear their prayer.*[54] And, again, *And do thou not worship for the people and do not intercede for them in prayer and petition, for I will not hear them what time they invoke me in the time of their affliction.*[55]

Furthermore, the same one who *prefers mercy to sacrifice* says in an earlier verse: *And do thou not worship for this people and do not ask that they obtain mercy and do not approach me on their behalf, for I will not listen;* [56] He means, even as they beg for mercy; He means, even as they weep and fast and offer their suffering to God in a spirit of penance. For God is *jealous* [57] and *He is not mocked* [58] by those, that is, who flatter Him on His goodness. And although He is patient, yet in Isaias He threatens an end of patience: *I have held my peace; will I always hold my peace and endure? I have been patient as a woman in labor; I will arise and cause them to wither.*[59] *For fire shall go before His face and burn up His enemies* [60] destroying not only the body but also souls in hell.[61]

The Lord Himself, moreover, shows in what sense He threatens those who judge: *For with what judgement you judge, will you be judged.* [62] Thus He has not forbidden us to judge, but rather He has taught us how to do so.[63] Accordingly, the Apostle also judges—and precisely in a case of fornication—that *such a man is to be handed over to Satan for the destruction of the flesh.* [64] Besides this, he makes it a matter of censure that the brethren are not *judged before the tribunal of the saints.* [65] Indeed, he also says: *What have I to do with judging those who are without?* [66] You forgive in order that you may be forgiven by God,[67] but the sins which are cleansed are those committed against a brother, not against God; for in our prayer we declare that we will *forgive our debtors.*[68]

It is not proper any longer, however, where there is question of scriptural authority, to pull alternately in opposite directions on a rope of contention such as this, [69] so that the latter texts seem to tighten the reins of discipline while the former loosen them as if it were something uncertain, the former prostituting the remedy of penance through leniency, the latter excluding it completely through severity. But now the authority of scriptural teaching [70] will remain unimpaired, without the contradiction of one text by another, if [71] the remedy of penance is applied according to its own proper forms [72] without indiscriminate indulgence, and if, before this is done, the cases where it is required [73] are themselves set forth without ambiguity.

REMISSIBLE AND IRREMISSIBLE SINS

We agree that the cases where penance is required are sins. These we divide according to two issues: [74] some will be remissible, others irremissible. [75] Accordingly, no one doubts that some deserve correction, others condemnation. Either pardon or punishment balances the account [76] of every sin, pardon after correction, punishment after condemnation. [77] With reference to this distinction we have already premised certain scriptural antitheses, some retaining, others forgiving sins. [78] But John will also teach us: *If anyone know that his brother sins a sin which is not unto death, he shall pray and life will be given him because he sins not unto death.* This will be remissible. *There is a sin unto death; not for this do I say that anyone should pray.* [79] This will be irremissible. Accordingly, where there is room for prayer there also is room for remission. Where there is no room for prayer there, likewise, neither is there room for remission.

According to this distinction of sins the form of penance [80] is also determined. One will be such as is able to win pardon, that is to say, in the case of a sin which is remissible. The other will be such as is by no means able to win it, that is to say, in the case of a sin which is irremissible. And now it remains to consider, in particular, the position of adultery and fornication, and to determine in which class of sins they must be placed.

AN OBJECTION ANSWERED

3. But first I shall dispose of an objection which is raised by the opposition respecting that form of penance which we assert categorically is without pardon. 'If there is a kind of penance,' they say, 'which is without pardon, then you should not perform it at all, for nothing should be done which is fruitless. And penance will be performed without fruit if it be without pardon. But now every kind of penance ought to be performed;[81] therefore every kind will win pardon, lest it be without fruit. For if it should be without fruit, it ought not to be performed. But it is performed without fruit, if it is to be without pardon.'[82]

Quite consistently do they raise this objection since they have unlawfully assumed power over the fruit—forgiveness, I mean—of this penance also.[83] Penance will indeed be without fruit as far as they are concerned who receive peace from men;[84] as far as we are concerned, however, who bear in mind that the Lord alone forgives sins, and I mean, of course, mortal sins,[85] it will not be without fruit. For when it is placed in the Lord's keeping and, thereafter, lies prostrate before Him, it will, on this very account, effect forgiveness all the more surely, since it asks it[86] of God alone, since it does not suppose that peace granted by men satisfies for its offenses, since it would rather suffer shame before the Church than be in communion with it.[87]

And so it stands before her doors,[88] warning others by its exemplary shame. It calls to its assistance the tears of the brethren[89] and returns home richer for their compassion than it would be for their company. And if it reaps not here the harvest of peace, it sows the seed of it with the Lord.[90] It does not lose its fruit but rather makes provision for it. It will not fail of its reward, if it fail not in its duty. And so penance of this kind is not done in vain, nor is a discipline such as this harsh.[91] Both do honor to God. The former will more easily obtain what is asks, since it does not delude itself with fancies; the latter will be all the more helpful in that it is not guilty of presumption.[92]

A QUESTION OF TERMINOLOGY

4. Now that we have described the different kinds of penance, we may return to our classification of the sins we have mentioned before,[93] in order to see whether they be among those which may obtain pardon from men. In the first place, usage requires that we speak of fornication also as 'adultery.'[94] There is a certain familiar terminology which faith, withal, employs,[95] and, accordingly, throughout our little treatise,[96] we shall follow accepted usage. However, whether I say *adulterium* or *stuprum* the indictment[97] of carnal defilement is one and the same. For it makes no difference whether a man attack a woman who is married or single, since she is not his wife.[98] So, also, the place is a matter of indifference, whether purity be ruined in bedrooms or battlements.[99] Every murder, even outside a woods, is a felony.[100] In like manner, a man who has intercourse outside of marriage[101] makes himself guilty of

adultery and fornication, wheresoever the place and whosoever the woman. And so, among us, secret marriages,
also, that is to say, those which are not first contracted
before the Church, run the risk of being judged the next
thing to adultery and fornication.[102] Nor may they, under
the appearance of marriage, escape the charge of crime
when they have been contracted because of it.[103] But all
other frenzied lust, vicious and unnatural uses of the body
and of sex, we banish not only from the threshold of the
Church but also from any shelter within it,[104] since they
are not sins but rather monstrosities.[105]

GRAVITY OF ADULTERY PROVED BY THE OLD LAW

5. And now God's primeval law will serve to show us
how serious a crime we must judge adultery to be,
adultery with which fornication also is substantially
identified as far as the externally sinful act is concerned.[106]
For after condemning the superstitious worship of strange
gods and the making of idols, after commending the
observance of the Sabbath, after enjoining a reverence for
parents immediately after that which is due to God, it laid
down no other precept to strengthen and support the
aforementioned decrees than *Thou shalt not commit
adultery*.[107] For after chastity and sanctity of the spirit there
followed purity of the flesh. This, therefore, it immediately
safeguarded by outlawing adultery which is its enemy.[108]
Here, already, see what sort of sin it is whose repression is
ordained immediately after idolatry! Nothing second is
far from first, and there is nothing so close to the first as the
second. That which comes from the first is, in a sense,
another first. And so adultery, since it is the next thing to
idolatry—for idolatry is often made a matter of reproach to

the people under the name of adultery and fornication[109] —will share its fate as it does its rank, and be joined with it in punishment as it is in position.[110]

Furthermore, it mentions first: *Thou shalt not commit adultery*, and then subjoins: *Thou shalt not kill.*[111] Undoubtedly it gave the place of honor to adultery in setting it before murder, at the very apex of the holy law, among the principal statutes of the code of heaven, distinguished by reason of its proscription among capital crimes. One may discern the quality of anything from its position, its *status* from its rank and its merit from its environment.[112] There is also an eminence in evil, when it is placed at the peak or in the midst of the worst. Adultery, as I see it, has a certain retinue and pomp[113] of its own, with idolatry going on before to lead the way and murder, in attendance, bringing up the rear. Worthily, without a doubt, does she take her place between these two most lofty vertices of vice and, in their midst, with the prestige of equal guilt, she fills, as it were, the vacancy between.

INCONSISTENCY OF THE SENSUALISTS

Since she is enclosed within such flanks as these, supported by such engirdling ribs, who will tear her away bodily from that with which she is compacted, from her articulation with adjacent vice, from the encirclement of contiguous crime, so that she alone may be set apart to receive the fruit of penitence?[114] Will not idolatry hold her fast on one side and murder on the other? And if they were able to speak, would they not cry out: 'This is our quoin,[115] our bond of union. By her we three are one.[116] She separates us to unite us, and with her we are conjoined as she rises aloft between us. Divine Scripture has incorporated us in a single body; its letters are our luting nor can adultery itself exist without us.[117] Often indeed do I, *Idolatry*, play the pimp for adultery. My sacred groves, my hills and fountains, even the city temples know how much I do to procure the destruction of chastity.[118] And I also, *Murder*, not infrequently serve the interests of adultery. To say nothing of tragedies,[119] the poisoners of our day know, the sorcerers know, how much illicit love I punish, how many rivals I destroy, how many guards I do away with, how many informers and accomplices. Midwives, also, know how many adulterous conceptions are slaughtered. Even among Christians there is no adultery without us. Wherever an unclean spirit is active, there are idolatries; wherever a man is brought to death by defilement,[120] there is murder. Therefore the remedy of penance is either not for her, or it is for us also. Either we hold her back or follow with her.'

Thus speak the deeds themselves. But if the deeds speak not, then the idolater stands before us, the murderer stands before us and, in between them both, the adulterer also stands before us. They take their places all together, according to the prescriptions of penitence;[121] they shudder together in sackcloth and ashes; their groans and lamentations are the same; their prayers for suffrage are the same; their kneeling supplications are the same; the mother they invoke is the same.[122] What now, Oh discipline most gentle and humane? You must be so to all of them—for *blessed are the peacemakers*[123]—or, if not to all, then you must be with us.[124] The idolater and the murderer you condemn out of hand, and yet you withdraw the adulterer from their midst—the adulterer, who follows after the idolater, who goes before the murderer and who is an associate of both.[125] This is *respect of the person*.[126] You have disregarded the penances which are more deserving of pardon.[127]

The Old Law and the New

6. Of course,[128] if you show me the heavenly precepts and examples[129] which authorize you to open wide the door of penitence to adultery alone, and fornication with it, then our contest will be fought out right along this line.[130] However, I must lay down the rule that you are not to stretch forth your hand to *the things of old* and you are not *to look back*.[131] For according to Isaias, *the things of old have passed away*;[132] and according to Jeremias, *newness is now made new*;[133] and according to the Apostle, *forgetting the things that are behind we stretch forth to those which are before*;[134] and according to the Lord, *the Law and the Prophets were until John*.[135]

For although, in beginning our study of adultery, we have stressed the Law, yet, quite properly, we look upon the Law as having that *status*[136] which Christ has not destroyed but has fulfilled.[137] For the burdens of the Law and not its help are *until John*; the yoke of *works* has been cast off, not the yoke of moral precepts;[138] *freedom in Christ*[139] has done no injury to virtue. There remains, in its entirety, the law of piety, sanctity, humanity, truth, chastity, justice, mercy, charity and purity; and *blessed is the man who will meditate day and night*[140] upon this law. David also says of it in another place: *The law of the Lord is irreproachable, converting souls; the judgements of the Lord are upright, delighting hearts; the commandment of the Lord shineth afar, enlightening the eyes*.[141] So, also, the Apostle: *Therefore this law is, in truth, a holy one and the commandment is holy and perfect;*[142] he means, of course, *Thou shalt not commit adultery.* Moreover, he says earlier: *Do we therefore make void the Law by faith? God forbid; rather we establish the Law;* [143] in those things, that is, which since they are now reprobated in the New Testament also, are prohibited by a commandment which is even more comprehensive. Instead of ' *Thou shalt not commit adultery,*' ' *Whosoever looks with a view to concupiscence has already committed adultery in his heart.*' [144] And instead of ' *Thou shalt not kill,*' ' *Whosoever says to his brother, Racha, shall be liable to the punishment of hell.*' [145] Ask yourself whether the law against adultery is preserved when it is supplemented by a law which prohibits concupiscence.

Biblical Examples

But if there are any precedents which favor your own desires, [146] they may not be held up in opposition to this discipline which we defend. For in vain is a law superimposed which condemns not only external acts but also the sources of sin, I mean concupiscence and desire, if pardon is granted to adultery nowadays on the pretext that it was granted in times past. What is the advantage of today's stricter legislation? Is it, perhaps, that pardon may be granted more easily to your lechery? [147] You may, then, pardon the idolater, also, and every apostate, since we find that as often as the chosen people were guilty of these things, so often were they restored to their former estate. [148] With the murderer, also, you may communicate, because Achab effaced by prayer the blood of Naboth; [149] and David, by confession, purged himself of the slaughter of Uriah and the adultery which caused it. [150] Then you may pardon incests because of Lot; [151] and fornications compounded with incest, because of Juda; [152] and filthy marriages with prostitutes because of Osee; [153] and not only successive but even simultaneous polygamy, because of our fathers.[154] For, surely, it is only right that now the same pardon be granted to everything which was formerly indulged, if pardon for adultery be vindicated by some example or other dug up out of the past.

As far as that goes, we, too, have examples from this same past in favor of our own way of thinking, examples of a judgement on fornication which was not only not remiss but rather immediately executed.[155] It is quite enough, I should think, that so great a number of the chosen people, twenty-four thousand, perished at one stroke after they had fornicated with the daughters of Madian.[156] I prefer, however, for the glory of Christ, to derive ecclesiastical discipline from Christ.

Let us grant, if the Sensualists wish it, that in the ancient days every kind of impurity was allowed. Let us grant that before Christ the flesh was wanton, even that it was lost before it was sought out by its Lord. It was not yet worthy of the grace of salvation; it was not yet ready for the obligation of sanctity. It was still reckoned as being *in Adam*, sinful,[157] quickly lusting for what seemed to it beautiful,[158] preoccupied with things base, repressing prurience with fig leaves. The poison of lust and infecting filth were everywhere within it, and well were they able to cling to it, since as yet there were no waters which themselves had cleansed it.[159]

But when the Word of God descended into flesh which not even marriage had unsealed,[160] and when the Word was made flesh[161] which not even marriage was ever to unseal, flesh which approached the tree of suffering, not of incontinence, and tasted there the bitter, not the sweet,[162] flesh which belonged to heaven, not to hell[163] and which was girt with flowers of sanctity and not with leaves of lust, flesh which imparted its own purity to the waters [164]—from this time on, all flesh which is in Christ loses its old, residual stains. Now it is something different. Now it emerges new, not from the slime of sperm, not from the filth of concupiscence, but from pure water and the Holy Spirit. [165]

Why, then, do you turn to the past to find excuses for it? When it received pardon for adultery, it was not called the *body of Christ*, [166] nor the *members of Christ*, [167] nor the *temple of God*. [168] If, therefore, after it has changed its condition and, *being baptized in Christ has put on Christ*, [169] and if, after it has been *redeemed at a great price—the blood, that is, of the Lord and the Lamb* [170]—you seize upon any precedent or precept or norm or opinion which has pardoned or which holds pardonable adultery and fornication, you have also from us a definitely determined period for reckoning the temporal limits of this matter. [171]

THE PARABLES OF THE LOST SHEEP AND THE DRACHMA

7. You may begin, then, with the parables. [172] There is that account of the lost sheep which our Lord sought out and carried home on His shoulders. [173] Let the very pictures on your chalices be taken into consideration, [174] if even they will reveal how that sheep is to be understood and whether it points to the restoration of a Christian or a pagan sinner. Of course we must insist at the outset, [175] on the basis of the natural law, the law of ear and tongue, [176] and of good sense, that answers are always given according to their occasions, that is to say, they are given to the questions which occasion them. The occasion here, I take it, was the angry muttering of the Pharisees that the Lord received pagan publicans and sinners and communicated with them

at table. When the Lord, in answer to this, used the figure of the restoration of a lost sheep, of whom must we suppose that He used the figure if not of a lost pagan? For a pagan was in question, not a Christian—since as yet none existed. Or must we suppose [177] that the Lord, replying like a sophist, ignores the case [178] in question, which He should be settling, and concerns Himself with one which belongs to the future?

'But, properly speaking, a "sheep" is a Christian and the "flock" of the Lord is the congregation of the Church and the good shepherd is Christ, and therefore, in the sheep, we are to see a Christian who has wandered from the flock of the Church.' Well, then, you will have it that the Lord gave an answer to your own preconceived idea and not to the muttering of the Pharisees! You will be obliged, however, to defend this idea in such a way as to deny that those points have application to a pagan which you think are peculiar to a Christian. [179] Tell me, is not the whole human race God's one 'flock'? Is not the same God of all nations also their Lord and shepherd? Who is more 'lost' from God than the pagan, as long as he remains in error? [180] Who is more 'sought out' by God than the pagan, when he is called back by Christ? In fact, this sequence [181] is more evident in the case of pagans, since men do not become Christians after having been pagans without first being 'lost,' then 'sought out' by God and 'brought back' by Christ. Therefore we, in our turn, must safeguard this sequence by interpreting this kind of figure of those to whom it first applies. But you, I take it, would have him refer to a sheep which was lost not from a flock but from a chest or coffer! [182]

Accordingly, although He calls the remaining number 'just,' [183] He does not indicate that they are Christians when He speaks in this way, for He is dealing with Jews and rebuking them especially because they were angry at the hope of the heathen. In order to show, by way of contrast with the malicious spite of the Pharisees, His own gracious kindness even to a single pagan, He indicated that He preferred the salvation of one sinner through repentance to their salvation through righteousness.[184] Or will you argue that the Jews were not 'just' and not such as 'had no need of penitence' because they had the Law and the Prophets to govern their conduct and excite their fear?[185] We conclude that He represented them in the parable not as they were but as they should have been, so that they might be put to the blush all the more in hearing that penitence was necessary for others and not for themselves.

In line with this we interpret the parable of the drachma,[186] also, as having reference to a pagan, occasioned as it was by the same situation; and this, even though it was lost in the house, as it were in the Church; and although it was found by the light of a lamp, as it were by the word of God. This whole world, however, is one house for all men.[187] In it the grace of God shines for the pagan, who is found in darkness, rather than for the Christian, who is already in God's light. Finally, both the sheep and the drachma are lost but once. If they were portrayed as types of the Christian sinner who is lost after Baptism, He would have mentioned that this was their second loss and restoration.[188]

CORRECT INTERPRETATION OF THE PARABLES

And now I shall withdraw, for a moment, from the position I have taken in order to strengthen it all the more by my withdrawal, for in this way, also, I shall be able to refute the assumption of my opponents. Granted, now, that a Christian sinner is intended in both parables, still it does not follow that we are to say he is one who may be restored by penance after the crimes of adultery and fornication. For although he is said to be 'lost,' we may still ask what kind of loss this is, since the sheep was lost because it strayed, not because it died, and the drachma was lost because it was latent, not because it was destroyed. In this sense something which is safe may be said to be 'lost.' [189]

Therefore one of the faithful, also, is 'lost' if he has sinned by going to see a wildly exciting chariot race, a bloody gladiatorial combat, a filthy play, a frivolous exhibition of athleticism; [190] or if he has made use of any magic rites at play or at banquets on pagan festivals or in the performance of public office or while cooperating in another's idolatry; [191] or if, perhaps, with some equivocal expression, he has recanted or blasphemed. [192] For some such cause as this he has been put outside the flock. Or, it may be that he himself has left it out of anger, pride, jealousy or, finally, as often happens, because he refuses chastisement. He must be sought out and brought back. [193] That which can be saved is not wholly lost, unless it persists in remaining outside. You will interpret the parable correctly if you restore a sinner who is still living; but who will not say that the adulterer and fornicator is dead just as soon as he has sinned? How can you presume to restore to the flock someone who is dead, on the authority of that parable which restores a sheep which is not dead?

Then, also, if you remember when the prophets upbraid the shepherds, I think it is Ezechiel who says: *Ye shepherds, behold ye drink milk and are clothed in wool; that which is strong ye have slain, that which is weak ye have neglected; that which was broken, ye have not bound; that which was cast out, ye have not brought back; that which was lost, ye have not sought out.*[194] Does he reproach them because of the dead—for having neglected to bring that, also, back to the flock? Quite clearly he states that they have caused the sheep to be lost and to be devoured by the beasts of the field; nor, if they are abandoned, could they avoid being lost in death and devoured. But he does not say that they should be restored *after* they have been lost in death and devoured.[195]

Moreover, according to the parable of the drachma, it is possible that even in the house of God, the Church, there should be certain lesser sins,[196] which are proportioned to the measure and weight of that drachma.[197] These are hidden there, soon they are discovered there, and, at once, they are forgiven there—with joy at their correction.[198] Adultery, however, and fornication are not a drachma's weight, but a talent's.[199] To hunt them out one needs, not the feeble glimmer of a lamp for a light, but the blaze of the entire sun.[200] The guilty man is excommunicated at once, just as soon as he is discovered. He remains there no longer; neither does he bring joy to the Church which finds him, but rather sadness. She invites not the congratulations of her neighbors, but rather the grief of the congregations roundabout.[201]

And so even when this interpretation of ours is put in opposition to theirs, the parables of the sheep and the drachma will refer all the more clearly to a pagan, in as much as they can not have reference to a Christian who is guilty of that sort of sin.[202] Therefore our adversaries do them violence when they interpret them of a Christian.

THE PRODIGAL SON

8. Most interpreters of the parables are deceived by the

same illusion which results, quite commonly, when garments are patched with purple.[203] When you think that you have brought together the right combination of colors and you believe that their tones harmonize with each other, then when both materials have been leached[204] and their sheen heightened, the manifest contrast brings forth into the light the whole defect. So also, apropos of the parable of the two sons, deceived by certain allusions which are momentarily apt, they wander in obscurity away from the true light of that typical sense which is furnished by the very substance of the parable.[205]

For they take the two sons as types of two peoples, the elder Jewish, the younger Christian. They cannot, then, arrange thereafter that the younger son be a Christian sinner who is to receive pardon unless they make the elder a Jew. But if I show that the Jew does not suit the type represented by the elder son, it will be admitted, in consequence, that the Christian is not typified by the younger. Now although the Jew is called a 'son' and an 'elder son' since he is first by adoption,[206] and although he resents the Christian's reconciliation with God his Father (this is a point which our opponents seize upon most eagerly) yet the statement: *Behold how many years I serve thee and I have never transgressed thy commandment*,[207] cannot be one which the Jew makes to the Father. For when was the Jew not a transgressor of the law? *hearing with the ear and not hearing*,[208] *holding in hate him who reproves at the gates, and scorning holy speech*.[209] So, also, neither can that be the word of the Father to the Jew: *Thou art always with me and all things that are mine are thine*. For the Jews are proclaimed apostate sons, *begotten*, indeed, and *raised on high*, but *they have not considered the interests of God* and *they have abandoned the Lord* and they have provoked to wrath the Holy One of Israel.[210] I suppose we may say that *all things* are given to the Jew, when he is denied the enjoyment[211] of every good gift of creation, including the very promised land of his fathers.[212] For the Jew today, no otherwise than the younger son, after *wasting the substance of God*, is a beggar *in a foreign land* and, even until now, he serves its princes, that is, the princes of this world.

Let Christians, therefore, seek some other as their brother, for the parable will not allow him to be a Jew.[213] Much more aptly, with faith as a point of comparison,[214] would they have identified the Christian with the elder son and the Jew with the younger—if the order of succession established from the womb of Rebecca for each of the two peoples permitted this reversal.[215] But then this would also be inconsistent with the conclusion.[216] For it is proper that the Christian should rejoice and not grieve over the salvation of the Jew, since all our hope is joined with the expectation which Israel has for the future.[217] And so, though some points may be pertinent, yet intelligent persons will see that in others the similarity of the types breaks down.[218]

And even though there might be a mirror-like correspondence in all respects, yet the one special danger in interpretations is that a facile typology be turned in a direction other than that which is required by the substance of each particular parable.[219] We recall that actors, too, when they suit allegorical gestures to their songs, express things which are quite remote from the current plot, scene and character—and yet they do it most harmoniously![220] But this eccentric ingenuity is a matter of no importance; it has nothing to do with Andromache![221] So, also, heretics, working out[222] these parables with perfect consistency, interpret them as they please and not as they ought. Why 'with perfect consistency'? Because from the beginning they have fashioned the very substance of their doctrines to agree with the details of the parables. Of course, since they are not bound by the rule of faith,[223] they are free to hunt up and piece together things which seem to be typified by the parables.

SOME PRINCIPLES OF EXEGESIS

9. We, however, do not take the parables as sources of doctrine, but rather we take doctrine as a norm for interpreting the parables. Therefore we make no effort to twist everything so that it fits our own explanation, striving to avoid every discrepancy.[224] Why a 'hundred' sheep? and why, indeed, 'ten' drachmas? and what does that 'broom' stand for? Well, when he wanted to show how pleased God is at the salvation of one sinner, he had to mention *some* numerical quantity from which *one* could be described as 'lost.' And in view of the ordinary procedure of a woman who looks for a drachma in the house, he had to supply the assistance of a broom and lamp. Curious questions of this sort lead to conclusions which are suspect and, as a rule, they seduce men from truth through the subtleties of an artificial exegesis. There are some things, however, which are introduced into the parable with a view to its literal sense,[225] as elements of its structure, design and essential constitution, so that they may lead us [226] to that which it is intended to illustrate.

The two sons, evidently, are introduced for the same reason as the drachma and the sheep, for they have their origin in the same situation as the parables with which they are conjoined, that is, in the same grumbling of the Pharisees against our Lord's association with the heathen.

But if anyone does not believe that in Judea, subjugated as it was long since by the power of Pompey and Lucullus,[227] the publicans were pagans, let him read Deuteronomy: *There shall be no weigher of tribute from among the sons of Israel.*[228] The name 'publican' would not have been so odious before the Lord had it not been that of aliens who demanded toll for passage through the very air itself and over land and sea.[229] And when sinners are mentioned in the text, along with publicans,[230] this does not prove immediately that they were Jews, even though some of them may have been. Rather, only one group is distinguished, the heathens, since the text[231] places side by side some who are sinners by reason of their office, that is, the publicans, and others who are sinners by reason of their character, that is, those who are not publicans. Moreover, He would not be blamed for taking food with Jews but rather with pagans, since the Jewish law forbids communicating with them at table.[232]

The Prodigal a Type of the Pagan Sinner

Now, as to the prodigal son, we must consider first of all, that which is more useful, since typology can not be allowed if it is dangerous to salvation, even though it may balance as perfectly as a scale. We see, however, that the interpretation affected by our opponents destroys the whole economy of salvation, which is founded on the preservation of discipline. For if it is a Christian who, wandering far from his Father and living like a pagan, wastes the substance which he has received from God his Father (this means, of course, Baptism and the Holy Spirit and, in consequence, the hope of eternity), and if, stripped of his soul's good gifts,[233] he has even given himself over in bondage to a prince of this world (who else but the devil?), and been appointed by him to herd swine (this means, of course, to serve unclean spirits), and if he has recovered his senses so as to return to his Father— then, according to this parable, not only adulterers and fornicators, but idolaters also and blasphemers and renegades and apostates of every kind may make satisfaction [234] to the Father. In very truth a similitude such as this destroys the whole substance of the sacrament. [235] For who will fear to throw away what he is able, afterwards, to recover? Who will try to keep in perpetuity something which he is able to lose temporarily? [236] Security in sin stimulates the very desire to commit it.

Therefore, the apostate, too, may recover his former vesture, which is the cloak of the Holy Spirit, and receive, once more, the ring, which is the seal of Baptism. [237] For him, once more, Christ will be slain [238] and he will recline upon that couch from which those who are not worthily attired (to say nothing of those who have been stripped of their raiment) [239] are wont to be taken by the executioners and cast out into the darkness. [240] Therefore we have taken a step forward, if it is inexpedient that the account of the prodigal son be referred to a Christian. [241]

But if it is true that the figure of the dutiful son does not apply to the Jew, then our interpretation will be governed, simply, by the intention of the Lord. [242] Now the Lord, we know, *came to save that which was lost*, [243] a physician more necessary to the sick than to the well. [244] This He taught symbolically in parables and preached openly in His discourses. What man is lost and who is sick if not the man who is ignorant of God? Who is safe and sound, if not the man who knows God? These two types, brothers by birth, [245] will also be symbolized in this parable. Ask yourself whether or no the pagan has, as his portion, his origin in God the Father and an understanding and natural knowledge of God.[246] For this reason the Apostle makes the accusation that *in the wisdom of God, the world, through wisdom, has not known God,*[247] that wisdom, of course, which it had received from God.

This, then, is the substance which he wasted, far from the Lord[248] by reason of his disordered habits, amid the delusions, temptations and lusts of the world. Here, pressed with hunger for the truth,[249] he gave himself over to the prince of this world. He put him in charge of swine (to tend that herd which is on intimate terms with demons)[250] where he would not have food sufficient for life[251] and, at the same time, where he would see others, working for God, richly nourished with heavenly bread. He remembers God, his Father, and after making satisfaction to Him, he returns. He receives back his former vesture, that state, I mean, which Adam lost by his transgression.[252] Then, for the first time, he also receives a ring, and, after he has been questioned, this seals the pact of faith;[253] and so, thereafter, he feeds upon the richness of the body of the Lord, I mean the Eucharist.[254]

Here, then, is the prodigal son. He is one who was never antecedently virtuous. He was a prodigal from the beginning, because he was not a Christian from the beginning.[255] And it is such a one whom the Pharisees see, with regret, in the persons of the publicans and sinners, returning from the world to his Father's embrace. Therefore, only when it is directed against someone like this[256] is the envy of the elder brother meaningful, not because the Jews were virtuous and obedient to God, but because they, who certainly should have been with the Father always, begrudged salvation to the Gentiles. Thus the Jew deplores the very first vocation of the Christian, not his second restoration; for the former is evident even to the pagans, while the latter, since it takes place in the churches, is not even known to the Jews.[257]

Concluding Comment on the Parables

I think that the interpretations which I have given are more consistent with the substantial teaching of the parables, the harmony of their parts and the preservation of discipline. But if our opponents desire to make the sheep, the drachma and the dissolute son types of the Christian sinner in order that they may grant the gift of penitence[258] to adultery and fornication, then other capital sins also must be pardoned, or else, adultery and fornication, which are on a par with them, must continue to be regarded as unpardonable.[259]

It is more to the point, however, that an argument should not be extended beyond the limits of the subject matter with which it is concerned.[260] As a matter of fact, if it were permitted to extend the meaning of the parables beyond their intent, we should rather ascribe to martyrdom the hope which they offer.[261] For this, alone, will be able to reinstate the son who has wasted all his substance. It will proclaim with joy that the drachma has been found, no matter where it was, even amid the dung; and it will bring back the sheep to the flock on the master's shoulders, though it may have wandered through every kind of wild and dangerous country. But if needs must be, we prefer to have an incomplete rather than an incorrect understanding of the Scripture. So, too, we should preserve the thought of the Lord as carefully as His command. Bad exegesis is no less serious than bad conduct.[262]

PENANCE AND PARDON NECESSARY FOR PAGANS

10. Therefore the yoke has been removed which requires that these parables be not interpreted of the pagans.[263] It is understood and even acknowledged unconditionally that they must be interpreted in no other way than their substantial truth allows. Nevertheless our opponents still insist that 'the preaching of penitence is not meant for the heathen because the sins of the heathen, being imputable to ignorance,[264] are not its proper subject matter, since it is only from nature that ignorance has its culpability in the sight of God.[265] Moreover, the pagans fail to understand the remedies since they fail to understand the diseases. The reason for penance, however, is clearly appreciated when sin is committed knowingly and willingly, and when there is an awareness of what sin and grace[266] both mean. He falls upon his knees in tears who knows what he has lost and what he will regain if he offers to God the sacrifice of that penitence to which God invites His children, of course, rather than outsiders.'[267]

Did Jonas, then, on this account,[268] think that penance was unnecessary for the pagan Ninivites, when he tried to avoid his duty of preaching? Or was it not, rather, because he foresaw that the mercy of God would be poured out on the heathen also, and so feared that it would prove him a false prophet?[269] Actually it was because of a pagan city which did not yet know God and which sinned in ignorance that the prophet was almost lost.[270] And he would have been, were it not for the fact that what he endured was a type of the Lord's suffering,[271] by which pagan penitents, also, would be redeemed.

Moreover, it is well to remember that John, when he *made ready the paths of the Lord*,[272] preached penance to soldiers and publicans no less than to the sons of

Abraham.[273] And the Lord Himself believed that the men of Tyre and Sidon would have done penance, had they seen the evidence of His miracles.[274] I must insist, then, that penance is much more appropriate for those who sin by nature than for those who sin deliberately,[275] since a man will be much more worthy of its fruit [276] who has not yet received it than one who has received it and abused it. Remedies which are new will be better appreciated than those which are familiar.

I suppose the Lord is more favorably disposed to the ungrateful than He is to the ignorant, and pardons more quickly those who have been rejected than those who have not yet been tested—and this so that He may be pleased rather than angered when His mercy is abused, and so that He may not the more willingly grant to outsiders that mercy which He has wasted on His children. For thus He would adopt the Gentiles, while the Jews make a mockery of His forbearance! [277] But what the Sensualists want is that God, who judges the just man, should *prefer the penance rather than the death* of that sinner who has preferred death to penance. If this is so, then we merit when we sin! [278]

Come now, you funambulist,[279] walking on a tightrope of purity and chastity and every sort of sexual asceticism, you who, on the slender cord of a discipline like this, far from the path of truth, advance with reluctant feet, balancing the flesh by the spirit, moderating your desires by the faith, guarding your eyes through fear, why do you watch your step so anxiously? Go right ahead, if you can and if you so desire, since you are just as safe as if you were on solid ground.[280] For if any wavering of the flesh, any distraction of spirit, any wandering glance, causes you to lose your equilibrium—remember God is good! It is to His own and not to the heathen that He opens His arms. A second penance will receive you and, after you have been an adulterer, you will again be a Christian.[281]

The Shepherd of Adulterers

Thus would you speak to me, Oh kindliest of God's exegetes. And I would assent, if the book of the Shepherd[282] which alone is favorable to adulterers deserved to be included within the sacred canon,[283] and if it had not been judged apocryphal and false by all the councils of the churches, even your own![284] It is adulterous itself and therefore favors its associates. In other ways, too, it serves as your sponsor.[285] Perhaps that shepherd will favor you whom you picture on the chalice, himself a debaucher of the Christian sacrament, worthy to be both an idol of drunkenness and a protector of the adultery which follows upon the cup. From this you will drink nothing more gladly than you do 'the sheep of a second penance.'[286]

But I drink the Scripture of that Shepherd who cannot be broken.[287] John offers me this at once, along with baptism and the duty of penitence, when he says: *Bring forth fruits which are proper to penance and say not that we have Abraham for our father* (lest they again yield, he means, to the blandishments of sin by presuming on the kindness shown their fathers); for *God can raise up from these stones children to Abraham.*[288] This refers to us, also,[289] as to persons who should sin no more and who should *bring forth fruits proper to penance.* For what is the ripened fruit of penance but a change of life? But if the fruit of penance is, rather, pardon,[290] this, in its turn, is impossible if sin be not discontinued. Thus the discontinuance of sin is the root of pardon, so that pardon may be the fruit of penance.[291]

THE EXAMPLE OF CHRIST

11. And so, in our study of the Gospel,[292] we have now thoroughly investigated the question of the parables. But if the Lord, by His actions also, favored sinners in some similar way, as, for example, when He even permitted a sinful woman to touch His body, washing His feet with her tears and drying them with her hair and, with ointment, making preparation for His burial,[293] and as when He showed the Samaritan woman (whose sixth marriage made her not so much an adulteress as a prostitute) who He was,[294] something He did not readily do for anyone[295] —this in no way favors our adversaries, even if He had granted pardon to those who were already Christians.[296] For we say now: 'This is allowed to the Lord alone. May His power to pardon be at work in our own day!'[297]

But as far as those times are concerned when He dwelt on earth, we lay down the principle that it does not prejudice our case in any way if He granted pardon to sinners, even to Jews.[298] For the Christian discipline begins with the New Testament and, as we have already said, with the redemption of the flesh, that is, with the passion of the Lord.[299] No one was perfect before the economy of faith[300] was revealed; no one was a Christian before Christ was taken up into heaven;[301] no one was holy before the Holy Spirit came from heaven to establish this discipline.[302]

THE APOSTOLIC DECREE

12. But as for those who, in and through the apostles,[303] have received another Paraclete Whom they now no longer possess even in the apostles since they have not acknowledged Him in His own prophets[304]—come, let

them now prove to us from the writings of the apostles[305] that stains of the flesh which is sullied once again after Baptism may be washed away by penance.[306] In the writings of the apostles, also, we see that the substance of the Old Law remains unchanged as far as its teaching on the gravity of adultery is concerned, else, under the new moral code, adultery might be considered less serious than it was under the old.[307] When the Gospel first thundered and shook the things of old to their foundations, then the apostles, debating the necessity of retaining the Law, issued, on the authority of the Holy Spirit, this first decree for those who had already begun to join them from among the Gentiles: *It has seemed good*, they say, *to the Holy Spirit and to us to lay no further burden upon you than that of those things from which you must abstain, from sacrifices, from fornications and from blood; abstaining from these things you will do well, with the assistance of the Holy Spirit.*[308]

It is sufficient that here, too, adultery and fornication have the place of honor reserved for them between idolatry and murder.[309] For the 'prohibition of blood' we shall understand as referring much more properly to human blood.[310] Then, again, how do the apostles wish us to regard those crimes which they single out from the Old Law for special attention[311] and which are the only ones they insist must necessarily be avoided? Not that they allow the others, but these are the only ones which they mention as certainly irremissible, they who, out of consideration for the pagans, made the remaining burdens of the Law remissible.[312]

Why, then, do they remove so heavy a yoke from our necks, except that they may lay upon them, in perpetuity, these *compendia*[313] of the Law? Why do they relax so many bonds, if not to bind us forever to duties which are more imperative? They have loosed us from a multitude of obligations so that we may be forced to discharge those whose neglect is more dangerous. The matter has been settled by compensation;[314] we have gained much so that we may give something. Compensation, however, is not revocable, unless, withal, it be revoked by the repetition of adultery, murder and idolatry! For the obligation of the whole Law is again assumed, if the condition which excuses from its observance is violated.[315]

But it is not lightly that the Holy Spirit has made a contract with us. He has even offered the contract spontaneously; therefore it is all the more to be respected. No one but an ingrate[316] will break an engagement he has made with Him; thereafter, He will neither accept what He has remitted nor will He remit what He has retained.[317] The *status* of a final testament[318] is forever immutable, and it is only with the end of the world that this judgement and the reading of this decree[319] will have an end. Clearly enough He has refused to pardon those sins which He has set aside for retention.[320] He has refused what He has not definitely granted.[321] It is for this reason that the churches do not grant peace either to idolatry or to murder.[322] To my mind, it is unbelievable that the apostles abandoned their own definitive decree, but if there are any who can believe it, they will have to prove it.

THE INCESTUOUS CORINTHIAN NOT PARDONED BY PAUL

13. Here, too, we are well aware of their false suppositions. Indeed, they actually suppose that the Apostle Paul, in *Second Corinthians*, granted pardon to the selfsame fornicator—that wicked heir of his father's marriage[323]—whom in *First Corinthians* he decreed was to be

given over to Satan for the destruction of the flesh;[324] as if he himself erased his earlier words[325] when he wrote: *Now if anyone has been a cause of sadness, he has not saddened me but, in a measure—not to be too severe—all of you. For such a one a rebuke which is given by many is sufficient; so that now you should forgive and support him, lest, perchance, he be overwhelmed by too much suffering. Therefore I beseech you to assure him of your love for him. For to this end, also, have I written, that I might, in putting you to a test, know that you obey me in all things. But if you forgive anyone, I also; for I, too, if I have forgiven anything, have forgiven it in Christ, lest we be cheated by Satan; for we are not unaware of his designs.*[326]

Where is there any mention here of one who has committed fornication? Where is there mention of one who has defiled the marriage bed of his father? Where is there mention of a Christian who has gone beyond the shamelessness of the Gentiles? For would he not also, most assuredly, have absolved with special pardon one whom he had condemned with special indignation?[327] He shows his mercy less plainly than his wrath! His severity is more evident than his leniency! And yet anger is, as a rule, less explicit than is indulgence; there is greater hesitancy in unpleasant than in pleasant things.[328]

It is obvious that there is question here of indulgence for a lesser fault, which, perhaps, may not have been taken seriously at all, for it is the custom that no grave sin is ever forgiven without at least proclaiming the fact clearly, to say nothing of indicating the nature of the sin.[329] Even you yourself, when you lead the penitent adulterer into church to beg the intercession of the brethren,[330] place him on his knees in their midst, covered with sackcloth and ashes, in an attitude of humiliation and fear, in the presence of the widows, in the presence of the priests, moving all to tears,

kissing the footprints of all, embracing the knees of all.[331]
And for the salvation of a man like this, good shepherd and
blessed bishop that you are,[332] you preach of mercy in the
most alluring terms possible. In the parable of the sheep,
you look for your goats,[333] and lest your sheep again escape
the fold—as if that which was *never* permitted should now
be permitted no longer!—you fill the others with fear at
the very moment when you are granting indulgence.[334]

Would the Apostle, then, have pardoned so casually the
abandoned licentiousness of a fornication aggravated by
incest, without demanding from the guilty man at least
those legally established forms[335] of penance which you
should have heard him mention? Would there have been
no warning of what was to come? Would he have said
nothing about the future?[336] What is more, he even goes
so far as to ask that they *assure him of love,* as if he is
repairing an injury, not as if he is pardoning a fault.[337] And
yet 'love' is the word I hear, not 'communion.' Just as he
writes to the Thessalonians: *But if anyone does not obey our
word by this letter, note that man and do not associate with him,
so that he may be moved to fear; not looking upon him as an
enemy, but admonishing him as a brother.*[338] In the same way
he could have said that love alone is given to a fornicator,
and not communion also. But to an incestuous man, not
even love is given; him he would surely have commanded
to be removed from their midst and, much more, I am
sure, from their hearts.[339]

'But he feared that they might be *cheated by Satan* in the
loss of that man whom he had himself *delivered up to Satan,*
or that the man might be *overwhelmed* by too much grief
whom he had *handed over for the destruction of the flesh.*'[340]
Here they go so far as to interpret *destruction of the flesh* as
referring to the ritual of penance which may seem to

satisfy [341] God by mortification of the flesh, through fasts, filth, every sort of neglect and deliberate harsh treatment. Their purpose is to argue from this that that fornicator, or rather, that incestuous man, was *handed over to Satan* by the Apostle not for his *destruction* but for his correction, as if, thereafter, he would obtain forgiveness by reason of the *destruction*—that is, the affliction—of the flesh, and as if he did, on this account, actually obtain it. [342]

HYMENAEUS AND ALEXANDER

We know that the Apostle also *handed over to Satan Hymenaeus and Alexander so that they might be corrected unto not blaspheming*, as he writes to his beloved Timothy. [343] And he himself says that *a thorn was given him, an angel of Satan to buffet him, lest he exalt himself.* [344] If they touch on this point, also, in order to make us see that those who were *given over to Satan* by him were given over for their correction and not *for their destruction*, we may ask what resemblance there is between blasphemy and incest on the one hand and, on the other, a soul which is entirely innocent of these things, one, even, which was exalted in no other wise than by the highest sanctity and perfect purity. This exaltation was checked in the Apostle by *buffets*, if you will; that is, by ear or head ache, as they say. [345] Men guilty of blasphemy and incest, however, were deservedly *delivered over* completely into the possession of Satan himself, not to an angel of his. For there is a difference in this, also, and it is one of capital importance, that those men, as we read, were *handed over to Satan by* the Apostle, whereas an *angel of Satan was given to* the Apostle. [346] Finally, when Paul calls upon the Lord, what does he hear? *Consider my grace as sufficient; for virtue is made perfect in infirmity.*[347] This they cannot hear who are *given over to Satan.*

Moreover, if the crime of Hymenaeus and Alexander, I mean their blasphemy, is *irremissible in this world and the next,*[348] then the Apostle, against the judgement[349] of the Lord, would not have *handed them over to Satan* with a hope of pardon, sunk as they were in blasphemy even after having embraced the faith.[350] Therefore he calls them *castaways of the faith,*[351] since they were no longer sustained by the ship of the Church;[352] for pardon is denied to those who fall into blasphemy after Baptism.[353] Pagans and heretics, however, daily emerge from blasphemy.[354] Even though he said, *I handed them over to Satan so that they might receive the discipline of not blaspheming,*[355] yet he meant this for others[356] who had to be taught from the example of those who were *given over to Satan*—and this means 'excommunicated'—that blasphemy must not be committed. So, also, it was for his *destruction* and not for his correction that he *handed over* the incestuous fornicator *to Satan*—and he had already gone over to him by sinning worse than a pagan—so that others might learn that fornication must not be committed.[357]

Finally, he says: *for the destruction of the flesh,* not its 'affliction.'[358] Thus he condemns that very substance which led to the man's downfall and which was already lost when Baptism was lost; *so that the spirit,* he says, *may be saved in the day of the Lord.*[359] And here it might be asked whether the spirit of this same[360] individual will be saved or not. Can a spirit be saved in these circumstances, polluted by so great a crime? when the flesh has already been given over to perdition for this crime? Will it be saved through chastisement?[361] If so, then those whose opinion is opposed to ours must hold that there is a chastisement in which the flesh has no part; and thus we give up the resurrection of the flesh.[362] We must conclude, therefore, that he speaks of that *spirit* which is thought of as being in the Church[363] and which must be shown forth *safe in the day of the Lord*[364]—that is, free from the contagion of impurity after the incestuous fornicator has been expelled. He adds, indeed: *Know ye not that a little leaven spoils the whole lump?*[365] And yet incestuous fornication was not a little leaven but a lot.

POINTS OF CONTRAST BETWEEN FIRST AND SECOND CORINTHIANS

14. And now that I have disposed of these objections that have been raised I shall return to *Second Corinthians* in order to prove that that other statement of the Apostle's: *Let that rebuke be enough for such a man which is given by many*[366] has no application to the fornicator. For when he declared that he was to be *handed over to Satan for the destruction of the flesh*, it is evident that he condemned rather than rebuked. It was a different man, therefore, for whom he was willing that a rebuke suffice, since his judgement on the fornicator was one of condemnation, not rebuke.

Moreover, I propose this question for your consideration. Were there others, also, mentioned in the first epistle, who grieved the Apostle by their disorderly conduct and who, as the second epistle expresses it, were saddened by reason of the rebuke which they received from him?[367] Could it have been one of these who received pardon in that epistle? We may remark, in this connection, that the whole first epistle was written, so to speak, not with ink but with gall. It is passionate, indignant, scornful, threatening, harsh; and with respect to each of its various charges, it is directed against certain individuals as chief offenders.[368] For their schisms and rivalries and dissensions and presumptions and lofty notions and quarrels had made it necessary that they feel the weight of his displeasure, that they be checked by chiding, improved by imperious treatment and intimidated by severity.

And what is the displeasure like which spurs them to humility? *I give thanks to God that I baptized no one of you except Crispus and Caius, lest anyone should say that I baptized in my own name.*[369] *Nor did I judge that I know anything among you except Jesus Christ and Him crucified.*[370] And also: *I think that God has chosen us apostles last of all, as victims of beasts, for we are made a spectacle to the world and to angels and to men.*[371] And also: *We are made as the refuse of the world, the offscouring of all.*[372] And also: *Am I not free? Am I not an apostle? Have I not seen Christ Jesus our Lord?*[373]

On the other hand, with what hauteur was he forced to say:[374] *But with me it is a small matter to be judged by you or by man's tribunal; neither am I conscious of any guilt?*[375] And also: *My glory none shall make void.*[376] *Do you not know that we shall judge angels?*[377] And, then, what freedom and frankness in his reproaches! How sharp the bared edge of his spiritual sword! *You are already rich. You are already sated. You already reign.*[378] And, again: *If anyone thinks that he knows anything, he does not yet know as he ought to know.*[379] And does he not smite one of them in the face[380] when he says: *For who singles thee out? or what hast thou that thou hast not received? But if thou hast received, why dost thou glory as if thou hadst not received?*[381] And does he not slap them in the mouth? *But some knowing what they do, even now eat idol-offerings as such.*[382] *But sinning in this way and shocking the weak consciences of the brethren, they will sin against Christ.*[383]

And now he descends to particulars.[384] *Or do we not have the right to eat and drink and take women about with us, as do the other apostles and the brethren of the Lord and Cephas?* [385] Again: *If others have a share in power over you, do we not even more?* [386] So, also, he pricks them individually with his pen. *Therefore let him who thinks he stands take heed lest he fall;* [387] and again: *If anyone seems to be contentious, we have no such custom, neither has the Church of God.* [388] When his final sentence closes with a curse like this: [389] *If anyone does not love the Lord Jesus, let him be anathema, maranatha,* [390] then certainly he castigated a definite individual.

But I will insist rather on those passages where the Apostle speaks with greater warmth, and where that same fornicator gave trouble to others also: *Some are puffed up, as if I were not coming to you. But I shall come quickly, if the Lord permits, and I shall learn not the speech of those who are puffed up but the power; for the kingdom of God is not in speech but in power. And what is it you wish? Shall I come to you with a rod or in a spirit of leniency?* [391] And then what followed? *It is common talk among you that there is even fornication in your midst and such fornication as is not found even among the Gentiles, that a man should have his father's wife. And you are puffed up and have not rather mourned, so that he who has committed such a crime should be taken from amongst you.* [392]

For whom should they mourn? For one who was dead, of course. Before whom should they mourn? Before the Lord, of course, so that in some way or other *he should be taken from amongst them.* Evidently this does not mean that he should be excommunicated—for something within the competence of the presiding officer [393] would not be asked of God—but rather that he should be more completely taken away from the Church by that death, also, [394] which is common to all and especially proper to that same flesh which was already a rotting corpse, corrupt with a decay which is irremediable. And, therefore, in so far as it was possible for him to be *taken away* betimes,[395] the Apostle decreed that *such a one should be handed over to Satan for the destruction of the flesh.*[396] For a curse followed flesh which was *given over to Satan*, so that it might be deprived of the sacrament of the Blessing,[397] never again to return to the camp of the Church.[398]

We see, therefore, that in this passage the Apostle's severity touches two men, one of whom is *puffed up* and the other *incestuous*. It is armed with a rod in the one case, with a judicial sentence in the other; a rod with which he threatened, a judicial sentence which he executed; the former he continues to flourish, the latter he fulminates at once; with the one he *rebuked* and with the other he *condemned*. We may be sure, then, that thereafter the man who was rebuked trembled under the threat of the rod, the man who was condemned perished in the infliction of punishment. The former perseveres because he fears a blow, the latter disappears from amongst them, because he suffers a penalty.[399]

When the same Apostle writes his second letter to the Corinthians it is quite clear that he grants a pardon, but it is uncertain to whom he grants it, since neither the person nor the offense is advertised. Let us look at things in the light of the text.[400] If the incestuous man is placed before our eyes, there, also, is the proud man by his side. Obviously the proper proportion of things is preserved[401] when the proud man is rebuked and the incestuous man condemned. The proud man is pardoned but rebuked; the incestuous man, as it appears,[402] was not pardoned, since he was condemned. If pardon was being granted a man who it was feared would be *consumed by too much grief,*[403] then the person rebuked was still in danger of being consumed, losing heart because of the threat and grieving because of the rebuke. But a man who was condemned both by reason of guilt and by judicial sentence was looked upon as already *consumed* [404] since he was incapable of grief and could only endure a punishment which, before his suffering, could have been a cause of grief. [405]

If the reason for granting pardon was *lest we be cheated by Satan*, [406] then, surely, care was being exercised to avoid the loss of something which had not, as yet, perished. One does not take precautions over something which is lost, [407] but over something which is still safe and sound. Now a man who was damned, and damned even to possession by Satan, was already lost to the Church when he committed so great a crime, to say nothing of when he was rejected by her with a curse. How could she fear *to be cheated* of one whom she had already lost because he was snatched away, and whom she could not have kept because he was already damned? Finally, when is it proper for a judge to show indulgence? in a case which he has settled by a definitive sentence or in one which he has held over by an interlocutory decree [408]—especially that judge who is not wont to *build up what he has torn down, lest he be considered a transgressor*? [409]

Now tell me, if the first epistle had not *saddened* so many persons, if it had not *rebuked* anyone or *terrified* anyone, if it smote none but the incestuous man, if it inspired fear in no one on his account, if it brought consternation to no one who was *puffed up*, would it not even then be better for you to suppose, and more consistent with the faith for you to argue, that there was among the Corinthians at that time some entirely different person who, involved in the same affair, was *rebuked, terrified, stricken with grief*, and who, as a result, received pardon thereafter—since the lesser gravity of his offense allowed it—rather than to suppose that this pardon was granted to an incestuous fornicator? [410]

For this is something which you should have read in the very character of the Apostle, even if you did not read it in his epistle. His purity impresses it more plainly than does his pen, so that you should surely not have stained Paul— an *Apostle of Christ*, [411] *teacher of the nations in faith and truth*, [412] *a vessel of election*, [413] a founder of churches, a censor of morals—with a charge of inconstancy so great that he either heedlessly condemned a man whom he was soon to absolve or heedlessly absolved a man whom he had not heedlessly condemned, even though it be that this condemnation was for the uncomplicated impurity of simple fornication, not to speak of incestuous marriage and impious lust and parricidal licentiousness such as he could not even compare with that of the Gentiles for fear that it might be explained as a matter of custom. This was fornication which he judged *in absentia*, lest the culprit profit by delay, [414] and which he condemned after invoking the Lord's own power, lest his sentence seem to be that of a man. [415] We must conclude, then, that he made a mockery of his own *spirit*, [416] of the *angel of the Church*, [417] and of the *power of God*, [418] if he revoked a sentence which their counsel had led him to pronounce.

FURTHER PROOFS THAT PAUL DID NOT FORGIVE INCEST

15. If you place the latter portions, also, of that epistle alongside the threatening language of the Apostle, neither will they justify the forgiveness of incest; [419] for the Apostle must not be put to the blush here either, [420] as if

his later declarations were inconsistent with his earlier. For how is it possible [421] that just after he grants the incestuous fornicator the right to renewed fellowship [422] in ecclesiastical peace, he at once begins to speak about avoiding impurity and checking immorality [423] and encouraging chastity, as if he had decreed nothing contradictory to this just a little while before?

Consider this contrast, for example: *Therefore discharging this ministry in accordance with the mercy which we have received, we do not fail; on the contrary, we renounce secret deeds of shame.* [424] Can this be said by the same man who forgave public deeds which were criminal and not merely shameful? [425] Can that same man pardon any impurity whatever [426] who, in listing his own labors, after speaking of *hardships* and *afflictions*, *fasts* and *watchings*, makes distinctive mention of chastity also? [427] Can that same man receive back to communion all sorts of reprobates, who writes: *For what has justice in common with iniquity? What fellowship has light with darkness? What harmony is there between Christ and Belial? Or what part has the believer with the unbeliever? Or what agreement has the temple of God with idols?* [428]

Ought he not to be answered at once: 'And how will you separate things which you formerly joined when you forgave the sin of incest?' For when incest is brought back into the body of the Church, *justice* and *iniquity* are joined, and *darkness* is at one with *light*, and *Belial* is in harmony with *Christ*, and the *unbeliever* has part in the sacraments [429] along with the *believer*. And as to idols, it is their affair [430] that the very violator of the temple of God [431] is one with the temple of God. For in this selfsame place he says, besides: *For you are the temple of the living God, since He declares: I will dwell and move among you and I will be their*

God and they will be my people. Therefore come out from amongst them; be separated and touch not an unclean thing.[432] This, also, Oh Apostle, you unfold,[433] and you do it at the very moment when you yourself stretch forth your hand to one who is an abyss of filth.[434] What is more, you even add: *Having, therefore, this promise, dearly beloved, let us cleanse ourselves from all defilement of the flesh and of the spirit, perfecting purity in the fear of God.*[435] Tell me, pray, did a man who impresses such thoughts as these upon our minds take back into the Church a notorious fornicator? Or does he not write in this way lest you suppose now that he did take him back?[436]

These words of his ought to serve as an antecedent norm for interpreting passages which follow, just as they serve as a prescriptive rule for those which go before.[437] Towards the close of his epistle he writes: *lest when I come again God humiliate me and I grieve for many of those who sinned before and did not do penance for the uncleanness of which they were guilty through fornication and debauchery.*[438] In saying this, of course, he did not decree that it was necessary to take back into the Church, if they did penance, those whom he would find in the Church;[439] but, rather, he decreed that tears be shed for them and that, without delay, they be expelled from the Church so that their penance might be without fruit.[440] It is impossible, moreover, that he should have said anything about 'communion' in this passage who earlier had denied it to *light* and *darkness*, to *justice* and *iniquity*.

Those persons are all ignorant of the Apostle who interpret any text of his in a way which is out of harmony with the character and the aims of the man himself and opposed to the norms and rules of his teaching, presuming that one who inculcates perfect chastity—and this in his own person also—one who detests all impurity and demands its expiation, one who is everywhere consistent in such matters, should have restored ecclesiastical communion to an incestuous man rather than to someone guilty of a lesser offense.[441]

CONSISTENCY OF THE APOSTLE

16. It is necessary, then, that we continue to reveal to them the character of the Apostle. I shall show that in *Second Corinthians* he is just the same sort of person [442] that I have found him to be in all of his other letters. In his first epistle he was the first of all to speak about the *temple of God*: [443] *Know you not that you are the temple of God and that the Lord dwells within you?* [444] And he it was, also, who, in order to keep the temple holy and inviolate, wrote a special law safeguarding the temple: *If anyone destroy the temple of God, him will God destroy; for the temple of God is holy and this temple you are.*[445] Tell me, now, who could ever restore someone whom God has completely destroyed, that is to say, someone who has been *handed over to Satan for the destruction of the flesh*, especially in view of the words which follow: *Let no one deceive himself,*[446] that is, let no one presume that what God has destroyed can again be restored?

So, also, in another passage, when, among other crimes, or rather *before* other crimes, he affirmed that adulterers and fornicators and the effeminate and sodomites will not possess the kingdom of God, he said by way of preface: *Do not err* [447]—as you will, of course, if you suppose that they may possess it. But those who are deprived of the kingdom are certainly not permitted to enjoy the life of the kingdom. He adds, besides: *And such were some of you, but you have been washed, but you have been sanctified in the name of the Lord Jesus Christ and in the spirit of our God.*[448]

Thus, in as much as he excuses those sins which are committed before Baptism, by just so much does he make those irremissible which are committed after it, since a second Baptism is not permitted.[449]

Then, too, in the passages which follow, you must recognize Paul as an unshakeable pillar of virtue.[450] *Food for the belly and the belly for food; God will destroy both the one and the other. The body is not for fornication but for God.*[451] For God says: *Let us make man to our image and likeness. And God made man; to the image and likeness of God did He make him.*[452] *The Lord is for the body.*[453] *For the Word was made flesh.*[454] *But God has raised up the Lord and He will raise us up also by His power.*[455] This, of course, is because of our body's union with Him. And therefore He says: *Know you not that your bodies are members of Christ?*[456] For Christ, too, is the temple of God: *Destroy this temple and in three days I will build it up again.*[457]

Shall I, then, take the members of Christ and make them members of a harlot? Know you not that a man who is joined to a harlot becomes one with her? For they will be two in one flesh. But a man who is joined to the Lord is one spirit with Him. Flee fornication.[458] If I think that this can be cancelled by pardon, how can I flee it, since to do so I must again become an adulterer? I shall gain nothing if I do flee it. I shall continue to be one body with that to which I remain joined in communion.[459]

Every sin that a man commits is outside his body; but the man who commits fornication sins against his own body.[460] To prevent you from seizing upon this text in order to justify fornication as an act committed against something which is your own and not the Lord's, he dispossesses you of yourself and, according to his previous disposition,[461] he gives you over to Christ: *And you are not your own*, adding at once: *For you have been bought at a price*, that is, the blood of the Lord. *Glorify God and bear Him in your body.*[462] Consider whether one who gives this command would grant pardon to a man who dishonors God, who casts Him forth from his body and, what is more, who does this by committing incest.

PAUL'S ATTITUDE TO MARRIAGE

If you wish to have an exhaustive knowledge of the Apostle,[463] so as to understand how ruthlessly he puts the axe of censure to every thicket of lust, how he roots it out and pulls it up so that nothing may ever again be permitted to grow there, then see how eager he is that souls should abstain even from the legitimate fruit of nature, I mean the apple of marriage.[464] *Now concerning the things whereof you wrote me: It is good for a man not to touch a woman. Yet for fear of fornication let each man have his own wife. Let the husband render to the wife her due, and the wife to the husband.*[465] Who does not see that it was in order to prevent fornication that he, all unwillingly, removed the pin which held this pleasure in check?[466] Now if he either has granted or does grant indulgence to fornication, this means that he has acted against the purpose of his own remedy. He will then be obliged to place the check of continence upon marriages,[467] if he no longer fears fornication—the fear of which leads to their permission. For it is not feared when it is pardoned.[468]

And yet he declares that he has *allowed* the use of marriage, not *commanded* it; for he wishes all to be like himself.[469] But when things which are licit are only allowed, how can they hope for things which are illicit?[470] He says that *it is good for the unmarried, also, and for widows so to remain*, according to his example. *But if they are wanting in strength, let them marry, because it is better to marry than to burn.*[471] With what fires, pray, is it worse to burn—those of concupiscence or of punishment?[472] But if fornication is pardoned, then its concupiscence does not cause one to burn.[473] It better accords, however, with the spirit of the Apostle that he should guard against the fires of punishment.[474] And if it is the punishment which burns,[475] then fornication is not pardoned, since punishment awaits it.

After this he prohibits divorce, also, and in its place he requires either perseverance in widowhood or peaceful reconciliation.[476] This is according to the Lord's precept against adultery, for: *Whoever puts away his wife, except on account of adultery, causes her to commit adultery and he who marries a woman who has been put away by her husband commits adultery.*[477] What excellent remedies the Holy Spirit has provided to prevent the recurrence of something which he is unwilling to *allow* for a second time![478] Then he says that it is best in every way *for a man so to remain. Art thou bound to a wife? Seek not to be freed*, lest you give occasion to adultery. *Art thou freed from a wife? Seek not a wife*, that you lose not the opportunity which is given you. *But if you take a wife and if a virgin marries, there is no sin. Yet such will have tribulation of the flesh.*[479] In these passages, also, his permission is one of toleration.[480] He declares, however, that *the time is short*,[481] so that *those who have wives should be as those who have them not. For the figure of this world is passing away*,[482] since, as is clear, the world no longer needs to *increase and multiply.*[483]

Accordingly, it is his wish that we live *free from care*, for *the unmarried are occupied with the Lord, how they may please*

God, whereas the married are preoccupied with the world, how they may please their spouse.[484] Therefore he asserts that the man who *keeps his virgin* does better than one who marries her off.[485] So, also, he judges that a Christian woman is more blessed who, after losing her husband, embraces the opportunity of remaining a widow.[486] And he proposes all these counsels of continence as coming from God. *I think,* he says, *that I also have the Spirit of God.*[487]

Who, then, is this brazen promoter of all impurity—a most faithful advocate, surely, of adulterers, fornicators and the incestuous, since it is to honor such as these that he has taken up this case against the Holy Spirit—that he should read out in public a statement which bears false witness against His Apostle?[488] Nothing of this kind has Paul treated with indulgence; rather he makes it his effort to do away completely with every necessity of the flesh,[489] even in cases where there is just cause for excusing it. Obviously he is indulgent—but to nuptials, not to adultery. Obviously he is tolerant—but of marriage, not fornication. Moreover, he tries to avoid indulging even what is natural; how, then, can he coddle what is criminal?[490] He endeavors to prevent a union which is blessed for fear that one which is accursed may be excused.[491] All he could do was cleanse the flesh of filth, for of lesser stains he cannot cleanse it.[492] But it is the practice of perverse and ignorant heretics, yes and of Sensualists[493] generally, to arm themselves, as occasion offers, with some ambiguous text opposing a whole host of definite declarations found throughout Sacred Scripture.[494]

CONDEMNATION OF IMPURITY

17. Challenge the forces of the Apostle.[495] Look at his

epistles. They all do battle for [496] purity, for chastity, for sanctity. They all assail the works of lust, lechery and licentiousness. What, for example, does he write to the Thessalonians? *For the support we gave you came not of deceit nor uncleanness.* [497] And, again: *this is the will of God, your sanctity; that you abstain from fornication; that everyone learn to possess his vessel in sanctity and honor, not in the licentiousness of concupiscence like the Gentiles who know not God.* [498] What do the Galatians read? *The works of the flesh are manifest.* What are these works? He mentions, in the very first place, fornication, impurity and lasciviousness; *and concerning these things I warn you, as I have warned you before, that they who do such things will not attain the heritage of the kingdom of God.* [499]

And the Romans—is any lesson impressed upon them more than that a man should not sin after Baptism? [500] *What, therefore, do we say? Do we persevere in sin so that grace may abound? By no means. We who are dead to sin, how shall we still live in it? Do you not know that we who have been baptized into Christ Jesus have been baptized into His death? For we were buried with Him by means of Baptism into death so that just as Christ has arisen from the dead, so also we may walk in newness of life. For if we have been buried together in the likeness of His death, we shall also be in the likeness of His resurrection, knowing this, that our old self has been crucified with Him. But if we have died with Christ, we believe that we shall also live with Him, knowing that Christ, risen from the dead, dies now no more and death no more has dominion over Him. For the death that He died, He died to sin, once for all, but the life that He lives, He lives unto God. Thus do you, also, consider yourselves as dead to sin, but alive to God in Christ Jesus.* [501] Therefore since Christ is dead, once for all, no one who follows after Christ in death [502] can ever again live to sin, especially to a sin so great. Else, if fornication and adultery can be forgiven a second time, so also will Christ be able to die again.[503]

The Apostle continues, then, with the command that *sin should not reign in our mortal body.* Well did he know the weakness of this flesh: *For just as you have given over your members to serve uncleanness and iniquity, so now also give them over as servants of justice unto sanctity.*[504] For although he declared that *no good dwelt in his flesh,*[505] yet this was according to the Law of the letter[506] under which he lived. According to the law of the spirit, however, which he applies to us, we are free from the infirmity of the flesh: *for the law of the spirit of life,* he says, *has set me free from the law of sin and death.*[507]

Though it may be that he is discussing this matter, at least in part, from the viewpoint of Judaism, nevertheless the totality and plenitude of these prescriptions are meant for us.[508] It was for us, laboring under the Law, that *God sent His son in the flesh, in the likeness of sinful flesh; and because of sin He condemned sin in the flesh, so that the righteousness of the law,* he says, *might be fulfilled in us who walk according to the spirit and not according to the flesh. For they who walk according to the flesh, savor what is of the flesh and they who walk according to the spirit, savor what is of the spirit.*[509] *But the inclination of the flesh,* he declared, *is death,*[510] and, accordingly, *hatred of God* Himself; and *those who are in the flesh*—he means *in the inclination of the flesh*—*cannot please God.*[511] He says, besides: *If you live according to the flesh, you will die.*[512] What do we understand by *the inclination of the flesh* and *the life of the flesh* except those things *which it is shameful to mention?*[513] For whatever else is of the flesh, even the Apostle would have spoken of by name.[514]

In like manner he writes to the Ephesians also, warning them for the future as he speaks to them of the past: *In whose company we also were, yielding to our carnal desires and the pleasures of the flesh.*[515] Thereafter he stigmatizes them as ingrates, because they denied what they were, Christians I mean, by giving themselves over to *the working of all impurity. Not in this way*, he says, *have you learned Christ.*[516] Then, again, he speaks thus: *He who was wont to steal, let him steal no longer.*[517] He does not say, however, 'He who up to the present time was wont to commit adultery, let him not commit adultery;' or 'He who up to the present time was wont to fornicate, let him not fornicate.' He would have added these injunctions, also, if it had been his practice to grant pardon to such sins,[518] or if he had been at all willing that it should be granted—he who, wishing to avoid even verbal pollution, says: *Let no filthy speech whatever proceed from your mouth.*[519]

He says, again: *But let not fornication or impurity of any kind be so much as mentioned among you, as becomes saints.* So far is it from being pardoned! *This you realize, that no fornicator or impure person has part in the kingdom of God. Let no one lead you astray with empty words; it is for this reason that the wrath of God falls upon the children of unbelief.*[520] Who *leads astray with empty words* but the man who preaches that adultery can be forgiven? He fails to see that the very foundations of adultery have been sapped by the Apostle when he represses drunkenness and revelry, as, for example, in this text also: *And be not drunk with wine, for in that is debauchery.*[521] To the Colossians, moreover, he shows what earthly *members* they should *mortify: fornication, uncleanness, lust, evil desire and filthy speech.*[522]

Surrender, at last, to such numerous texts as these that one passage to which you cling. The few are eclipsed by the many, the uncertain by the certain, the obscure by the clear.[523] Even if it were certain that the Apostle had pardoned the fornication of that Corinthian, yet this would be but another instance of something which he did on one occasion only, against his own regular practice and in view of the circumstances of the time. He circumcised Timothy—him only—and yet he abrogated circumcision.[524]

Scripture Refuses Pardon to Adultery

18. 'But these passages,' he says, 'have to do with the condemnation of impurity in general and the commendation of purity in general.[525] They do not, however, exclude the possibility of pardon. This is not refused by the very fact that sins are condemned, since it is possible to receive forgiveness just as long as the condemnation lasts which forgiveness cancels.'[526] It was to be expected that the Sensualists, in their wisdom, would think of this objection also, and therefore we have put off to this place all mention of those explicit regulations,[527] existing even from ancient times, which bear on the refusal of ecclesiastical fellowship in cases of this kind.

For example, as early as the Proverbs of Solomon, which we call παροιμίαι,[528] it is expressly stated that there is no atonement possible for adultery: *But the adulterer, through want of understanding, brings destruction upon his own soul. He endures suffering and disgrace. His ignominy will never be effaced, for the wrath of a husband is swollen with jealousy and he will not spare on the day of judgement.*[529] If you suppose that this is said of a pagan, yet it is surely the faithful of whom you hear in Isaias: *Go out from among them and be separated. Touch no unclean thing.*[530] At the very beginning of the Psalms you have the *blessed man who walks not in the counsel of the ungodly nor stands in the way of sinners nor sits in the chair of pestilence.*[531] And it is he who says later on: *I have not sat with the council of vanity, neither will I enter in with those who do evil. I have hated the assembly of the wicked and I will not take my seat with the impious.* And also: *I will wash my hands among the innocent and I will encompass thy altar, O Lord*[532]—as if he, all alone, were many.[533] *For, in truth, with the holy thou wilt be holy and with the innocent man thou wilt be innocent and with the perverse thou wilt be perverse.*[534] And, in another place: *But the Lord saith to the sinner: Why dost thou speak of my righteousness and take up my testament in thy mouth? If thou sawest a thief, thou didst run with him, and with adulterers thou didst make thy portion.*[535]

Accordingly, the Apostle also, deriving his doctrine from this source, says: *I wrote to you in a letter not to associate with fornicators. I meant not, of course, the fornicators of this world* etc., *else it would be necessary to depart from the world. But now I write to you that if anyone called a brother among you should be a fornicator or an idolater* (for what else is so intimately bound up with it?) *or a deceiver* (for what else is so closely joined with it?) etc., *with such a one you should not even take food*[536]—to say nothing of the Eucharist.[537] *For a little leaven*, withal, *corrupteth the whole mass.*[538] In like manner he wrote to Timothy: *Impose not hands hastily upon anyone, and do not be a partner in the sins of others.*[539] And to the Ephesians also: *Do not, then, become partakers with them; for you were once darkness.*[540] And even more pertinently: *Have no fellowship with the unfruitful works of darkness, but rather rebuke them. For of the things that are done by them in secret it is shameful even to speak.*[541] What more shameful than impurities? Moreover, if he commands the Thessalonians to *withdraw from a brother who even walks idly*,[542] how much more from one who commits fornication!

These are, in effect, the precepts of Christ, who *loves the Church*, and who *delivered Himself up for her that He might sanctify her, cleansing her by the baptism of water in the word, and that He might present the Church to Himself glorious, having no stain or wrinkle*—he means, of course, after Baptism—*but that she might be holy and without reproach*.[543] He means that from this time on she should be without a wrinkle of old age,[544] like a virgin, without the stain of fornication, like a bride, without the disgrace of sin, like one made clean.

What if at this point you also conceive the objection that communion is indeed withdrawn from sinners, especially from those polluted by sins of the flesh, but that this is only temporary, that is, it is to be restored after the course of penance[545] in accordance with that mercy of God which *prefers the penance of the sinner to his death*?[546] It is absolutely necessary that this foundation of your erroneous opinion be refuted. We say, therefore, that if it had been a part of the divine mercy to reveal itself even to those who had sinned after Baptism, the Apostle would then express himself thus: *Have no fellowship with the works of darkness*[547]—unless they have done penance! And: *With such as these you should not even take food*[548]—except after they have wiped the shoes of the brethren in their prostrations! And: *If anyone destroy the temple of God, him will God destroy*[549]— unless he shall have shaken from his head in church the ashes of every hearth.[550]

If his condemnation was temporary and conditional rather than permanent in its severity, then he should have indicated exactly how long and under what conditions the things which he condemned were under condemnation.

He takes his stand with us, however, when in all of his epistles he commands us not to receive a sinner like this if he has already embraced the faith, and excommunicates him,[551] without any hope that this is conditional or temporary, if he has been received. For in this way he shows that the penance which the Lord chooses is that which is *preferred to the death of the sinner* before he embraces the faith and before he is baptized. He must be washed [552] once for all by the grace of Christ, who once for all died for our sins.[553]

The Apostle confirms this even in his own person. For when he declares that *Christ has come to save sinners*, of whom he is himself *the first*, what does he add? *And I have obtained mercy because I acted ignorantly, in unbelief.*[554] Accordingly that mercy of God by which He *prefers the penance of a sinner to his death*,[555] is meant for those who are still in ignorance and still unbelievers. It is to save these that Christ has come. It is not meant for those who [556] have already come to a knowledge of God and learned the mystery of faith.[557] But if those who are still in ignorance and unbelief meet with the mercy of God, it is penance,[558] assuredly, which attracts this mercy to itself. This is without prejudice to that other kind of penance, performed after Baptism, which for lesser sins can obtain pardon from the bishop or for greater and irremissible ones from God alone.[559]

St. John's Teaching in the Apocalypse

19. But why speak of Paul at such length, when it appears that John, too, lends some measure of support to our opponents? For in the Apocalypse he seems to promise, rather clearly, the patronage of penitence to fornication, in that passage where the Spirit announces to the angel of the

Thyatirenes that He *holds it against him because the woman,
Jezabel, who says she is a prophetess, continues teaching and
seducing my servants to commit fornication and to eat of things
sacrificed to idols. And I gave her a space of time to do penance
but she did not wish to do it because of her fornication. Behold I
shall put her in a bed and her adulterers with her so that they will
have great suffering, unless they shall have done penance for her
works.*[560]

Fortunately the apostles are at one in what concerns the
canons of faith and discipline. *For whether it be I or they*, he
says, *thus do we preach.*[561] It is a matter of importance, then,
to the Christian religion as such, that one should not
believe John granted anything which Paul refused.[562]
Whoever regards this consistency of the Holy Spirit will
be guided by Him to an understanding of His words. For
the woman, whom he quite properly urged to the performance of penance, was a heretic, one who undertook
to teach what she had learned from the Nicolaites and to
introduce it stealthily into the Church.[563] Who doubts that
a heretic, deceived by the instruction which he has received,
obtains pardon and is admitted into the Church after he
comes to know of his error and expiates it by penance?[564]
So, also, among us, a heretic, as being just like a pagan—
yes, and even more than a pagan—is brought into the
Church through the Baptism of truth, after he is washed
clean of both characters.[565]

If, however, you are certain that it was *after* she had
embraced the living faith that that woman died the death
of heresy—so that you may claim for her, as a Christian
sinner and not as a heretic, the pardon which comes of
penance—so be it. Let her do penance, then, but in order
that she may put an end to her adultery and not that she
may also be restored to communion.[566] For this will be

the penance which we, too, more than you, recognize as necessary. And yet we reserve pardon to God alone.[567]

Moreover, this same Apocalypse, in later passages, has unconditionally condemned[568] to *the pool of fire, shameless ones and fornicators*, as well as the *cowardly and the unbelieving and murderers and sorcerers and idolaters.*[569] These are men who were guilty of such crimes *after* they had embraced the faith. Surely one can see here no reference to pagans, since it is of the faithful that he asserts: *They who overcome shall possess the inheritance and I will be their God and they will be my sons;* and then he continues thus: *But for the cowardly and the unbelieving and the shameless ones and fornicators and murderers and sorcerers and idolaters there is a portion in the pool of fire, which is the second death.*[570] And then, again: *Blessed are they who act according to the commandments that they may have power over the tree of life and over the gates so that they may enter into the holy city. Outside with dogs, sorcerers, fornicators and murderers.*[571] These, of course, are persons who do not act according to the commandments. And, certainly, they alone can be put out who were once within. Moreover, it was written earlier: *What have I to do with judging those who are without?*[572]

THE EVIDENCE OF HIS FIRST EPISTLE

In the epistle of John, also, they find a passage to their purpose. At the very outset it is said: *The blood of His son purifies us from every sin.*[573] Shall we, then, sin at all times and in every way, since He cleanses us at all times and from every offense? But if not 'at all times' then neither after embracing the faith; and if not 'from every offense' then neither from fornication![574] What is the thought with which he begins? He had stated that *God is light*, that *darkness is not in Him* and that *we lie if we say that we have fellowship with Him and walk in darkness.* Then he says: *But if we walk in the light, we shall have fellowship with Him and the blood of Jesus Christ our Lord cleanses us from every offense.*[575]

Do we sin, then, while we walk in the light? And while we walk in the light will we be cleansed? By no means! For he who sins is not in the light but in the darkness. In saying this he shows, also, how we shall be *cleansed from sin while we walk in the light,* wherein sin cannot be committed. He means that we are made clean by God not as those who sin but as those who do not sin. For *while we walk in the light and have no fellowship with darkness* we shall conduct ourselves as men who are 'made clean' not because sin has been removed but because it has not been committed. For this is the virtue of the Lord's blood, that those whom it has once made clean from sin and then placed in the light, remain clean[576] from that time on, if they continue to walk in the light.

'But,' you say, 'he continues:' *If we claim that we have no sin, we deceive ourselves and the truth is not in us. If we confess our sins, He is faithful and just, so that He will forgive them for us and cleanse us from all iniquity.*[577] This does not mean 'from impurity' does it? If it does, then it means 'from idolatry' also![578] But there is something else in the passage. For look you, he adds this also: *If we say that we have not sinned, we make Him a liar, and His word is not in us.*[579] And yet again: *My dear children, these things I have written to you in order that you may avoid sin; but if anyone sins, we have an advocate with God the Father, Jesus Christ, the just one; and He is a propitiation for our sins.*[580] It should be clear from this, you argue, that we do commit sin and also that we do receive pardon.

But suppose, when I read on, I find a passage with a different meaning?[581] For he denies that we sin at all and he insists strongly on this point, making[582] no concession of this kind whatsoever. He calls our attention to the fact that our sins have been effaced by Christ, once for all, to be pardoned no more thereafter. We may conclude, then, that he proposes the following texts as an admonition to chastity. *Everyone*, he says, *who has this hope, makes himself holy, because He also is holy. Everyone who commits sin, commits iniquity also, and sin is iniquity; and you know that He appeared in order to take away sins.*[583] This means, of course, that they were not to be committed after this time. For he continues: *Everyone who remains in Him sins not. Everyone who sins has neither seen nor known Him. My dear children, let no one lead you astray. He who practices justice is just, even as He is just. He who commits sin is of the devil, because the devil sins from the beginning. For to this end the son of God appeared, that He might destroy the works of the devil.*[584] And He does destroy them, when He frees man through Baptism, *cancelling* on his behalf *the decree of death.*[585] And therefore *everyone who is born of God sins not, because the seed of God remains in him; and he cannot sin because he is born of God. In this the children of God and the children of the devil are distinguished.*[586] In what, if not in that the former do not sin once they have been born of God, whereas the latter, because they are of the devil, do sin, just as if they had never been born of God?[587] And if he adds, as he does: *He who is not just is not of God*,[588] how shall he who is not chaste be God's again, once he has ceased to be so?[589]

The next thing we shall be forced to say, then, is that John has forgotten himself, asserting in the first part of his epistle that we are not without sin, yet now requiring us to avoid sin completely; there flattering us with some hope of pardon, and yet here refusing the name of *children of God* to all who sin. But perish the thought! For we have not forgotten that distinction of sins which was our point of departure[590]—and now John also confirms it. It is a fact that there are some sins which beset us every day and to which we all are tempted.[591] For who will not, as it may chance, fall into unrighteous anger and continue this even beyond sundown,[592] or even strike another or, out of easy habit, curse another, or swear rashly, or violate his pledged faith, or tell a lie through shame or the compulsion of circumstances?[593] In the management of affairs, in the performance of duties, in commercial transactions, while eating, looking, listening—how often we are tempted! So much so that if there were no pardon in such cases, no one would be saved. For these sins, then, pardon is granted through Christ who intercedes with the Father.[594] But there are also sins quite different from these, graver and deadly, which cannot be pardoned: murder, idolatry, injustice, apostasy, blasphemy; yes, and also adultery and fornication and any other violation of the temple of God.[595] For these Christ will not intercede with the Father a second time.[596] He who has been born of God will not commit them at all; if he should commit them, he will not be a child of God's.[597]

Thus an explanation of the apparent contradiction in John will be found in the fact that he is making a distinction between classes of sins when he asserts, in one place, that the sons of God *do* sin and, in another, that they *do not*. For he was looking forward to the close of his epistle and, with this in mind, he first composed these passages, intending to say very clearly in his conclusion: *If anyone knows that his brother is committing a sin that is not unto death, he shall make supplication and the Lord will give life to him who does not sin unto death. But there is a sin unto death; not for this do I say that anyone should make supplication.*[598] He, too, recalled that God forbade Jeremias to pray for the people when they were guilty of mortal sins.[599] *All unrighteousness is sin, and there is a sin unto death; but we know that everyone who is born of God sins not*[600]—not, that is, a sin unto death. And so you are now left with no choice but this: either to deny that fornication and adultery are mortal sins, or else to admit that they are irremissible and that we are not even permitted to make supplication for them.[601]

THE EPISTLE TO THE HEBREWS

20. The Scriptures composed by the apostles themselves are the principal determinants of that discipline which, like a priest, guards the perfect sanctity of the temple of God and roots out from the Church, everywhere, every sacrilegious act committed against chastity—with never a word about its restoration.[602] I should like, however, over and above this, to add the testimony of one of the apostles' companions which aptly confirms, as a secondary authority, the teaching of the masters.[603] For there is also extant a book entitled *To the Hebrews*, written by Barnabas,[604] a man well accredited[605] by God since Paul associates him with himself in the observance of continence: *Or is it only Barnabas and I who have not the right to do this?*[606] And surely the epistle of Barnabas has found wider acceptance among the churches than has that apocryphal *Shepherd* of adulterers.[607]

Now he warns the disciples to *leave all that is at the beginning and strive, rather, for what is perfect, not laying the foundations of penitence once again on works that are dead.*[608]

For it is impossible, he says, for those who were once enlightened, who have tasted the heavenly gift and shared the Holy Spirit and tasted the sweet word of God, when they fall away, as the world comes to an end, to be renewed once more to penitence, crucifying in themselves and dishonoring the son of God. For the earth that drinks in the rain that often falls upon it and produces vegetation that is good for those who till it, receives the blessing of God; but that which brings forth thorns is reprobate and nigh unto a curse, and its end is to be burnt. [609] A man who learned this from the apostles and who taught it with the apostles knows that a second penitence was never promised to the adulterer and fornicator by the apostles. For he was a perfect interpreter of the law and he preserved, in actuality, the types which foreshadowed it. [610]

PRESCRIPTIONS OF LEVITICUS

It was in reference to this point of discipline, for example, that a decree was passed concerning the leper: *But if a changing appearance spread out over the skin and cover the skin completely from head to foot, as far as can be seen, and if the priest, when he looks at this, shall declare that he is clean because he is turned completely white—then he is clean. But when in such a man there shall be seen flesh color, he is defiled.* [611] Thus he wished us to understand that the man who is changed from his former carnal state to the whiteness of faith (which the world considers a blemish and a stain) and who is completely renewed, is clean. He is no longer spotted, no longer mottled with both the old and the new. [612] But if, after its removal, something of the 'old,' which was thought dead to sin, again appears in its old condition in his flesh, [613] he is judged defiled and is no longer purified by the priest. So also is adultery an irremovable blemish when it returns once more from the past and sullies the purity of that new coloring from which it was effaced. [614]

The same was true of a house. If it was reported to the priest that there were any stains or pocks in its walls, he ordered everything removed from the house before he entered to inspect it; thus the things which belonged to the house would not be unclean. After this the priest entered into it and if he found there greenish or reddish pocks which appeared to be sunk down below the surface of the wall, he would go to the door and close up the house for seven days. Then he returned on the seventh day and if he saw that that contamination had spread over the walls, he would order the stones upon which the contamination of leprosy was found to be removed and thrown away outside the city into an unclean place, and other stones, smooth and sound, to be taken and put in place of those that were there before, and the house to be plastered with new mortar. [615]

Certainly, then, when we approach Christ, the High Priest of the Father, we must, first of all, within the period of a week, remove from the house, which is our person, all *impedimenta*, so that the house itself which remains—our body and soul—may be clean. And when the Word of God enters therein and finds stains of red and green, then at once the deadly, bloody passions—and note that the Apocalypse represents death on a green horse and a swordsman on the red[616]—must be rooted up and cast out and away; and in their place smooth and solid stones must be laid, which are suitable for building—such as may be changed into children of Abraham[617]—so that, in this way, a man may be fit for God. [618]

But if after its rehabilitation and transformation the

priest again observed in that same house any of the old pocks or stains, he pronounced it unclean and ordered its timbers and its stones and its whole structure to be torn down and cast forth into an unclean place.[619] This typifies the man, body and soul, who is transformed after Baptism, that is to say, after the entrance of the priest,[620] and then takes up once more the scabrous contaminations of the flesh. He is cast forth outside the city into an unclean place, that is to say, he is *given over to Satan for the destruction of the flesh*,[621] nor is he ever again established in the Church after his ruination.

Similarly, when a man had intercourse with a maid-servant who was promised to another but not, as yet, either purchased or freed, it is written: *Care shall be taken of her and she shall not die, because she was not as yet freed for him to whom she was pledged.*[622] So, also, flesh which was not yet made free by Christ, to whom it was pledged, escaped punishment, even though it was defiled. We conclude, therefore, that after it has actually been made free, it does not receive pardon.[623]

Privileges Peculiar to the Apostles

21. Since the apostles understood this better than others, naturally they were more solicitous about it than others.[624] And now, at length, I come to that point in my argument[625] where I make a distinction between the *doctrine* of the apostles and their *power*.[626] Doctrine gives direction to a man; power marks him out with a special character.[627] The power of the Spirit is a thing apart, for the Spirit is God.[628] What, then, did He teach? *There must be no fellowship with works of darkness.*[629] Observe His commandment! And who had power to forgive sins? This no one can do

but He Himself: *for who forgives sins but God alone?*[630] This means, of course, mortal sins committed against Him and against His temple.[631] For as far as you yourself are concerned, you are commanded in the person of Peter to forgive offenses committed against yourself even seventy times seven times.[632]

Therefore if it were proved that the blessed apostles themselves showed indulgence to any sin of such a character that it could be pardoned by God alone and not by man, they would have done this because power was given them and not because doctrine allowed it.[633] Moreover,[634] the apostles raised the dead to life,[635] something which God alone can do. They healed the sick,[636] something which no one but Christ can do. They even inflicted punishments, something which Christ did not wish to do, for it was not fitting that He should strike who came to suffer. Ananias was smitten[637] and Elymas also,[638] Ananias with death and Elymas with blindness; this itself proves that Christ, too, had the power to do these things.[639]

So it was with the prophets also. They pardoned murder —and adultery which was joined with it—to those who were penitent; this was justified by the fact that they also gave proof of their severity.[640] Now then, apostolic man,[641] show me samples of your prophetic works so that I may recognize your divine authorization; after this, claim for yourself the power to forgive such sins. If, however, you have been entrusted with no office beyond that of teaching moral doctrine,[642] and if your presidential authority is that of a servant and not a master, then who do you think you are, or how exalted, that you grant pardon for sin?[643] You show yourself neither prophet nor apostle; therefore you lack the power in virtue of which pardon is granted.

'But the Church,' you say, 'has power to forgive sins.'

I know this better than you do and I regulate it better,[644] because I have the Paraclete Himself saying in the person of the new prophets:[645] 'The Church can forgive sin, but I will not do it lest others also sin.'[646] But what if a false prophetic spirit said this? This can not be the case, since the Destroyer would rather have commended himself by his clemency and he would have set others in the way of sin.[647] Or if, here too, he tried to ape the Spirit of truth, then the Spirit of truth can, indeed, grant pardon to fornication[648] but will not do it when it brings harm to many.

THE POWER OF THE KEYS IS PERSONAL TO PETER

And now I put a question to you about this opinion of yours: Where do you get this right which you claim for your Church?[649] If it is because the Lord said to Peter: *Upon this rock I will build my Church; I have given you the keys of the kingdom of heaven;* or: *Whatsoever you shall bind or loose on earth, will be bound or loosed in heaven,*[650] then you presume that the power of binding and loosing has devolved upon you also, that is, upon every church which is akin to Peter.[651] Who are you to pervert and to change completely the manifest will of Christ, who grants this to Peter personally?[652] *Upon you,* he says, *I will build my Church;* and, *I will give the keys to you,* not to the Church; and, *Whatsoever you shall loose or bind,* not what they shall loose or bind.

This is also clear from the sequel. In him was the Church built, that is, through him.[653] He himself first used the key —and see what it was:[654] *Men of Israel, give ear to what I say. Jesus of Nazareth, a man destined for you by God* etc.[655] He himself, thereafter, was the first to open the gate of the kingdom of heaven in the Baptism of Christ,[656] wherein sins are *loosed* which were formerly *bound* and those are *bound* which were not loosed in the way of true salvation.[657] Besides this, he *bound* Ananias in the bonds of death, and he also *loosed* the lame man from his crippling disease. Moreover, in that well-known dispute about the observance of the Law, Peter was the first of all to be moved by the Spirit, and after some introductory remarks on the vocation of the Gentiles, he said: *And now why do you tempt the Lord in this matter of putting a yoke on the brethren which neither we nor our fathers were able to bear? But we believe that it is through the grace of Jesus that we will be saved, just as they.*[658] This statement both loosed the precepts of the Law which were abrogated and, at the same time, it bound those which remained in force. We conclude, then, that the power of loosing and binding which was committed to Peter has nothing to do with forgiving the capital sins of the faithful.[659]

Since Christ told him to forgive even seventy times seven times a brother who offended him, certainly he would not afterwards have commanded him to bind anything, that is, to retain it,[660] except, perhaps, such sins as a man might commit against the Lord and not against a brother. For the fact that it is sins against man which are pardoned, settles it antecedently that those committed against God must not be pardoned.[661]

What, then, does this have to do with the Church, and I mean yours, you Sensualist? For this power is Peter's personally and, after that, it belongs to those who have the Spirit—to an apostle or a prophet.[662] For the Church is itself, properly and principally, the Spirit Himself,[663] in whom there is a trinity of one divinity, Father, Son and Holy Spirit.[664] He unites in one congregation that Church which the Lord said consists of three persons.[665] And so, from this time on, any number of persons at all, joined in this faith, is recognized as the Church by Him who founded and consecrated it.[666] Therefore it is true that the Church will pardon sins, but this is the Church of the Spirit, through a man who has the Spirit; it is not the Church which consists of a number of bishops.[667] For it is the Lord and not the servant who has this sovereign right. It belongs to God Himself, not to a priest.[668]

Martyrs and the Forgiveness of Sins

22. But you grant this power even to your martyrs.[669] Just as soon as anyone is put in bonds—and by collusion they are easy enough [670] in the merely nominal custody of these days—at once adulterers solicit him, at once fornicators approach him. Petitions echo round and pools of tears are shed by every *débauché*. There are none more eager to buy their entrance into prison than those who have lost their right of entrance into church.[671] Violence is done to men and women in the dark, well known as the ordinary place of debauchery, and peace is sought from those who are in danger of losing it themselves.[672] There are others who have recourse to the mines and come back as communicants from a place where a second martyrdom is already necessary for sins committed after the first.[673]

Who, pray, while he dwells on earth and in the flesh, is without fault? Who can be called a martyr while he lives in the world, a suppliant with pennies in hand, at the mercy of physicians and money-lenders?[674] Even suppose that his head is already poised beneath the sword,[675] suppose his body is already extended on the cross,[676] suppose he is at the pillar and the lion already loosed,[677] suppose he is at the stake and the fire already laid [678]—at the very moment, I mean, when he is in secure possession of martyrdom—who will even then permit a man to pardon sins which are reserved to God alone? He has condemned them as irremissible; nor have the apostles themselves, who to my best knowledge were also martyrs, judged that they may be pardoned. [679] Paul, be it noted, had already fought with beasts at Ephesus when he decreed *destruction* for the incestuous man. [680]

It should be enough for the martyr that he has washed away his own sins. It is the mark of a man who is either ungrateful or proud to bestow on others with careless abandon what he has himself received at a great cost. [681] Who has ever redeemed the death of another by his own, except the Son of God alone? And He, in His very passion, brought salvation to a thief. [682] Indeed, it was for this purpose that He came—to die for sinners, [683] though He Himself was free from sin and wholly just. So, also, you who set yourself up as His rival in forgiving sins, if you have committed no sin yourself—then suffer for me! But if you are a sinner, how will the oil in your tiny lamp suffice both for you and for me? [684]

I have, besides, another way of recognizing the presence of Christ. [685] If Christ is in the martyr so that the martyr may absolve adulterers and fornicators, let him reveal the secrets of the heart and so pardon sins—then he is Christ! [686] It was in this way that our Lord Jesus Christ revealed His power: *Why do you think evil in your hearts? For what is easier to say to a paralytic: your sins are forgiven you, or arise and walk? Therefore so that you may know that the son of man has power to forgive sins on earth, I say to you, paralytic: Arise and walk.* [687] If the Lord took such great care to prove His power that He revealed thoughts, and if He restored health at a word of command precisely in order to prevent disbelief in His power of forgiving sins, then I may not believe that any other person has this power unless he furnishes these same proofs.

Now, however, when you demand from a martyr pardon for adulterers and fornicators, you yourself acknowledge that crimes of this kind can not be pardoned except by personal martyrdom, yet you presume that this same effect will follow from the martyrdom of another.[688] Martyrdom, as I see it, will be *another Baptism*.[689] *For I have*, He says, *yet another Baptism*.[690] And so water and blood flowed from the wound in our Lord's side, in preparation for both Baptisms.[691] If, then, I am able to free another by the second Baptism, I ought also to be able to do so by the first.[692]

A FINAL WORD

I must insist upon this point right up to the very last:[693] Whatever authority there is, whatever argument, for granting the peace of the Church to the adulterer and fornicator, this should also be used to assist the repentant murderer and idolater.[694] Especially is this true of the apostate[695]—and surely of one whom savagery has overcome after he has struggled with torments in the agony of martyrdom. It would, in fact, be unworthy of God and of His mercy—the mercy of Him who *prefers the repentance of the sinner to his death*[696]—that those who have fallen in the heat of lust should more easily reenter the Church than those who have fallen in the heat of battle.[697]

Indignation forces us to speak. Will you restore[698] bodies which are polluted in preference to those which are bloodied? Which penitence is more deserving of mercy[699]

—that which prostrates flesh titillated by lust or torn by torture? In any judicial process, when is pardon granted with greater justice—when it is sought by one who sinned willingly or by one who sinned in spite of himself?[700] No one is willingly forced to apostatize and no one unwillingly commits fornication. Lust suffers no violence except its own; that which gives pleasure knows no compulsion.[701] On the other hand, what ingenuities of the executioner,[702] what varieties of torments enforce apostasy! Who was more of an apostate—he who gave up Christ amid agonies or amid delights? he who suffered while losing Him, or he who while losing Him wantoned?

But these scars were cut in a Christian combat. They are, assuredly, efficacious in the sight of Christ, since a desire for victory won them,[703] and so, they too are worthy of honor because it was only in not overcoming that they were overcome.[704] The very devil himself regards them with dismay. They have experienced misfortune, but they are chaste. In the performance of penance they grieve before the Lord but they do not blush. They will be forgiven once again because in their apostasy they made reparation.[705] In their case, only, may we say: *the flesh is weak*.[706] But flesh which overcomes the Spirit—there is none so strong as that![707]

LIST OF ABBREVIATIONS

AC   F. J. Dölger, Antike und Christentum. Münster i. W.
ACW   Ancient Christian Writers, edit. J. Quasten and J. C. Plumpe. Westminster, Md.
ANF   Ante-Nicene Fathers. Buffalo and New York
BALAC   Bulletin d'ancienne littérature et d'archéologie chrétienne. Paris
BLE   Bulletin de littérature ecclésiastique. Toulouse
BTAM   Bulletin de théologie ancienne et médiévale. Louvain
DACL   Dictionnaire d'archéologie chrétienne et de liturgie. Paris
DB   Enchiridion symbolorum, 21st ed., ed. by H. Denzinger, C. Bannwart, J. B. Umberg
DCA   Dictionary of Christian Antiquities, edit. W. Smith and S. Cheetham. Hartford
DCB   Dictionary of Christian Biography, edit. W. Smith and H. Wace. London
DTC   Dictionnaire de théologie catholique. Paris
ERE   Encyclopedia of Religion and Ethics, edit. J. Hastings. New York and Edinburgh
ETL   Ephemerides Theologicae Lovanienses. Louvain
HTR   Harvard Theological Review. Cambridge, Mass.
IER   Irish Ecclesiastical Record. Dublin
ITQ   Irish Theological Quarterly. Dublin
JBL   Journal of Biblical Literature. Philadelphia
JTS   Journal of Theological Studies. London
LF   Library of the Fathers. Oxford
LMB   Le musée belge. Louvain
MSR   Mélanges de science religieuse. Lille
NRT   Nouvelle revue théologique. Tournai
PJ   Philosophisches Jahrbuch der Görresgesellschaft. Fulda
RAC   Reallexikon für Antike und Christentum, edit. Th. Klauser. Leipzig
RB   Revue biblique. Paris
RE   Realenzyklopädie der classischen Altertumswissenschaft, edit. E. Pauly, G. Wissowa. Stuttgart
RHE   Revue d'histoire ecclésiastique. Louvain
RJ   Enchiridion Patristicum, 11th ed., ed. by M. Rouët de Journel

RSR Recherches de science religieuse. Paris
SE Sacris Erudiri. Brugge
TG Theologie und Glaube. Paderborn
TLL Thesaurus linguae latinae. Leipzig
TQ Theologische Quartalschrift. Tübingen
TS Theological Studies. Woodstock, Md.
VC Vigiliae Christianae. Amsterdam
ZKT Zeitschrift für katholische Theologie. Innsbruck
ZNW Zeitschrift für die neutestamentliche Wissenschaft und die Kunde der älteren Kirche. Giessen

D'Alès I A. D'Alès, *La théologie de Tertullien* (Paris 1905)
D'Alès II A. D'Alès, *De paenitentia* (Paris 1926)
D'Alès III A. D'Alès, *L'édit de Calliste* (Paris 1914)
Borleffs I J. W. Ph. Borleffs, 'Observationes criticae in Tertulliani De paenitentia libellum,' *Mnemosyne* 60 (1932) 254–316
Borleffs II J. W. Ph. Borleffs, 'Un nouveau manuscrit de Tertullien,' VC 5 (1951) 65–79
Galtier I P. Galtier, *De paenitentia* (Rome 1950)
Galtier II P. Galtier, *L'Église et la rémission des péchés aux premiers siècles* (Paris 1932)
Galtier III P. Galtier, *Aux origines du sacrement de pénitence* (Rome 1951)
Hoppe I H. Hoppe, *Syntax und Stil des Tertullian* (Leipzig 1903)
Hoppe II H. Hoppe, *Beiträge zur Sprache und Kritik Tertullians* (Lund 1932)
Poschmann I B. Poschmann, *Paenitentia secunda. Die kirchliche Busse im ältesten Christentum bis Cyprian und Origenes* (Bonn 1940)
Poschmann II B. Poschmann, *Der Ablass im Licht der Bussgeschichte* (Bonn 1948)
Poschmann III B. Poschmann, *Busse und Letzte Ölung* (Handbuch der Dogmengeschichte, edit. M. Schmaus, J. Geiselmann, H. Rahner 4.3, Freiburg 1951)
Teeuwen I St. W. J. Teeuwen, *Sprachlicher Bedeutungswandel bei Tertullian* (Studien zur Geschichte und Kultur des Altertums 14.1, Paderborn 1926)
Teeuwen II St. W. J. Teeuwen, 'De voce *paenitentia* apud Tertullianum,' *Mnemosyne* 55 (1927) 410–19

NOTES

ON PENITENCE

INTRODUCTION

[1] For a more detailed study of this subject, particularly with reference to the teaching of the New Testament, see E. Redlich, *The Forgiveness of Sins* (Edinburgh 1937).

[2] Poschmann III 20.

[3] The words of Christ which are cited in justification of this claim occur in Matt.16.19; 18.15–18; John 20.19–23.

[4] For the more recent literature on the penitential doctrine and discipline of the *Pastor Hermae*, see J. Quasten, *Patrology* (Westminster 1950) 1.104 f.

[5] Evidence for the existence of post-baptismal ecclesiastical penitence before the year A.D. 250 has been collected and studied by O. Watkins, *A History of Penance* (London 1920) 1.3–222; A. D'Alès, *L'édit de Calliste* (Paris 1914); B. Poschmann, *Paenitentia secunda. Die kirchliche Busse im ältesten Christentum bis Cyprian und Origenes* (Bonn 1940). P. Galtier, *Aux origines du sacrement de pénitence* (Rome 1951), gives particular attention to New Testament texts and to the literature of the sub-apostolic period. For Cyprian, see A. D'Alès, *La théologie de saint Cyprien* (Paris 1922); K. Rahner, 'Die Busslehre des hl. Cyprian von Karthago,' ZKT 74 (1952) 252–76; M. Bévenot, 'The Sacrament of Penance and St. Cyprian's *De lapsis*,' TS 16 (1955) 175–213. For Origen, E. Latko, *Origen's Concept of Penance* (Quebec 1949) and K. Rahner, 'La doctrine d'Origène sur la pénitence,' RSR 37 (1950) 47–97, 252–86, 422–56.

[6] The best recent studies on Tertullian's theology of penance are those of C. Daly, 'The Sacrament of Penance in Tertullian,' IER 69 (1947) 693–707, 815–21; 70 (1948) 730–46, 832–48; 73 (1950) 159–69, and K. Rahner, 'Zur Theologie der Busse bei Tertullian,' *Abhandlungen über Theologie und Kirche. Festschrift f. K. Adam, hrsg. v. M. Reding* (Düsseldorf 1943) 139–67. See, also, the bibliographies in Quasten, *op. cit.* 2.301 f., 314 f., 335.

[7] The following may be listed as representatives of the viewpoint that Tertullian's treatises on penance prove that it was not the practice of the early Church to forgive serious sins: J. Sirmundus, *Historia paenitentiae*

publicae (Paris 1651) 1–9; F. Funk, 'Zur altchristlichen Bussdisciplin,' *Kirchengeschichtliche Abhandlungen und Untersuchungen* 1 (1896) 151–81; A. Harnack, *History of Dogma* (tr. from the 3rd German ed. by N. Buchanan, London 1896) 2.108–12; L. Duchesne, *Histoire ancienne de l'Église* (Paris 1916) 1.518–20. The contrary opinion has been defended by J. Morinus, *Commentarius historicus de disciplina in administratione sacramenti paenitentiae* (Anvers 1682) 670–85; P. Monceaux, *Histoire littéraire de l'Afrique chrétienne* (Paris 1902) 1.432; G. Esser, *Die Bussschriften Tertullians de paenitentia und das Indulgenzedikt des Papstes Kallistus* (Bonn 1905). D. Petavius, *De vetere in ecclesia ratione poenitentiae diatriba. Dogmata theologica* 8 (Paris 1867) 182, favors the first opinion; however, in a later work, *Diatriba de poenitentia et reconciliatione veteris ecclesiae moribus recepta, ibid.* 451, he states that, *re altius et accuratius perspecta*, he has come to the conclusion that it was never the practice of the universal Church to refuse pardon to capital sins. References to other representatives of these two schools may be found in Poschmann I 283 f.

[8] Tertullian reveals a thorough familiarity with Latin and Greek letters; he has read widely in medical literature; in philosophy and law he has a specialist's learning. The judgement of antiquity is summed up in the famous eulogy of Vincent of Lerins, *Commonitorium* 24: *Quid enim hoc viro doctius? Quid in divinis atque humanis rebus exercitatius? Nempe omnem philosophiam et cunctas philosophorum sectas, auctores, assertatores sectarum, omnesque eorum disciplinas, omnem historiarum atque studiorum varietatem mira quadam mentis capacitate complexus est.*

[9] E. Norden voices the common opinion of classical literary critics when he says that 'Tertullian is, without doubt, the most difficult of all authors who wrote in Latin.' *Die antike Kunstprosa* (2nd ed. Leipzig 1909) 2.606. For complete bibliographies on his language and style, see Quasten, *op. cit.* 2.250 f. and J. Waszink, *Tertullianus. De anima. Edited with Introduction and Commentary* (Amsterdam 1947) 601–603 and 610–20.

[10] The word 'penitence' has been chosen for the English title of this treatise since it avoids the controversial connotations which attach to the terms 'repentance' and 'penance' and since it most closely approximates the various senses of *paenitentia* which Tertullian supposes or explains in the course of his composition. The persons whom he addressed had a definite notion, carried over from classical Latin and from their ordinary speech, of what *paenitentia* meant. At the beginning of his discourse Tertullian insists that for the Christian this concept is not enough. To the pagan *paenitentia* signifies nothing more that a feeling of regret for something which he did in the past. To the Christian,

however, it means sorrow for sin and conversion to a new way of life. It includes a fear of God's punishments, the performance of painful actions by way of satisfaction and, in terms of its relationship to ecclesiastical ritual, it means Baptism (*paenitentia prima*) and exomologesis (*paenitentia secunda*). Thus it encompasses everything which at any time and in any way is required of the sinner who seeks the forgiveness of God. There is no one word in any modern language which will convey all of these meanings and, for this reason, Teeuwen is of the opinion that the title should always be given in Latin in order to avoid misconceptions and misrepresentation; cf. St. W. J. Teeuwen, 'De voce *paenitentia* apud Tertullianum,' *Mnemosyne* 55 (1927) 410. That *paenitentia* means more than repentance in the sense of *mutatio mentis* (μετάνοια) and *conversio* is clear from Tertullian's use of the word with such verbs as *amplexari* (4.2), *invadere* (2.13 ; 4.2), *capessere* (6.1), *cogere* (2.10), *adsumere* (6.1), *adhibere* (2.12), *adimplere* (6.4), *includere* (6.1), *suscipere* (5.1), *fungi* (5.2). It is interesting that in the first edition of his translation (Kempten 1870) Kellner entitles the treatise *Über die Busse*; in the Cologne edition of 1882 he has *Über die Bekehrung*; and in the Kempten-Munich edition of 1912 the title is again *Über die Busse*.— For the spelling *paenitentia* rather than *poenitentia*, see Teeuwen, *op. cit.* 419. Other uses of the word and its derivatives in early Christian writers may be seen in A. Blaise-H. Chirat, *Dictionnaire latin-français des auteurs chrétiens* (Strasbourg 1954) 588 f.

[11] On Tertullian's use of the sermon form in many of his compositions, see Monceaux, *op. cit.* 1.366. Other references to Tertullian as a preacher are given by G. Diercks, *Tertullianus. De oratione* (Bussum 1947) xcix f., and E. Dekkers, *Tertullianus en de Geschiedenes der Liturgie* (Brussels-Amsterdam 1947) 39 f.

[12] Cf. St. Pacian's treatise, *Parainesis sive exhortatorius libellus ad poenitentiam*.

[13] Rauschen's opinion is discussed below, *De paen.* note 110.

[14] Tertullian uses a great variety of words and images in speaking of the salutary effect of *paenitentia*: we find, for example, *venia, reconciliatio, restitutio, pax, communio, salus, remedium, iasis, curatio, emendatio, planca, merx, ianua, reaedificatio, reformatio, redintegratio, oblitteratio, indulgentia, ignoscentia, expiatio, satisfactio, compensatio*. Related verbs are: *absolvere, revocare, sanare, mederi, reviviscere, purgare, mundare, emendare, expungere, dispungere, donare, in ecclesiam recipere, redigere, reddere.*

[15] E. Noeldechen, *Die Abfassungszeit der Schriften Tertullians*. TU 5 (Leipzig 1888) 59–62.

[16] A. Harnack, *Die Chronologie der altchristlichen Litteratur* (Leipzig

1904) 2.271 f. For other literature on this subject, see O. Bardenhewer, *Geschichte der altkirchlichen Literatur* (Freiburg 1914) 2.417.

[17] P. de Labriolle, *Tertullien. De paenitentia, De pudicitia.* Texte et trad. (Paris 1906); H. Kellner, *Tertullians ausgewählte Schriften* (Kempten-Munich 1912) 1.224-46; C. Mohrmann, *Tertullianus. Apologeticum en andere Geschriften* (Utrecht-Brussels 1951) 275-300.

TEXT

[1] *Caeci sine domini lumine.* The words may be read closely to give a causal sense to the prepositional phrase; that is, they are blind *because* they are unenlightened by the Lord. Compare Ps. 145.8: *Dominus illuminat caecos.* Both the *Codex Trecensis* and the *Codex Ottobonianus* have *homines,* in place of *hominum* read by the earlier editors. For this usage in Tertullian see Hoppe I 17.

[2] The word is *paenitentiam.* Cf. above, note 10 to the Introduction for the various senses of *paenitentia* in this treatise. In the translation 'repentance,' 'penance,' and 'penitence' will be used as seems most appropriate in each context.—Tertullian follows his regular custom here of repeating the title of a treatise in the opening sentence. In this case, as also in the *De pudicitia* and *Adversus Valentinianos,* the substantive of the title is the first word of the opening sentence.

[3] For *natura tenus norunt.* Not infrequently in Tertullian *tenus* has the force of 'only so far as.' Thus, in *Apol.* 40.7, the apples of Sodom are said to be apples *oculis tenus,* that is, only as far as appearances go. In *Adv. Marc.* 1.24 the salvation promised by Marcion is called an imperfect salvation because men are *anima tenus salvos, carne deperditos*; their souls alone are saved, their bodies are lost. So here, those who do not have a Christian conception of penitence understand it *natura tenus,* or 'only so far as nature instructs them.'

[4] This definition is important and must be analyzed in detail. The text reads: *Paenitentiam . . . norunt passionem animi quandam esse quae obveniat de offensa sententiae prioris.* The meaning of the words *passionem animi* may be illustrated from *De anima* 12. Discussing the unity of the soul in this chapter Tertullian says that *anima* and *animus* are not separate substances but that the *animus* is an essential function (*officium*) of the *anima* (*De an.* 12.6); it is that by which the soul thinks and acts (*De an.* 12.1). Tertullian contends, against Aristotle, that since the *anima* is *passibilis,* the *animus,* by concomitance, is also *passibilis* (*De an.* 12.3). The *passiones* are then described as *sentire, sapere* and *moveri,* that is, sensation, thought and emotion (*De an.* 12.4). In its broadest sense, therefore, a *passio animi* is any kind of psychic state or experience. Strictly and literally, it is an affection of the mind (*animus*) but by metonymy, it may also be called an affection of the soul (*anima*). For Tertullian *passio* often means a painful experience, suffering or distress, so that a *passio*

animi might be considered not merely an 'affection of soul' but, more precisely, an 'affliction of soul.' Thus we might translate '. . . a kind of unpleasant emotion which is the result, etc.'

S. McComb, in his article 'Repentance,' ERE 10.734, states that Latin theology was 'incapable of rising to the full compass of the New Testament idea of repentance' and erred in making the emotional primary in repentance. This process, he asserts, begins with Tertullian, as may be seen from his definition of *paenitentia* in *De paenitentia* 1.1. We must remember, however, that the definition of the word which is given here is not Tertullian's, nor does it represent the Christian concept of *paenitentia*. It is explicitly said to be a pagan notion and it is cited by Tertullian only to be rejected as inadequate.

Offensa is here the equivalent of *offensio*, as often in Tertullian; cf. F. Dölger, 'Missa als militarischer Fachausdruck,' AC 4 (1934) 272. The word has both an objective and a subjective sense. Objectively and primarily it is the offense itself; subjectively and secondarily it is the dislike, disgust, hatred which results from the offense. Translators are agreed in taking the subjective sense in the present definition: Thelwall (disgust), Dodgson (dislike), Kellner (Misbilligung), De Labriolle (regret), Mohrmann (spijt). Thus *paenitentia* would be defined as a kind of emotion which is caused by regret for a past decision. This interpretation, however, is not completely satisfactory. It is clear from the whole sentence that the *offensa* is the cause of the *passio animi* which we call *paenitentia*. It seems tautological, then, to interpret *offensa* as itself a subjective state of regret or dislike or disapproval. It is as though we were to say 'repentance is caused by regret,' or 'a *passio animi* is caused by a *passio animi*.' Regret for the past act is intrinsic to the very act of repentance itself, it is not merely an extrinsic cause which excites repentance.

There is no real difficulty about taking *offensa* here in the original, objective sense of the word. The *passio animi* of which there is question is one which results from a past action and it is this past action which is itself the *offensa*. The past action is a former decision which gives offense; it is this past action, therefore, which is now found offensive or regrettable. Thus there is an identification of *offensa* with *sententiae prioris*, explained grammatically by construing the genitive as appositional rather than objective. Repentance is a *passio animi* which is caused by the 'offense' or the 'offensiveness' of a past decision. This is quite different from saying that it is caused by 'regret for a past decision.'

The *offensa* which excites *paenitentia* is identified with a past *sententia* and this *sententia* may be understood as an act of either the mind or the will. Possibly both ideas are latent in the word since both judgement and choice entered into the action which is now the cause of repentance. The reading *prioris*, instead of *peioris*, is all but certain. It has been accepted by all recent editors and is supported by the *Codex Trecensis* and *Ottobonianus*; moreover, it is in perfect accord with the analysis of *paenitentia* which has here been given. Compare *Ad nat.* 1.1.10: *Non paenitet nisi pristinorum* and, especially, the important passage on the nature of *paenitentia* in *Adv. Marc.* 2.24, where Tertullian says that God's 'repentance' is a *simplex conversio sententiae prioris*.

⁵ Tertullian's fondness for word play is illustrated by his use of *ratio* in this and the following sentences. When he speaks of the *ratio paenitentiae* he refers to the nature or essence of penitence, particularly as this essence is an object of knowledge or understanding. When he says that God is the *auctor rationis* he is thinking rather of *ratio* as the power or faculty which apprehends essences. In the sentence which follows he states that God created all things by reason; here *ratio* is related to or identified with the *Logos* or *Verbum*, without whom 'was made nothing that was made.' John 1.3. For this last sense of *ratio* in Tertullian see especially *Adv. Praxean* 5–7; also E. Evans, *Tertullian's Treatise against Praxeas* (London 1948) 43 and J. Waltzing, *Tertullien Apologétique: Commentaire analytique, grammatical & historique* (Paris 1931) 120, 144. F. de Pauw, 'La justification des traditions non écrites chez Tertullien,' ETL 19 (1942) 11, has counted three hundred and forty passages in Tertullian where the word *ratio* occurs and he concludes that, with the exception of *deus*, *dominus* and the like, it is probably the substantive used most frequently in his works.—A summary of Tertullian's teaching on creation may be found in D'Alès I 109–12. The sequence of the three words used here, *providit, disponit, ordinavit* is logical and suggests that God, in creating, first plans what is to be done, then settles on a definite order in the universe and, finally, carries His plan into execution.

⁶ *Ratio res dei est.* Other examples of the use of *res* in the sense of 'proper possession' have been collected by G. Thörnell, *Studia Tertullianea* (Upsala 1918) 2.63 f. Reason is the proper possession of God; it is shared by those who know Him, while it is wanting in those who know Him not. The rational character of the work of God is mentioned, also, in *Apol.* 11.5; *Adv. Marc.* 1.23; *De an.* 16 and *De res. mort.* 3.— The Latin word *res*, like the English word 'property,' can mean both 'attribute' and 'wealth' or 'goods.' Here, too, Tertullian is indulging in word play. *Ratio* is a *res dei*; that is, it is a property of God's, an operative attribute which is manifest in creation; yet *ratio* is also a treasure of God's to which strangers have no access. This context suggests that it would probably be better not to translate *thesaurus* by 'treasure house' (Thelwall) or 'Schatzkammer' (Kellner). Possibly

Tertullian's idea might be best conveyed by the word 'substance,' which, like 'property,' suggests both 'nature' and 'wealth.' There is an interesting parallel in *Adv. Marc.* 1.22, where the *bonitas dei* is said to be laid up *in thesauris naturalium proprietatum.* For the Stoic notion that *ratio* is the original essence of God, cf. C. De Lisle Shortt, *The Influence of Philosophy on the Mind of Tertullian* (London n.d.) 57 f.

[7] This is in striking contrast with the supposed anti-intellectualism of Tertullian. In passages stressing the paradoxes of Christianity and in others which deal with the existence of mysteries, Tertullian appears to speak disparagingly of human reason; cf. *De bap.* 2; *Adv. Marc.* 2.2; *De res. mort.* 3; and the frequently quoted phrases from *De praesc. haer.* 9: *credibile quia ineptum . . . certum quia impossibile.* It is incorrect, however, to say that he condemned the use of reason in the investigation of religious truth. His principle is: *Quaerendum est donec invenias et credendum ubi inveneris (De praesc. haer.* 9); and, again, . . . *qui studuerit intellegere, cogetur et credere (Apol.* 18). Human reason is to be used, but the best that it can achieve of itself is a superficial understanding of things; *ratio autem divina in medulla est, non in superficie, et plerumque aemula manifestis (De res. mort.* 3).

It is true that Tertullian's strictures on philosophy and philosophers are vigorous and sarcastic, but he blames the philosophers for abusing their intelligence, not for using it. It is their pride he castigates (*philosophus, gloriae animal, De an.* 1.2), since it is their pride which leads them to corrupt the truth (*Apol.* 46). In a number of places he speaks of the pagan philosophers as the 'patriarchs of heretics;' cf. *Adv. Herm.* 8; *De an.* 3.1; *Adv. Marc.* 1.13. His denunciation of Aristotle is particularly fierce. He is the 'wretched inventor of dialectics' and dialectics is not a legitimate use of reason but rather the 'art of building up and tearing down;' it is 'evasive in its conclusions, forced in its conjectures . . . productive of contentions, it makes difficulties of everything and really settles nothing' (*De praesc. haer.* 7). For Tertullian and philosophy, see the literature listed by Quasten *op. cit.* 2.321 f. On the estimate of Aristotle in other early Christian writers, cf. J. Waszink—W. Heffening, 'Aristoteles,' RAC 1.657–67.

Tertullian's statement that 'all things are to be understood by reason' appears to conflict with his earlier declaration that pagans have but an inadequate concept of repentance because they know it only *natura tenus.* Of course it is not unusual to discover contradictory utterances in Tertullian, but here, perhaps, a solution is to be sought in his understanding of the word *ratio.* That which is *natura tenus,* he would say, is really *sine ratione,* at least in the sense that men who are not enlightened by God are without the light of that substantial *Ratio* or Wisdom which is identified with the *Verbum* and which has come into the world to enlighten all men (John 1.1-10). Quite possibly, for Tertullian, it would suggest a kind of contradiction in terms to speak, as philosophers do today, of the *lumen rationis naturalis*.

[8] Not infrequently in Tertullian pagans are called *extranei* (cf. *Apol.* 1.2; 16.4) and this seems to be the meaning connoted here.

[9] An allusion to the end of the world, which Tertullian, even in his Catholic writings, considered to be quite close at hand. Compare *Apol.* 32.1, where he speaks of the *vim maximam universo orbi imminentem . . . ipsam clausulam saeculi . . . comminantem*. In this passage he asserts that Christians pray that the end of the world may be delayed (*precamur differri*); in *De orat.* 5 he says they pray that it may be hastened.

[10] *Deversentur*; cf. TLL 5.852 for other instances of this word in the sense of *se gerere*.

[11] This expression (*illam . . . adhibent*) is one of several in the present context which show that Tertullian regards *paenitentia* as an *actio* as well as a *passio*; it is something one does, not simply something one feels or experiences; cf. *figere paenitentiam in corde*; *paenitentiam incubare*; *in actu paenitentiae*; *per paenitentiam delinquere, recte facere*. Such expressions show that, even for pagans, *paenitentia* is, in some sense, a matter of personal, voluntary activity and not merely a psychic state resulting from a cause over which one has no immediate control.

[12] The justice of this accusation may be seen in references to classical authors given in any Latin lexicon, s.v. *paenitere*. For the reading *liberalitatis* (*Codex Ottobonianus*) in place of *libertatis*, cf. J. Borleffs, 'Un nouveau manuscrit de Tertullien,' VC 5 (1951) 69.

[13] *Prout quid in ingratiam cecidit. Ingratia* can also mean 'disfavor' or 'unpleasantness,' but this alternative, though it would make good sense in the present passage (i.e. 'when, for one reason or another, a good action displeases them, pagans reproach themselves for having performed it.'), is improbable in the light of *De paen.* 2.10, where *ingratia* certainly means ingratitude and where the reference is obviously back to the present sentence. Compare *De pud.* 17.14 and *Adv. Marc.* 2.24. In the latter passage Tertullian says that, as a rule, men repent when they recall some evil they have done, although at times repentance follows *ex alicuius boni operis ingratia*. This is translated by P. Holmes, ANF 3.316, as 'the unpleasantness of some good action,' but *ingratia* is best taken here, also, as meaning 'ingratitude.'

[14] *Inrogare* is a legal term used regularly with such words as *poena, multa, supplicia*, etc., to indicate that something is set as a sanction or inflicted as a punishment. Tertullian wishes to say here that the *paenitentia* which follows upon their good actions is a kind of sanction which

the pagans impose upon themselves in order to guard against future benefactions.

15 Reading *ad augmentum perversae emendationis*. The expression is difficult but probably means little more than that pagans become worse instead of better when they repent. Their penance is perverted because it involves regret for having practiced virtue. The reading of the *Codex Ottobonianus* is *strumentum perversae emendationis*. This gives a very good sense, i.e. '... they would never use *paenitentia* as a means or instrument of a sinful conversion (as they do when they repent their good deeds).'
—It is interesting to compare *Martyrium Polycarpii* 11, where the proconsul calls upon Polycarp to repent his Christianity and the saint replies that it is not the practice of Christians to repent what is good in order to adopt what is evil.

16 Those who know God will have a right understanding of what repentance is and will realize that it is to be restricted to things that are sinful. Since they will also fear God, they will sin less frequently and, as a result, they will have fewer occasions to practice repentance. Thus both sin and repentance are held within limits (*modum temperarent... tenerent*) by the knowledge and fear of God.

17 Fear of God's punishments is repeatedly proposed in Scripture as a motive for repentance and amendment of life; cf. Ps. 2.12; Prov. 15.27; Eccli. 1.27; 5.7 ff.; Matt. 10.28; Lc. 3.3 ff.; John 5.14. This is true, also, throughout the patristic period. Tertullian's mind is frequently and clearly expressed. In the *De paenitentia* alone, besides the present passage, he refers to the fear of God as a motive of repentance and amendment in cc. 5, 6, 7, 9, 10 and 12. See, also, Clement of Alexandria, *Stromata* 7.12 and Gregory the Great, *Hom. in 1 Reg.* 5.11. St. John Chrysostom states simply that if the fear of God's punishments were not a good and salutary motive for repentance, Christ would not have spoken so frequently and at such length on the subject of hell (*Ad pop. Antioch. de statuis* 15.1). Other references may be found in D'Alès II 69. There is some ambiguity in St. Augustine's teaching, particularly in his explanation of the distinction between what he calls *timor servilis* and *timor castus*. It has been shown, however, that the servile fear he deprecates is not the fear of hell, *per se*, but rather a fear which, *per accidens*, does not exclude an affection for sin. The question has been studied by R. Rimml, 'Das Furchtproblem in der Lehre des heil. Augustin,' ZKT 45 (1921) 244-49.

18 The concept of *paenitentia* revealed here clearly includes more than simple regret for a past action. Throughout the whole chapter it suggests the idea of a complete conversion to God in a new life; cf. Teeuwen II 411; A. Dirksen, *The New Testament Concept of Metanoia*

(Washington 1932) 53; H. Pohlmann, *Die Metanoia als Zentralbegriff der christlichen Frömmigkeit* (Leipzig 1938).—The present chapter of the *De paenitentia*, along with chapters 4 and 6, is widely quoted by theologians in discussing the necessity of repentance for justification. See, for example, Galtier II 51 f. and E. Doronzo, *De poenitentia* (Milwaukee 1949) 1.478 f.

[19] Tertullian's views on original sin are well summarized in D'Alès I 120–27. See, also, R. Roberts, *The Theology of Tertullian* (London 1924) 162 f. and J. Morgan, *The Importance of Tertullian in the Development of Christian Dogma* (London 1928) 172, 182 f., 219. This question is treated below, *De paen.*, note 201.

[20] *Cum saeculi dote*. The world (*saeculum*) is a gift of God's to man (Gen. 1.28 f.). After the sin of Adam, man is accursed and the world, also, is accursed with him (Gen 3.17 f.). For *dos* in the sense of *donum*, see Waszink, *op. cit.* 99. The sentence is also capable of another interpretation, as follows. Man was condemned, and, from this time on, the human race (*saeculum*) has, as a kind of endowment (*dos*), all of the miseries to which it is subject.

[21] Reading, with Borleffs, *maturuisset*. If *maturavisset* is preferred, we might interpret the sentence to mean that God condemned man after the fall of Adam but, moved by mercy, He promptly revoked the sentence of condemnation and thus gave us the first example of *paenitentia*.—For man as the 'image' of God, see the discussion in H. Karpp, *Probleme altchristlicher Anthropologie* (Gütersloh 1950) 53–56 and I. Hübscher, *De imagine Dei in homine viatore* (Louvain 1932) 5.—The words *sententia recissa* recall the expression *offensa sententiae prioris* used in the definition of *paenitentia* which opens the treatise; there, however, *sententia* meant, simply, a subjective decision or determination of some kind; here it is thought of, principally, as an objective, juridical sentence which was carried into execution. The sense in which God is said to 'repent' is explained more fully in *Adv. Marc.* 2.24.

[22] Literally, 'He gave voices to all the prophets.' The words *ei praedicandae* have been restored by Borleffs from the *Codex Trecensis*. It is worth noting that Tertullian does not restrict the function of the prophets to foretelling future events; compare *Apol.* 18.2, 5. For his use of the *dativus finalis*, see Hoppe I 26 f.

[23] In post-Augustan Latin *mox* is often used simply for *post* or *postea*.

[24] The meaning of the sentence appears to be this. The outpouring of grace which illuminates the world through the Holy Spirit is identified with the conferring of grace in Christian Baptism. This is distinguished from the Baptism of John, which is exclusively a Baptism of penance (Acts 19.2–6), effecting neither the forgiveness of sins nor the grace of

the Spirit (cf. *De bap.* 10). The Baptism of John was instituted before the Baptism of Jesus and was intended for those who were, later on, to receive the Baptism of Jesus and thus enter into the inheritance promised to the chosen people. See *De bap.* 10–12 for a detailed description of the differences between the two Baptisms.

25 Suggested by Matt. 3.2, in the Vulgate: *Poenitentiam agite, appropinquavit enim regnum coelorum*. Tertullian has freely adapted the second part of the verse to read: *iam enim salus nationibus appropinquabat*. The change of tense shows that he intends this as his own comment and not as a direct quotation of the text; see Borleffs I 77 f. and II 67. *Enim* is affirmatory rather than causal; for this use cf. references in Diercks, *op. cit.* 165.

26 The expression *vetus error*, standing by itself, is ambiguous and it seems best to preserve this ambiguity in the translation. It might, possibly, mean some former personal transgression (*error* is, originally, a wandering or deviation) which has stained the soul. It is more likely, however, that there is a reference here to original sin and its consequences. Certainly in *De test. an.* 3 Tertullian asserts that the human race is 'infected' as a result of Adam's sin; in *De an.* 40.1 he says that the soul, before Baptism, is *immunda*, while in *De an.* 41.14 he speaks of a *malum animae* which comes *ex originis vitio* and which is a veil *pristinae corruptionis* removed by Baptism (*De an.* 41.4). The idea that the soul, before Baptism, is veiled in darkness and ignorance occurs frequently in Tertullian, as does, also, the parallel scriptural concept of Baptism as an enlightening (cf. Eph. 5.8–14). See, for example, the opening sentence of the *De baptismo*, where we read that, through the sacrament, *ablutis delictis pristinae caecitatis in vitam aeternam liberamur*. There is an interesting discussion of this whole subject in F. Dölger, 'Die Sünde in Blindheit und Unwissenheit,' AC 2 (1930) 222–26.

27 Père Galtier argues from this passage that the forgiveness of sins in ecclesiastical penance is similar, in its effects, to the forgiveness of sins in the sacrament of Baptism, since in both cases the Holy Ghost comes to the soul as a consequence of the rite which is administered by the Church. It seems clear, however, that Tertullian is thinking here of penance in its broadest sense and not, specifically, of the ecclesiastical penance which he will describe in later chapters of the present treatise; cf. Galtier I 119 f. and the same author's article 'Confirmation ou absolution,' RSR 5 (1914) 201–35, 339–94. For Tertullian's teaching on the indwelling of the Holy Spirit see D'Alès I 264–68 and the literature cited by Waszink, *op. cit.* 456 f.

28 Violence is done repentance when it is twisted and perverted to include a regret for virtuous actions.

[29] The efficacy of divine grace is mentioned frequently by Tertullian but nowhere more emphatically than in the present passage. Not only does God help man perform good actions but these actions *are* the actions of God Himself; cf. *De an.* 21.6; *Ad mart.* 1; *Ad ux.* 1.8 and, especially, *Adv. Marc.* 2.24. With equal emphasis he insists that man's will remains free; cf. *De monog.* 14 and *Adv. Marc.* 2.5–10. The problem of reconciling the efficacy of grace with the freedom of man's will did not seriously engage his attention, although in *De exhort. cast.* 2 he touches it briefly in discussing the question of responsibility for moral evil in the world.

[30] *Viderit ingratia . . . viderit gratia.* For Tertullian's use of *viderit* and *viderint* cf. Waszink, *op. cit.* 112.

[31] *Bonum factum deum habet debitorem, sicuti et malum, quia judex omnis remunerator est causae.* This is one of the earliest and most explicit statements by a Christian writer of the patristic period on the subject of condign merit. Compare Cyprian, *De op. et eleem.* 14: *Pervenire ad videndum deum potes, dum deum et moribus et operibus promereris.* The first official pronouncement of the Church is in canon 18 of the second council of Orange: *Debetur merces bonis operibus, si fiant* (DB 191). See K. Wirth, *Der Verdienstbegriff bei Tertullian* (Leipzig 1892) and, below, *De paen.*, note 92.—*Omnis* is here taken with *judex*; if it is read with *causae*, we might translate,'. . . there is no account which is not settled by a judge.'

[32] For references to *disciplina* in this sense, cf. J. Waltzing, *op. cit.* 335. The meaning of the word *disciplina* in Tertullian has also been studied by V. Morel, 'Disciplina. Le mot et l'idée représentée par lui dans les œuvres de Tertullien,' RHE 40 (1944–45) 5–46 and W. Dürig, *Disciplina. Eine Studie zur Bedeutung des Wortes in der Sprache der Liturgie und der Väter*, SE 4 (1952) 245–79.

[33] The difference which seems to be indicated here between *peccatum* and *delictum*, sin and transgression, is hardly more than verbal. St. Augustine, *Quest. in Hept.* 3.20, states that *peccatum* may be regarded as *perpetratio mali*, *delictum* as *desertio boni*, but this, too, is a rational and not a real distinction. Tertullian uses *delictum* much more frequently than *peccatum*; *delictum* occurs about two hundred and fifty times in his writings, *peccatum* only thirty-five times.

[34] *A suo auctore respectus.* Thelwall sees here a reference to Luke 22.61, 'the Lord, turning, looked at Peter,' and translates, 'our spirit having been "looked back upon" by its own Author;' but the allusion is forced and can hardly have been intended by Tertullian. For the use of *respicere*, see G. Thörnell, *Studia Tertullianea* (Upsala 1918) 2.56 f.

[35] *Dominica praecepta.* The adjective *dominicus* in Tertullian almost

always means 'the Lord's.' Compare *passio dominica* (*De praesc. haer.* 36.3; *De pud.* 10.4); *dominicum corpus* (*De pud.* 9.16); *similitudines dominicae* (*De paen.* 8.4); *dominica resurrectio* (*De res. mort.* 6.2.) For *dominica* as referring to the Lord's day, Sunday, cf. *De cor.* 3 and *De ieiun.* 15. The phrase *dominica sollemnia* (*De fuga in persec.* 14.1; *De an.* 9.4) probably is to be understood of Sunday Mass (see the literature listed by Waszink, *op. cit.* 166) although F. Dölger, 'Das *Martyrium* als Kampf mit dem Teufel,' AC 3 (1932) 188 and 'Zu *dominica sollemnia* bei Tertullianus,' AC 6 (1940) 108-15, contends that it means simply, 'the service consecrated to the Lord.' The substantive, *dominus*, is used indifferently of Christ, the God Man, and of God considered absolutely. In the *De paenitentia*, for example, Borleffs I 284 f., lists four passages where the reference is to Christ and twenty-seven where the reference is simply to God. Tertullian explains his own understanding of the word in *Apol.* 34.1, where he says that *dominus* is the *cognomen* of God and adds, *dominus meus unus est, deus omnipotens et aeternus.* For the different connotations of *dominus* and *deus*, see *Adv. Hermog.* 3.

[36] The present chapter contains Tertullian's most detailed description and analysis of the nature of sin. The definition he gives here, *id a quo deus arceat*, is substantially the same as Augustine's *factum vel dictum vel concupitum contra legem aeternam* (*Contra Faustum Manich.* 22.27). For Tertullian's teaching on this subject see H. Motry, *The Concept of Mortal Sin in Early Christianity* (Washington 1920), especially 50-55. See, too, A. E. Wilhelm-Hooijbergh, *Peccatum. Sin and Guilt in Ancient Rome* (Groningen 1954) 98-102.—It is worth pointing out that the opening pages of the *De paenitentia* furnish a brief synthesis of Christian ethics. This synthesis may be phrased thus: (1) The divine law is the foundation of moral obligations; (2) conscience interprets man's immediate duty; (3) free will is the principle of merit or demerit; (4) the whole man, composite of body and soul, is put to the test in this life and rewarded or punished in the next; cf. D'Alès I 263 f.

[37] Literally, 'a great essence (*grande quid*) of goodness.' Compare, also, *Adv. Marc.* 2.3, where Tertullian states that God's goodness is known simultaneously along with Himself, and 2.4, where, in a beautiful passage on creation, *Goodness* is hypostatized and described as the cause of all that is good in the world.

[38] Tertullian speaks frequently of the composition of man and of the unity of body and soul in this composite; cf. *De res. mor.* 14-16, 40; *De an.* 40, 41, 58. In these passages he asserts that the soul acts *in* the flesh and *with* the flesh and *through* the flesh. Even thought itself is an act of the flesh. The soul has no activity apart from the flesh as long as it is in the flesh, and all that the flesh does, it does in company with the soul.

The word 'man' is a kind of tie or pin (*fibula*) which binds together these two substances and shows that they cannot be, unless they are united.

All of this would suggest that Tertullian was not far from the Aristotelian notion of the soul as the form of the body, yet it must be admitted that there are other passages in his works which are quite inconsistent with this conception. For example, the body is described as a house in which the soul dwells (*De an.* 38.4, 6; *De res. mor.* 41, 46; *De pud.* 20, with reference to 2 Cor. 5.1). It is the *calix animae* (*De an.* 40.2); the *vagina animae* (*De res. mor.* 9); the *vasculum animae*, because it 'receives and contains the soul' (*De res. mor.* 16). The soul is itself corporeal (*De an.* 5–8); it has length, breadth, height, color, and the same configuration as the human body (*De an.* 9). In answering the objections of the Platonists that the soul cannot be corporeal, since two bodies can not be in one and the same place at the same time, Tertullian insists that philosophy is here out of touch with reality, since the fact of pregnancy is an obvious refutation of the objection; in order to emphasize the reasonableness of his solution, he adds that there is a case on record of a Greek woman who gave birth to quintuplets (*De an.* 6.8).

It is clear, then, that although Tertullian teaches the unity of man in a composite of body and soul, his notion of this unity is quite imperfect. Body and soul are two complete substances which exist together; they do not possess the substantial unity of an *unum per se*, described and demanded by Aristotelian and scholastic psychology. The soul is diffused through the body as air is diffused through the pipes of an organ (*De an.* 14.4) and its ruling power is localized in the heart (*De an.* 15.4). There is no justification in *De an.* 32 for the assertion of De Lisle Shortt, *op. cit.* 64, that in this chapter Tertullian teaches, with the Stoics, that the soul permeates the body of man exactly as the world soul is diffused throughout its parts. For the μῖξις of body and soul, described in Stoic psychology, and the influence of this idea on Tertullian, see G. Rauch, *Der Einfluss der stoischen Philosophie auf die Lehrbildung Tertullians* (Halle 1890) 27–29.

[39] Cf. Gen. 2.7, and compare *Scorp.* 6: *alterum manus dei, alterum flatus*. The origin of the soul from the breath of God was treated in Tertullian's lost work *De censu animae* and is briefly considered in *De an.* 3–4.

[40] *In vitam aut in iudicium*. For other examples of *iudicare* in the sense of *condemnare, punire*, cf. Waltzing, *op. cit.* 343. The doctrine of the resurrection of the body is treated at length in Tertullian's work *De resurrectione mortuorum* (*De resurrectione carnis*); see the synopsis and analysis in D'Alès I 142–52.

[41] *Paenitentia* here and in the following paragraph clearly means more

than the *passio animae* described in the opening sentence of the present treatise. Tertullian has said above (c. 2) that the *justice* of God demands the repentance of man. The purpose of penitence is to restore the sinner to the friendship of God and thus to effect his salvation. Penance is required precisely because God is offended. This would seem to imply some appreciation of the fact that *paenitentia* includes not only regret for a past action and a purpose of amendment for the future, but also involves an effort to make reparation or satisfaction to God for the offenses which have been committed against Him. The fundamental distinction between pagan and Christian penitence is this. Pagan penitence is indifferent to the offensiveness of the past action in the sight of God; Christian penitence is concerned primarily, if not exclusively, with this consideration. Since both body and soul have shared the guilt of sin, each must have its part in the penance which is demanded after sin. For a comprehensive list of scriptural and patristic passages on the necessity of penance, see Doronzo, *op. cit.* 1.478 f. Other references to this subject in the present treatise may be found in cc. 4 and 6; cf. below, *De paen.*, note 87.

⁴² *Hoc eo praemisimus ut non minorem alteri quam utrique parti, si quid deliquerit, paenitentiae necessitatem intellegamus impendere.* The correlatives *alter* and *uterque* indicate here an opposition between 'the one' and 'the other' rather than between 'one' and 'both;' cf. W. Freund-E. Andrews, *A New Latin Dictionary*, s.v. *uterque*, B 3 for other examples of this usage. If Tertullian is understood to say that penance is *no less* necessary to either part of man, if it sins, than it is to both parts (Thelwall, Dodgson, De Labriolle, Kellner) then he states the opposite of what the context requires, since we would expect him to say that penance is *no more* necessary to one part, if it sins, than it is to both. The subject of *deliquerit* is not expressed but, in the interpretation given here, is understood from *utrique*, rather than from *alteri parti*; that is, 'there is no less obligation for one part to do penance than there is for the other, even though it is the other which has sinned.'

⁴³ Tertullian's description of sins as 'spiritual' and 'corporeal' did not find favor with later writers and has no place in the language of moral theology today. The classification, however, corresponds roughly to the familiar distinction between internal and external sins; cf. H. Davis, *Moral and Pastoral Theology* (London 1946) 1.229-35, and, below, *De paen.* note 47.

⁴⁴ The statement seems to allow for a distinction between material and formal sin. Formal sin supposes subjective guilt, resulting from the free choice of an objectively sinful act; material sin exists when an objectively sinful act is performed without subjective guilt. Sin which

is 'imputed to accident, necessity or ignorance' is not sin which the agent commits *sciens volens*, and, to that extent, it is only material or objective sin. Cf. *De pud.* 19.24 and Motry, *op. cit.* 63 f.

[45] *Adiectionem legi superstruere*, for *legem . . . adimplere* in the Vulgate, Matt. 5.17.

[46] *Comminus*; compare Lucretius 4.1051.

[47] The text here, Matt. 5.28, is cited regularly as scriptural authority for the distinction between internal and external sins; for its use in Tertullian see *De an.* 15.4; 40.4; 58.6; *De idol.* 2; *De exhort. cast.* 9; *De resur. mort.* 15; *De pud.* 6. In all of these passages, except *De exhort. cast.* 9 (*stupravit*), he refers to the sin which is committed by a lustful glance as adultery (*adulteravit, moechatus est*, for the Greek ἐμοίχευσεν), not *stuprum* or *fornicatio*; cf. G. Aalders, *Tertullianus' Citaten uit de Evangeliën en de oud-Latijnsche Bijbelvertaligen* (diss. Amsterdam 1932) 35. The following sentence suggests that Tertullian further distinguished internal sins as sins of thought and sins of desire, but this is not expressly stated and can not be shown with certainty from the passage. In *Apol.* 36.4, however, he asserts that there are four ways in which sin can be committed, scl. by evil thoughts, desires, words and deeds.—C. Mohrmann, *op. cit.* 282, considers that *matrimonium* is an *abstractum pro concreto*, to be translated as the equivalent of *uxor*; for *cadere*, compare Plautus, *Pers.* 656.

[48] The meaning of the word *repraesentare* in Tertullian has been widely discussed, particularly in controversial literature dealing with the real presence of Christ in the Eucharist. D'Alès, *op. cit.* 356–60, lists fifty-two examples of the verb *repraesentare* and its derivatives, *repraesentatio* and *repraesentator*. In thirty-three instances it has a concrete, physical sense, that is, the object is actually *re praesens*; in seven places it has the subjective sense of an imaginative or intellectual representation; in twelve examples it is used of a juridical or pictorial representation. It may be noted, in connection with the use of the word in the present passage, that in the materialistic psychology of Stoicism even intellectual apprehension supposes a quasi-physical representation of the external object. The soul does not actively abstract the universal from the particular; rather it resembles a *tabula rasa* on which the senses inscribe a picture of external, corporeal reality. It is in this sense, probably, that we should understand such expressions as *imaginario fructu repraesentat* (*De monog.* 10); *repraesentantes faciem uniuscuiusque* (*De praesc. haer.* 16) and *animus sibi repraesentat* in the present passage. Cf. A. Virieux-Reymond, *La logique et l'épistémologie des Stoïciens* (Lausanne n.d.) 51–66; see, also, the careful exegesis of the whole passage in Borleffs I 80–82.

[49] The expression is *conscientiae tuae confessione*. *Conscientia* may be translated as 'consciousness' or 'conscience.' If the first meaning is adopted, the sentence could be paraphrased as follows: There is an acknowledgement of guilt, a confession, in the very assertion which the sinner makes, 'I willed, but I did not act.' This is an assertion made by, or based on, the interior knowledge which a man has of himself (*confessio conscientiae*), and it condemns the man who makes it, since it proves that he knew what he willed was evil. For this meaning of *conscientia*, see Waltzing, *op. cit.* 200 and 227. However, the expression also gives an intelligible sense if we understand it to mean that a man's conscience attempts to excuse itself by saying that no external deed followed upon the internal act of the will. This excuse is a *confessio conscientiae*, an actual avowal of guilt, since our conscience should impel us to do what our will has led us to desire, unless our will itself desires what is evil.

[50] The strong voluntarist tendency in Tertullian's character is conspicuous in the closing paragraph of this chapter. See the analysis in B. Nisters, *Tertullian: Seine Persönlichkeit und sein Schicksal* (Münster i. W. 1950) 73–80; cf., also, A. Quaquarelli, 'Liberta, peccato e penitenza secondo Tertulliano,' *Rassegna di scienze filosofiche* 2 (1949) 16–37.

[51] Tertullian teaches here, clearly and emphatically, that there are no unforgivable sins. He speaks in general terms of the efficacy of penitence but appears to be thinking primarily of sins committed before Baptism and of their forgiveness through the penance which is associated with that sacrament (*paenitentia prima*). For this reason the sentence ought not to be cited as proof (e.g. RJ, *Index Theologicus* 522; B. Otten, *Institutiones dogmaticae* (Chicago 1925) 6.69) that, before his lapse into Montanism, Tertullian taught that all sins, no matter how grave, could be forgiven by ecclesiastical absolution in the sacrament of Penance (*paenitentia secunda*). Actually this was his belief at the time he wrote the *De paenitentia* but the fact is better established by later chapters in the treatise, taken in conjunction with statements in the *De pudicitia*.

In saying that God grants pardon to all repentant sinners Tertullian is simply repeating the teaching of Scripture and the common doctrine of the early Church; cf. pertinent texts from the patristic period in C. Boyer, *De paenitentia* (Rome 1942) 166. For references in Tertullian's own works to God's loving kindness towards sinners, see the impressive list of passages collected by C. Daly, *op. cit.* 69 (1947) 819–20. Tertullian's Montanist interpretation of the *peccatum ad mortem* (1 John 5.16) may be seen in the treatise *De pudicitia* 2.14 and 19.25–28.

[52] An abbreviation of Ezech. 18.21–23.

[53] Ezech. 33.11. The subject of *inquit* is indefinite, as it often is in

Tertullian when the verb is used to introduce a quotation from Scripture. The repetition of *inquit, dicit* is awkward, but appears to be the correct reading; cf. Borleffs I 49; for Tertullian's method of joining multiple quotations from Scripture, *ibid.* 85 f. The texts from Ezechiel cited here have been of the greatest importance in the history of penitential theology, particularly in the evolution of the Church's teaching on the necessity of sorrow for sin (Galtier I 32 f.) and the efficacy of perfect contrition; cf. P. Anciaux, *La théologie du sacrement de pénitence au XIIe siècle* (Louvain–Paris 1949) 52. The Hebrew *schub*, translated in the Vulgate by *paenitere* and *agere paenitentiam*, means, literally, *converti*, and is used to describe the return of men and nations to God consequent upon their recognition of the evil which comes of sin; cf., besides the passages in Ezechiel, 2 Par. 6.24; 7.14; 3 Kings 8.33; Joel 2.12; Jer. 31.19. The idea of conversion, present in the Hebrew *schub*, persists in the words μετάνοια (cf. Dirksen, *op. cit.* 219) and in *paenitentia*, as Tertullian understands the term; cf. Teeuwen II 411.

⁵⁴ *Ut naufragus alicuius tabulae fidem.* Compare Plato, *Phaedo* 85d, Seneca, *De beneficiis* 3.9.2, *dare tabulam naufrago*, and Cicero, *De officiis* 3.23.89, *tabulam de naufrago arripere.* Tertullian Christianized this popular figure, using it to describe the salvation of man through the means of grace given him by God. Quite possibly he was influenced in making this application by St. Paul's words in I Tim. 1.19, *circa fidem naufragaverunt*; compare *De pud.* 13.19 f. In the phrase *alicuius tabulae fidem, fides* has a pregnant sense; it is that which brings safety or security. The expression, *secunda tabula post naufragium*, used so frequently of the sacrament of Penance in Christian tradition, is certainly derived from Tertullian's language in the *De paenitentia*, although he nowhere phrases the formula in precisely these terms. As far as can be ascertained, this was first done by St. Jerome, *Epist.* 130.9. For other references, see Oehler, *op. cit.* 1.649 f. In its 14th session, the Council of Trent distinguishes the sacrament of Penance from the sacrament of Baptism, and condemns the view that the former is not properly called the *secunda tabula post naufragium*; DB 912. The precise meaning of the formula has engaged the attention of numerous theologians and divergent interpretations have developed; cf. Peter Lombard, *Lib. sent.* 4. 14.1; St. Thomas, *Summa theol.* III, q. 84, art. 6; *Catech. Conc. Trid.* 2.5.1; *Suarez, Tractatus de poen.* 1.1.4.

Teeuwen II 414 says that Tertullian thinks of Baptism as a ship which enables men to reach the haven of salvation. If they sin, their repentance is the *planca salutis* which will save them. There is some inconsistency, however, in speaking of Baptism as the ship which saves men, if it is also the *prima planca salutis* which is given to them after this ship is wrecked. The discussion of a *naufragium post baptismum* does not begin until chapter 7 of the treatise, and the *tabula salutis* which is given to men after post-baptismal sin is the *secunda* and not the *prima tabula salutis*; cf., below, note 111. It is probably more correct to suppose that Tertullian here speaks of *paenitentia* in general as a *tabula salutis*, prescinding for the moment from the distinction between *prima* and *secunda paenitentia*. A *tabula salutis* is first given to men in Baptism; it is given, secondly, if they sin after Baptism. These are the two *plancae salutis* referred to below, *De paen.* 12.9. Thus the *naufragus* who finds a *planca salutis* in penitence is any sinner, whether he has sinned before or after his Baptism. Suarez, *loc. cit.*, states that *homo natus est naufragus* and that Baptism, as the *prima tabula salutis*, saves him from the effects of original sin as well as from the effects of personal sin committed before Baptism. This conception is not foreign to Tertullian's thought on the efficacy of Baptism but it probably does not enter into consideration here.

55 Isa. 40.15.

56 Osee 13.3. Compare Dan. 2.35 and Matt. 3.12.

57 Jer. 19.11. Compare Rom. 9.21.

58 Ps. 1.3.

59 Cf. Matt. 3.10.

60 Reading *non odisse*, rather than *nosse*. *Nosse* has the support of the MSS and is defended by Borleffs I 83 f. *Non odisse* is a conjecture of Rhenan's, adopted by most later editors. The sentence is then interpreted to mean that a man, in order to obey God, must love what God loves, just as a servant, in order to obey his master, must love what his master loves. It is precisely in such a conformity of wills that the essence of obedience consists. If *nosse* is retained, the sentence may be taken to mean that servants are not even permitted to learn about things which displease their masters, since if they do not know what displeases them, they will not do it; *nihil est volitum nisi praecognitum*. Thus there will be no conflict between the judgement of master and servant, and in this conformity of minds (*in similitudine animorum*) the true essence of obedience is found. Understood in this way, the final words of the sentence hint at, though they do not completely or exactly express, the principle of 'obedience of judgement' discussed by later writers. It may seem that the expression, *in similitudine animorum*, is more consistent with the reading *nosse* than *non odisse*, since *animus*, as a synonym for *mens* (*De an.* 12.1) appears to suggest conformity of intellect rather than of will. *Animus*, however, is the principle of all psychic life and its use here is not decisive in favor of either reading.

⁶¹ The fact that God decrees repentance proves that it is a good act. The same argument is used by St. Thomas (*Summa theologica* 3, q. 84, art. 1) to prove that penance is a virtue. Tertullian's statement is also cited by contemporary theologians in discussing the controversial question of whether or not repentance, as understood in Catholic dogma, is morally good, bad or indifferent; cf. E. Doronzo, *op. cit.* 1.270.

⁶² The English form of the oath is 'as I live,' or 'by my life;' cf. above, note 53. The Hebrews swore by the living God (*vivit dominus*); God swears by His own life (*vivo ego*); see the interesting explanation which Tertullian gives of God's oath *per semetipsum* in *Adv. Marc.* 2.26. For other references in Tertullian to the taking of oaths, cf. *Apol.* 28.3 and 32.2; *Ad nat.* 1.10 and 1.17; *Ad Scap.* 2; *De cor.* 11; *De idol.* 11 and 20; *De pud.* 19.24. On *Apol.* 9.9, see F. Dölger, 'Das Blutbündnis im griechisch-römischen Verschwörungseid,' AC 4 (1934) 209. The taking of oaths was not absolutely forbidden to Christians; there are, however, frequent warnings in the writings of the Fathers against vain and indiscriminate swearing. Adjurations commonly used in a pagan society involved, almost inevitably, some recognition of heathen divinities, and the idolatry implicit in such forms could hardly have been tolerated. A special problem arose over the practice of swearing by the emperor's genius. Tertullian says that this is prohibited to Christians (*Apol.* 32.2), although they may and do swear by his safety; cf. Waltzing, *op. cit.* 218 f. for the meaning of this latter oath. In formal attestations, Christians swore by the most high God, by the mystery of the Incarnation, by Christ, by the Holy Spirit, by the Gospels, by the Alleluja; see G. Mead, 'Oaths,' DCA 2.1415–18. On the practice of swearing by the altar, cf. F. Dölger, 'Die Heiligkeit des Altars und ihre Begründung im christlichen Altertum,' AC 2 (1932) 168.

⁶³ Tertullian plays on the words *adseveratio* and *perseverare*. God has promised salvation as the reward of penitence; when, confiding in this promise, we persevere in its practice, we ensure its fruit, salvation, as a permanent possession.

⁶⁴ *Enim*, used here as a simple introductory particle, without demonstrative or corroborative force.

⁶⁵ The word *gratia* refers, in general, to the favor of God. In the first part of the sentence it means a favor which God grants the sinner as a help in the performance of penance; in the second it means the favor or approval which the sinner finds in God's sight as a result of his penance. The distinction between actual and habitual grace is not described in technical language until the medieval period but may be seen here, in rudimentary form, if the word *gratia* is understood in the

twofold sense it appears to have in the present sentence. At any rate, theologians have cited this passage as proof of Tertullian's belief: (1) that the grace of God (actual grace) inspires the virtuous acts of men (D'Alès I 270, 286), and (2) that the grace which is lost by sin (habitual grace) is restored by penance (Galtier II 52). For this second point, see also the valuable study by K. Rahner, 'Sünde als Gnadenverlust in der frühkirchlichen Literatur,' ZKT 60 (1936), especially 491-507.

[66] The first four chapters of the *De paenitentia* are introductory. With this fifth chapter Tertullian begins to treat more explicitly and in greater detail of penance as a *conversio*. The catechumens whom he addresses are converts from sin to Christianity, and they will seal their 'penance-conversion' by the reception of Baptism. Baptism, therefore, is both a penitential rite and a rite of conversion. Once the Christian has received it (*semel*= once for all) he is a member of a society of saints and he must never return to a life of sin; cf. Heb. 6.6; 1 John 3.9; 5.18. Thus the notion of *dolor* (a *passio animi quae obveniat de offensa sententiae prioris*; c. 1.1) recedes from the concept of *paenitentia* and the idea of conversion predominates; cf. Teeuwen II 411.

Tertullian writes: *paenitentiam ... numquam posthac iteratione delicti resignari oportere*. The word *resignari* is significant as revealing an identification between Baptism and the penitence of which Tertullian here speaks. *Signare* is to seal and *resignare* is to unseal or violate a seal, as *serare* is to lock and *reserare* to unlock, *claudere* is to close and *recludere* is to open. To return to a life of sin is, therefore, to violate the seal of Baptism, and this is quite properly described as *paenitentiam resignari*. Other uses of *resignari* and its derivatives may be seen in *De virg. vel.* 5; *Adv. Marc.* 1.28; 4.10; *Ad nat.* 1.5; *De orat.* 22; *Apol.* 6.4; *De carne Christi* 23; *De resur. mort.* 39; *De cultu fem.* 1.1. For Baptism as a sign or seal, see below, c. 6. Probably the concept has a scriptural foundation in such texts as 2 Cor. 1.22; Eph. 1.13; 4.30. The expression is frequent in St. Augustine and, particularly, in the Greek Fathers. Pastor Hermae, *Sim.* 8.6.3, has θλᾶν τὴν σφραγῖδα a very close approximation of the thought in the present sentence. Further details may be seen in F. Dölger, *Sphragis, eine altchristliche Taufbezeichnung* (Paderborn 1911).

[67] This penance is, *in concreto*, a conversion which is begun by turning away from sin and sealed by receiving the sacrament of Baptism. Quite possibly Tertullian includes in the phrase, *paenitentia functus*, the performance of such *opera paenitentiae* as the confession of sins, fasting, vigils, prostrations and similar practices which customarily preceded the actual reception of Baptism; cf. *De bap.* 20; Hippolytus, *Apost. trad.* 20; Justin, *Apol. prima* 61. Origen, *In Luc. hom.* 21, insists that the forgiveness of sins in Baptism is dependent upon a true, internal

conversion; candidates must first 'bring forth fruits worthy of penance' and only then approach the sacrament. It is worth noting, in this connection, that Baptism was conferred at Eastertide and that the penitential season of Lent was regarded as a period of appropriate preparation for the catechumens who were to receive the sacrament; cf. Cyril of Jerusalem, *Catech.* 1.5; Chrysostom, *Hom.* 10 *in Matt.* 3.5; Leo M., *Serm. de Quad.* 5.3. The performance of external works of penance testifies to the internal conversion which is required of those who are to be introduced into the Christian way of life. Possibly this prebaptismal penance was also thought of as contributing its part in effecting the actual forgiveness of sin (cf. *De paen.* 2.6), although this is denied by B. Poschmann II 1 f.; cf., also, Teeuwen II 415. It is Poschmann's contention that Baptism was conceived as a *magna indulgentia* in which sins were remitted solely through the merits of the passion of Christ and not by reason of personal works of penance performed by the sinner himself. Baptism is thus contrasted with *paenitentia secunda*, in which the sinner was obliged to perform works of penance proportioned to his offense in order to make amends to God and avert the divine anger. For a valuable note on the difference in efficacy between the sacraments of Baptism and Penance precisely with relation to the personal-subjective contribution of the sinner and the ecclesiastical-objective contribution of the Church, see K. Rahner, *Zur Theologie der Busse bei Tertullian*, 166 f. A more general treatment of the question may be found in J. Stufler, 'Die verschiedenen Wirkungen der Taufe und Busse nach Tertullian,' ZKT 31 (1907) 372–76: cf. also, below, *De paen.* note 103. On the catechumenate as a period of probation to test the sincerity of the candidate's petition and to prove his ability to lead the sinless life demanded of a Christian, see F. Dölger, 'Das Garantiewerk der Bekehrung als Bedingung und Sicherung bei der Annahme zur Taufe,' AC 3 (1932) 260–77, and E. Schwartz, *Bussstufen und Katechumenatsklassen* (Strassburg 1911). For confession before Baptism, cf. Doronzo, *op. cit.* 2.371, 387 f.

[68] The contrast is between *ab ignorantia segregaris* and *contumaciae adglutinaris*; the clearer a man's knowledge of God and of God's law, the greater is his wilful disobedience when he returns to a life of sin.

[69] *Exceptio*, in legal terminology, is a plea of the defendant alleging a circumstance which bars a claim without denying its *prima facie* validity; cf. W. Buckland, *A Textbook of Roman Law from Augustus to Justinian* (2nd ed. Cambridge 1932) 653 ff.; J. Stirnimann, *Die Praescriptio Tertullians im Licht des römischen Rechts und der Theologie* (Freiburg i. S. 1949) 17–20.

[70] *Deum . . . ignorari non licet*; compare Wisd. 13.1–9; Rom. 1.19 f. The *bona caelestia* which lead logically to a knowledge of God include all of the gifts of God to men, the visible gifts of created nature as well as personal favors granted to individuals. The existence of God must be admitted because, as a recent apologist has phrased the argument which Tertullian here uses, man needs someone to whom he can say 'Thank you' for the world.

The fact that man can know God is one of Tertullian's strongest and most frequently expressed convictions; see, especially, *Adv. nat.* 2.8; *Adv. Marc.* 1.10; *Scorp.* 2; *De test. an.* 2; *De res. mort.* 3; and, above, note 7. Although he acknowledges the validity of the demonstration *a posteriori* (*Adv. Jud.* 2; *Apol.* 17.4), he nowhere elaborates the argument in detail. He is content, for the most part, with assuming the fact of God's existence as a self-evident truth; it is recognized by innate intuition, *ex testimonio animae*. It may be admitted that not all of Tertullian's arguments for the existence of God are such as commend themselves to modern readers; see, for example, *De an.* 47.2, where he states that almost all men (*paene maior pars hominum*) come to a knowledge of God through visions. On the relationship between reason and revelation in man's knowledge of God's existence, see L. Fuetscher, 'Die natürliche Gotteserkenntnis bei Tertullian,' ZKT 51 (1927) 1–34; 217–51, and J. Stier, *Die Gottes und Logoslehre Tertullians* (Göttingen 1899).

[71] Reading *negat beneficum, cum beneficium non honorat*; Borleffs has *beneficium . . . beneficum*.

[72] *Quemadmodum ei potest placere cuius munus sibi displicet?* In Borleff's construction of this passage, II 88, *ei* refers to the sinner rather than to God, and *cuius* is elliptical for *is cuius*. Others interpret the sentence as meaning that the sinner will not be pleasing to God if he is not pleased with the gifts of God.

[73] *Leviter in dominum.*

[74] *Aemulus*, or *aemulus dei*, is used *passim* in the writings of Tertullian as a designation of Satan. To the partial list in Oehler's index may be added: *De cor.* 6; *De pat.* 5; *De bap.* 5; *De praesc. haer.* 40; *De cultu fem.* 1; the adjectival use is illustrated in *Apol.* 2.18, *ratio aemulae operationis*, and the verbal in *Adv. Prax.* 1, *varie diabolus aemulatus est veritatem.*—The renunciation of Satan was, from the beginning, part of the ritual of Baptism; for an early formula, see Hippolytus, *Apost. trad.* 21.9. On the object of this renunciation, cf. J. Waszink, 'Pompa diaboli,' VC 1 (1947) 13–41. The use of the words *cum . . . diabolo paenitentia sua renuntiasset* affords further proof of an identification between Baptism and *paenitentia* in this chapter of the treatise. Compare

De cor. 3. The scriptural basis of this renunciation is suggested in 1 Peter 3.21.

[75] The concept of the sinner as a captive slave of Satan is a familiar one in ancient Christian literature. The captivity which has made man the booty (*praeda*) of Satan is the result of original sin, cf. *Adv. Marc.* 5.17, *diabolo captante naturam quam et ipse iam infecit delicti semine inlato*; from this captivity he is freed by the sacrament of Baptism (*De bap.* 9): *Liberantur de saeculo nationes per aquam scilicet et diabolum dominatorem pristinum in aqua oppressum derelinquunt*; cf. J. Rivière, 'Tertullien et les droits du démon,' RSR 6 (1926) 199–216. Texts relating to the notion of Baptism as a redemption (ἀπολύτρωσις) have been collected by A. D'Alès, *De baptismo et confirmatione* (Paris 1927) 99.

[76] *Per aliam paenitentiae paenitentiam*, literally, 'by another repentance for his repentance.' There is an interesting parallel, first noted by Rigault, in Pliny, *Epist.* 10.7: . . . *ne agat poenitentiam poenitentiae suae.*

[77] Tertullian is the first Christian writer to speak of penance explicitly as *satisfying* God for sin. Although we need not suppose that he understood this term in the precise, technical sense which it acquired in later centuries, specified by such distinctions as *satisfactio de condigno* and *de congruo*, *pro reatu culpae* and *pro reatu poenae*, still it can hardly be denied that the generic notion of satisfaction as a compensation made to God for the debt incurred by sin is a constituent part of his penitential theology. This is particularly clear in the chapter which immediately follows; cf. below, note 88. Tertullian was certainly aware of the juridical meaning of the word *satisfacere* in cases of material indebtedness; cf. *Digests* 46.3.52: *Satisfacere pro solutione est*, and the important qualification in *Digests* 13.7.9: *omnis pecunia exsoluta esse debet aut eo nomine satisfactum esse. Satisfactum autem accipimus quemadmodum voluit creditor, licet non sit solutum.* This juridical sense of the term *satisfacere* is easily transferred to express the idea of satisfaction for sin. Sin involves the contraction of a debt in the moral order; compare Matt. 18.21–35, Luke 7.36–50. The performance of external works of penance, or better, the whole penitential process beginning with an aversion from sin and including, besides personal works of penance, the intervention of the Church in the *prima* or *secunda paenitentia*, is a means of paying the moral indebtedness which the sinner has contracted by offending God. External works of self-affliction, therefore, are not only proofs of internal penance and a means of averting the divine wrath (Dodgson, *op. cit.* 369) but they are also, in a true sense, a necessary and effective means of making amends to God by a *compensatio pro debito peccati*. That this concept of satisfaction is essentially the same as that of modern theologians may be seen by comparing it with the brief analysis given

by L. Lercher, *Institutiones theologiae dogmaticae* (3rd ed. Innsbruck 1949) 4.2.167 f. The treatise *De paenitentia* is of the greatest importance in illustrating Tertullian's notion of theological satisfaction; see, in particular, cc. 6.4; 7.14; 8.9; 9.2 f., 5; 10.2; 11.3. The idea is also found in other treatises of his; cf. *De bap.* 20; *De orat.* 23; *De pat.* 13; *De cultu fem.* 1.1; *De ieiun.* 3; *De pud.* 9.9 and 13.14. It may be admitted that in the present passage we have nothing of this beyond the use of the words *per paenitentiam domino satisfacere* and *satis habere.* Any effort to attach a technical sense to these expressions, taken in isolation from the context of the whole treatise, is weakened by Tertullian's statement in the passage that man also *per paenitentiae paenitentiam satisfacit diabolo.* Among the best recent analyses of the concept of theological satisfaction is that in Galtier I 421–35. There is a useful listing of patristic passages bearing on the subject in A. Deneffe, 'Das Wort *satisfactio,*' ZKT 43 (1919) 158–78. For a more complete account of the literature see F. Diekamp, *Theologiae dogmaticae manuale* (Paris 1946) 4.348; on the identification of *paenitentia* and *satisfactio* in Tertullian see Teeuwen I 25 ff.

[78] *Licet actu minus fiat* is ambiguous. It can mean either that the *honor* given to God in mind and heart is not given by external acts, since man continues to sin, or it can mean that the satisfaction which is given to God by internal acts is not given by external acts also. In the first interpretation, *minus* is taken as a softened negation, 'even though God is not honored externally;' in the second, *minus fiat* is opposed to the idea of *satis fiat,* suggested in the words *aiunt se satis dominum habere.* Compare *De bap.* 13, where Tertullian condemns certain adversaries who deny the necessity of Baptism and insist that faith alone is sufficient to please God. It is Tertullian's view that faith is a necessary disposition for Baptism, not a substitute for it. De Labriolle I, Introd. 39 f., thinks it possible that the *hypocritae* of the present passage and the *scelestissimi* of *De bap.* 13 are representatives of a group of Gnostics who attempted to introduce into Christianity the notion that external actions are a matter of indifference provided that one's internal comprehension of divine things remains unimpaired. This particular development of Gnosticism is discussed by E. De Faye, *Gnostiques et gnosticisme* (Paris 1925) 413–28. Batiffol is of the opinion that the error which Tertullian attacks here had already been censured in the Pastor Hermae; cf. P. Batiffol, *Études d'histoire et de théologie positive. Première série* (Paris 1926) 70.

[79] An alternative translation might be, 'whose conversion (*paenitentia*) does not last.'

[80] There appears to be little appreciable difference between a

repentance which is undertaken only once (*semel*=once for all) and one which is permanently preserved. Both expressions point up the dominant thought of this and the preceding chapter: when a conversion has been once effected, it must not be violated by subsequent sin.

81 Reading *debitos* (*Codex Trecensis*), rather than *deditos domino*. In this same chapter (6.19), however, the *Codex Trecensis* has *domino deditus*, which Borleffs considers an error for *debitus*.

82 *Novitiolis*. This is, apparently, the first reference in Christian literature to religious recruits as 'novices.' The *novitioli* mentioned here are, of course, the catechumens. Later in this and the following chapter, they are called *auditores* and *audientes*. There are other allusions to the catechumenate in *De bap.* 20; *De praesc. haer.* 41; *De cor.* 2. For *novitiolus* as a military term, see Teeuwen I 107 and F. Dölger, 'Sacramentum infanticidii,' AC 4 (1934) 200; cf., also, the literature cited in W. Le Saint, *Tertullian. Marriage and Remarriage* (ACW 13, Wesminster 1951) 146 f. treating of the Christian way of life as a warfare with the world and the devil. The words *cum maxime incipiunt*, appearing in this context, echo the words *cum maxime formantur* in *De bap.* 1. See J. Borleffs, 'La valeur du *Codex Trecensis* de Tertullien,' VC 2 (1948) 193.

The fact that Tertullian, in a number of treatises, addresses himself directly and explicitly to the catechumens (e.g. *De bap.*, *De paen.*, *De orat.*, *De spect.*, *De cultu fem.*) affords rather conclusive evidence that he occupied an official position in the church at Carthage, possibly that of the *doctor audientium* referred to by St. Cyprian, *Epist.* 29; cf. also, *Passio SS. Perpetuae et Felic.* 13 and *De praesc. haer.* 3, 14. The interesting suggestion has been made that problems arising out of his regular instructions to the catechumens, particularly the opposition excited by his exaggerated asceticism, occasioned his defection from the Church; cf. Nisters, *op. cit.*, 124 f. The disputed question of his ordination to the priesthood can not be settled by an appeal to the circumstance that he held the position of catechist, since, as is clear from the example of Origen, laymen could be and were appointed to that office. It must be added, however, that most of the catechists mentioned in ancient Christian literature were clerics. Hippolytus, *Apost. trad.* 19, says that the 'teacher of the catechumens' is to lay hands upon them before their Baptism, then he is to pray and dismiss them. 'Whether the teacher be an ecclesiastic or a layman, let him do the same.' See the note in G. Dix, *The Treatise on the Apostolic Tradition of St. Hippolytus of Rome* (London 1937) xxvii. For the literature dealing with the question of Tertullian's priesthood, see Bardenhewer, *op. cit.* 2.379–81 and additional references in Quasten, *op. cit.* 2.248. An excellent account of the catechumenate is given by P. de Puniet in his article 'Catéchuménat,' DACL 2.2579–2621.

83 Cf. Deut. 32.2; compare Ovid, *Metamorph.* 10.62 (*aure haurire*), and Horace, *Odae* 2.13.32 (*aure bibere*).

84 *Includere eam neglegunt.* This failure is not found in their neglect of Baptism, as Oehler, Thelwall and others suppose, but rather in their unwillingness to give up completely a life of sin before they are actually baptized. This is convincingly shown in Teeuwen II 412–14 from an examination of various expressions in this chapter bearing on the defective repentance of catechumens. It remains possible, however, that their repentance is also thought of as defective because it fails to include the external works of penance which are required of the candidates before their actual reception of Baptism; cf. above, note 67 and, below, *De paen.*, note 103.

85 Although their day is passed, they pride themselves, as it were, upon the external appearance of beauty which still remains to them and encourage themselves with the delusive hope that they will continue to remain attractive. In some such way as this the sinner who fails to perfect penance, i.e. who fails to give up a life of sin before he is baptized, will turn from the specious pleasures of the world by his enrollment in the ranks of the catechumens and yet, at this very time, through the sinful desires which he encourages now more than ever, he cultivates the vain hope that he may still enjoy a life of self-indulgence. The sentence is typical of the forced and obscure imagery which is so marked a characteristic of Tertullian's style. *Adulari* is difficult; for the meaning here cf. Hoppe II 89 f.

86 In military language the word used here, *commeatus*, signifies a furlough or a leave of absence from one's station. In its more general sense *commeatus* means any space or period of time, and this general sense is frequently found in Tertullian; cf. Oehler's note on *De fuga in persec.* 9, Waszink, *op. cit.* 377 and D'Alès I 68.

87 This text is often cited by theologians in discussing the necessity of penance as a virtue; cf. Doronzo, *op. cit.* 1.478 f. The price at which the Lord has agreed to sell (*addicere*) His merchandise (*venia delictorum*) is man's penitence (*adimpletio paenitentiae*). Hence, if the established price is not paid, sin is not forgiven.

88 The words are *hac paenitentiae conpensatione redimendam proponit impunitatem.* There is a quasi-contract here in which God promises to accept an *impletio paenitentiae*, that is to say, the *vera paenitentia*, or *integer metus* or *veritas paenitentiae* described throughout the chapter (cf. above, note 84), as compensatory payment, a *quid pro quo*, in place of the punishment which the sinner has deserved. This concept is

fundamental in the traditional Christian view of satisfaction for sin, and finds its scriptural justification in such texts as Prov. 15.27; 16.6; Dan. 4.24; Tobias 4.11; Luke 3.7 f. and 13.3; 1 Cor. 11.31 f.; 2 Cor. 7.10. For the force of the word *conpensatio* compare *Apol.* 50.15, where Tertullian says that the martyr wins a full pardon from God for all his sins *conpensatione sanguinis sui*. Cf. also Buckland, *op. cit.* 703–7 and the literature there listed for the meaning of *conpensatio* in Roman jurisprudence.

[89] A careful study of this sentence may be seen in Borleffs I 90–94. The principal difficulty it presents is in the reading *versus* (*Codex Trecensis*) for *rasus*, found in other codices and generally accepted by earlier editors. Tertullian refers to three ways in which money might be falsified, and he seems to intend a progression in his listing from the least to the most objectionable form of falsification. First, a legitimate coin could be altered in weight by trimming away from its edge a part of the gold or silver of which it was minted (*scalptus*); secondly, a coin might be minted in iron or bronze and then plated with silver or gold (*versus*); third, it could be a counterfeit coin made of lead or a lead-silver alloy (*adulter.*) It is admitted that the ordinary term for plated coin is not *nummus versus* but, rather, *nummus tinctus, nummus infectus* etc. Borleffs argues, however, that Tertullian uses the expression *vertere capillos* (*De virg. vel.* 12; *De cultu fem.* 2.6) and, since *vertere capillos* can mean *tinguere* or *inficere capillos*, by analogy *vertere nummum* (*nummus versus*) can mean *tinguere* or *inficere nummum* (*nummus tinctus* or *infectus*).

[90] The reading *mercem* for *mercedem* gives an excellent sense and it is defended by Rauschen, though it has no justification in the manuscripts.

[91] A true conversion (*veritas paenitentiae*) is one in which sin is completely abandoned. The wording of the objection is of importance in determining the meaning of such difficult phrases in the chapter as *paenitentiam includere, infida paenitentia, metus integer* etc.

[92] Since deliverance from sin is merited by the sinner through repentance, this repentance must precede deliverance and must not be deferred until after the time of deliverance. Thelwall is hardly correct in interpreting the words *ut possimus mereri* as a parenthesis meaning 'so far as merit we can.' D'Alès I 270 states that the text supposes the distinction between merit *de condigno*, in which God rewards man *ex justitia*, and merit *de congruo*, in which He rewards Him *ex liberalitate*. The element of condignity will be present in the quasi-contract (cf. above, note 88) by which God binds Himself to grant both impunity from sin and the reward of eternal life to those who pay the price which He demands. This also suggests the close relationship which

exists between the notion of merit and satisfaction. It is through *paenitentia* that man satisfies the debt which he has contracted by sin, and, at the same time, merits the reward which God will grant to those whose conversion is complete and permanent. For the last point, see Morgan, *op. cit.* 43; for other references to Tertullian's teaching on merit, cf. above, note 31 and J. Tixeront, *History of Dogmas* (tr. from the 5th French ed. by H. L. B., St. Louis 1910) 1.319 f.

[93] The sinner must repent his sins *before* he is baptized or he will not repent them at all. This is clear from the example of slaves and soldiers, who forget their past offenses once they have secured their freedom. On the branding of soldiers for violations of military discipline, see F. Dölger, 'Sacramentum militiae,' AC 2 (1930) 271. The word *notae*, however, may here mean simply the ignominy or infamy which a soldier has suffered because of offenses committed during his term of service. Compare *De paen.* 12.9, where Tertullian refers to himself as a *peccator omnium notarum*.

[94] All of the early evidence points to the practice of Baptism by immersion. See, for example, the detailed description in Hippolytus, *Apost. trad.* 20–21, where the words 'going down into the water' occur frequently. Tertullian here writes *aquam inituris*.

[95] Dodgson and others, of whom Rigault says *splendide nugantur*, see here a reference to Baptism by aspersion. Tertullian is thinking, rather, of the ritualistic sprinkling practiced in various pagan cults; cf. *De bap.* 5. An insincere convert or initiate into one of these cults will not receive so much as a single sprinkling of the water which is used in their ritual; *a fortiori*, an insincere convert to Christianity will not be admitted to the waters of Baptism by the authorities of the Church.

[96] Matt. 10.26.

[97] I John 1.5.

[98] The 'symbol of death' is the sacrament of Baptism. Cf. Rom. 6.3–5 and Col. 2.12. The sinner who is baptized in the dying Christ dies mystically to sin and rises with Christ to newness of life. St. Paul's great figure is well explained by F. Prat, *The Theology of St. Paul* (London 1933) 1.221–23 and 2.256–60. Other references to the literature on baptismal symbolism are given in R. Refoulé, *Tertullien. Traité du baptême* (Sources chrétiennes 35, Paris 1952) 19.

[99] For this meaning of *fides* (security) see above, note 54. Borleffs II 76, however, believes that the expression *paenitentiae fidem adgressi* should be translated by 'the faithful accomplishment of penitence' or something of the kind. This interpretation is supported by the phrase *a paenitentiae fide* which occurs below (6.16) and which seems to refer to the faithful performance of a genuine repentance.

[100] Matt. 7.26.

[101] The words *auditorum tirocinia* led early commentators to suppose that Tertullian is here referring to a class of candidates for Baptism called the *audientes*, who were not members of the catechumenate or who formed one of several distinct groups within it; see, for example, de l'Aubespine's note, quoted by Oehler, *ad loc.*, and J. Bingham, *Christian Antiquities* (London 1834) 2.12–17. Bingham argued for a fourfold division of the catechumenate, in which the second grade or degree was that of the *audientes*. Such a definite division, if it existed at all, can not be proved from the works of Tertullian. The catechumens who had finished their period of probation and who were about to receive Baptism were called the *electi* (Rome) or *competentes* (Africa). Tertullian designates them simply as *ingressuri baptismum* (*De bap.* 20). Cf. C. Mohrmann, *Die altchristliche Sondersprache in den Sermones des hl. Augustin* (Nimeguen 1932) 90 and Dekkers, *op. cit.* 167–69.

[102] The word play on *fides . . . a fide* in this passage is discussed by Thörnell, *op. cit.* 4.126. For Baptism as an *obsignatio fidei* see above, note 66. Other references may be found in D'Alès I 326. On faith as a necessary disposition for the reception of the sacrament, cf. D'Alès, *op. cit.* 281, 336 f. A contrasting opinion of Tertullian's views on this subject is given by Batiffol, *op. cit.* 71, without the support of any convincing argument.

[103] The words *abluimur . . . quoniam iam loti sumus*, 'we are baptized because we are already clean,' involve an oxymoron which exaggerates the efficacy of personal repentance to the detriment of the efficacy of Baptism. Baptism effects the forgiveness of sins because the disposition which is necessary for its reception (*metus integer*) has already effected their remission! The rite is objectively efficacious and yet a conversion (*prima audientis intinctio*) is first required which is itself efficacious. This same difficulty occurs in the treatise *De baptismo*. In chapter 13 of that work Tertullian asserts that under the Old Law faith without Baptism was sufficient for justification, whereas in the New Law the *obsignatio baptismi* is also required. If, then, Baptism is necessary for the forgiveness of sins, it is quite inconsistent to state, as Tertullian does in chapter 18 of the treatise, that a perfect faith (*fides integra*) is assured of salvation, and that on this account the actual reception of the sacrament may be deferred. Here, again, the problem is that of reconciling the objective efficacy of Baptism with the efficacy of a 'perfect' personal penance; cf. above, note 67. Both are necessary, and yet the latter is sufficient by itself! The apparent antinomy is partially solved in modern theology by the distinction between Baptism *in re* and *in voto*, and it may be that this distinction is implicit in Tertullian's explanation. On the primacy

of the parallel problem in contemporary studies on the sacrament of Penance, see Poschmann III 111.

It is worth noting that while Tertullian clearly states that *paenitentia* is efficacious without the actual reception of Baptism, he does not say that Baptism is efficacious without personal repentance. D'Alès I 338 remarks in this connection that Tertullian fails to consider the question of baptismal efficacy in the case of a sinner who approaches the sacrament without the proper dispositions, *qui ficte accedit*. Against this, however, it may be pointed out that the words *furto aggredi* and *deus thesauro suo providet* (*De paen.* 6.10) show that he was not completely unaware of the problem or greatly embarrassed by it. It is obvious that his whole treatment of this subject would have been much more satisfactory if he had known the distinction between a valid and a fruitful reception of the sacrament. Further commentary on this passage may be found in F. Dölger, 'Das Garantiewerk der Bekehrung als Bedingung und Sicherung bei der Annahme zur Taufe,' AC 3 (1932) 262. For an interesting study of the problem in Origen see J. Daniélou, *Origen* (tr. from the French by W. Mitchell, London 1955) 54 f.

[104] The *prima audientis intinctio* referred to here is not to be confused with the *paenitentia prima* which includes the actual reception of Baptism. Tertullian wishes to emphasize that a man's first cleansing is effected by his own personal penitence and not by the rite of Baptism, which is ordinarily spoken of as the *prima paenitentia*.

[105] *Metus integer* is that reverence for God and fear of His punishments which has led the candidate for Baptism to give up sin completely; cf. Teeuwen II 413 and, above, note 84. The translation follows the reconstruction of the passage given in Borleffs II 98; for a different version, cf. the note to Mohrmann's translation, 289.

[106] Sinlessness is demanded of the Christian as a matter of special obligation because on the occasion of his Baptism he solemnly renounces Satan and all his works (cf. Hippolytus, *Apost. trad.* 21) and because, if he sins thereafter, he is subject to the punishment of excommunication.

[107] *Vera paenitentia functum.* The nature of this 'proper penance' is explained above, note 84. The expression *paenitentia fungi* occurs also in *De paen.* 5.2; *De pud.* 1.6; *Adv. Marc.* 2.17. In *De paen.* 9.5 Tertullian has *exomologesis . . . fungatur.*

[108] In *De bap.* 18 there is much that resembles Tertullian's strictures here on the presumptuous and premature reception of the sacrament. He reminds those whose duty it is to administer Baptism of the words of our Lord, 'cast not your pearl (*margaritam*, in Tertullian's version) before swine' (Matt. 7.6) and St. Paul's admonition to Timothy,

'Impose not hands lightly, lest you share in another's sins' (1 Tim. 5.22). This latter text is commonly thought of as referring to the rite of ordination, although Galtier I 185 considers that it has to do rather with the imposition of hands in the ritual of penance. For the use of the text in reference to ecclesiastical penitence, cf. *De pud.* 18.9 and St. Pacian, *Epist.* 3.39; *Parain. ad paenit.* 15.

[109] *Disciplina* is here synonymous with *doctrina*; compare *De pat.* 7, *patientiae disciplina*. In such uses as this the notion of doctrine or teaching is predominant but the word also connotes the existence of definite moral obligations which the doctrine supposes and imposes; cf. Morel, *op. cit.* 23 and Durig, *op. cit.* 250–54.

[110] This opening sentence of the chapter indicates the beginning of a transition from the consideration of pre-baptismal to that of post-baptismal penitence. The thought is difficult to get at because of the tortuous language in which it is expressed but it may be paraphrased thus: When Christians consider the subject of penitence they should be concerned with the penitence which is necessary before Baptism. They should know nothing of penitence after Baptism because they should never sin once they have received the sacrament. The 'servants' of Christ are all the baptized, or, perhaps, all who are seeking to do the will of Christ; the *audientes* are the catechumens, although this identification is denied by Rauschen in his note to *De paen.* 1.1. It is his belief that the treatise *De paenitentia* was not addressed primarily to the catechumens but was intended for all Christians. The *audientes*, he contends, are all those of whom it is said: *servis tuis dicere vel audire contingat*. On the meaning of *servus Christi* and *servus dei* see Teeuwen I 126.—This passage has been closely imitated by St. Pacian in one of his letters to Sympronian, *Epist.* 1.5. For the influence of Tertullian on Pacian, cf. S. Gonzalez Rivas, *La Penitencia en la Primitiva Iglesia Española* (Salamanca 1949) 73–78.

[111] *Spes* has a concrete, objective sense; it is that in which hope is placed, in this case, *paenitentia*. So *fides*, in a similar context (above, 4.2), is that which brings security, namely *paenitentia* as a *tabula salutis naufrago*. Thus the *prima spes*, or *prima paenitentia*, is a repentance for sins which had been committed before Baptism; the *secunda* and *ultima spes*, or *paenitentia secunda*, is that for sins committed after Baptism.

[112] If the *paenitentia secunda* spoken of in these final chapters of the treatise is exclusively a personal, private matter between the soul and God, it is difficult to see how it can be thought of as involving a *spatium delinquendi*, with a definite *terminus post quem non*. A penitence which is *ultima* (7.2) and *semel* and *amplius numquam* (7.10) supposes the

existence of a time after the completion of *paenitentia* when sin is still possible but *paenitentia* is no longer possible. Such a *paenitentia* can hardly be one which is exclusively a personal, private aversion from sin and conversion to God.

[113] Reading *redundantiam* (*Codex Trecensis*) rather than *redundantia*, but construing *faciat* after *quasi eo* rather than after *absit ut.*

[114] This is a possible reference to the waters of Baptism.

[115] The concept of sin as an *opus mortis* is first suggested in Gen. 2.17; compare Wisd. 1.12; Rom. 6.2 ff.; Eph. 2.5; Apoc. 20.6, 14.

[116] The difficulty which has hitherto been found in the interpretation of this sentence disappears if we read *dominationis suae* in place of *damnationis suae*, the text received before the discovery of the *Codex Trecensis* and *Codex Ottobonianus*. On the apparent imitation of this passage by St. Pacian, *Epist.* 1.5, *tot titulos damnationis impressit*, see Borleffs II 68.

[117] Cf. 1 Cor. 6.3.

[118] A good synopsis of Tertullian's demonology is given in D'Alès I, 156–61.

[119] The sins listed here are spoken of in general terms, but Tertullian refers definitely enough to sins of the flesh and loss of faith, specified later in the canonical triad of *peccata capitalia* as adultery and apostasy. It is precisely because God foresees that men will fall into these particular sins that He has granted a second penitence through which and in which post-baptismal sins can be forgiven. The point is of importance in showing that at the time Tertullian wrote the *De paenitentia* he did not exclude from *paenitentia secunda* those sins which in the *De pudicitia* he said the Church could not forgive.

[120] This is one of the most significant single passages in the treatise *De paenitentia*. The translation is made from the following text: *Deus clausam licet ignoscentiae ianuam et intinctionis sera obstructam aliquid adhuc permisit patere.* For the justification of this reading, rather than *clausa . . . ianua et . . . obstructa*, hitherto generally received, see Borleffs I 99 f. *Aliquid* is not the object of *permisit* but is adverbial with *patere*. Teeuwen II 414 believes that the *et* between *ianua* and *intinctionis* is the equivalent of *scilicet*, but this hardly changes the essential sense of the sentence.

Considerable attention has been given to the meaning of the word *ignoscentia* in this passage. Ancient Christian writers frequently distinguish between a forgiveness of sins called *aphesis* and a forgiveness through *metanoia*; cf. Poschmann II 1 f. Both *aphesis* and *metanoia*, understood generically, are possible after Baptism as well as before it. Strictly speaking, however, *aphesis* is the forgiveness of sins in Baptism, a forgiveness of sins which is possible only once. Sins committed after

Baptism can also be forgiven but this is through *metanoia*, and such a forgiveness is not properly called *aphesis*. Since there are no Latin equivalents for each of these two Greek words, *ignoscentia* is forced to do duty for them both. Tertullian says that the door of pardon (*ignoscentia*) is closed and locked through Baptism, yet he at once states that it remains somewhat open. What he means is that *ignoscentia* through *aphesis* in Baptism is possible only once, yet *ignoscentia* through *metanoia* may be had after Baptism. A comparative study of this distinction in the writings of Hermas, Clement of Alexandria and Tertullian may be found in Galtier I 196–99. For Cyprian's use of the word *remissa* (*remissio*) see D'Alès, *La théologie de saint Cyprien*, 233 f., 277, 287. There is an interesting parallel to Tertullian in *De op. et eleemos.* 2: *Semel in baptismo remissa peccatorum datur, assidua et iugis operatio baptismi instar imitata dei rursus indulgentiam largiatur. Remissa* corresponds to *aphesis*, and the *indulgentia* which is had through a work *ad instar baptismi* corresponds to forgiveness through *metanoia*, as this is described in the Pastor Hermae (e.g. *Mand.* 4.3), Clement of Alexandria (e.g. *Strom.* 4.24) and in the present passage of Tertullian.

[121] *Conlocavit in vestibulo paenitentiam secundam quae pulsantibus patefaciat. Patefacere* is an active verb, used here either absolutely or with *ianuam* understood. It is not penance which is open to those who knock but it is penance which itself opens the *ianua ignoscentiae* to those who knock; by their penance they ask for pardon, and by this action (cf. below 9.1, *paenitentiae . . . non sola conscientia praeferatur, sed aliquo etiam actu administretur*) the door of pardon is opened. Their *paenitentia* is a *pulsatio* and their *pulsatio* effects a *patefactio*. On the *vestibulum* as a *locus paenitentiae*, see A. D'Alès, 'Limen ecclesiae,' RHE 7 (1906) 16–26 and the same author's work, *L'édit de Calliste*, 409–21. It is tempting to see in Tertullian's reference to penance *in vestibulo* an allusion to the first of the four stages of public penance so frequently described in accounts of the penitential practice of the Oriental church; cf. Gregory Thaumaturgus, *Epist. canon.* 11. This is inadmissible, however, since such definite and distinct penitential stages had no place in the discipline of the West.

There has been some controversy over the question of whether it was the custom in the Western church to segregate public penitents in a special *locus paenitentiae*. H. Leclercq, 'Pénitents,' DACL 14.251–58, is of the opinion that the penitents were excluded from communion but were permitted to enter the church and assist at the sacred mysteries. This view has also been defended by H. Koch, 'Die Büsserentlassung in der alten abendländischen Kirche,' TQ 82 (1900) 481–534, and 'Der Büsserplatz im Abendlande,' in the same review 85 (1903) 254–70.

See, too, C. Chartier, 'L'excommunication ecclésiastique d'après les écrits de Tertullien,' *Antonianum* 10 (1935) 341 f. Whatever may have been the practice in other localities and at other times, the evidence of Tertullian points to the conclusion that in Carthage shortly after the year 200 it was customary to separate penitents guilty of serious sin from the body of the faithful and to require of them the performance of exomologesis *ad limen ecclesiae*.

J. Grotz, in his important study *Die Entwicklung des Bussstufenwesens in der vornicänischen Kirche* (Freiburg 1955) 350, discusses the bearing of this passage on his thesis that, in Christian antiquity, excommunication was not of the essence of ecclesiastical penance. Grotz is of the opinion that the Church, before the Montanist crisis, knew but one form of penance, and that was the exomologesis described in *De paen.* 7-9. This exomologesis did not involve separation from the Church, since it was performed *in vestibulo ecclesiae* and was under the direction of ecclesiastical authorities. Grotz insists that persons thus *in* the Church and cared for *by* the Church must not be regarded as 'excommunicated' from the Church. There is some ambiguity here, one feels, in the use of the word 'excommunicate.' 'Communion' can mean (1) membership in the Church, and (2) the reception of the Eucharist. If we understand 'excommunication' as a cutting off from '*communio*' in the first sense, the public penitents were not excommunicated; if we understand it as a cutting off from '*communio*' in the second sense, they were.

The close juxtaposition of *ianua* and *vestibulum* in this context makes it appear extremely unlikely that the expression *ianua ignoscentiae* is to be understood in a merely metaphorical sense, with reference to a form of private penance which reconciles the sinner to God apart from any concomitant public reconciliation to the Church; Poschmann I 290-93. Understood metaphorically, the *ianua ignoscentiae* is the door which admits to God's forgiveness; but at the same time it is, in a literal sense, the door which allows physical entrance into the church. If a man is excluded from the Church by a serious sin committed after Baptism, he must stand in the vestibule, before the door of the church, and there perform the exomologesis which is necessary to secure readmission into the Church. His readmission into the physical body of the church is a symbol of his readmission into the mystical body of Christ, through a restoration of *pax* and *communio cum ecclesia*. In their turn *pax* and *communio cum ecclesia* suppose a reconciliation to God through Christ, since reconciliation to the living body is inconceivable apart from reconciliation to Christ, who is its head. Therefore a twofold effect follows from the *pulsatio ad ianuam* of exomologesis. Tertullian states that a door is opened to those who knock. Literally this is the physical door of the church, metaphorically it is the spiritual door of pardon for sin. This opening of the *ianua ignoscentiae* is not exclusively the removal of an ecclesiastical excommunication, but neither is it exclusively a pardon which God grants the sinner independently of the Church. It consists in a reconciliation of the sinner to God (7.14) and a restoration of the baptismal blessings lost by post-baptismal sin (7.11-13) through a reconciliation of the sinner to the Church symbolized by his readmission into the physical body of the church. E. Rolffs, *Das Indulgenzedikt des römischen Bischofs Kallist* (Texte u. Unters. 11.3, Leipzig 1893) 38, states that *paenitentia secunda* is placed at the *ianua ignoscentiae* and not at the *ianua ecclesiae*, but this interpretation appears to ignore the whole symbolism of the passage; cf. D'Alès III 148.

[122] *Amplius numquam quia proxime frustra.* The pardon received through *paenitentia secunda* has been frustrated by subsequent sin. It would be an abuse, then, to grant forgiveness again. The sentence might also be translated: 'Never again, however, because the next time will be in vain.' *Paenitentia secunda* may not be repeated because if it is attempted again it will be without fruit. This second interpretation supposes that the *paenitentia secunda* of which Tertullian speaks is public and ecclesiastical, since there is no reason why a private and personal contrition for sin in the presense of God alone should be fruitless, no matter how often it is repeated. In either translation the essential sense of the sentence remains unchanged: *paenitentia secunda* is permitted only once after Baptism. On this point the teaching of Christian antiquity is clear and unanimous; cf. B. Poschmann, *Die abendländische Kirchenbusse im Ausgang des christlichen Altertums* (Munich 1928) 57-68, 97-104. No doubt one reason for the initerability of *paenitentia secunda* was the analogy which it bore to the *paenitentia prima* and *unica* of Baptism; this point is treated by D. Nerney, *Adnotationes in Tractatum de paenitentia* (Rome 1933) 8 f. The preceding words, *iam semel quia iam secundo*, suggest that precisely because it is *paenitentia secunda* (exomologesis) as distinguished from *paenitentia prima* (Baptism) it may not be repeated. That which is *secunda* can be had only 'once,' else it would be *tertia*—and no *paenitentia tertia* is recognized in the Church.

[123] 'This once' refers to the single possible reception of *paenitentia secunda*, not the 'once' of *paenitentia prima*. It is as though Tertullian would ask, 'Do you wish a *paenitentia tertia* or *quarta*?' Since he envisages the possibility of a relapse into sin after the *paenitentia secunda*, we must conclude that the reconciliation of the sinner by the Church was not delayed until the hour of death. On the forgiveness of those who relapsed after the performance of *paenitentia secunda*, cf. Galtier I

267–74 and R. Mortimer, *The Origins of Private Penance in the Western Church* (Oxford 1939) 8 f.

[124] After *paenitentia secunda* you have the favor of God once more. This you no longer deserved, since you lost it by committing sin after the *paenitentia prima*.

[125] God gives the sinner His favor in *paenitentia prima*. When this favor is given again in *paenitentia secunda*, it is not merely repeated but it is a greater favor than it was originally, since, as Tertullian immediately adds, 'to give back is a greater thing than to give.' This is of particular significance as showing that the effect of *paenitentia secunda* is more than an external reconciliation of the sinner to the Church by the removal of ecclesiastical penalties. That which is given back through *paenitentia secunda* is identified with that which was originally received through *paenitentia prima*. But in *paenitentia prima* the forgiveness of sins is a forgiveness *coram Deo*, not merely *coram ecclesia*; it is a *planca salutis* which will save the sinner from punishment at the hands of God, not simply from punishment at the hands of ecclesiastical authority. *Paenitentia secunda*, therefore, will, in its turn, effect an actual forgiveness of sin *coram Deo* and, as the second *planca salutis*, will truly save the sinner from the punishment which his post-baptismal sins have deserved.

[126] Here, again, Tertullian has influenced the thought and expression of St. Pacian; cf. *Epist.* 1.5: *Pigeat sane peccare sed poenitere non pigeat. Pudeat periclitari sed non pudeat liberari.*

[127] The translation is based on the reading *iteratae valetudinis*, rather than *iterandae valetudinis*. If *iterandae* is preferred (it is found in the *Codex Trecensis* and is defended by Borleffs, 'La valeur du Codex Trecensis de Tertullien,' VC 2 (1948) 195) the sentence might be translated: 'For the restoration of health medicine must be repeated.'

[128] If God wills that the sinner give satisfaction for his offense by the performance of *paenitentia secunda*, then He also wills at least implicitly, to accept the satisfaction when it is properly offered. Thus in the words *et quidem volentem* Tertullian expresses one of the conditions necessary for theological satisfaction, scl. God's willingness to accept a penitential work as compensatory. On the relationship of this acceptance to the notion of satisfaction *de condigno* and *de congruo*, see Doronzo, *op. cit.* 3.300, 313–18.

[129] *Revolve.* See Borleffs I 101 f. and compare Pacian, *Epist.* 1.5, where this passage and others of the present chapter are quoted with only slight verbal alterations.

[130] Apoc. 2.4. That this is the word of the Holy Spirit appears from Apoc. 2.7.

[131] Apoc. 2.20 f.

[132] Apoc. 3.2.

[133] Apoc. 2.15.

[134] Apoc. 3.17.

[135] Even though the Christians of whom St. John speaks have committed the grave sins charged against them, still the very fact that God threatens them with punishment unless they repent proves that they will receive pardon if they do repent. It seems a valid assumption that the penitence in question is that of the *paenitentia secunda* referred to in the preceding chapter and described more fully in the chapter which immediately follows. This is one of the proofs used to show that the exclusion of *peccata capitalia* from exomologesis in the *De pudicitia* represents a change in Tertullian's thought from his orthodox position in the *De paenitentia*. It should be observed that Tertullian here mentions explicitly the sins of adultery and idolatry (apostasy). In a work of this same period he says that adultery is forgiven by penance, through patience; *De pat.* 12 and cf. D'Alès II 25.

[136] Tertullian's language throughout this chapter is in striking contrast with his intolerance in the *De pudicitia*. This is particularly evident in his use of the Scripture texts and parables of mercy which follow. Cf., for example, *De pud.* 2, 7, 8, 9; and compare, also, the list of texts compiled in the work *Exhortatio de paenitentia*, formerly attributed to St. Cyprian. This work begins with the statement that 'all sins may be forgiven to him who turns to God with his whole heart.'

[137] An approximation of Jer. 8.4, as the verse stands in the Vulgate.

[138] Osee 6.6; Matt. 9.13; 12.7.

[139] Luke 15.10. On the Marcionite and Catholic translations of Luke utilized by Tertullian see A. Higgins, 'The Latin Text of Luke in Marcion and Tertullian,' VC 5 (1951) 1–42.

[140] Omitting *reditu*, a conjecture of Pamelius which was suggested by Pacian's imitation in *Parain. ad paenit.* 12: *Heus tu, peccator . . . vides ubi de tuo reditu gaudiatur.* The sense of *de tuo gaudeatur* is given by Borleffs I 103 f.

[141] Luke 15.8–10.

[142] Luke 15.4–7. The popularity of the parable of the Good Shepherd in Christian antiquity and its influence on the development of penitential discipline is remarked in Mohrmann's note, *ad loc.* The Good Shepherd is the symbol of Christ's redeeming love restoring the repentant sinner to safety within His fold; at the same time the parable exemplifies the mercy which Christ expects the shepherds of His Church to show in restoring to communion those who have been separated from the Church by sin; cf. Galtier I 112.

¹⁴³ Luke 15.11–32.

¹⁴⁴ In *De pud.* 9.16, possibly, also, 9.11, Tertullian sees a reference to the Eucharist and the reception of communion in the banquet prepared for the prodigal son. Some commentators have argued, *a pari*, that the same allusion is to be found in this passage of the *De paenitentia*. If this is true it confirms the view that the *paenitentia secunda*, as described in the treatise *De paenitentia*, involved not only a pardon granted privately to the sinner by God but also an absolution in the external forum restoring the sinner to communion with the Church. See G. Esser, 'Nochmals das Indulgenzedikt,' *Der Katholik* 2 (1907) 302 f. and J. Stufler, 'Zur Kontroverse über das Indulgenzedikt des Papstes Kallistus,' ZKT 32 (1908) 31.

¹⁴⁵ A reference to the 'portion of his inheritance' which the Christian received at the time of his Baptism and squandered by post-baptismal sin. In *De pud.* 8 and 9 Tertullian explicitly rejects the notion that the prodigal is a type of the Christian sinner.

¹⁴⁶ The *Codex Trecensis* breaks off at this point and does not resume until 12.9, with the closing words of the treatise.

¹⁴⁷ Luke 15.21.

¹⁴⁸ The meaning of *confessio* in Tertullian is discussed below, note 152.

¹⁴⁹ The desire to make satisfaction for his offenses prompts the sinner to acknowledge that he has committed them. It is interesting to note that when the theology of confession was developing during the early medieval period many Scholastics considered that the shame evoked by the act of confession was itself a part of sacramental satisfaction; cf. P. Anciaux, *La théologie du sacrement de pénitence au XIIᵉ siècle* (Louvain 1949) 610.

¹⁵⁰ The opposition between *non sola conscientia praeferatur* and *aliquo actu administretur* makes it clear that in Tertullian's view sins committed after Baptism are not forgiven by an internal repentance which is in its inception and which remains throughout its course a private matter between the soul and God. He insists that for the forgiveness of post-baptismal sin an external penitential process is also required, and in the chapters which follow he warns repeatedly that neglect of this process endangers the sinner's salvation. That the concept of *paenitentia secunda* as an external penitential process is not an invention of Tertullian's appears from the evidence of other early writers and from his own statement that, under the name of exomologesis, *paenitentia secunda* was widely known among the churches (*magis exprimitur et frequentatur*); cf. H. Swete, 'Penitential Discipline in the First Three Centuries,' JTS 4 (1903) 321–37 and the literature cited above in note 5 to the Introduction.

One is tempted to see in the expression *actu administretur* the implication that *paenitentia secunda* was a process administered by ecclesiastical authorities. This, however, is better proved by other arguments, since *administrare* in Tertullian often means little more than *agere* or *exercere*. The *administratores spectaculorum*, for example, referred to in *De spec.* 22, are those who perform in the games, not the magistrates who produce them. We may understand, *a pari*, that the *administratores secundae paenitentiae* are the sinners who perform penance and not the authorities who direct it; see Thörnell, *op. cit.* 3.4 and compare *De paen.* 12.8; *exomologesis . . . ministerium paenitentiae*; and *De cultu fem.* 2.8 : *gravitas . . . instrumentum administrandae pudicitiae.*

[151] The word ἐξομολογεῖσθαι is used in Scripture and the church fathers to designate a number of different religious obligations or observances. Four principal meanings may be distinguished: (1) to give praise to God; (2) to confess sins to God; (3) to confess sins to men; (4) to do public penance for sin. Texts illustrating these four uses may be found in D'Alès II 80 f. The last three meanings are not mutually exclusive and it is sometimes difficult to determine which of the three is primarily intended in a given passage.

The noun, exomologesis, occurs eleven times in the *De paenitentia* (9.2, 3, 5; 10.8; 12.1 (*bis*), 5, 7, (*bis*) 8, 9). It is also found in *De orat.* 7 and *De pat.* 15. *De paen.* 9.2 is copied *verbatim* by Isidore of Seville, *Etymol.* 6.19.76; *De paen.* 12.7 is imitated by St. Pacian, *Parain. ad paenit.* 10. In the present passage Tertullian uses exomologesis as a technical term to describe the complexus of penitential acts performed before the Church as works of satisfaction for post-baptismal sin. These penitential acts constitute, in themselves, a public confession of guilt, a confession which is made to God (*De paen.* 9.2) but which, by its very nature, is also a confession to the Church (*De paen.* 10.1). In *De orat.* 7 Tertullian says that a petition for pardon is itself a confession of guilt; we may conclude, *e converso*, that exomologesis, as a confession of guilt, is also a petition for pardon; cf. Poschmann I 286. Compare, also, *Adv. Marc.* 2.24, where Tertullian explains that the word for *paenitentia* in Greek is not derived *ex delicti confessione* (ἐξομολόγησις) but *ex demutatione* (μετάνοια).

The relationship between exomologesis and *paenitentia secunda* is that of a part to a whole. Exomologesis is the *actus externus* of *paenitentia secunda* (*De paen.* 9.1), its *ministerium* (*De paen.* 12.8) in somewhat the same way as *metus* is said to be the *instrumentum* of pre-baptismal penitence (*De paen.* 6.23) and *gravitas* the *instrumentum administrandae pudicitiae* (*De cultu fem.* 2.8). By synecdoche, then, in the *De paenitentia* the word exomologesis is sometimes used when the whole of *paenitentia secunda* is intended; cf. Teeuwen II 416 f. In the *De pudicitia* the figure of synecdoche is reversed and the whole is used for the part. In this latter treatise Tertullian nowhere employs the word exomologesis; however, the public penance there referred to (e.g. *De pud.* 5.14 and 13.7) is clearly identified with the exomologesis described in the *De paenitentia*. Accordingly, the word *paenitentia* is used occasionally in the *De pudicitia* to designate the process which is called exomologesis in the *De paenitentia*.

Other early references to the discipline of public penance as exomologesis may be found in Irenaeus, *Adv. haer.* 1.13.5, and, quite frequently, in Cyprian; e.g. *Epist.* 4.3; 16.2; *De lapsis* 16. For further details see G. Mead, 'Exomologesis,' DCA 1.644–50; Watkins, *op. cit.* 1.114–18; Galtier I 186–99; D'Alès III 426–30. The external penitential actions which Tertullian particularizes here in the *De paenitentia* constitute what later writers call the *actio paenitentiae*, as distinguished from the *impositio paenitentiae* and the *absolutio paenitentiae*; cf. Galtier I 222 f. This *actio paenitentiae* did not differ greatly from the penitential practices required before the reception of Baptism; as technical terms, however, both *actio paenitentiae* and exomologesis are restricted to post-baptismal penitence. Liturgical aspects of this question are treated by Dekkers, *op. cit.* 217–30, and J. Jungmann, *Die lateinischen Bussriten in ihrer geschichtlichen Entwicklung* (Innsbruck 1932) 238–95.—For *magis exprimitur*, cf. Hoppe II 85 f.

[152] No certain argument can be drawn from the *De paenitentia* to prove that confession of sins *secundum numerum* and *speciem* existed in the church of Carthage at the close of the second century. As has been said above (note 151), however, a confession of sin *coram ecclesia* is implicit in the very act of exomologesis. Obviously, a confession to the whole Church is, inclusively, a confession to ecclesiastical authority, but how circumstantial this public confession was it is impossible to determine from the text of Tertullian. It may be pointed out that since the whole process of exomologesis was considered necessary for forgiveness and salvation (*De paen.* 9–12), the confession of sin which it implies was also considered necessary for forgiveness and salvation.

Various indirect arguments are given to show that in addition to the generic confession of sins implicit in exomologesis the sinner was also obliged to confess his sin or sins *in specie* to the bishop. In the case of a sinner who was excommunicated for a serious offense (cf. *Apol.* 39.4) and who, thereafter, sought readmission into the Church, such a confession would not be necessary, since his sin would already be *publici juris*. Public penance, however, may also have been required for sins which were not as yet a matter of common knowledge. In such cases a detailed and explicit confession to the bishop would have been required. It was the duty of the bishop, as the final authority in all matters of ecclesiastical discipline, to determine who was to undertake exomologesis and when it might be terminated by restoration to communion through the *ianua ignoscentiae*. Thus either he or his delegate would determine the actual duration of the public penance. Presumably the duration of this penance was proportioned not only to the intensity of the penitent's contrition but also to the number and gravity of the sins which he had committed; cf. Poschmann II 1–7; and Rahner, *op. cit.* 144 f. Other references in Scripture and tradition to confession of sins may be found in Galtier I 368–410 and Doronzo, *op. cit.* 3.348–464, 849–988. On the difference between confession before Baptism and in exomologesis, cf. A. D'Alès, *Tertulliani de baptismo* (Rome 1933) 46–48. For Tertullian's use of the word *confessio*, see Teeuwen I 74 f.

[153] The works of penitence which Tertullian describes in this chapter are not merely canonical penalties required by the Church as a proof of internal sorrow and conversion. They are, in a true sense, compensatory works of satisfaction which propitiate God and redeem sin. This is evident is such phrases as the following: *paenitentia deus mitigatur* (9.2); *misericordiae inlicem* (9.3); *illa quae peccant tristi tractatione mutare* (9.4), but see, below, note 156; *in peccatorem ipsa pronuntians pro dei indignatione fungatur et temporali afflictatione aeterna supplicia non dicam frustretur sed expungat* (9.5); *in quantum peperceris tibi, in tantum tibi deus, crede, parcet* (9.6). Tixeront, *op. cit.* 1.339, sees in the words *satisfactio confessione disponitur* a reference to the detailed confession of sins which made it possible for the bishop to determine and impose external works of satisfaction proportioned to the sinner's guilt. This interpretation is not impossible, although *disponitur* is ambiguous and may mean simply that when sin is confessed in exomologesis the penance which gives satisfaction to God is *eo ipso* properly performed.

[154] Here *disciplina* probably means an ecclesiastical ordinance. For other uses of the word in this sense, cf. Morel, *op. cit.* 37.

[155] Compare *De pud.* 5.14. The performance of penance in sackcloth and ashes is referred to frequently in Scripture. Tertullian, it will be observed, speaks of *lying* in sackcloth; compare *Apol.* 40.15: *in sacco et cinere volutantes*. So, also, Cyprian says that penitents are obliged *solo adhaerere, in cinere et cilicio . . . volutari*; *De lapsis* 35. Additional references may be found in Oehler's note *ad loc.* and H. Edmonds–B. Poschmann, 'Busskleid,' RAC 2.812–14. To these may be added the interesting note in Commodianus, *Instructiones* 2.8, where the influence of Tertullian's language seems quite clear. It is well known

that many of the early ascetics asked to be placed on the earth to lie and die in ashes and sackcloth; see, for example, Sulpicius Severus, *Epist.* 3, on the death of St. Martin of Tours, and St. Jerome's description of the death of Paula, *Epist.* 108. On the use of ashes in the performance of penance, cf. C. Schneider, 'Asche,' RAC 1.725–30, and J. Jungmann, *op. cit* 58–60. This description of exomologesis is copied closely in Isidore of Seville, *Etymol.* 6.19.79.

[156] *Illa quae peccant tristi tractatione mutare.* The thought is not perfectly clear. Tertullian probably wishes to say that the penitents 'change,' that is, put off or get rid of, their sins by the harsh treatment which they inflict upon themselves. The concept of exomologesis as a compensatory work of satisfaction for sin is suggested if we think of this 'change' as an 'exchange.' It is possible, however, that they change sin for suffering, or harsh treatment (cf. *De paen.* 12.7), in the sense that they change over from a life of sin to a life of penance. Kellner translates *tristi tractatione* as 'durch das bittere Andenken,' and understands the words to mean that penitents cancel their sin by their bitter thoughts about them. Oehler believes that *tractatione mutare* means *tractare et iterum tractare,* therefore *retractare.*

[157] Tertullian's viewpoint shifts in this chapter from the first person plural (9.2) to the second and third person singular (9.4). Rigault's suggestion of *suum* for *tuum* is helpful but without manuscript authority.

[158] This text may not be used to prove that in the exomologesis there was a detailed confession of sin to ecclesiastical authorities, followed by episcopal absolution. The expression *presbyteris advolvi* testifies to the place of prominence which the clergy occupies in the Christian community. When the sinner confesses *coram ecclesia,* he humbles himself before all the brethren and begs the intercession of all; he turns to the clergy, in particular, because of their position of authority in the Church and because of the special efficacy which, by reason of their office, attaches to their intercessory prayer.

[159] *Adgeniculari* regularly means to 'kneel before,' not to 'embrace the knees;' cf. TLL 1.1305, but see, below, note 176 and *De pud.*, note 331. The *cari dei* are all faithful Christians, although it may be that certain definite groups within the Church are intended more specifically, for example, the martyrs and confessors, cf. E. Preuschen, 'Zur Kirchenpolitik des Bischofs Kallist,' ZNW 11 (1910) 155, or the widows, cf. K. Adam, *Der Kirchenbegriff Tertullians* (Paderborn 1907) 84 f. Compare *De pud.* 13.7: *prosternens in medium ante viduas, ante presbyteros.* Manuscript evidence favors the reading *aris dei* rather than *caris dei,* and this is retained by Borleffs; against this, see Mohrmann's note *ad loc.*

[160] Through the intercession of the priests and those of the faithful who are especially dear to God the sinner's prayer for pardon becomes the prayer of the whole Church and, thus, the prayer of Christ Himself; cf. *De paen.* 10.6. This, of course, does not infringe upon the bishop's power to absolve the sinner at the conclusion of his public penance; cf. Galtier I 140–48 and Rahner, *op. cit.* 152–54. The close relationship between the communion of saints and the doctrine of the forgiveness of sins is evident in many beautiful passages to be found in ancient Christian literature. See Poschmann II 7–9, 82–86 on the importance of this privileged intercession in the history of indulgences and the development of the doctrine of the *thesaurus ecclesiae*; cf., also, Poschmann I 256 f., 319.

[161] *De periculi timore.* For *periculum* in the sense of 'punishment' compare *Apol.* 5.2.

[162] *Expungere*, a word in technical use to describe the cancellation of a debt when payment is received. There is an interesting and suggestive parallel in *Apol.* 2.15, where Tertullian writes that in Roman juridical procedure, *sententia opus est: debito poenae nocens expungendus est, non eximendus*; only when justice is done may a criminal's name be erased from the list of the condemned; cf. Waltzing, *op cit.* 33 and Hoppe I 132.

[163] Dodgson translates, 'the fouler the fairer.' St. Jerome, *Epist.* 54.7, write of the penitent Magdalen, *quanto foedior, tanto pulchrior.*

[164] When Tertullian says that exomologesis absolves a man from sin by condemning him to penance (*cum condemnat, absolvit*) his language closely resembles that of a number of theologians who, in later centuries, describe the Church's power to forgive and to retain sin as a power to forgive by retaining. In the discipline of exomologesis sin was retained when the sinner was authoritatively bound to penance; it was forgiven when he completed his penance and was readmitted to communion with the Church. This primitive retention of sin is considered to have its modern counterpart in the priest's imposition of a sacramental penance. The imposition of such a penance contributes to the ultimate forgiveness of sin, and thus the priest may be said to loose by binding, to forgive by retaining; cf. St. Bonaventure In IV, dist. 18, p. 1, q. 2, a. 1, *data est . . . potestas ut ligando solveret*; and Suarez, *De sacramento poenitentiae*, Disp. 16.2.16, *ligando simul solvit*. This question is ably treated by P. Palmer, 'How Does the Priest Retain Sins?' TS 11 (1950) 240–58.

D'Alès III 166 considers that the series of antitheses in this sentence proves that exomologesis was terminated by an ecclesiastical absolution. It is clear that at the close of exomologesis the penitent was absolved from sin, and since exomologesis was an ecclesiastical process, the absolution which it effected was an ecclesiastical absolution and not merely a private pardon granted to the sinner by God. In the present sentence, however, Tertullian neither asserts nor implies that this absolution was episcopal or sacerdotal. In fact, the obvious sense of his words is that forgiveness results from the exomologesis itself, and not from any action on the part of ecclesiastical authorities who reconciled the sinner to the Church after he had performed public penance. That such reconciliation took place and was granted by the bishop can be proved elsewhere, but it would be wiser not to look for it here.

[165] Disease is frequently spoken of in patristic literature as a type of sin. So, also, priests are described as physicians whose duty it is to know and cure the various diseases of the soul; cf. references in Galtier I 379-82. In this they continue the work of Christ the Savior; compare Evodius, *Epist. ad Valent.* 1.17: *Medicus salvator Christus*, and see F. Dölger, 'Der Heiland,' AC 6 (1950) 241-72. Although Tertullian does not state here explicitly that priests act as physicians in the administration of penance, St. Pacian, in a close imitation of the present passage (*Parain. ad poenit.* 8-9), does identify the sick man who refuses to reveal his disease to the physician with the sinner who refuses to reveal his sin to the priest. In both cases disaster follows as the result of a false shame. From such passages it appears that the priest, as physician, exercised a special power in the forgiveness of sin, although it is not certain that this was always thought of as a power to grant sacramental absolution. For the important teaching of Clement of Alexandria and Origen on confession, even to lay persons, as a means of spiritual therapy, see Poschmann III 34-38.

[166] This is one of many expressions in the present chapter which suggest that Tertullian considered the performance of public penance to be necessary even in the case of secret sin. It is his contention, throughout the chapter, that a sinner endangers his salvation (e.g. *damnatum latere*, 10.8) who, out of a sense of shame, refuses the public confession involved in exomologesis.

[167] The feeling of shame which accompanies confession is itself an appropriate part of the satisfaction which the sinner makes to God for his offense. See above, notes 149, 153.

[168] *Prodactae.* Other examples of this participle in Tertullian are listed by Waszink, *op. cit.* 507.

[169] Reading *pro te*, rather than *per te*. Compare Pacian, *Parain. ad poenit.* 8: *cui pro te melius est perire*; see J. Van der Vliet, 'Ad *Tertulliani De pudicitia* et *De paenitentia*,' *Mnemosyne* 20 (1892) 282.

[170] *Risiloquium* is a coinage. Compare *maliloquium* (*De spec.* 2; *Apol.*

45.3); *turpiloquium* (*De pud.* 17.18); *spurciloquium* (*De res. mort.* 4); *minutiloquium* (*De an.* 6.7). For *si forte*, cf. Oehler's long note on *De cor.* 5 and Waszink, *op. cit.* 161 f.—The words *periculum eius . . . onerosum est* are difficult and various interpretations of the sentence are possible. *Periculum* appears to be suggested by *detrimentum* and *perire* in the preceding sentence. Shame may be said to suffer injury (*detrimentum*) or to be lost (*mihi melius est perire*) when it is ignored or put aside in the interest of one's eternal salvation; one does what is right in spite of a feeling of shame. This is a salutary loss and one which should not be burdensome, since it is experienced in the presence of sympathetic and understanding brethren. Shame is also endangered, however, when it is excited by the derision and mockery of those who attempt to exalt themselves at the expense of the humiliation of others. It is especially in this latter case that the danger to shame may be called *onerosum*, since the efforts which one makes to overcome it in such circumstances are particularly painful.

[171] Compare 1 Cor. 12.4–11; Eph. 4.3. These passages in St. Paul are closely joined with his teaching on the Mystical Body of Christ, to which Tertullian is about to refer.

[172] *Quid consortes casuum tuorum ut plausores fugis?* The sentence may also be translated, 'Why do you flee from those who share in your misfortunes (i.e. your lapses into sin) as from men who rejoice (clap their hands) over them?'

[173] Cf. 1 Cor. 12.26.

[174] *In uno et altero ecclesia est.* Three interpretations may be given to these words. (1) The Church is found both in the whole body and in each single member of the body, i.e. in the *unus* and *alter* referred to in the preceding sentence. (2) The Church is found in each separate member of the Mystical Body of Christ, i.e. in *any one* or *another* of the faithful. (3) Where there are two of the faithful, i.e. *one* and *another*, gathered together, there is the Church; cf. Matt. 18.20. This third sense is the one which has been adopted in the translation. In *De exhort. cast.* 7 Tertullian writes: *Ubi tres, ecclesia est, licet laici*; cf. also *De bap.* 6: *Ubi tres, id est, Pater et Filius et Spiritus Sanctus, ibi ecclesia, quae trium corpus est*; and in *De pud.* 21.16: *ipsa ecclesia . . . ipse est spiritus, in quo est trinitas unius divinitatis, pater et filius et spiritus sanctus.* It may be noted that under the influence of Montanism Tertullian departs more and more from his concept of the Church as the Mystical Body of Christ and begins to think of it exclusively as the internal church of the Spirit; cf. Adam, *Der Kirchenbegriff Tertullians* 92.

[175] Cf. Colos. 1.24; Acts 9.5. In a famous passage on the nature and work of the Church Tertullian says (*Apol.* 39.1): *Corpus sumus de*

conscientia religionis et disciplinae unitate et spei foedere ; cf. also *De monog*. 13, where, in a close approximation to Col. 1.24, he writes: *corpus Christi quod est ecclesia*. E. Mersch, *The Whole Christ* (tr. from the 2nd French ed. by J. Kelly, Milwaukee 1938, 371–73), believes that Tertullian's teaching on the Mystical Body was defective even during his Catholic period, and considers that the thought of this passage in the *De paenitentia* may represent popular contemporary preaching on the subject rather than the author's own reflection. In any hypothesis, however, it remains one of the most beautiful expressions of the doctrine of the Mystical Body and the communion of saints in ancient Christian literature.

[176] *Christum contrectas*. *Contrectare* (*tracto*) originally connotes physical contact or handling; cf. 1 John 1.1; Col. 2.21. *Contrectabilis* is a neologism in Tertullian (*De an*. 57.12) used to describe the condition of a body which is risen from the dead and reunited with the soul. Tropically, however, *contrectare* can mean 'to look upon' or 'to turn to.' If Tertullian intends the original sense of the word here, we must suppose that in the course of exomologesis the penitents actually clung to the feet or embraced the knees of the brethren whose intercession they besought. It is difficult to determine from the wording of the passage just how we are to picture the posture of the penitents. *Protendis te* means, literally, 'stretch yourself out towards.' This may be done by prostrating oneself at the feet of another or, simply, kneeling with arms extended towards the person whose favor is sought. The latter position is suggested by a line in Petronius 17: *Protendo supinas manus ad genua*. Quite probably much was left to the individual's own fervor and to the inspiration of the moment, so that at different times and in the case of different penitents, various positions of humility and supplication, all more or less natural and traditional, would have been assumed. We need not suppose that such matters were determined in detail by definite rubrics. It is well known, also, that no great distinction was made in Christian antiquity between kneeling and prostration as positions of prayer. No doubt this fact contributes to the ambiguity of Tertullian's language. It is interesting to observe that the third class of penitents (cf. above, note 121) are said, indifferently, γόνυ κλίνειν (*Conc. Neocaes*., c. 5) and ὑποπίπτειν (*Conc. Nicaen*., c. 11). Further particulars may be found in H. Leclercq, 'Génuflexion,' DACL 6.1017–21. For other pertinent passages in Tertullian see *Adv. Marc*. 3.18; *Ad ux*. 2.8; *De pud*. 5.14 and, especially, *Apol*. 40.15: *in sacco et cinere volutantes . . . deum tangimus*.

[177] Cf. John 11.41 f. With less probability we might translate, 'What a son requests is always easily obtained.' It is evident from this whole passage that no restrictions are placed on the sins for which

pardon is asked and obtained in exomologesis through the intercession of Christ and the Church. This contrasts sharply with the harshness of *De pud.* 19.25, where Tertullian insists that there are some sins for which Christ is not an *exorator patris*, sins, that is, *quae veniam non capiant*. The contrast between the *De paenitentia* and the *De pudicitia* on this point has been studied at length by C. Daly, *op. cit.* 69.815–21; 70.730–46, 845–48; see, also, Galtier I 201–05. Of course there would be no contradiction between the two treatises if, in the *De paenitentia*, Tertullian said simply that all sins are forgiven by God and, in the *De pudicitia*, denied that all can be forgiven by the Church; if in the *De paenitentia* he asserted that all sins for which Christ begs pardon are forgiven and in the *De pudicitia* he denied that Christ actually asks pardon for all sins.

[178] The opposition is between *existimatio hominum* and *conscientia dei*. *Existimatio* may also connote the *good opinion* of men. Thus the sinner who shuns exomologesis shows that he considers God's awareness of his guilty state to be of less consequence than the preservation of his reputation among men.

[179] The question raised by the words *palam absolvi* in this sentence has been the subject of much controversial comment. Is the absolution to which Tertullian refers an absolution granted by God alone or is it also, in some sense, an absolution granted by the Church? It may be admitted that absolution is public in the sense that it is effected by an exomologesis which is public, but the problem is to determine, further, whether exomologesis itself included an act of ecclesiastical reconciliation which made the absolution of the sinner a matter of public knowledge. In other words, is it possible or even, perhaps, necessary to say that the words *palam absolvi* indicate that the absolution effected by exomologesis was public not only because the external acts of the penitent were public, but also because the absolution was itself publicly granted by the authority of the Church?

It may be useful here to list briefly the principal arguments which lead to the conclusion that the absolution which followed upon the performance of *paenitentia secunda* was, in some sense, ecclesiastical. (1) The exomologesis described in the *De paenitentia* is the same as that described in the *De pudicitia*. The latter, at least in the case of lesser sins, was terminated by ecclesiastical reconciliation (cf. *De pud.* 18.17); therefore we may presume that the former (i.e. the exomologesis of which there is question in the *De paenitentia*) was also. Tertullian has less reason to speak of the Church's intervention in the *De paenitentia* since his chief interest here is the necessity of personal penance, whereas in the *De pudicitia* he is particularly concerned with the precise subject of episcopal claims. When he acknowledges, in this latter treatise, that he himself formerly did not restrict the Church's power to absolve from sins of the flesh, we may suppose that the ecclesiastical absolution which he says he admitted as a Catholic was an absolution granted after the performance of public penance for those sins which, as a Montanist, he called *irremissibilia*. That he is thinking of serious sins in the *De paenitentia* is also clear from the fact that he says they are punished by damnation if they are not forgiven through exomologesis. (2) In the *De pudicitia* such words as *absolvere* and *restituere* have reference to ecclesiastical reconciliation; therefore, *a pari*, they must be thought of as ‐having this same sense in the *De paenitentia*, unless the contrary can be proved. (3) *Paenitentia secunda* is permitted only once; accordingly, if the friendship with God which it restores is lost by sin, it is not recoverable by exomologesis. A *terminus post quem non* is understandable when we are thinking of a penance which is concluded by an ecclesiastical act of reconciliation; it is less easily understood, however, of a penance which is exclusively a matter between the soul and God. An absolution which is granted only once (*semel*) would seem to be an ecclesiastical absolution; but since the same absolution which is granted *semel* is also said to be granted *palam*, we must conclude that when it is designated as a public absolution, it is public precisely *qua* ecclesiastical. (4) The *paenitentia secunda* of exomologesis closely parallels the *paenitentia prima* of Baptism. The latter was terminated by the intervention of ecclesiastical authority admitting the candidate to the communion of saints; therefore we may suppose that when communion was restored after the performance of public penance, this restoration would be accomplished and made known by some external act on the part of the Church. This supposition is confirmed if it can be shown that Tertullian considers the feast prepared for the Prodigal Son, referred to in *De paen.* 8.6, to be a type of the Eucharistic banquet; cf. above, note 144. (5) *Paenitentia secunda* is performed *in vestibulo ecclesiae* and is described as a *pulsatio* which opens the *ianua ignoscentiae*. Exomologesis, as a *pulsatio*, is certainly public, but no less public is the actual opening of the door of pardon which comes in response to and as a result of the sinner's *pulsatio*. The whole symbolism of this description supposes that the *paenitentia secunda* was concluded by some public act of ecclesiastical authority readmitting the penitent to communion with the Church, unless we are to suppose that the sinner who knocked upon the door of the church was also empowered to open it himself whenever he felt that his penance was complete. The conclusion seems inescapable that the *palam absolvi* of the present passage is identified with the opening of the *ianua ignoscentiae* described above, *De paen.* 7.10. (6) Finally, the expression *palam absolvi* itself implies an act of reconciliation by the Church. Absolution is public when it can be known as such, that is to say, when it can be recognized as having been received. This is possible when absolution is granted externally by the Church; it is not possible when it is granted internally by God alone. In the first case there is an absolution *in existimatione hominum*; in the second it remains exclusively *in conscientia dei*. Tertullian asks whether it is better to be condemned in secret (*damnatum latere*) or to be absolved in public. If there is no external reconciliation with the Church and by the Church, then the absolution which is granted by God remains secret just as truly as the condemnation of the sinner by God remains secret when he refuses to undertake the performance of exomologesis. It may be mentioned, in passing, that the ecclesiastical superintendence of public penance is clearly and repeatedly affirmed by St. Cyprian, writing at Carthage less than fifty years after Tertullian; see, for example, *De lapsis* 29: *satisfactio et remissio facta per sacerdotes* and *Epist.* 43.3: *per episcopos et sacerdotes domini domino satisfiat.*

If the arguments synopsized here are accepted as valid, then we must see in the ancient exomologesis a religious rite which, in its intrinsic constituents, is substantially the same as that which is now called the sacrament of Penance. In the external performance of *paenitentia secunda* we can distinguish the three acts of the penitent which form the sinner's own contribution to the sacramental sign. They constitute the material or quasi-material element of the sacrament, scl. a manifestion of sorrow, a confession of sin, at least *in genere*, and the performance of commensurate works of penance determined by the Church as satisfaction for sin. The formal constituent element of the sacrament is an ecclesiastical absolution which, at least indirectly, reconciles the sinner to God.

There are two ways in which this contribution of the Church to the efficacy of exomologesis is conceived and described. According to the well-known thesis of B. Poschmann, the whole sacramental causality of the Church's intervention in exomologesis is found in the readmission of the sinner to *pax* and *communio* with the body of the faithful. Ecclesiastical absolution reconciles the sinner to the Church. It is a transaction in the external forum, and only indirectly and mediately does it effect a remission of sin *coram Deo*. P. Galtier, on the contrary, along with many others, insists that in granting *pax* and *communio* the Church also reconciles the sinner to God, not only removing the *poena ecclesiastica* of excommunication, but also absolving the penitent from the guilt of sin itself and from the eternal punishment which is its due.

It should be noted that when Tertullian speaks of the efficacy of exomologesis, he is thinking of what is effected by all of its parts *simul sumptae*, when the whole penitential process is complete. He makes no effort to distinguish or to determine the special causality of its various elements considered distributively, ascribing, for example, formal efficacy to the intervention of the Church and viewing the acts of the penitent as the material element in a judicial process or as mere conditions which are required for absolution. The whole effect of exomologesis is sacramental; therefore all of its necessary constituents, *simul sumptae*, including the pardon granted to the sinner by the Church, will be sacramental. Ecclesiastical reconciliation *in sensu diviso* from the acts of the penitent in exomologesis has no more sacramental significance or efficacy than have the acts of the penitent themselves *in sensu diviso* from the ecclesiastical reconciliation which terminates the process in which they occupy so conspicuous a place. The whole is necessary for salvation; therefore all of its essential parts, contrition, satisfaction, confession and ecclesiastical absolution, are also necessary for salvation.

Prescinding, therefore, from the question of just what Tertullian thought was effected by the *venia episcopi*, we may say, in conclusion, that he considers the effect of exomologesis *complete sumpta* to be a restoration of the sinner not only to communion with the Church but also to friendship with God. This is apparent, for example, in the close parallel which he sees between the *prima* and *secunda paenitentia*. Both are *plancae salutis* which save the sinner from eternal death. Moreover, Baptism makes a man, for the first time, a friend of God. This gift of friendship is included among the blessings which are lost by post-baptismal sin and restored by exomologesis; cf. *De paen.* 7.11; 8.6-8. The same internal efficacy of exomologesis is evident in Tertullian's juxtaposing of the phrases *damnatum latere* and *palam absolvi*. Since the sinner's condemnation is a condemnation by God in the internal forum, it would seem that his absolution also must be thought of not only as the lifting of an ecclesiastical penalty but also as an absolution in the internal forum from the guilt of sin itself. Further proof of this may be seen in Rahner, *op. cit.* 156; Galtier I 115-20; D'Alès I 344-48; D'Alès III 158-60; cf. also E. Fruetsaert, 'La réconciliation ecclésiastique vers l'an 200,' NRT 57 (1930) 379-90. It may be pointed out that the sacramental nature of the ancient public penance has long been recognized by theologians; see, for example, Suarez, *De poenitentia* 21.2.9.

[180] Following Rauschen: *Malo (peccando) ad miserum pervenitur.* This is, as Borleffs remarks in his apparatus, a *locus nondum sanatus.*

[181] Tertullian's interest in and knowledge of medicine are revealed *passim* in his writings; cf. P. de Labriolle, 'La physiologie dans l'œuvre de Tertullien,' *Arch. gén. de méd.* 83 (1906) 1317–28; A. Harnack, *Medicinisches aus der ältesten Kirchengeschichte* (TU 8.4, Leipzig 1892). In *De an.* 2.6 he writes that he studied medicine, 'the sister of philosophy'; compare, also, *De carne Christi* 20; *De an.* 25; *Adv. Marc.* 2.16 for further evidence of his familiarity with medical theory and practice.

[182] Cf. Matt. 6.16.

[183] *In coccino et Tyrio.* For *Tyrium*, cf. *De cultu fem.* 1.8; *De pallio* 4 and the note in A. Gerlo, *Tertullianus: De pallio* (Wetteren 1940) 141 f.

[184] Borleffs reads this as an imaginary question which the insincere penitent puts to himself as he gazes into his mirror.—For references to the *acus* used in parting and arranging the hair, cf. TLL 1.469. Tertullian seems to be thinking of the *acus discriminalis* (Isidore of Seville, *Etymol.* 19.31), an ornamental pin popular in the elaborate coiffures of the day. The word suggests that Tertullian alludes to a female penitent who refuses to permit her hair to hang loose and unkempt in the traditional manner of penance and mourning. See, for example, Jerome's description of the public penance which Fabiola performed 'weeping, in sackcloth, filthy and with dishevelled hair (*sparsum crinem*),' *Epist.* 77.4.—On the powder used in caring for and beautifying the teeth, cf. RE, s.v. *dentifricium*. Scribonius Largus, *Compositiones medicamentorum* 59, says of it: *splendidos facit dentes et confirmat*; cf. also references given in Oehler *ad loc.*—The instrument used in manicuring the nails is designated as *bisulcum aliquid*. For the meaning of *repastinare*, see Waszink, *op. cit.* 525. Perhaps 'some bifurcate thing to plow around the nails' would better preserve the implications of the Latin.

[185] Sin is an injury done to God and it is this injury which makes compensatory works of satisfaction necessary as a matter of justice. Mortification of the flesh, as a particularly effective means of satisfying God for sin, is extolled with fervor and Montanist exaggeration in the treatise *De ieiunio*.

[186] Other references to the obsequious conduct of candidates for public office may be seen in TLL 3.237 f., s.v. *candidatus*.

[187] The *fasces*, bundles of birch or elm rods bound around an axe, were carried by lictors before the higher Roman magistrates as symbols of civil authority. On the method of electing the various public officials and the term of office which each enjoyed, cf. J. Reid, 'The Roman Constitution,' in *A Companion to Latin Studies*. Ed. by J. Sandys (3rd ed. Cambridge 1943) 272–81.

[188] Tertullian's version of this text (Isa. 5.18) is quite close to the

Septuagint but differs considerably from the Vulgate: *Vae qui trahitis iniquitatem in funiculis vanitatis.* The sense of the original Hebrew seems to be that the wicked disposition of sinners is a kind of cord which binds their sins upon them; cf. E. J. Kissane, *The Book of Isaiah* (Dublin 1941) 1.64. Other illustrations of Tertullian's dependence upon the Septuagint have been gathered by D'Alès I 235–37. Perhaps Tertullian wishes to say that persons who have offended God and who then refuse repentance add new sins to those of which they are already guilty. It is possible, however, that his understanding of the text is closer to the Hebrew original than is indicated in the present translation. If so, we might render his version, 'Woe to those who bind on their sins as with a great rope.' It is by *paenitentia* that the cord of wickedness is broken and the bonds of sin removed; for *funes peccatorum* see Prov. 5.22 and a variant reading in *De pud.* 1.6.

[189] In this final chapter of the treatise Tertullian emphasizes the efficacy of exomologesis and its necessity for salvation. His principal purpose is to exhort sinners to acts of personal penitence; therefore he disregards, though he does not deny, the ecclesiastical character of exomologesis. The fact that the penitence of Nabuchadonezzer and Adam and the neglected penitence of the Pharaoh were non-ecclesiastical and yet are called exomologesis does not prove that throughout the treatise *De paenitentia* Tertullian attributes the efficacy of exomologesis exclusively to the personal efforts of the repentant sinner; cf. above, note 179 and Teeuwen II 416 f. The use of the word exomologesis in Christian antiquity parallels the use of the words 'penance' and 'confession' today. All three words primarily signify the performance of personal acts of penance; by metonomy, however, they are also used to designate the whole external penitential process of which ecclesiastical absolution is a part; cf. above, note 151 and below, note 198. Other examples of the use of exomologesis without reference to the Church's role in public penance may be found in *De ieiun.* 9 (the repentance of David) and 10 (the austerities of Daniel).

[190] Tertullian's eschatology is extremely primitive. It was his belief that the souls of the martyrs alone were admitted to Paradise before the Last Judgement. All others were *apud inferos*, where they experienced either *refrigeria* (*in sinu Abrahae*) or *supplicia* (*in gehenna ignis*). See the detailed treatment in *De an.* 7, 55–58, and Waszink's excellent notes on these chapters, *op. cit.* 153, 553–93. Tertullian's conception of the *gehenna ignis* is marked by the crudest realism. It is a *thesaurus* or *clibanus* or *furnus* or *stagnum ignis* somewhere beneath the earth; volcanoes are the actual vent-holes of hell and not, as D'Alès says (I 287, 427), merely types or images which call to mind the eternal flames. Compare

Apol. 47.12 and 48.14 f.; cf. also the allusions to Aetna and Vesuvius in Minucius Felix, *Octavius* 35.3, and the more detailed description in Pacian, *Parain. ad paenit.* 11. It is possible, perhaps even probable, that the present reference in Tertullian was inspired by the eruption of Vesuvius which, according to Dio Cassius 76.2, occurred in 203 A.D. Further passages dealing with Tertullian's teaching on the punishment of fire and the eternity of hell may be found in *De res. mort.* 17, 43, 44; *Adv. Marc.* 1.27; 3.24; 4.34; *Ad ux.* 1.4; *De fuga* 12; *De praescrip. haer.* 2; *De pud.* 1.5; 19.7.—It was a common opinion of the Fathers that hell is located within the interior of the earth; numerous references are given by M. Richard, 'Enfer,' DTC 5.102. However, St. Augustine (*De civ. dei* 20.16) and St. Gregory the Great (*Dial.* 4.42) assert that the location of hell is unknown. St. John Chrysostom, *In Epist ad Rom. Hom.* 31.5, insists that it is much more profitable to ask how hell can be avoided than to ask where it is.

[191] In the *Codex Ottobonianus, iacula exercitatoria*; for the meaning cf. Borleffs II 70 f.

[192] The difference between the Baptism of Jesus and the Baptism of John is treated in *De bap.* 10–12; cf. above, note 24.

[193] The plant dittany (*dictamnum*) received its name from Mt. Dicte in Crete, where it grew in great abundance. The curative properties to which Tertullian refers are described in a number of places by the elder Pliny, e.g. *Hist. nat.* 8.27; 25.92; 26.142. Cf. also Aristotle, *Hist. animal.* 9.6; Cicero, *De nat. deorum* 2.126 and Vergil, *Aeneid* 12.412. Other references may be found in Borleffs II 71–73 and Van der Vliet, *op. cit.* 284 f. Kroymann's conjecture of *edendam* for *medendum* has been confirmed by the *Codex Ottobonianus*.

[194] There is some difficulty in taking *hirundo* as the subject of *excaecaverit* and various emendations have been suggested: *excaecaveris* (Junius); *si quis excaecaverit* (Scaliger); *si excrementum excaecaverit* (Preuschen).—On the celandine or swallow-wort, see Pliny, *Hist. nat.* 8.27; 25.50. In the latter passage he states that the herb is efficacious in restoring vision *etiam erutis oculis.* Tertullian says that through the use of celandine the swallow *novit oculare* (give eyes to) its young. This same curious belief is mentioned by St. Basil, *In Hexaem. Hom.* 8. Aristotle does not speak of the swallow-wort, but in *Hist. animal.* 2.17 and 6.6 he states that if the eyes of a swallow chick are gouged out, they will grow back again. Modern students consider that the swallow-wort received its name from a fancied resemblance of its pods to the outstretched wings of a swallow, or because of a popular belief that the plant blossomed in the spring with the arrival of the swallows and withered with their departure in the fall.

[195] Dan. 4.29-33. The lion is mentioned in the Septuagint and in the version of Theodotion, but not in the Vulgate or the Aramaic original. Tertullian speaks of both the lion and the eagle, but the order of the two words within the sentence is uncertain. The translation given here follows the reading of Pamelius. The passage has been imitated by St. Pacian, *Parain. ad paenit.* 9. Cf. also St. Paulinus of Nola, *Epist.* 4; St. Jerome, *Epist.* 107.2 and Tertullian, *De pat.* 13.

[196] *Felicitatem* has been restored to the text from the *Codex Ottobonianus* (Borleffs II 73 f.) and is supported by St. Pacian, *Parain. ad paenit.* 9.

[197] Exod. 14.

[198] Cf. above, notes 151, 189. For Tertullian *paenitentia* and exomologesis are distinguished as internal disposition and external act. Exomologesis is an *instrumentum* or *ministerium* (*minister*, the abstract for the concrete) of *paenitentia* in the sense that it is the means or instrument by which the interior sorrow of the penitent is proved genuine through his performance of external works of penance.

[199] The *duae humanae salutis plancae* are *paenitentia prima* (Baptism) and *secunda* (exomologesis). Here, again, Tertullian indicates his belief that the public penance, *complete sumpta*, reconciles the sinner to God and not merely to the Church.

[200] *Peccator omnium notarum*; cf. above, note 93. Tertullian rather frequently refers to himself as a sinner and a man of no importance. Compare *De paen.* 4.2; *De bap.* 20; *De orat.* 20; *De exhort. cast.* 13.

[201] Tertullian says, simply, that Adam was the first member of the human race to sin against God (*offensae in dominum princeps*); he does not say that he was the *princeps humanae offensae*. If *humanae* is taken as modifying *offensae* in this way, it might be possible to see in the sentence an allusion to original sin as a *peccatum naturae* committed by Adam, the *caput* or *princeps generis humani*. For a discussion of the solidarity between Adam and the human family with respect to the guilt of original sin, see P. Galtier, *Les deux Adam* (Paris 1947) 52-68. A partial list of patristic references to original sin as the sin of Adam which infects the whole human race is given in RJ, *Index Theologicus* 302. For Tertullian's teaching on the subject, see the studies cited above, note 19. The formula *princeps et generis et delicti* is found also in *De exhort. cast.* 2.

[202] The references to Adam in this final sentence are obscure and the logic of the whole paragraph rather elusive. Tertullian probably means to say that it is more important to practice repentance than it is to write about it; yet since he is, as a child of Adam, born to repent and since he has imitated his father in the commission of sin, he is obliged to imitate him also in the practice of penance, and not only in its practice

but also in extolling its excellence. Thus he is justified in having written something about the subject, although he will now pursue it no farther. That Adam did penance for his sin and was saved is a firm conviction of Tertullian's, expressly stated here, and against Tatian in *De praescr. haer.* 52. Compare, also, *Adv. Marc.* 2.2 and 2.10. In *Adv. Marc.* 2.25 Tertullian describes the elements of Adam's exomologesis. His confession was made when he answered the questions of God in the garden (Gen. 3.9–11); penitential works were imposed upon him by God (Gen. 3.17–19); therefore, *etsi deditus morti est, spes ei salva est.* Both Adam and Eve were *candidati restitutionis, ut confessione relevati.* Tertullian asserts that Adam was not silent on the subject of penitence after his restoration to Paradise. The allusion is not clear but, possibly, he means to say no more than that the fact of Adam's salvation through exomologesis itself gives testimony to its excellence and value. There are highly imaginative accounts of the penance and pardon of Adam in the apocryphal literature; see, for example, the *Vita Adae et Evae,* translated by R. H. Charles in *The Apocrypha and Pseudepigrapha of the Old Testament* (Oxford 1913) 2.123–54; also the *Evangelium Nicodemi,* translated by A. Walker in ANF 8.437 f. For further details see P. de Labriolle, 'Vestiges d'apocryphes dans le *De paenitentia* de Tertullien, 12.9,' BALAC 1 (1911) 127 f.

The phrase *in paradisum suum* is ambiguous since Tertullian uses the word 'Paradise' indifferently to signify both the garden of Eden and the Paradise of the elect in heaven. *Suus* means 'his own' or 'that which is proper or peculiar to him'; Hoppe I 103. Thus Tertullian appears to believe that the Paradise to which Adam was restored was the same as that in which he was originally placed. This would seem to be 'his own particular Paradise' as distinguished from the Paradise *in coelis* which all repentant sinners win by their performance of exomologesis. It should be pointed out, however, that Tertullian is not unsympathetic to the notion that this Paradise *in coelis* is physically identified with the garden of Eden; cf. *De res. mort.* 26. Accordingly, the Paradise which was 'his own' originally and to which he was restored by his performance of exomologesis could also be the Paradise *in coelis* which all the just will eventually enjoy after the Last Judgement; cf. above, note 190. In other words, the fact that it is 'his own' Paradise does not necessarily exclude the possibility that it is also the Paradise promised to all repentant sinners. For Tertullian's views on the location of Paradise, cf. *De an.* 55; *Apol.* 47.13; *Adv. Marc.* 5.12. It is clear from these and other passages in his writings that he does not identify it with the *sinus Abrahae* (Luke 16.22) or situate it *apud inferos,* as has sometimes been erroneously supposed. Unfortunately Tertullian's detailed discussion of this subject in the treatise *De paradiso* has been lost. For a valuable study of the early Christian conception of Paradise and the use of the word as a synonym for heaven see H. Leclercq, 'Paradis,' DACL 13.1578–1615; cf. also C. Mohrmann, *Die altchristliche Sondersprache in den Sermones des hl. Augustin* (*Lat. christ. primaeva* 3, Nijmegen 1932) 132.

ON PURITY

INTRODUCTION

[1] This work is generally referred to in English as the treatise on *Modesty*, the title given it in Thelwall's translation. In modern usage, however, the word 'modesty' does not correspond exactly to *pudicitia* as Tertullian understands the term in this treatise. He is concerned, throughout, with the defense of a virtue which is violated by sins of adultery and fornication. This is the virtue of purity or chastity, not precisely and certainly not primarily the virtue of modesty. What we call 'modesty' today is a safeguard of what Tertullian calls *pudicitia*; compare *De cultu fem.* 2, where he declares that the virtue of purity (*pudicitia*) is necessary for salvation, and that this virtue will be preserved by the avoidance of extremes (i.e. by modesty) in dress and ornamentation. In *Apol.* 50.12 he states that the pagan persecutors, in condemning a Christian girl *ad lenonem potius quam ad leonem*, acknowledge that Christians consider the violation of chastity (*pudicitia*) a more dreadful punishment than death; cf. below, note 31. In *Apol.* 35.5 he distinguishes *modestia, verecundia* and *pudicitia*, paralleling these virtues with *probitas, sobrietas* and *castitas* in the preceding paragraph. See, also, Novatian's treatise *De bono pudicitiae*, a work which deals very definitely with the virtue of chastity and, at the same time, closely imitates, in a number of passages, the *De pudicitia* of Tertullian. That *pudicitia*, in other early Christian writers as well as in classical Latin, quite frequently means sexual purity, may easily be seen from the dictionaries. Tertullian's concept of *pudicitia* is illustrated, also, by his use of the word *impudicitia* in this present treatise; cf. 6.14; 14.17; 15.4; 16.22; 18.1, 11. In all of these places, and particularly in 14.27 and 18.11, 'impurity' is closer to his meaning than is 'immodesty.' As early a commentator as J. Pamelius, *Tertulliani opera* (Cologne 1617) 716, found difficulty with the title of this treatise. He remarks that the contents of the work would be more clearly indicated if it were called *Adversus paenitentiam* rather than *De pudicitia*, but he suggests that the latter title was chosen because, in attacking adultery and fornication as he does in his book, Tertullian is really writing in defense of purity (*pudicitia*).

[2] It will be observed that throughout this section of his work Tertullian's argument is largely one of rebuttal. His opponents appeal to definite passages in Scripture which they insist justify their forgiveness

of serious sins, e.g. the parables of mercy, the example of Christ, the teaching and example of the apostles. These arguments he examines in order and attempts to refute either by substituting his own interpretation of the passages in question or by setting over against them other passages which appear to destroy their force.

[3] For *peccata gravia*, cf. 3.13; 19.20; 21.14; 19.28; 21.2; 18.17; 19.25. For *peccata levia*, 1.19; 2.10; 7.20; 18.17; 19.22–24. For *peccata irremissibilia*, 2.12, 14, 15; 16.5; 9.20; 13.19.

[4] See the bibliography in Quasten, *op. cit.* 2.314 f.

[5] Cf. *De pud.* 5.8, 15; 6.7 f.; 9.20; 12.5, 11; 19.15.

[6] The dogmatic argument is found in a number of the older manuals of theology; see, for example, D. Palmieri, *De poenitentia* (Rome 1879) 93 f. It is defended, also, by J. Stufler in a series of articles in the *Zeitschrift für katholische Theologie*, 1907 to 1914; cf. in particular, 'Die Bussdisziplin in der abendländischen Kirche bis Kallistus,' ZKT 31 (1907) 433–73. The best evaluation of the dogmatic argument is that of J. Umberg, 'Absolutionspflicht und altchristl. Bussdisziplin,' *Scholastik* 11 (1927) 321 ff.

[7] That such parties of rigorists existed in Africa is clear from St. Cyprian, *Epist.* 55.21: *Et quidem apud antecessores nostros quidam de episcopis istic in provincia nostra dandam pacem moechis non putaverunt et in totum paenitentiae locum contra adulteria clauserunt.*

[8] This is the view of Galtier I 201–6, Daly, *op. cit.* 70.845–48 and many others. Mortimer, however, *op. cit.* 11, asserts, 'it is not true that Tertullian nowhere says he is combating an innovation,' and B. Botte, in his review of Daly's study, BTAM 6 (1950–53) 104 f., remarks that the problem is not to be solved by insisting that Tertullian's position in the *De pudicitia* represents a break with an earlier tradition which he had supported in the *De paenitentia*. Perhaps it is safest to say that rigorism and tolerance were in conflict from the beginning of the Church's history, and that Tertullian, who in his early years as a Christian favored a policy of moderation and leniency in dealing with sinners, eventually came to reject this policy and insist upon severity, not so much because he considered tolerance an innovation but because he considered that it was forbidden by the new revelation of the Paraclete.

[9] Poschmann I 330; cf., also, D'Alès III 203 f.

[10] Galtier I 209–20.

[11] Cf. Noeldechen, *op. cit.* 150–54; Harnack, *Chronologie* 286.

[12] The *editio princeps* is that of M. Mesnartius (Paris 1545), incorrectly attributed to J. Gagneius by editors up to and including Rauschen. There is no extant manuscript of the *De pudicitia*, though some pages of the text have been preserved in the *Codex Ottobonianus*.

TEXT

[1] Tertullian speaks somewhat similarly of this aspect of chastity in *Apol.* 9.16–20.

[2] This may be an echo of the opening verses of Juvenal's *Sixth Satire*: *Credo pudicitiam Saturno rege moratam in terris.* Cf. G. Highet, *Juvenal the Satirist* (Oxford 1954) 183, 297 for other possible borrowings from Juvenal in the works of Tertullian.

[3] Tertullian is here thinking of *natura, disciplina* and *censura* as determinants of morality in the natural order. The same three influences, Christianized, aɪ mentioned in a succeeding paragraph.—The rhythm and style of this carefully constructed introduction are noted by Norden, *op. cit.* 2.943 f. For the thought, apparently an echo of Aristotle, *Nicomachean Ethics* 10.9, cf. P. Keseling, 'Aristoteles bei Tertullian, *De pud.* 1.1,' PJ 57 (1947) 256 f. On 'nature' as a norm in Tertullian see the chapter on this subject in A. Lovejoy, *Essays in the History of Ideas* (Baltimore, 1948) 308–38. In Novatian's *De bono pudicitiae* 3 there is a close imitation of this sentence. Novatian's dependence on Tertullian has been studied by C. Daly, 'Novatian and Tertullian,' ITQ 19 (1952) 33–43.

[4] Cf. Matt. 24.12; 2 Thess. 2.10; 2 Tim. 3.1–5. Tertullian, of course, was in complete sympathy with the Montanist belief in the proximity of the parousia.—For *magis vincunt*, cf. Hoppe II 86.

[5] It seems clear from the expression *eiuratio libidinum* that the virtue of *pudicitia*, as Tertullian conceives it, is more than a matter of external modesty.

[6] Reading *qui minus non castus fuerit*, i.e. 'who is rather less unchaste.' Dekkers prefers *qui non nimis castus fuerit*.

[7] *Viderit saeculi pudicitia cum saeculo ipso.* For the meaning of *viderit* see above, note 30.

[8] A literal translation of this difficult sentence is all but meaningless; its thought, however, may be conveyed in the following paraphrase. The world neglects the practice of purity and no longer even knows what the virtue demands or in what it consists. The responsibility for this rests with the world itself and it is a matter of no concern to the Christian. If the world's impurity is congenital, then the world's own nature or natural bent must be held responsible; if impurity has been learned, then worldly education is responsible; if it has been forced

upon the world, then the world's enslavement to sin and Satan bears the responsibility.

[9] Other instances of *stare* in the sense of *perseverare* or *permanere in statu suo* may be found in *De pud.* 2.11 and 14.19; so, also, *Apol.* 40.2; *Scorp.* 10; *De ieiun.* 13.

[10] The text is in dispute and no certain interpretation of the passage is possible; cf. Van der Vliet, *op. cit.* 274. It seems, however, that Tertullian is here contrasting Christian and pagan purity just as in the introduction to *De paenitentia* he contrasted Christian and pagan repentance. He states that even if purity had been preserved among pagans it would have been of no advantage to them, since it would have been practiced for merely natural motives (*non apud deum egisset*). Thus pagan *pudicitia*, since it is a vain and fruitless good, is worse than no good at all.

[11] Reading *et coactam (censuram)* rather than *et coacta (iudicia)*. The sentence serves as a transition from Tertullian's strictures on pagan purity to his specific charge of laxity in the same matter leveled against the author of the Edict he is now about to discuss.

[12] On the Edict as a source of Roman law, cf. Buckland, *op. cit.* 8 ff., 17 f. An *edictum peremptorium* was one which put an end to all further discussion or debate. It is defined in *Digests* 5.1.70: *Peremptorium edictum inde hoc nomen sumpsit quod perimeret disceptationem, hoc est, ultra non pateretur adversarium tergiversari.* J. Stelzenberger's translation of *peremptorium* as 'sehr gefährlicher' is inadmissible; cf. F. Dölger, 'Bewertung von Mitleid und Barmherzigkeit bei Tertullianus,' AC 5 (1936) 264.—*Audio etiam* suggests that the issuance of this Edict is simply another incident in an already existing controversy and not the original cause of it.

[13] The text here is unsatisfactory. The translation follows a reading which is a conflation of suggestions proposed by Rauschen and von Hartel: *Adversus hanc* (that is, the *ratio christianae pudicitiae*) *nunc—nec dissimulare potuissem—audio edictum esse propositum, et quidem peremptorium.*

[14] The author of this Edict cannot be identified with certainty. For a synopsis of the problem and references to the literature, see the Introduction p. 47. The use of the titles *Pontifex Maximus* and *episcopus episcoporum* does not prove that the directive originated at Rome since these titles were not applied to the Roman Pontiff until a much later date. Tertullian is speaking ironically in order to excite resentment at what he considers an unwarranted exercise of episcopal authority. The irony would appear to be all the greater if he refers to a bishop of Carthage rather than to the bishop of Rome. For an interesting explanation of Tertullian's choice of the expression *Pontifex Maximus*, see

F. Dölger, 'Ächtung des Ehebruchs in der Kultsatzung,' AC 3 (1932) 140 f.

[15] *Quod est*, meaning 'that is to say.' We might also translate, 'because he is (i.e. claims to be) the bishop of bishops.'

[16] *Ego et moechiae et fornicationis delicta paenitentia functis dimitto.* It is generally supposed that the wording of the decree as given here represents a verbatim citation of the directive which was issued by Tertullian's episcopal opponent. Harnack, for example, sees in this formula the 'style of the curia' and recognizes the *imperatoria brevitas* of the Roman Church; cf. 'Die älteste uns im Wortlaut bekannte dogmatische Erklärung eines römischen Bischofs,' *Sitzungsberichte d. preuss. Akad. der Wiss.* 7 (1923) 52. It is quite likely, however, that Tertullian gives no more than the substance of the legislation which he is opposing and that its form is simply his own parody of the solemn phrasing used in contemporary imperial Edicts. Examples of such Edicts may be found in P. Girard, *Textes de droit rom.* (2me ed. Paris 1895) 154 f. and C. Bruns, *Fontes iuris rom. ant.* (6me ed. Paris 1893) 238 f. The use of the first person singular is typical of legislation by Edict. Thus Tertullian wishes the expression 'I forgive sins of adultery and fornication' to be understood as meaning 'I decree that such sins are to be forgiven.' The Edict is phrased as a statement of its author's personal practice, but it is to be taken as a determination, by episcopal authority, of the Church's law for the reconciliation of sinners guilty of fornication and adultery. Preuschen, *ad loc.*, suggests that the law may have been promulgated in the course of a sermon preached by the Catholic bishop and relayed to Tertullian (*audio etiam ...*) by someone who had heard it. See the careful analysis of the wording of this decree in P. de Labriolle, *La crise montaniste* (Paris 1913) 416–18.

The expression *paenitentia functis* in this Edict is considered by many historians of penance as proof that in Christian antiquity a private absolution from sin was not granted before the performance of public penance; cf. Galtier I 228 and G. Rauschen, *Eucharist and Penance in the First Six Centuries of the Church* (St. Louis 1913) 221. The whole passage is of the greatest importance as evidence that in the primitive Church forgiveness of sins was not viewed as an exclusively personal matter between the soul and God but involved, also, the intervention of ecclesiastical authority. The *paenitentia* of which there is question here is the exomologesis, and quite clearly, in the Catholic practice, it is terminated by a pardon from sin granted by the bishop or at his bidding. For this see D'Alès II 148; Rahner, *op. cit.* 148; Rauschen, *op. cit.* 243. That this was a direct pardon of sin itself (*delicta dimitto*) and not merely the removal of an ecclesiastical excommunication is argued by Galtier

II 30 f. The *editio princeps* has *moechiae et fornicationis funes*, i.e. the bonds of sin; cf. *De virg. vel.* 14, *funes delictorum*, and above, *De paen.* note 188. *Paenitentia fungi*, however, is used frequently of the performance of penance; cf. above, *De paen.* 5.22 and 6.22.

[17] The formula *Bonum Factum* was used in Latin Edicts as a good omen in somewhat the same way as the words ἀγαθῇ τύχῃ were added to treatises, decrees and the like by the Greeks. The sense seems to be about the same as that of the popular expression, *quod di bene vortant*; hence the translation here might be, 'God favor it.' Compare Plautus, *Paenulus. Prol.* 16 and 45; Suetonius, *Vitellius* 14 and *Julius Caesar* 80. Isidore of Seville, *Etymol.* 1.23 (*De notis iuridicis*) says that in juridical documents certain common expressions were regularly abbreviated by their initials: *scribebatur enim, verbi gratia, per B et F, 'bonum factum.'*

[18] The reference is to a house of prostitution. A *titulus* was a super-scription over the door of the *cella meretricis*, giving the name of the prostitute. The word occurs in the same sense in *De an.* 34.4 and, possibly, *Ad nat.* 1.16.12. Cf. Juvenal, *Satires* 6.123; Martial, *Epigr.* 11.45 and other references given in H. B. Swete's commentary on Apoc. 17.5, *The Apocalypse of St. John* (3rd. ed. Reprinted 1951. Grand Rapids) 217.

[19] The word *paenitentia* in this sentence is used, by synedoche, for *venia*. The point is of interest as showing how naturally Tertullian thought of penitence as including ecclesiastical absolution.

[20] The concept of the Church as the bride of Christ derives, no doubt, from the Old Testament concept of Israel as the bride of Yahweh; cf. Osee 2; Isa. 62.5; Jer. 3.1-14, 20. For the New Testament, 1 Cor. 6.15 f.; 2 Cor. 11.2; Eph. 5.23-33; compare, also, Matt. 9.15; John 3.29 and parallel passages in the other Evangelists. The allusion is frequent in Tertullian; cf. *De exhort. cast.* 5; *Adv. Marc.* 5.12; *De monog.* 5 and 11. In this last passage Tertullian writes: *et coniungent vos in ecclesia virgine, unius Christi unica sponsa.*

[21] The Church is a society of saints. Her members do not commit sins of adultery and fornication. If anyone should do so, he is excommunicated and can never again be a member of the body of Christ.

[22] Matt. 21.13; Mark 11.17; Luke 19.46. The 'temple of God' in this passage refers to the temple of Jerusalem as a type of the Christian Church.

[23] *Erit igitur et hic adversus psychicos titulus.* In his Montanist works Tertullian uses the epithet *psychicus* (cf. 1 Cor. 2.14) as a term of reproach for Catholics. A detailed explanation of this usage is given in de Labriolle, *op. cit.* 138-43; see, also, Evans, *op. cit.* 187 f. In addition to the present instance the word occurs in *De pud.* 6.14; 10.8; 16.24; 18.2;

21.16. The English word 'sensualist' is not a completely satisfactory translation of *psychicus*, yet it approaches the idea which Tertullian wishes to convey and is certainly preferable to the transliteration 'psychic.'—*Titulus* has been interpreted as meaning 'count in my indictment of' (Thelwall) or 'argument against the Sensualists' (Rauschen; cf. Oehler's note to *Apol.* 1.4); Kellner supposed that it refers to the designation of the Church as a virgin. The correct explanation, however, was given as early as Pamelius. At the time Tertullian wrote the *De pudicitia* he had already composed some half-dozen Montanist tracts against the Catholics. This work, also, he says will be directed against them. For *titulus* in the sense found here, see below, *De pud.* 20.2: *Exstat enim et Barnabae titulus ad Hebraeos*; cf., also, W. von Hartel, *Patristische Studien. Sitzungsberichte Wiener Akad. Philos.-hist. Klasse* (Vienna 1890) 4.13.

24 Literally, '... It is also against a sharing in my own opinion formerly (*retro=antea*; cf. Hoppe I 113) held amongst them.' The 'opinion' formerly held and now rejected seems to be the Catholic doctrine that the sin of adultery may be forgiven by the Church. Mortimer, however, *op. cit.* 13, states that the expression must be understood in a more general sense, i.e. 'Here is another book I am writing against the people I was formerly associated with; another book which opposes the line of easy toleration which I took then.' This is a possible interpretation, although the word *sententia* appears to be too definite and explicit a term for one's general attitude to moral questions.

25 *Praeiudicium*, a favorite word of Tertullian's. For its technical sense in legal language, cf. A. Beck, *Römisches Recht bei Tertullian und Cyprian* (Halle 1930) 87 f. As a form of *praescriptio* it is described in Buckland, *op. cit.* 648 f.; see, also, the note on *praeiudicia, ibid.* 561. The argument used here makes it clear that even at this time Christians appealed from Tertullian the Montanist to Tertullian the Catholic in attacking his teaching on irremissible sins.

26 For the appearance of this thought in later liturgical prayer see C. Coebergh, 'Le pape saint Gélase Iᵉʳ auteur de plusieurs messes et préfaces du soi-disant sacramentaire léonien,' SE 4 (1952) 50 f. Tertullian's conviction that in matters of belief the majority is always wrong quite probably contributed to his defection from the Church, just as originally it may have been one of the psychological reasons for his conversion. His temperament made it difficult for him to be happy except as spokesman for a militant minority, and one suspects that where a minority did not exist, he would find it necessary to create one.

27 1 Cor. 13.11, omitting the clause *cogitabam ut parvulus.*

[28] Cf. Gal. 1.14 and context; compare, also, 2 Thess. 2.15.

[29] Gal. 5.12.

[30] *Nomen* often means the 'essence' of a thing, or the 'thing itself;' cf. *De virg. vel.* 1; *De car. Christi* 12; *Apol.* 23.4. Thus, in the present passage, *nomen christianum*, by periphrasis, signifies Christianity, just as in *Apol.* 25.2 and 3 *nomen Romanum* signifies Rome. *Nomen* in the sense of 'being' or 'person' or 'essence' is familiar to us in the petition of the Lord's prayer, *sanctificetur nomen tuum.*—*Disciplina*, as appears from the phrases . . . *quam testatur* and *eam punire contendat*, means the whole Christian ideal and practice of purity and not, as Morel supposes, *op. cit.* 39, the Montanist law which excluded adulterers from penance.

[31] The prostitution of Christian women is mentioned repeatedly in the *Acta Martyrum* as a particularly vicious feature of the early persecutions; cf. F. Augar, *Die Frau im röm. Christenprocess* (TU 28.4, Leipzig 1904) and P. Allard, *Ten Lectures on the Martyrs* (tr. from the French by L. Cappadelta, New York 1907) 199–207.

[32] 1 Cor. 7.9. Tertullian discusses this text at length in his treatises on marriage; cf. *Ad ux.* 1.3; *De exhort. cast.* 3; *De monog.* 3. In all of these passages he interprets the words *melius est nubere quam uri* to mean that marriage is not an absolute good but is called good only in comparison with something that is very bad. See, also, St. Jerome, *Adv. Jovin,* 1.7, 9. In the present passage Tertullian asserts that his opponents, of all people, ought to be least indulgent to sins of adultery and fornication, since they permit remarriage precisely as a remedy against these sins. It is better to remarry, they argue, than to burn with a concupiscence which leads to sexual excesses. Since they have made this concession they should be the more severe with those who commit sins of adultery and fornication in spite of it.

[33] Tertullian wishes to say that there is no point in permitting multiple marriage if adultery is so easily condoned. Why supply a remedy when you pamper the disease? On the other hand, adultery itself will continue unchecked if the only remedy employed against it is the useless concession of multiple marriage. This interpretation retains *si remedia vacabunt* with Dekkers, against Rauschen's substitution, *si remedia praecavent*. Other examples of *vacare* in the sense it bears here are given by Hoppe I 139 f.

[34] This sentence is quoted by Norden, *op. cit.* 2.611, as typical of the Sophist dialectic and as illustrating Tertullian's position in a stream of literary tradition which had its origin some five or six hundred years before his birth.

[35] The distinction appears to be between *delicta modica* and *maxima* (Ursinus, followed by Oehler, Rauschen, Kellner-Esser) not between

delicta modica and *media* (Mesnartius, followed by Preuschen, De
Labriolle, Reifferscheid-Wissowa, Dekkers). This same distinction
(*modica-maxima*) is found in the following sentence and, below, 13.6.
As noted in the Introduction, p. 47, Tertullian seems to recognize a
distinction between mortal and venial sins (cf. Motry, *op. cit.* 158) but
there is some difficulty in determining precisely how we are to classify
the *delicta cotidianae incursionis* (*De pud.* 19.23) which may possibly form
a quasi-intermediate class between them; cf. Rahner, *op. cit.* 143, Daly,
op. cit. 70.731–39, and Grotz, *op. cit.* 345 f. Esser's statement, in his note
to Kellner, that Tertullian knows no *delicta media* is misleading and
cannot be proved. Galtier II 281 understands *et* to be conjunctive, not
disjunctive; that is to say, he considers sins which are *modica* and *media*
to form one class which are distinct from the *peccata gravia* which
Tertullian says are irremissible. For the bearing of this distinction on
the problem of private penance, see below, note 198. It may be said
here, briefly, that Tertullian's principal division of sins in the *De
pudicitia* is between those which are *remissibilia* (2.12, 14, 15) and those
which are *irremissibilia* (2.12, 14, 15; 16.5; 18.18) or *inconcessibilia* (9.20).
In terms of their gravity he describes some sins as *maxima* (1.19 *bis*;
13.6), *capitalia* (9.20; 21.14), *mortalia* (3.3; 19.28; 21.2), *exitiosa* (19.25),
maiora (18.18) and *gravia* (19.25). Others are *mediocria* (7.20), *modica*
(1.19 *bis*; 13.6) and *leviora* (18.17).

[36] *Post fidem.* Other examples of *post* in brachylogy may be found
in Hoppe I 141 and Waltzing, *op. cit.* 348. For *post fidem*, cf. Teeuwen
I 30 and 91 f.

[37] *Infamantes paracletum disciplinae enormitate* may also mean, 'at the
risk of bringing the Paraclete into disrepute because of the severity of
His discipline.' For the Montanist doctrine on second marriage see
especially Tertullian's treatise *De monogamia*.

[38] *Limitem liminis . . . figimus.* Tertullian is speaking here as a Montanist and not as an orthodox Christian. The Montanists condemned to
perpetual excommunication, without distinction, those Christians who
committed adultery and fornication, as well as those who contracted
a second marriage after the death of husband or wife. For the *limen
ecclesiae* as a place of penance see the notes on *De paen.* 7.10.

[39] The heartless cruelty of this sentence is unparalleled, even in a
work conspicuous for intolerance and severity. Tertullian sums up in
one brief, shocking declaration the spirit and theme of his whole
treatise: Montanists require public penance of those who have contracted second marriage and who have committed sins of fornication
and adultery. In such cases, however, they refuse to grant the pardon
and peace with which exomologesis was ordinarily terminated by the

Church. For Tertullian's use of the word *pax* in the sense of ecclesiastical forgiveness of sins, see Teeuwen I 62–64.

40 The combination *misericors et miserator* occurs six times in the Bible: Ps. 85.15; 102.8; 110.4; 111.4; 144.8; James 5.11.

41 Cf. Exod. 34.6 f.; Joel 2.13.

42 Osee 6.6; Mich. 6.6–8; Matt. 9.13 and 12.7.

43 Ezech. 18.23; 33.11. In *De res. mort.* 9, *Adv. Marc.* 2.13 and 4.10, *De paen.* 4.2 these texts are cited to prove the mercy of God. Tertullian studies them as difficulties against the Montanist thesis in *De pud.* 10.8, 18.12 and 22.12.

44 1 Tim. 4.10. The implication of the text, as here cited, is that forgiveness should be granted especially to the baptized, if they should fall into sin. Tertullian has *salutificator*, the Vulgate *salvator*; compare *De ieiun.* 6, *De res. mort.* 47, *Adv Marc.* 5.15. For *salutificator* as *salutis artifex* (*De carne Christi* 14) see Dölger's interesting note, 'Christus salutificator,' AC 6 (1950) 267–71; cf. also H. Rönsch, *Das Neue Testament Tertullians* (Leipzig 1871) 709 and Teeuwen I 18.

45 Luke 6.36; Matt. 5.7, 9. The word *pacifici* is used by Tertullian with an allusion to the *pax* which was given to the sinner when he was restored to communion with the Church.

46 Col. 3.13; Eph. 4.32.

47 Matt. 7.1; Luke 6.37; compare Rom. 2.1.

48 Rom. 14.4. The same text is quoted in *De ieiun.* 15 against Catholics who condemn Montanist xerophagies.

49 Luke 6.37.

50 Following Rauschen's construction of the text. Dekkers and most other editors read the sentence as a rhetorical question. For *et nos et contrariis*, cf. Thörnell, *op. cit.* 2.81.

51 The texts to be cited will prove the strictness of God's justice. They will, at the same time, be such as prompt us to lead virtuous lives. For the legal term *provocare*, cf. Beck, *op. cit.* 88 f.

52 Cf. Job 5.18; Deut. 32.39.

53 Isa. 45.7.

54 Jer. 14.11 f.

55 *Ibid.* 11.14, but with notable verbal variations from the Vulgate.

56 *Ibid.* 7.16.

57 *Zelotes*; cf. Exod. 20.5; 34.14. Compare the Septuagint text in Deut. 4.24; 5.9; 6.15; Jos. 24.19; Nah. 1.2.

58 Gal. 6.7. Tertullian quotes *qui naso non deridetur*, a rather literal version of the Greek θεὸς οὐ μυκτηρίζεται. The Vulgate has, simply, *Deus non irridetur*.

59 Isa. 42.14, but very free.

⁶⁰ Ps. 96.3.

⁶¹ Matt. 10.28.

⁶² Matt. 7.2.

⁶³ *Docere* may mean not only 'to teach how to do a thing,' but 'to teach that it should be done.' Possibly this second sense is to be preferred in the context. Tertullian wishes to say that if men judge as they should, then God will judge them favorably because of their zeal in safeguarding the observance of His law.

⁶⁴ 1 Cor. 5.5. The specific sin to which St. Paul refers was a sin of incest. The Greek word (*ibid.* 5.1) is πορνεία. The Vulgate regularly translates πορνεία as *fornicatio*; the only exception in the New Testament is Apoc. 19.2, where we find *prostitutio*. Tertullian translates πορνεία as *stuprum* (*Ad ux.* 2.2, with a reference to Matt. 5.32 and 19.9), or *fornicatio* (in addition to the present passage, cf. *De pud.* 15.10, 16.6–8, 17.2, 19.2, quoting respectively, 2 Cor. 12.21; 1 Cor. 6.13, 18; 1 Thess. 4.3; Apoc. 2.21), or *moechia* (*De pud.* 16.17, quoting Matt. 5.32), and *adulterium* (*Adv. Marc.* 4.34, quoting Matt. 5.32). See H. von Soden, *Das lateinische Neue Testament in Africa zur Zeit Cyprians* (TU 3.3, Leipzig 1909) 73 f. for the use of *adulterium, fornicatio* and *moechia* in Cyprian's Bible text. On Tertullian's interpretation of Matt. 5.32, cf. J. Bonsirven, *Le divorce dans le Nouveau Testament* (Paris 1948) 65–68.

⁶⁵ 1 Cor. 6.1.

⁶⁶ *Ibid.* 5.12. *Enim*, introducing this quotation, is a simple affirmative particle, without causal or conclusive significance. It is often used by Tertullian to open a discussion or, as here, in place of *enimvero*; cf. Waltzing, *op. cit.* 100. The point seems to be that St. Paul, in denying that he judges pagans, affirms implicitly that he does judge Christians. The Church, then, will be derelict in her duty if she does not follow his example and pass a condemnatory judgement on her members when they have violated God's law.

⁶⁷ Cf. Matt. 6.14; Luke 6.37.

⁶⁸ In the Lord's Prayer we ask that God forgive us our trespasses as we forgive those who trespass against us. When we forgive, we grant pardon to men for sins committed against men, not for sins committed against God. Accordingly, when the Church forgives sins after exomologesis, this forgiveness must be restricted to sins committed against men and must not be extended to include the forgiveness of sins committed against God. The distinction between sins committed against men and those committed against God is found, also, below, 21.15. Harnack, *History of Dogma* 2.113, influenced, possibly, by such texts as these, has asserted that the Church forgave violations of her own laws, but not violations of the laws of God. This is refuted by P.

Batiffol, *Études d'histoire et de théologie positive* (7me ed. Paris 1926) 77 f.
and D'Alès I 487. It should be noted, however, that Harnack, *ibid.* n. 1,
confesses himself unable to clarify the concept of a 'sin committed
against God, as we find it in Tertullian, Cyprian and other Fathers.'
The sense in which, according to the mind of Tertullian, the three
capital sins of adultery, murder and apostasy are 'sins against God' is
well explained in D'Alès III 208–11 and Poschmann I 336 ff., 411 ff.
Idolatry as a sin against God is self-explanatory; *impurity* is a violation of
God's temple, sanctified by Baptism; men were created according to
God's image, and when life is taken in *murder* this image is wantonly
destroyed. For the identification of the 'sin against God' with the sin
of idolatry or apostasy (during the centuries of persecution the two
sins were commonly regarded as two aspects of the same offense, since
one formally apostatized by offering incense to the gods), see D'Alès,
La théologie de saint Cyprien 283–88.

⁶⁹ This figure is found, also, in *Adv. Marc.* 4.4; *Adv. Jud.* 1; *De res.
mort.* 34. In *De cor.* 3 Tertullian speaks of such rival appeals to Scripture
as 'drawing a saw to and fro through the same cut.'

⁷⁰ *Terminus* is here taken as the equivalent of *sententia*; compare *De
pud.* 13.19, *terminus domini*, i.e. the definite decision of the Lord. Thus
Tertullian says that the authority of Scripture *in suis terminis* (i.e.
sententiis, in what it teaches and requires) will be preserved etc. Thelwall's 'within its own limits' and De Labriolle's 'dans ses propres
limites' are literally correct, but it is not clear just what the 'authority
of Scripture in its own limits or sphere' would mean in this context.

⁷¹ The text is not certain; the translation follows the reading *si et*,
with Ursinus, Kroymann and Rauschen.

⁷² The words *suis condicionibus determinetur* are difficult, and the
interpretation given here is adopted with considerable hesitancy. Cf.
below, 2.15: *Secundum . . . differentiam delictorum paenitentiae condicio . . .
discriminatur.* This suggests that the phrase *condicio paenitentiae* refers to
the 'condition' or 'form' of penance as it is terminated or not by
ecclesiastical absolution, rather than to the 'conditions' upon which it
is granted. The first 'form' or penance is that which is done for capital
sins; in this case exomologesis is required but God alone grants
forgiveness. The second 'form' is that which is done for lesser sins;
here exomologesis is also required but in this case the bishop grants
absolution.

⁷³ In this and the following sentence *causa* appears to combine three
meanings: (a) that of a 'case' in which penance is done; (b) an occasion when it is done; (c) the reason why it is done.

⁷⁴ *In duos exitus.* The word *exitus* seems strange here; we would

expect something like *genera* or *species*. The sense, however, is plain. *Exitus* looks to the final outcome of sin; in some cases sin ends in forgiveness, in others it does not.

[75] Throughout the rest of the treatise Tertullian attempts to justify this classification of sins as remissible and irremissible; see Poschmann I 303–320. For various views on the relationship of Tertullian's remissible and irremissible sins to the modern distinction between venial and mortal sin, see Motry, *op. cit.* 75–100. There is considerable dispute as to the exact meaning of the words *capitalia, mortalia* and *irremissibilia* in the writings of Tertullian. The terms are not demonstrably convertible, yet they are all used to designate serious sin. When Tertullian says that certain sins are irremissible he means, as has been noted above, that they are irremissible by the Church, not that they are irremissible by God. It must be emphasized that the expression 'irremissible sin' is not found in the *De paenitentia.*

[76] *Dispungit.* In post-Augustan mercantile language *dispungere* was used to describe the cancellation of a debt or the settling of an account. The word occurs twenty-three times in Tertullian's works. Three meanings may be distinguished: (a) to bring to a close; to complete; (b) to examine; (c) to pay for or to recompense; cf. Waszink, *op. cit.* 394 and Hoppe I 130. The third meaning is the one intended here; hence the translation might be, 'absolves from' or 'cancels the debt of every sin.' Compare *expungere,* above *De paen.* note 162.—It may be argued from these words that in Christian antiquity ecclesiastical absolution was thought of as forgiving sins *coram Deo* and not exclusively *coram ecclesia,* since *venia* (episcopal pardon after *castigatio*) is described as having the same effect (*dispungit*) in cancelling the debt of remissible sin as *poena* (public penance followed by divine though not ecclesiastical forgiveness) has in cancelling the debt of irremissible sins.

[77] *Venia ex castigatione, poena ex damnatione.* According to the well-known thesis of P. Galtier, private penance existed in the early Church in the sense that lesser sins were forgiven by ecclesiastical authority without requiring the enrollment of the sinner in the ranks of the public penitents. The present passage from the *De pudicitia* is adduced in support of this thesis; cf. Galtier I 245–48 and, for a more complete treatment, II 272–83. Galtier argues that *castigatio* is a lesser form of ecclesiastical punishment, distinguished from the extreme form of the public penance. It consisted, probably, in the imposition of some relatively light penalties such as moderate fasting, with brief abstention from communion, accompanied by official reprimands, more or less severe. *Castigatio,* then, is private penance, distinguished from *poena,* which is the public penance exacted for capital crimes. *Castigatio,* like

correptio, is primarily medicinal, looking to the amendment of the sinner; *poena* is a retributive penalty, inflicted in the interest of justice. This distinction between *castigatio* and *poena* is illustrated by the contrast between *castigationes* and *censura* in *Apol.* 39.4, and by the penance imposed upon Marcion and Valentinus who are said to have been 'more than once expelled from the Church;' *De praesc. haer.* 30. The repeated reconciliations which this implies point to the existence of an ecclesiastical penalty and pardon distinct from the public penance which, as all admit, could be administered only once. Both Catholics and Montanists, then, distinguish two types of ecclesiastical penitence: *castigatio*, private penance (in Galtier's sense of the term) for lesser sins and *poena*, public penance for serious sins. They agree that *venia* may be given after *castigatio*; they disagree in that Catholics say episcopal pardon may be granted after *poena* for any sin whatever, whereas Montanists insist that public penance for irremissible sins can win a *dispunctio delicti* from God but not from the Church.

In this interpretation, therefore, *damnatio* means an ecclesiastical condemnation to public penance, without hope of pardon from the Church; *poena* is the public penance itself; *venia* is episcopal absolution; and *castigatio* is the lesser, private ecclesiastical penance. *Damnare* is used, occasionally, for *claudere* or *obstruere*, TLL 5.20, a meaning which suggests that the *poena ex damnatione* is that which is imposed in virtue of the Church's power to retain sins. Tertullian's thought may then be paraphrased as follows. Ecclesiastical penance must be done for sin, and yet not all sins are remitted by the Church after penance. Those which are remissible are subject to lesser penalties (*castigatio*); those which are irremissible are subject to the punishment of permanent excommunication (*damnatio*). The debt of sin is cancelled either by ecclesiastical absolution (*venia*) after correction (*castigatio*), or by God Himself, after the sinner has lived out the life of penance (*poena*) to which he was condemned by the Church. This interpretation remains controversial and is opposed by Poschmann I 309, Mortimer, *op. cit.* 16-18, and Grotz, *op. cit.* 354. Against Mortimer, cf. G. Joyce, 'Private Penance in the Early Church,' JTS 42 (1941) 18-42 and P. Galtier, 'Comment on écarte la pénitence privée,' *Gregorianum* 21 (1940) 183-202.

[78] This is an allusion to the contrasting texts cited earlier in the chapter. The antithesis of *dimittere* and *retinere* may have been suggested by John 20.23: *quorum remiseritis peccata, remittuntur eis: et quorum retinueritis, retenta sunt.* For the exegesis of this text in patristic literature, cf. H. Bruders, 'Matt. 16.19; 18.18 und Jo. 20.22-3 in frühchristlicher Auslegung,' ZKT 34 (1910) 659-77.

[79] I John 5.16, cited also, below 19.27. Both Montanists and Nova-tians constantly appealed to this verse in order to justify their distinction between remissible and irremissible sins. Orthodox writers, however, interpreted the *peccatum ad mortem* as one which separated the sinner from Christ. Life is had through union with Him; a sin which destroys this union and this life is a 'mortal' sin. A Christian who has committed a *peccatum ad mortem* is separated from the body of Christ by excommunication. This is not to say, however, that it is impossible for him to be restored to life in Christ after the performance of public penance. Hence a 'mortal' sin, considered etymologically, is not necessarily one which means the eternal death of the soul; cf. Galtier I 175 f. and A. Brooke, *A Critical and Exegetical Commentary on the Johannine Epistles* (repr. from ed. of 1912, Edinburgh 1948) 145–48.

[80] For this meaning of *condicio*, see above, note 72.

[81] Other instances of the distributive sense of *omnis* in *De pudicitia* are given in Galtier I 114. Tertullian's opponents argue that every form (*condicio*) of penance is good, whether it be for graver or lesser sins. Moreover every form of penance is obligatory. But if there were any form of penance without pardon, it would be useless and could not be made a matter of obligation. Hence no such form may be admitted.

[82] Rauschen considers this last sentence 'repetitious, superfluous and inept,' and he has bracketed it in his text. It is interesting to compare the argument which Tertullian attributes to the Catholics of his day with an argument which Cyprian used less than fifty years later in combating the heresy of Novatian. Both Montanists and Novatians restricted the Church's power to pardon grave sins, the Montanists being particularly concerned with sins of the flesh, the Novatians, at least during the early years of the heresy, with the sin of apostasy. Cyprian insists that penance without ecclesiastical pardon is inconsistent with the mercy of God; to exact public penance and then refuse absolution is to drive men to despair and lead them to abandon penance itself; cf. *Epist.* 55.17, 28. For Cyprian's teaching on penance, cf. D'Alès, *La théologie de saint Cyprien* 272–302; Poschmann I 368–424 and the comments of Quasten, *op. cit.* 2.380 f.—It appears from this that the Catholic party granted pardon to all serious sins, including sins of murder and apostasy. Tertullian says his opponents argue that penance would be done in vain, if it were not followed by pardon; but they certainly required that it be done for murder and apostasy; therefore we must suppose that, at some time, perhaps only at the hour of death, they granted pardon to these sins also, lest the penance required for them be done in vain.

[83] This sentence and its context point up sharply the issue between

Catholics and Montanists. Its significance is ably discussed by J. Stufler, 'Zur Kontroverse über das Indulgenzedikt des Papstes Kallistus,' ZKT 32 (1908) 9 f.; cf., also, D'Alès III 176 ff. Tertullian admits that the Church has a power to forgive sin. He rejects as a usurpation, however, the claim that this power may be used in favor of those who have committed adultery. The argument of his opponents is a logical one (*merito opponunt*), on the assumption that they actually have the power over this sin which they claim. If this power is theirs and if it is *not* exercised after exomologesis, then, truly, penance remains without fruit. But it is without fruit only for those who suppose that there is no forgiveness to be had except from men. Tertullian's words imply that the Church claimed not only a power to forgive grave sins but also a kind of monopoly in their forgiveness, as though God had contracted not to pardon sinners if the Church did not. That precisely this claim was made by orthodox writers of Christian antiquity may be seen in the *catena* of patristic texts regularly cited by theologians in developing the argument from tradition for the necessity of the sacrament of Penance; cf. Galtier I 289–99; Doronzo, *op. cit.* 2.382–402. The words *extra ecclesiam nulla salus* were applied by the Fathers just as naturally to the excommunicated sinner who refused exomologesis as they were to the pagan who refused Baptism.

Père Galtier considers that the words *huius quoque paenitentiae* suggest the existence of two types of penance in the Church, one private and the other public; for the argument, see Galtier II 275 f. This interpretation is attacked by Mortimer, *op. cit.* 18 f. One feels that the words are best taken as referring to the form (*condicio*) or type of penance which, in the Montanist discipline, is without ecclesiastical absolution.

[84] Tertullian's language throughout this chapter indicates his belief, even as a Montanist, that when pardon is legitimately granted by the Church, it effects forgiveness of sins *coram Deo* and not merely *coram ecclesia*. If ecclesiastical pardon were effective merely in reconciling the sinner to the Church, it would be difficult to explain why Catholics assert that when ecclesiastical pardon is refused to a sinner, the fruit of penance, i.e. God's forgiveness, is lost. It would also be difficult to understand why Montanists protest against ecclesiastical pardon for *peccata gravia*, if they did not believe that God ratifies the Church's sentence when it is legitimately pronounced. Since the Church is said to usurp the power of God in forgiving *peccata gravia*, she claims a power which belongs to Him alone, that is, a power to forgive such sins *secundum reatum culpae* and not merely *secundum reatum poenae ecclesiasticae*. This argument is further developed in Galtier I 116 f. and II 30–33.

[85] A succinct statement of the Montanist thesis, with a possible allusion to Mark 2.7 and Luke 5.22: *Quis dimittit peccata nisi solus deus?*— The expression 'mortal sin' is found for the first time in Tertullian, and it occurs only in *De pud.* 3.3, 19.28, 21.2; see the detailed study in Motry, *op. cit.* 101–23. It was suggested to him, quite probably, by the *peccatum ad mortem* of 1 John 5.16 to which he alluded in the preceding chapter. Thus the familiar phrase 'mortal sin' was coined by Tertullian in the heat of controversy to express the Montanist interpretation of St. John's 'sin unto death.' To him it meant a sin which excluded a Christian from communion with the Church for life and which could be forgiven by God alone; cf. above, *De pud.* note 79. *Mortalis* is also a natural substitute for *capitalis*, the ordinary term employed in legal language to describe an offense which is punished by death; Teeuwen I 71. It has already been noted, however, that, although *peccata capitalia* and *mortalia* are closely related, an examination of the passages in which these terms occur reveals that they are not always synonymous; Motry, *op. cit.* 85–100. In classical Latin *mortalis* means 'subject to death' or 'liable to die;' it does not mean 'causing death' or 'bringing death.' The concept of sin as a cause of physical or spiritual death is found in the Bible from Gen. 2.17 to Apoc. 20.14, yet nowhere in the Vulgate is sin referred to as *mortale*. Num. 18.22, however, has *peccatum mortiferum* and James 1.15, *peccatum vero cum consummatum fuerit generat mortem*.

[86] Other uses of *exorare* may be seen in *De paen.* 10.6; *De pud.* 13.7; 19.28. In *De pud.* 19.25 f. Tertullian says that Christ is an *exorator patris* for those guilty of lesser sins, but not for Christians who have committed major crimes.

[87] *Communicare* here means 'to be joined in membership with' (*pacem habere cum*), rather than 'to receive the Eucharist.' On the close relationship between these two meanings of the word see F. Dölger, 'Der Ausschluss der Besessenen von Oblation und Kommunion nach der Synode von Elvira,' AC 4 (1934) 111 f. The thought which is conveyed in both cases by the word 'communion' has been given by Isidore of Pelusium, *Epist.* 1.228, who says that it is so called because *nobis coniunctionem cum Deo conciliat, nosque regni ipsius consortes ac participes reddit.*

[88] The public penance alluded to in this chapter is clearly identified with the exomologesis which Tertullian described in the *De paenitentia*; see, for example, cc. 7, 9, 10 and 12. For penance *in limine ecclesiae*, cf. *De paen.* notes 120, 121 and the literature there cited.

[89] Compare *De paen.* 9.4.—*Compassio* is a coinage of Tertullian's; cf. F. Dölger, 'Bewertung von Mitleid und Barmherzigkeit bei Tertullianus,' AC 5 (1936) 271.

[90] J. Stufler feels that there are passages in the *De pudicitia* in which Tertullian speaks as though God Himself will not pardon the 'irremissible' sins, while there are others where he clearly says that God alone will do so. The apparent contradiction disappears, he believes, if, in the light of the present sentence, we suppose that the former passages refer to forgiveness by God in this life and the latter to forgiveness in the next; cf. 'Zur Kontroverse über das Indulgenzedikt des Papstes Kallistus,' ZKT 32 (1908) 12. See, also, on the interpretation of this sentence, the conflicting views of G. Esser, 'Nochmals das Indulgenzedikt des Papstes Kallistus und die Bussschriften Tertullians,' *Der Katholik* 2 (1907) 194, De Labriolle, *La crise montaniste* 438 and Rauschen, *Eucharist and Penance* 161 f.—Père Galtier 116 f., is of the opinion that Tertullian's language in this sentence gives further evidence that his Catholic opponents claimed a power to reconcile the sinner to God and not merely to the Church. After the performance of exomologesis, 'irremissible' sin is pardoned by God Himself, at least in the next life. Since it is this same 'harvest of peace' which Catholics have 'usurped' and which they claim to 'reap' even in this life, it would appear that they are claiming a power to forgive sins *in foro interno*, restoring to the sinner that *pax divina* which is found in friendship with God, along with the *pax humana* which is found in communion with the Church.

[91] Compare *De monog.* 15, where Tertullian defends himself against the charge that his condemnation of second marriage is harsh and heretical.

[92] The distinction between *paenitentia* and *disciplina* is not sharply drawn, but Tertullian seems to mean that the former is the actual performance of exomologesis, while the latter is the regulation which requires that the Church refuse pardon after public penance to those who have committed serious sins. The performance of penance without hope of pardon in this life will be all the more efficacious in the sight of God since the sinner places his trust in Him alone and does not vainly imagine that ecclesiastical forgiveness is capable of absolving him from the guilt of major crimes. At the same time, the discipline which refuses ecclesiastical absolution for capital sins is of advantage to the sinner in that it requires him to throw himself on the mercy of God and to reject the presumptuous notion that there is any other way in which he can be saved. In this way the penance which the Montanists practice and the discipline which they preach give special honor and glory to God.

[93] The *census delictorum ipsorum* is that which was given in chapter 2, where sins were distinguished as remissible or irremissible. At the close of this chapter Tertullian asked to which of these classes the sins of

fornication and adultery belong. He now returns to this question, but before taking up in detail his proof that sins of adultery and fornication are irremissible (chapters 5 to 20) he endeavors to explain, in the present chapter, just how he will understand these terms throughout the treatise. Sins of the flesh are irremissible, but what sins are to be classified as sins of the flesh? It appears, from the present chapter, that Tertullian is thinking primarily, if not exclusively, of any and all sexual intercourse outside of marriage.—The 'remissible' sins referred to in chapters 2 and 3 are here spoken of as sins which 'receive pardon from men.' The expression furnishes further evidence of Tertullian's belief, even as a Montanist, that the Church in certain cases exercises a legitimate power to cancel the debt of sin by an authoritative act of absolution.

94 It is not clear whether Tertullian alludes to Christian or Montanist usage. Possibly we have here an early instance of the extension of the sixth commandment to include other sins of impurity besides the specific sin of adultery; cf. H. Noldin–A. Schmitt, *De sexto praecepto* (Innsbruck 1937) 1. It may be, too, that the identification of the terms adultery and fornication resulted from an inability on the part of early commentators to determine the exact sense of the word πορνεία in Matt. 5.32 and 19.9; cf. above, *De pud.* note 64.

95 *Fides* is the Christian religion, which has its own proper vocabulary, just as have philosophy, medicine, the law etc.

96 Or, with less probability, taking *omnis* in a distributive sense, the sentence might be translated: 'In each of our little works we follow accepted usage.'

97 *Elogium*; for the technical meaning of this word in Roman law, cf. Beck, *op. cit.* 126 and Waltzing, *op. cit.* 26.

98 Other examples of the causal sense of *dum* in brachylogy are given by Waltzing, *op. cit.* 307.—*Vidua*, contrasted with *nupta* (*nuptam alienam an viduam quis incurset*), seems to mean 'single' rather than 'widow' or 'widowed.' Ciacconius has deleted *alienam*; Rauschen and Kellner-Esser were tempted to do so. The phrase, however, may be taken simply as a pleonasm for 'married woman.'—Tertullian's language throughout this chapter shows that he recognizes a theoretical distinction between adultery and fornication but considers that, practically, the abuse of sex is no worse in the one case than in the other; compare *De exhort. cast.* 9 and *De monog.* 9.

99 The interpretation of this sentence must be left a matter of conjecture. For *turribus* (the *editio princeps* of Mesnartius), Ciacconius reads *curribus*; Preuschen, De Labriolle and Dekkers, *triviis*; von Hartel, *toris*; *ruribus* is suggested by Weymann. Rauschen considers *in*

turribus the equivalent of *in palatiis*; Kellner translates, 'unter der Stadtmauer' and Thelwall, simply, 'in towers.' There is an interesting parallel in *Apol.* 23.3; cf. Waltzing, *op. cit.* 170. Possibly Tertullian merely wishes to contrast a place which is public with one which is private, and to insist that the sin is the same whether committed in a location where we might ordinarily expect it or one where it would be less likely to occur. This idea would then be continued in the example which follows: *omne homicidium et extra silvam latrocinium est.*

[100] *Latrocinium*, in addition to its specific meaning of 'robbery' has also a generic sense of villainy or criminality, often with the implication of secrecy. The word is derived from λάτρις, a 'hired servant' or 'mercenary soldier,' but Isidore of Seville reflects what must have been a popular notion even before his day, when he writes: *Latro, dictus a latendo* (*Etymol.* 10.159). If the specific meaning of *latrocinium* is taken here, we may suppose that 'every murder is robbery' in the sense that it takes from a man his dearest possession, life itself; cf. *De an.* 25.5, where Tertullian speaks of the murder (*iugulatio*) of a child in its mother's womb as a *caecum latrocinium*. It may be, however, that in the legal language of the day a technical sense attached to the word *latrocinium* which now escapes us.

[101] *Aliter quam nuptus utitur.* Tertullian uses the word *nubere* to designate marriage by either the man or the woman.—On the absolute use of *utor*, cf. Waszink, *op. cit.* 179. Apparently Tertullian is thinking throughout this chapter of sins of deed, rather than of internal sins of thought and desire.

[102] Or, 'the same thing as adultery and fornication;' *iuxta moechiam et fornicationem iudicari*; compare *De monog.* 15: *Secundas nuptias . . . iuxta adulterium judicamus.*—*Penes nos*, in the present passage, may mean that this is a view peculiar to Montanists, rather than one which is common to all Christians. For further details on the Church's role in Christian marriage, cf. *Ad ux.* 2.2, 8 and *De monog.* 11. This subject has been studied by J. Köhne, 'Die kirchliche Eheschliessungsformen in der Zeit Tertullians,' TG 23 (1931) 645–54.

[103] *Inde consertae*, contracted, that is, as a result of the crime of adultery or fornication. The commission of such sins will often be followed by a marriage between the guilty partners, who attempt in this way to cloak their guilt. Tertullian's language is cryptic but he seems to be saying that among the sins for which penance must be done are sins of fornication and adultery, even though the guilty partners have married after their sin.

[104] *Non modo limine, verum omni ecclesiae tecto.* They are excluded not only from the threshold of the church but from the vestibule itself;

that is to say, they are not only excluded from absolution, but they are not even permitted to do public penance *in vestibulo*. Tertullian contrasts the threshold of the church with the *vestibulum* in front of it. This *vestibulum*, although open to the sky, was considered a part of the church, and penitents who were admitted to it enjoyed, to some extent, 'the shelter of the church.' Accordingly, Tertullian here states that sinners guilty of adultery and fornication are admitted to exomologesis but not to absolution, they are permitted to do penance *in vestibulo*, but the *ianua ignoscentiae* (*De paen.* 7) is not opened to them. Those, however, who have been guilty of unnatural vice are not even admitted *ad vestibulum*; that is to say, they are not even permitted to take their place in the ranks of those penitents who perform an exomologesis not terminated by ecclesiastical absolution. Cf. D'Alès III 414 and Poschmann I 306.

[105] It is difficult to say just which sins of the flesh Tertullian regards as *ultra iura naturae*, although, with the possible exception of masturbation, he would certainly include those which moralists today describe in the same phrase; cf. Motry, *op. cit.* 118–21. D'Alès, III 370, sees here a parallel to canon 17 of the Council of Ancyra, where certain sinners guilty of bestiality were required to do penance among the *hiemantes*. The interpretation of this canon, however, remains controversial, and, in any event, it is not clear that the sinners whom Tertullian separates *ab omni tecto ecclesiae* are to be thought of as forming a distinct class of penitents like the *hiemantes* or *flentes*; cf. C. Hefele–H. Leclercq, *Histoire des conciles* (Paris 1907) 1/1. 318–20.

[106] The *prima lex* given by Moses in the Decalogue is distinguished from the *secunda lex* given by Christ in the New Testament. Rigault suggests that the *prima lex dei* may be understood, simply, as that which God gave to men at the beginning of the world. Thus the sentence could be translated, 'From the very beginning, God's law is ready to hand to show us how serious etc.'—The phrase *secundum opus criminis* is taken with the words it follows rather than with those it precedes.— From this point to the end of the treatise Tertullian attempts to prove his thesis by an appeal, in order, to the teaching of the Old Testament (cc. 5–6), the teaching of the Gospel (cc. 7–11) and, finally, the teaching of other New Testament authorities, especially St. Paul (cc. 12–20). Compare the construction of *De monog.* 4–14.

[107] Exod. 20.14.

[108] 'Chastity and sanctity of the spirit' have reference to man's fidelity to God and consecration to Him alone. Just as idolatry is prohibited because it is a violation of the spiritual integrity or oneness which should exist between God and man, so adultery is prohibited

because it is a violation of the fidelity and 'oneness in flesh' which is demanded of men and women by monogamous marriage; cf. *De monog.* 4.

[109] The translation follows Thörnell's punctuation of the text and his interpretation of the words *nam et*; cf. *op. cit.* 2.88 f.

[110] The antitheses are between *sorte et serie, damnatione et dispositione.*

[111] Exod. 20.13; Deut. 5.17 f. Tertullian has reversed the familiar order of these two commandments as we know it from the Vulgate, and D'Alès III 198 suggests that the reversal may be deliberate in the interest of his argument. It should be noted, however, that the Septuagint, regularly reflected in Tertullian's quotations from the Old Testament, lists adultery before murder in both Exodus and Deuteronomy; cf. also Mark 10.19; Luke 18.20 (Greek text); Rom. 13.9. On the other hand, it is interesting that in *Adv. Marc.* 2.17, where the order is of no importance to his argument, Tertullian cites the commandments as *Non occides. Non adulterabis.*—This is the first allusion in Christian literature to the well-known canonical triad of idolatry (apostasy), adultery and murder. It is clear from the entire passage that Tertullian links the three together as *principalia delicta* because of their juxtaposition at the beginning of the Decalogue. He was also influenced in this, no doubt, by his understanding of the Apostolic Ordinance promulgated at the Council of Jerusalem (Acts 15.29); cf. below, *De pud.* 12.4. Rauschen, *Eucharist and Penance* 191, has noted that these three sins are frequently grouped together in the Rabbinic literature. The designation of these sins as 'irremissible' is due, of course, to Montanist influences; cf. K. Adam, *Der Kirchenbegriff Tertullians* (Paderborn 1907) 86 and the comparative study of all pertinent passages in the *De pudicitia* given by D'Alès III 197–208. That this trilogy does not exhaust the list of crimes which Tertullian regards as capital may be seen from *Adv. Marc.* 4.9 and *De pud.* 19.25; cf. Poschmann III 24 f.

[112] The expressions are: *de loco modum, de ordine statum, de confinio meritum.*

[113] *Suggestus.* On the various senses of this word in Tertullian cf. A. Englebrecht, *Neue lexikalische und semasiologische Beiträge aus Tertullian.* (Wiener Studien 28, 1906) 50–58.

[114] The *fructus paenitentiae* is *venia*; cf. *De pud.* 3.3 and compare Cyprian, *Epist.* 55.17, 29, and Vigilius, *Epist. ad Profuturum* 3. Evidence of the importance which Tertullian attaches to this feature of penitence is furnished by the fact that he uses the word *venia* six times in the *De paenitentia* and some forty-seven times in the *De pudicitia.*

[115] *Cuneus*; cf. TLL 4.1403–06.

[116] *Ab illa enim tria unitamur* (Rauschen), but the reading is uncertain.

Dekkers, following the *Codex Ottobonianus*, gives *ab idololatria metiamur*.

[117] The words of Scripture have, as it were, glued (*glutina nostra sunt*) these three sins together. If *ipsa* is taken as referring to Scripture, the sentence may mean that the sacred text is itself corrupted and destroyed when the three sins are separated.

[118] The debauchery which often accompanied worship of the gods is mentioned by pagan and Christian authors alike. Cf. *Apol.* 15.7, where Tertullian writes: *adiciam in templis adulteria componi, inter aras lenocinia tractari, in ipsis plerumque aedituorum et sacerdotum tabernaculis, sub isdem vittis et apicibus et purpuris, thure flagrante, libidinem expungi*; and Minucius Felix, *Oct.* 25.11: *Ubi autem magis quam a sacerdotibus inter aras et delubra conducuntur stupra, tractantur lenocinia, adulteria meditantur? Frequentius denique in aedituorum cellulis quam in ipsis lupanaribus flagrans libido defungitur*; compare, also, Juvenal, *Sat.* 6.314-45 and 9.24.

[119] Tertullian is thinking of plays in which the plot requires that murder be represented as serving the purposes of adultery. The *Agamemnon* suggests itself as a typical example of what he has in mind. Compare *De spec.* 17, where he speaks of the stage as being 'at once lustful and bloody.' A popular expression of this same close connection between murder and lust is found in the Roman maxim that every adulteress is a potential poisoner.—The crime of infanticide had assumed frightful proportions among the Romans in the second and third centuries, and Tertullian refers to it repeatedly; cf. *Ad nat.* 1.15; *Apol.* 9.6-8; *De virg. vel.* 14; *De an.* 25; *De exhort. cast.* 12; *De monog.* 16 (*carnifices obstetrices*). See F. Dölger, 'Das Lebensrecht des ungeborenen Kindes und die Fruchtabtreibung in der Bewertung der heidnischen und christlichen Antike,' AC 4 (1934) 1-61, especially the essay, 'Die Beseelung des Embryo und die Fruchtabtreibung in der Beurteilung Tertullians,' 32-37. The prevalence of abortion as a means of preventing the birth of children conceived in fornication or adultery is mentioned by Clement of Alexandria, *Paed.* 2.10 and Soranus, *Gynaeciorum* 1.19.60. St. Jerome, *Epist.* 123.4, makes the curious statement that St. Paul wishes young women to marry and bear children (1 Tim. 5.4) *ne metu partus ex adulterio filios necare cogantur*.

[120] An allusion to sin as the death of the soul; cf. above, *De pud.* note 85.

[121] *Adsistere* is either 'to stand by the door of the church' or, simply, 'to present oneself for consideration.' We might then translate, 'See the idolater, see the murderer, and see between them both the adulterer.' If the sins themselves do not speak of their close connection with adultery, then we may look at the sinners themselves who have

committed them, as they perform their public penance.—In this context *sedere* must mean simply 'to be present' or 'to remain' in a place, not 'to be seated' there. The *officium paenitentiae* is the ritual of obligatory, public penance described here and in the *De paenitentia*. For the use of *de*, 'according to' or 'in conformity with,' cf. Hoppe I 33.

122 Compare the description of exomologesis in *De paen.* 9–11: *sacco et cinere incubare . . . ingemiscere, lacrimari et mugire . . . caris dei adgeniculari, omnibus fratribus legationes deprecationis suae iniungere* (9.4); *ad fratrum genua protendis* (10.6); *in asperitudine sacci et horrore cineris* (11.1); *ambitum obeunt* (11.4); compare, also, *De pud.* 13.7. Quite obviously in both the *De paenitentia* and *De pudicitia* Tertullian is describing identical forms of public penance. The only difference is that in the present treatise ecclesiastical pardon is refused to those guilty of capital crimes, whereas no such restriction is suggested in the *De paenitentia*.—The reference to the Church as 'mother' is the last of many such in Tertullian. It is interesting that even in his Montanist writings he continues this usage; cf. J. C. Plumpe, *Mater ecclesia* (Washington 1943) 45–62.

123 Matt. 5.9. Tertullian's use of this text here and his allusion to it above, *De pud.* 2.1, suggest that it was one which his Catholic opponents appealed to in order to justify the milder discipline which they followed in granting absolution.

124 The Catholics must grant pardon to all three capital sins or follow the Montanist practice of refusing to pardon adultery also.

125 Most editors, including Dekkers, read this sentence as a question but Rauschen thinks it is to be taken rather as a statement of the Catholic practice which Tertullian condemns. Adultery is the *successor* of idolatry and the *antecessor* of murder in the sense explained earlier in this chapter; cf. notes 118 and 119.

126 Acts 10.34; Rom. 2.11; 1 Peter 1.17. Tertullian has *personae acceptatio*, the Vulgate regularly *personarum*.

127 The present passage furnishes one of the strongest arguments in support of the view that the early Church did not grant pardon for the sins of murder and apostasy until some time after the year 200 A.D. This question is treated in the Introduction, pp. 48–51.

128 *Plane*, ironically, for *sane*. See Thörnell, *op. cit.* 2.48 for Tertullian's use of the combination *plane, si* to indicate that, although a concession is made, a condition is attached which nullifies the concession. Apparently Tertullian here concedes that a matter about which he has no real doubt may still be debated on scriptural grounds. The condition which nullifies the concession is that his adversaries must prove from Scripture that adultery alone, and not murder and apostasy also, ought to be pardoned by the Church.

[129] The *exempla* and *praecepta caelestia* are those which are found in the Bible.

[130] The metaphor *ad hanc iam lineam dimicabit nostra congressio* is taken from the amphitheatre. In gladiatorial combats a line was drawn in the sand to limit the area in which an engagement was to take place. Numerous instances are given in Oehler's note to *Scorpiace* 4; to these may be added from St. Jerome, *Adv. Lucif.* 4.11; *Adv. Pelag.* 3.6; *Adv. Rufin.* 3.14.—*De pud.* 6.1 is cited by F. Diekamp–A. Hoffmann, *Theologiae dogmaticae manuale* (Paris 1946) 4.366, to prove that in the early Church other mortal sins besides those designated as *capitalia* were forgiven by ecclesiastical penance. This cannot be shown from the text. Tertullian demands scriptural evidence which authorizes his Catholic opponents to pardon adultery, while refusing to pardon murder and idolatry. His argument that if pardon is granted to adultery it should also be granted to murder and idolatry can hardly be quoted as proof that he allowed ecclesiastical absolution for mortal sins which were not *capitalia*, since (1) it is only *sub hypothesi* that he says the Church should pardon other sins, and (2) the 'other sins' to which he refers are capital sins of murder and idolatry, not mortal sins of lesser gravity.

[131] Compare Isa. 43.18 and Luke 9.62.

[132] This is probably suggested by Isa. 43.18, although neither the Vulgate nor the Septuagint has the equivalent of Tertullian's *transierunt*.

[133] Approximated in Jer. 4.3.

[134] Phil. 3.13.

[135] Matt. 11.13; Luke 16.16.

[136] *Status* means, literally, the 'condition' or 'situation' of the Law with respect to its binding force. As a technical legal term the *status* of a Roman citizen was the aggregate of rights which he possessed in the city and family. Tertullian suggests that the Law has a *status* which is different in the Old and the New Testament; it retains its rights in some respects but loses them in others. He asserts that when he appeals to the Law in his consideration of adultery, he is thinking of it as having the *status* or 'aggregate of rights' which it did not lose after the coming of Christ.

[137] Matt. 5.17.

[138] The contrast is between *opera* (Rom. 3.20; Gal. 2.16) and *disciplinae* (for the meaning here, cf. Morel, *op. cit.* 35). The 'burdens' of the Law are the *opera legis*; its 'remedies' are the moral precepts which help men to lead good lives.

[139] Cf. Gal. 2.4; 5.13.

[140] Ps. 1.2.

[141] Ps. 18.8 f., omitting *testimonium Domini fidele, sapientiam praestans parvulis.*

[142] Rom. 7.12, but quoted freely.

[143] Rom. 3.31.

[144] Matt. 5.27 f.

[145] Matt. 5.21 f., though Tertullian has garbled *racha* and *fatue, concilium* and *gehenna.*

[146] The words *vobis in sinu plaudent* are difficult. Precedents which 'favor you in the secrecy of your heart' seem to be those which favor a discipline that is 'according to your heart,' i.e. your desires.—*Opponentur,* in the apodosis of this sentence, is an instance of the future indicative used for a potential subjunctive; cf. Hoppe I 64 f. The construction is frequent in Tertullian.

[147] The text and interpretation of this sentence remain uncertain. The translation given here is based on a reading suggested by A. Kroymann, *Questiones Tertullianeae criticae* (Innsbruck 1893) 83.

[148] Another text which is used to show that it was not the practice of the African church at this time to pardon the sins of murder and apostasy. See, also, on the interpretation of this passage, Mortimer, *op. cit.* 11; D'Alès III 198 f. and 251.

[149] 3 Kings 21.27–9.

[150] 2 Kings 12.13.

[151] Gen. 19.33–5.

[152] Gen. 38.15–18.

[153] Osee 1.2; 3.1.

[154] In his treatises on marriage and remarriage Tertullian has occasion to discuss at length the problem presented by the polygamy of the patriarchs; cf. *Ad ux.* 1.2; *De exhort. cast.* 6; *De monog.* 6.

[155] *Repraesentati iudicii.* Compare Suetonius, *repraesentare tormenta poenasque, Claud.* 34; *iudicia repraesentata,* Quintilian 10.7.2. For other senses of *repraesentare* in Tertullian, see above, *De paen.* note 48.—D'Alès II 8 believes that this sentence suggests the judicial nature of ecclesiastical penance; cf. also below, 14.25, and a more satisfactory passage in *Apol.* 39.4. For other evidence in early Christian writers, see Doronzo, *op. cit.* 1.133 f.

[156] Num. 25.9. Tertullian has *una plaga,* which may also be translated 'in one plague;' cf. Num. 25.18.

[157] *Cum suo vitio,* an allusion to the *vitium originis* which the human race contracted in Adam. Compare *De ieiun.* 3 and, especially, *De test. an.* 3: *Homo a primordio circumventus, ut praeceptum dei excederet, et propterea in mortem datus, exinde totum genus de suo semine infectum suae etiam damnationis traducem fecit;* cf. the notes in W. Scholte, *Q.S.F.*

Tertulliani: *De testimonio animae* (Amsterdam 1934) 80 f., and Waszink's notes on *De an.* 39.4 and 40.1, *op. cit.* 446 f., 448 f. For Tertullian's teaching on original sin and its dependence on his doctrine of traducianism, see D'Alès I 40, 446 f., 448 f., and Roberts, *op. cit.* 160 ff., 248 ff.

[158] Gen. 3.6.

[159] Reading *inhaerebant usquequaque libidinum virus, iniectae sordes inhaerendi idoneae, quod nec ipsae adhuc aquae laverant.* The text is unsatisfactory and various reconstructions have been attempted; cf. M. Haguenin, 'Tertullien. *De pudicitia* 6.15,' RSR 2 (1911) 459 f. A. D'Alès, '*Tertulliania*,' RSR 27 (1937) 230 f. has proposed *non habentis idonee*, on the analogy of *rite non habeant, De bap.* 15 and *non a Christo habendo, De praesc. haer.* 37; i.e. the flesh was not what it should have been, since as yet Baptism did not exist to sanctify it. The interpretation given here owes most to a suggestion proposed by Esser in a lengthy note to Kellner's translation. Rigault, followed by Oehler (*ex lacte sordes*) and Rauschen (*lacteae sordes*), considered that the *libidinum virus* was a milky or viscous substance of some kind which Tertullian thought of as oozing from the fig leaves which Adam and Eve used in clothing themselves after their sin. This substance, *quasi venereae pruriginis virus, adhaesit pudendis ipsorum*, and it could not be washed away from the flesh 'because the waters themselves had not yet washed'; that is to say, they had not yet been sanctified as baptismal by Christ's own Baptism. This interpretation is rather elaborate and yet it may well be correct. Tertullian speaks of 'the contagion of concupiscence which is caused by fig leaves' in *De an.* 38.2, and numerous parallels to this from other early Christian writers are given by Waszink, *op. cit.* 436 f. See, too, H. Koch, 'Die Feigenblätter der Stammeltern bei Irenäus und bei Tertullian,' *Theologische Studien und Kritiken* 105 (1933) 39–50.

[160] The Virgin Mary. For the literature on Tertullian's Mariology, cf. Quasten, *op. cit.* 2.330. Tertullian teaches Mary's virginity *ante partum*, but denies it *in* and *post partum.*—For *resignare*, cf. Hoppe I 135, Rönsch, *op. cit.* 655 and compare above, *De paen.* note 66.

[161] John 1.14, given as *Sermo caro factus est.* Tertullian usually translates λόγος by *Sermo* (cf. Rönsch, *op. cit.*, especially 250–53), and he tells us that this was the current practice in Africa at the time he wrote; cf. *Adv. Prax.* 5, where he also expresses some dissatisfaction with the common usage, indicating that λόγος would be better translated by two words, *sermo et ratio*; compare *Apol.* 21.10 f. In *De res. mort.* 37 and 63, *Adv. Prax.* 15 and 26, and below, *De pud.* 16.7, he quotes John 1.14 in the same form which we have here. In *De carne Christi* 18, however, we have *Verbum caro factum est*, and in *Apol.* 21.17 he says that Christ, in performing His great miracles, showed Himself to be the

Verbum Dei, id est λόγον *illud primordiale, primogenitum.* For the relationship between *ratio* (λόγος ἐνδιάθετος) and *sermo* (λόγος προφορικός) see D'Alès I 84–96.

[162] The contrast between the tree of the forbidden fruit in the garden of Eden, which brings death, and the tree of the cross of Christ on Calvary, which brings life, is often mentioned in the Fathers. Apparently it was first pointed out by St. Justin, *Dial. cum Tryph.* 86. Tertullian's use of this work is well established, especially for passages in *Adv. Iud.* 10, where he discusses types of the cross of Christ. It is probable that the present passage, also, dealing as it does with the same subject, was influenced by the same source. The scriptural foundation for this contrast is St. Paul's designation of Christ as the second Adam; cf. 1 Cor. 15.

[163] A reference to the resurrection of Christ in the flesh, and His ascension into heaven.

[164] At the time of His baptism by John; compare Rigault's interpretation of *nec ipsae adhuc aquae laverant* in this same sentence, above, note 159. For the thought that water was sanctified by contact with Christ's body at the time of His baptism in the Jordan, see *Adv. Iud.* 8; compare, also, *De bap.* 9; Ignatius of Antioch, *Eph.* 18; Cyril of Jerusalem, *Catech.* 3.11.

[165] Cf. the Vulgate text of John 3.5: *nisi quis renatus fuerit ex aqua et spiritu sancto*; see, also, Eph. 5.26 and Titus 3.5. For Tertullian's teaching on the effects of Baptism, cf. Waszink's note on *De an.* 41.4 and the literature there cited; *op. cit.* 455 ff.—Tertullian uses the phrase *ex seminis limo* to point up what he considers a kind of parallel between the birth of all of Adam's descendants and the original creation of Adam himself *de limo terrae* (Gen. 2.7). On the word play *limo—fimo*, against the older reading, *limo—fumo*, see Oehler's note. Tertullian's traducianism is expressed most clearly in *De test. animae* 3. Compare, too, *De an.* 19, 27, 40, 41 and *De ieiun.* 3.

[166] 1 Cor. 12.27; Eph. 4.12; 5.30.

[167] *Ibid.*; 1 Cor. 6.15.

[168] 1 Cor. 6.19, where fornication is called a violation of the temple of the Holy Spirit.

[169] Gal. 3.27.

[170] Cf. 1 Peter 1.18 f.; Apoc. 12.11; 22.14. The reading *et agni* is a conjecture of Gelenius. The *Codex Ottobonianus* and the *editio princeps* have *et magnum*, which originally may have been a dittograph from the preceding *et magno redempta est.* Dekkers prefers *en manu.*

[171] The thought of *habes etiam temporis a nobis definitionem, ex quo deputetur aetas quaestionis* is compact but not difficult. Tertullian says that

if his adversaries insist upon appealing to ancient precedents, they should also remember that they have been shown within just what temporal limits these precedents have validity. They may excuse men who lived under the Old Law, but not those who live under the New.

172 Tertullian argues, in the present chapter, that the parables of mercy must be interpreted as having reference to the salvation of infidels. He insists that even if they are taken as referring to the forgiveness of Christians they would still have to be understood as justifying pardon for lesser sins and not for sins which bring death to the soul, such as adultery and fornication. This interpretation is quite different from that given in *De paen.* 8, where neither of these viewpoints is expressed; cf. D'Alès III 181 f.

173 Luke 15.4–7.

174 This is the first reference in patristic literature to the use of the chalice in the Church's liturgy; see, also, below 10.12. Early chalices were made of glass, silver or gold, although there is some evidence that wood and lead were occasionally used. On the shape and decoration of early chalices, cf. H. Leclercq, 'Calice,' DACL 2.1597 ff.—It is not completely clear how this allusion bears on the argument of the chapter. Perhaps Tertullian intends to say no more than that representations of the Good Shepherd with which the faithful were familiar furnish no argument that the lost sheep typifies the Christian and not the pagan sinner.—For the various ways in which the Good Shepherd was pictured in early Christian art, see the illustrations in H. Leclercq's lengthy article, 'Pasteur,' DACL 13.2272–2390.

175 *Praescribere* followed by the accusative with the infinitive is post-classical for *praescribere ut.* The technical, legal sense of this word is discussed by commentators on Tertullian's treatise *De praescriptione haereticorum*; see, also, Buckland, *op. cit.* 647–49.

176 A concrete way of saying, 'the laws which govern the use of language.' Tertullian's frequent allusions to the natural law reveal the strong and lasting influence of Stoicism on his thought; see T. Glover, *The Conflict of Religions in the Early Roman Empire* (London 1927) 314.

177 *Quale est, ut* . . . For this use see Hoppe I 68 and 82.

178 *Species*; cf. *Ad nat.* 1.18; *De idol.* 15. In legal language *species* designates a particular case to which a defendant must reply or upon which a judge is to pronounce; cf. *Digests* 9.2.5.

179 The Catholic who interprets the parable as referring to a Christian sinner will be obliged to show that such words as 'flock,' 'shepherd,' 'lost,' etc. can have no application to the salvation of a pagan. In the sentence which follows Tertullian rejects this view and attempts to prove that these words and the sequence in which they occur point

much more clearly to the salvation of an infidel than to the reclamation of a Christian.

[180] *Quamdiu errat*, suggesting deviation in doctrine and conduct as well as the physical straying of the sheep in the parable.

[181] *Ordo*; cf. note 179, immediately above.

[182] The interpretation of this sentence is not certain. The translation supposes that the objection is Tertullian's own and not, as Rauschen suggests, one which he puts in the mouth of his adversary. Hence the subject of *opinor* is Tertullian himself; the *tu velis* refers to an assumption of his opponent. Tertullian has shown that the whole human race is God's flock. When his Catholic adversary says that the lost sheep is a Christian, he denies, at least implicitly, that it is lost from a large number of sheep grazing freely. If it were lost from the Church, as his opponent supposes, it would be lost not from a wandering flock, but rather from a restricted place of safety or safekeeping, like a chest or coffer.—Tertullian here writes as though he wishes to refute a single adversary (*tu velis*); cf. also *De pud.* 7.1, 6, 8; 10.9–11; 13.7; 21.5, 9; 22.1. In other passages he speaks of his 'adversaries,' as if he is disputing with many; cf. 3.1, 3; 6.7; 10.1; 13.1.

[183] Luke 15.7.

[184] Catholics object that the ninety-nine who remain are called 'just'; therefore they may not be thought of as infidels. Tertullian answers that the *justi* are the Jews; therefore the ninety-nine who remain must not be thought of as Christians.

[185] *Habentes gubernacula disciplinae et timoris instrumenta legem et prophetas.* The law of Moses was the moral guide of the Hebrew people; the preaching of the prophets led them to fear the Lord. Tertullian says that the Jews may be understood as the ninety-nine 'just' not because they actually were just but because, with the helps which they had, they should have been.

[186] Luke 15.8–10.

[187] Compare *Apol.* 38.3: *Unam omnium rem publicam agnoscimus mundum.* This is another Stoic idea which Tertullian has Christianized.

[188] The forgiveness of the pagan is by Baptism, the *paenitentia prima*; the forgiveness of the Christian is by exomologesis, the *paenitentia secunda*; cf. *De paen.* 7.2; 12.5. Tertullian argues that since nothing is said in the parables of a second loss and restoration, we must understand them as referring to the forgiveness of the pagan, not the Christian sinner.

[189] In his alternative explanation of the two parables Tertullian says that the sheep and the drachma could be 'saved' because they were not permanently lost by death or destruction. He insists, however, that a Christian who has committed adultery and fornication is permanently

lost in the death of mortal sin and, therefore, the parables can have no application in his case.

[190] The same four forms of popular amusement are condemned in almost identical terms in *Apol.* 38.4. In both passages the same reasons are given why such *spectacula* are objectionable: the races cause a frenzy of excitement, the theatre portrays and arouses lust, the amphitheatre is the scene of cruelty and bloody murder, athletic contests are a foolish waste of time. See, too, *Adv. Marc.* 1.27: *voluptates circi furentis, caveae saevientis et scaenae lascivientis*, and *De cultu fem.* 1.9. Tertullian wrote at greater length on these subjects in the *De spectaculis*, especially cc. 16–19. Compare, also, Min. Felix, *Octav.* 37. 11 f.; St. Jerome, *Epist.* 43.3. Salvian closely imitates Tertullian in *De gubern. Dei* 6.11: *Quicquid immunditiarum est, hoc exercetur in theatris, quicquid luxuriarum in palaestris, quicquid immoderationis in circis, quicquid furoris in caveis; alibi est impudicitia, alibi lascivia, alibi intemperantia, alibi insania.* On this passage, cf. J. Waltzing, 'Tertullien et Salvien,' *LMB* 19 (1920) 39–43. For the whole subject of popular recreations at this time, see L. Friedlander, *Roman Life and Manners under the Early Empire* (tr. from the 7th German edition by J. Freese and L. Magnus, London n.d.) 2.1–130.

[191] Tertullian lists the situations in which a Christian would have occasion to practice the *artes curiositatis*, that is, magical and idolatrous observances of one kind or another. *Lusus* refers to private games of chance, rather than to the public spectacles. Plautus frequently notes that a person about to throw the dice will invoke the name of one of the deities. For further details on the idolatry practiced at pagan festivals, cf. *De idol.* 13–16. On the idolatry which was required of magistrates in the exercise of public office, *De idol.* 17. Various cases of cooperation in the idolatry of others are discussed in the same treatise, cc. 16–23.

[192] *In verbum ancipitis negationis aut blasphemiae impegit. Impingere* often suggests that one has been swept into an offense or fallen into it blindly or by chance; see, for example, *Apol.* 3.1. In a later chapter (19.25) blasphemy is placed among the irremissible sins, but this must be understood as malicious and deliberate blasphemy. For the view that blasphemy is merely a specification of apostasy, see Oehler's note *ad loc.*

[193] It is clear from these words that excommunication could be and was inflicted for the non-mortal sins here listed, and that the sinner was saved when the excommunication was removed by ecclesiastical authority. It is possible that this excommunication was relatively brief, and that it did not require the performance of public penance; cf. *De paen.* note 121, *De pud.* above note 77 and below note 198. Grotz, *op. cit.* 350–54, prefers not to call it an excommunication at all, since it did not mean a complete separation from the Church.—Tertullian uses the

verb *abrumpere* to describe a voluntary break with the Church; cf. *Adv. Valent.* 4. This is contrasted with *extra ecclesiam datus est*, which may mean an excommunication incurred *ipso facto* or imposed by judicial sentence. On the subject of excommunication in the early Church, cf. C. Chartier, 'L'excommunication ecclésiastique d'après les écrits de Tertullien,' *Antonianum* 10 (1935) 301-44, 499-536.

[194] Ezech. 34.2-4, with some verbal variations from the Vulgate and omitting the clause *gregem autem meum non pascebatis*.

[195] When the prophet censured the shepherds for neglecting their sheep, he did not blame them for failing to restore to the flock those which were permanently lost in death. So, also, the shepherds of the Church are not to be blamed if they refuse to take back into the Church those sinners who are spiritually dead as a result of adultery and fornication.—*Ingerere*, meaning 'to assert' or 'to insist,' is post-classical; for Tertullian's frequent use of this word in referring to the meaning of a scriptural passage, cf. Hoppe I 133.

[196] *Delicta pro ipsius drachmae modulo ac pondere mediocria.*

[197] The Greek drachma, referred to in the Gospel text, was worth, roughly, about 17¢, the equivalent of a Roman denarius.—For *ipse* as a strong demonstrative, see Hoppe II 112 f.

[198] Historians of the sacrament of Penance have discussed this passage at length in connection with the problem of the existence of private penance in the early Church. The problem, in so far as the evidence of Tertullian is concerned, is inseparable from the difficult question of his division of sins. Up to this point in the *De pudicitia* the following classes of sins have been mentioned: (a) monstrous crimes which exclude the sinner completely from the Church, even from the ranks of the public penitents (4.5); (b) capital sins which are punished by excommunication and public penance but for which no ecclesiastical pardon is granted, e.g. adultery and fornication (1.20 and *passim*); (c) sins which are punished by excommunication but which are forgiven by ecclesiastical authority (7.14-16); (d) the sins designated here (7.20) as *mediocria*. The problem is to determine, first, whether these *peccata mediocria* are identified with the sins mentioned in (c), i.e. those of lesser gravity which are punished by excommunication, and, second, whether they are identified with the *peccata cotidianae incursionis*, described in a later chapter (19.23 f.), or, third, whether they form a distinct, intermediate class of remissible sins, more serious than the *peccata cotidianae incursionis* but less serious than the non-mortal sins which are punished by excommunication (7.14-16). If (c) and (d) are identified, and if (d) is identified with the sins described in 19.23 f., then, of course, the sins listed in (c) must also be classified as *cotidianae incursionis*.

P. Galtier II 281 and others identify (c) and (d), and this identification is admissible if it can be shown that the *peccata mediocria* may be 'forgiven in the Church' (*statim ibidem cum gaudio emendationis transiguntur*; 7.20), and yet be such as are serious enough to be punished by separation from the Church (*ob tale quid extra ecclesiam datus est*; 7.16). This is possible if one understands 'forgiven in the Church' to mean 'forgiven by the Church,' and not 'forgiven to a Christian who remains in the Church' or 'who is not excommunicated.' Galtier I 247 f. supposes that the *castigatio* (cf. above, *De pud.* note 77) inflicted for the remissible sins referred to in c. 2.12 and for the *mediocria* referred to here, involved a brief separation from the Church, but he insists that it did not require the performance of public penance and that it was a punishment which might be imposed more than once in a lifetime. Thus, for the *peccata mediocria* there would have been a kind of private penance, distinguished clearly from the public penance demanded of those who had been guilty of the *peccata capitalia*.

Galtier II 281 identifies both (c) and (d) with the *peccata cotidianae incursionis* of 19.23. A comparison of 7.14–16 and 19.23 f. appears to justify this identification, although Rahner, *op. cit.* 143, asserts that they must be kept distinct, since the sins of 7.14–16 are punished by excommunication and since *peccata cotidianae incursionis* would hardly be serious or unusual enough to be punished so severely. Tertullian, however, states in 19.23 that all Christians are *tempted* to commit these sins each day; he does not say that they actually commit them every day. It is not impossible that after his lapse into Montanism Tertullian should have felt that the Christian who fell into such sins from time to time ought to be disciplined by a brief separation from the Church (the *extra ecclesiam datus est* of 7.16) and pardoned, thereafter, by what Galtier has called 'private penance.' This private penance, Galtier believes, existed for all remissible sins, that is, for sins which the Montanists considered to be non-mortal (7.14–16) and which they designated indifferently as *peccata cotidianae incursionis* (19.23), *mediocria* (7.20), *leviora* (18.18) and *remissibilia* (2.15).

It would appear from this that there is no evidence in the *De pudicitia* for the existence of a public penance terminated by ecclesiastical absolution, since the *peccata capitalia*, according to the Montanist thesis, are not to be forgiven at all by the Church, and since the *mediocria* or *leviora*, according to P. Galtier's understanding of this and other pertinent passages, are forgiven by the *castigatio*, or private penance. However, there is no real difficulty in admitting that Tertullian, as a Montanist, rejected a public penance (i.e. a major excommunication requiring enrollment among the public penitents) which was terminated by ecclesiastical absolution, since it was precisely here that Montanists and Catholics were at variance. Both Catholics and Montanists may have had a *castigatio* for lesser sins; both, also, had a public penance, the exomologesis, for *peccata capitalia*, but whereas the Catholics pardoned the *capitalia*, at least the sins of adultery and fornication, the Montanists did not. It must be admitted, against this explanation, that the penance done for *peccata leviora*, as described in 18.17, will hardly satisfy Galtier's definition of private penance, since as far as its external form is concerned, it is identified with the public penance which Montanists require for *peccata majora* and *irremissibilia*.

The alternatives, then, appear to be these. (1) The *mediocria* of 7.20 form a distinct class of intermediate sins, i.e. between the *peccata cotidianae incursionis* (19.23 f.), which were forgiven without excommunication and, possibly, without any formal ecclesiastical intervention whatever, and, second, the more serious non-mortal sins described in 7.14–16, which both Montanists and Catholics punished by a brief excommunication and forgave by ecclesiastical authority. This first alternative supposes three classes of remissible sins in the *De pudicitia*, but it does not exclude the possibility that the *mediocria* were forgiven by the kind of penance which P. Galtier designates as 'private.' At the same time it avoids the difficulties which must be met by those who hold for a form of private, ecclesiastical penance which is administered for sins serious enough to be punished by excommunication and yet light enough to be *cotidianae incursionis*, sins which separate a man from the Church (*extra ecclesiam datus est*) and yet which are found and forgiven in the Church (*intra domum dei ecclesiam*). (2) The *mediocria* are identified with the *peccata cotidianae incursionis* and also with the sins involving excommunication mentioned in 7.14–16, but this excommunication did not require that the sinner be enrolled among the public penitents and it was one which might be repeated a number of times.

P. Galtier, as has been seen, defends the second of these alternatives in arguing for the existence of private penance in the early Church; cf. I 247 f., 253; II 274 ff., 281 f., 287 f., 302. His interpretation of *De pud.* 7.14 is attacked by Mortimer, *op. cit.* 19 f. and supported by Joyce, *op. cit.* 28 f. For further comments on this important passage, cf. Daly, *op. cit.* 70.736 ff., 742 ff.; Rauschen, *Eucharist and Penance* 230 f.; Batiffol, *op. cit.* 80 f.; Poschmann I 306–308, III 24 f. The lengthiest discussion of the passage is in Motry, *op. cit.* 128–56, although his interest is limited to the classification of sins as mortal and venial and he does not consider the passage in its relation to the problem of private penance.

Grotz, *op. cit.* 440–42, is of the opinion that Tertullian, as a Catholic, recognized but two classes of sins: (1) *peccata modica* or *cotidianae incursionis*; (2) *peccata graviora*. Ecclesiastical penance (*exomologesis*) was required only for the *peccata graviora*; this was not, however, a penance which involved excommunication. Later on, as a Montanist, he distinguished three classes of sins: (1) the *peccata modica* or *cotidianae incursionis*, for which no ecclesiastical penance was required; (2) the *peccata mediocria* or *media*, which were pardoned by the Church after public penance; (3) the *crimina capitalia*, for which no ecclesiastical pardon was allowed, but which were punished by lifelong excommunication. This new distinction of sins Grotz sees as being closely bound up with the new concept of 'excommunication-penance' which, according to his central thesis, was introduced into the Church about the time of the Montanist crisis.

[199] It is estimated that the talent was worth about $2,000. Tertullian has chosen to ignore the parable of the king who forgave his servant a debt of ten thousand talents; Matt. 18.21–35.

[200] The contrast is between *lucernae spiculo* and *totius solis lancea*. For the use of these words, cf. Oehler's note *ad loc.* and F. Dölger, 'Sonne und Sonnenstrahl als Gleichnis in der Logostheologie des christlichen Altertums,' AC I (1929) 278.

[201] Reading *advocat* (Ursinus, Dekkers) rather than *advocant* (Mesnartius, Rauschen).

[202] This is awkward and the interpretation given here is tentative. Tertullian seems to say that the parables of the lost sheep and drachma can not refer to a Christian who is guilty of that kind of sin (i.e. adultery) which his opponents have in mind when, by a forced exegesis, they interpret the parables as referring to a Christian sinner. Therefore we have all the more reason (i.e. an added reason, over and above the arguments in the first part of the chapter) for saying that they are to be understood as referring to the salvation of a pagan. The alternative interpretation of the parable (beginning at 7.13) which Tertullian mentions (*etiam hac nostra . . . interpretatione*) is purely hypothetical; that is, even if the parable were to be taken as referring to a Christian there would still be no evidence from Scripture that the Catholic position is justified. The whole chapter furnishes an interesting example of Tertullian's habitual attitude in controversy—*Quidquid dixeris argumentabor*.

[203] *In vestibus purpura oculandis*. Thörnell, *op. cit.* 3.25, gives the meaning of *oculare* as *pannulis adsutis quasi oculis distinguere*, and defends the reading against emendations suggested by Kroymann (*clavandis*) and Leo (*colorandis*).

204 *Erudito mox utroque corpore.* The translation is based on Thörnell's interpretation of the passage, *op. cit.* 2.25–27.

205 Just as men are deceived by an apparent similarity of color in the original garment and the patch, so interpreters of the parable of the prodigal son (Luke 15.11–32) are deceived by an apparent similarity between the terms of the parable and certain points of doctrine which they wish to defend. When the garment is cleaned and treated by the fuller, the defective patchwork appears; so, also, when the parable is studied carefully in the light of the substantial truth it teaches, we are able to see the inaccuracies which disfigure the interpretations of this tendentious exegesis. Compare *De praesc. haer.* 39.

206 Cf. Exod. 4.22; Rom. 9.4. Compare, also, Isa. 1.2, quoted by Tertullian later in this same chapter.

207 Luke 15.29.

208 Cf. Isa. 6.9 f.

209 Amos 5.10.

210 Cf. Isa. 1.2, 4. The Vulgate has *blasphemaverunt sanctum Israel.* Tertullian's text, *in iram provocaverunt sanctum Israelis*, reflects the sense of the Septuagint: παρωργίσατε τὸν ἅγιον 'Ισραήλ.

211 Literally, 'every agreeable created thing has been snatched from his jaws.'—*Plane dicemus* is ironical.

212 Compare *Apol.* 21.5: *Dispersi, palabundi, et soli et coeli sui extorres vagantur per orbem.* Cf. also *Adv. Iud.* 13; *Adv. Marc.* 3.23.

213 Even if the younger son were taken as a type of the Christian sinner, it would still not be perfectly correct to speak of the elder as a type of the Jew, since this is inconsistent with features of the parable which have just been noted.

214 *Secundum fidei comparationem.* Thelwall translates, 'according to the analogy of faith,' with a reference to Rom. 12.6, but it is not clear what this would mean in the context. Perhaps Tertullian simply wishes to say that if one compares the Jewish and Christian religions (i.e. the faith they hold), one would be inclined to suppose that the former is typified by the wayward prodigal and the latter by his faithful and devoted brother.

215 Cf. Gen. 25.21–25; Rom. 9.10–13. The Church supplants the Synagogue just as the younger son, Jacob, supplanted his elder brother, Esau. Therefore the 'order of succession established from Rebecca's womb' requires that we consider the Jew as the elder son and the Christian as the younger. Compare *Adv. Iud.* 1 and *De an.* 26.2.

216 *Clausula* is the conclusion of the parable, where the elder son expresses resentment at the favor shown the repentant prodigal.

[217] Christ is the hope of the world; compare Tertullian's eloquent protest against the heresy of Docetism in *De carne Christi* 5: *Parce unicae spei totius orbis.* Israel hopes for the first coming of Christ; Christianity hopes for the second; see *Apol.* 21.15 f.; *Adv. Iud.* 7. The *reliqua expectatio* of the Jews is that which they still have at the time Tertullian writes; hence it is one which looks to the future. De Labriolle's emendation *cum aliqua expectatione* is unnecessary.

[218] Tertullian seems to understand this as a general principle which is applicable in the interpretations of all parables. We must look to the general sense of the parable and not expect that all of its details will fit, in all respects, the truth it is intended to illustrate.

[219] Reading *facilitas* (Junius; Dekkers), rather than *felicitas comparationum* (the *editio princeps*).

[220] The gestures which actors use to express the thought of the verses in a play are 'allegorical' just as the parables which are used in Scripture to express religious truth are 'allegorical,' i.e. figurative representations of an idea. The gestures of actors are graceful and harmonious, even though they are often irrelevant to the essential features of the particular play which is being staged. So also in interpreting parables, one may discover features which fit in with one's own subjective convictions or feelings but which have nothing to do with the substantial truth taught in the parable. Von Hartel, *Patristische Studien* 4.23, considers that this is an allusion to Livy 7.2.9, where Livius Andronicus is said to have introduced the custom of having a boy sing his verse while he himself accompanied the monody in pantomime. For the source of Livy's account, cf. J. Waszink, 'Varro, Livy and Tertullian on the History of Roman Dramatic Art,' VC 2 (1948) 233 f.

[221] The gestures of the actor flow from his own inventiveness, they have nothing to do with Andromache, that is, with the character of Andromache in the play of that name. The example of Andromache is chosen at random, just as in a somewhat similar context Shakespeare has Hamlet ask, 'What's Hecuba to him or he to Hecuba, that he should weep for her?'

[222] *Excludunt*, literally, 'hatch out;' but see the note in Van der Vliet, *op. cit.* 276 f.

[223] The *regula veritatis* or *regula fidei* is found in the traditional teaching of the living Church which comes down from the apostles; see the detailed explanation in *De praesc. haer.*, *passim*, and briefer statements in *De virg. vel.* 1 and *De monog.* 2. The subject has been treated by D'Alès I 201–13, 254–61; see, too, J. Quasten, 'Tertullian and "traditio,"' *Traditio* 2 (1944) 481–84, and E. Flesseman-Van Leer, *Tradition and Scripture in the Early Church* (Assen 1954) 145–185. It is strange that

Tertullian sees no inconsistency in appealing to the rule of faith in order to justify a position which is so obviously opposed to it.

224 Since we do not take the parables as sources of doctrine, we need not try to find religious truth in all of their details, nor need we labor to explain away everything in the parables which seems inconsistent with the truth which we know *aliunde*. Compare the condemnation of Valentinus in *De praesc. haer.* 38: *non ad materiam scripturas, sed materiam ad scripturas excogitavit*; cf. also, Irenaeus, *Adv. haer.* 2.27. Tertullian's theory of exegesis is sound but his application is not always correct or consistent. As a Montanist he abandons his rule of praescription, and although he 'takes doctrine as a norm' in interpreting the parables, he finds this doctrine, not in the traditional teaching of the Church, but rather in the new revelations of the Paraclete supposedly granted to the elect in the latter days.

225 *Simpliciter posita sunt*. For the use of *simpliciter* as a technical term to describe the literal as opposed to the allegorical meaning of Scripture, see parallel passages in *Ad ux.* 1.2; 2.2; *De an.* 35.2. A similar usage occurs in Hilary, Jerome and Rufinus; cf. references in Waszink, *De anima* 413. It may be said in general that Tertullian preferred the literal to the metaphorical interpretation of Scripture. As is evident from the present passage, he is completely out of sympathy with the elaborate allegorism of his Alexandrian contemporaries. In particular he deprecates the efforts made by some commentators to find mystical meanings in biblical numbers. The absurdities to which this method led later writers are familiar to all readers of St. Augustine.

226 *Perducant*. For variants, see Van der Vliet, *op. cit.* 277.

227 In 65 B.C. See Josephus, *Antiq. Iud.* 14.4 and *Bell. Iud.* 1.7. There is no mention of Lucullus (L. Licinius, the conqueror of Mithridates) in Josephus' account of Pompey's subjugation of Judea, though Pamelius thinks it not impossible that he may have taken part in the campaign; cf. J. Pamelius, *Tertulliani Opera* (Cologne 1617) 719 f.

228 Possibly an allusion to Deut. 23.19, although this text condemns usury and not the taking of tribute. St. Jerome, *Epist.* 21.3, rejects the statement of Tertullian that the publicans were foreigners: *Unde vehementer admiror Tertullianum in eo libro quem de pudicitia adversus paenitentiam scripsit et sententiam veterem nova opinione dissolvit hoc voluisse sentire, quod publicani et peccatores qui cum domino vescebantur ethnici fuerunt.*

229 Aelius Spartianus, in his life of Pescennius Niger, relates that when the Jews petitioned for relief from their heavy burdens of taxation, they were told that the Roman authorities wished to tax not only the land in Palestine but the air as well; cf. references in Oehler.

[230] Luke 15.1. The words *peccatores autem non statim Iudaeos ostendit* may contain a sneer, as though Tertullian's contemporaries considered *peccatores* and *Iudaei* synonymous.

[231] The subject of the verbs *adjungit, ostendit, distinxit* in these sentences is indefinite and, probably, impersonal, with 'Scripture' or 'the sacred writer' understood. Compare the use of *inquit* introducing a quotation from the Bible, above, *De paen.* note 53.—*Ethnicorum* is an appositional genitive with *unum genus.*—The logic of the sentence is elusive. Tertullian wishes to prove that both 'publicans' and 'sinners' referred to in the text are heathens and not Jews. He considers that they are mentioned together because the writer thinks of them as forming but one group or class, i.e. sinners. Thus Scripture pairs off 'the lame and the blind' as one group assisted by our Lord's miracles, or the 'Scribes and the Pharisees' as one group united in hatred of the Lord. Here 'publicans and sinners' are one group in need of the divine mercy. Since the publicans are not Jews, for the reason just given, i.e. the prohibition of Deuteronomy, it follows *a pari* that those who are simply classified as sinners along with them are not Jews either. There is no real reason why Tertullian should exclude the Jews from the parables of mercy, since he sufficiently refutes his opponents if he shows that the parables are not applicable to Christians who have fallen into serious sins.

[232] Acts 11.3; Gal. 2.12.

[233] For *mens*, by metonymy, as 'soul,' cf. *De an.* 12.1.—On the coming of the Holy Ghost in Baptism, see above, *De paen.* note 27 and the literature there cited.

[234] This is the satisfaction which is offered to God through the penitential works of exomologesis and which is crowned by ecclesiastical pardon; for parallel passages, cf. D'Alès III 427. The satisfaction of which there is question below, 9.16, is that which precedes the *paenitentia prima* of Baptism.

[235] The sacrament of Baptism. Compare *De bap.* cc. 1, 3, 4, 5, 9 and 12, where Baptism is called a sacrament in more or less the same sense in which the word is used here; for the more recent literature, cf. Refoulé–Drouzy, *op. cit.* 52. The substance of good gifts is compared with the substance which the prodigal received from his father. If it is possible to recover the 'substance' of Baptism so easily through exomologesis, no one will make an effort to avoid serious sins and, accordingly, the 'substance' of Baptism will be destroyed by the very fact that the parable promises its easy recovery.—On the contrast between *De pud.* 9.9–11 and *De paen.* 7.2 f., cf. D'Alès III 199 f.

[236] Literally, 'Who will try to keep in perpetuity something which he is able to lose not in perpetuity?'

237 It should be observed that the graces here described are effected, at least indirectly, by *paenitentia secunda*. It is precisely against this extension of the Church's power that Tertullian protests. We conclude that in Catholic belief the total effect of exomologesis was more than simply an external reconciliation to the Church; cf. Galtier I 120.— On Baptism as a seal, see above, *De paen.* notes 66, 102 and, below, 9.16. The use of the finger-ring as a signet was, of course, quite common from the very earliest times.

238 This appears to suggest that he is again permitted to assist at the sacrifice of the Mass and that Christ's redemptive death on the cross is renewed for him in the sense that its merits are again applied to save him from the effects of his sin. It is as though the crucifixion of Christ, which was the meritorious cause of his salvation through Baptism, takes place a second time in order that the sinner may be saved through *paenitentia secunda*; compare Heb. 6.6. Tertullian alludes directly to the father's command that the fatted calf be slain (Luke 15.23) to make a banquet for the penitent prodigal; cf. below, 9.16, where the communicant is said to 'feed upon the fatness (*opimitate*) of the body of the Lord.' Understood in this way, the sentence is of great importance in the argument from tradition for the sacrificial nature of the Eucharist. See, also, *De orat.* 19, and frequent references to the liturgical services of the Christians as *oblatio* and *sacrificium*; cf. D'Alès I 308-14, and the literature listed below, note 254.

239 The contrast is between pagans (*indigne vestiti*), who have never had the garment of grace, and Christian sinners (*spoliati*), who have lost it.

240 Matt. 22.11-14. The 'couch' from which the unworthy are forcibly removed and cast out into darkness is understood, by metonymy, of the Eucharistic banquet from which sinners are excluded by excommunication.

241 It has been proved above, 8.3-7, that the younger son cannot reasonably be taken as a type of the Christian sinner, since the elder son cannot be taken as a type of the Jew. Now we have also proved, and this is a step forward (*plus igitur*), that the Catholic interpretation is not only unreasonable but that it is even harmful to salvation (*saluti nocentissima*, 9.8).

242 Reading *integri* (Esser), not *integre*.

243 Matt. 18.11; Luke 19.10.

244 Matt. 9.12; Luke 9.31 f.

245 *Genus* frequently in Tertullian means *genus humanum*; cf. Waszink, *op. cit.* 290. The man who knows God and the man who does not are 'brothers by birth' because they are both members of the same human

race, children of Adam, the *auctor* (*De exhort. cast.* 2) and *princeps* (*De an.* 20.2) *generis*.—Tertullian's argument in this paragraph is a kind of sorites: the prodigal son is one who is lost; but one who is lost is one who does not know God; but one who does not know God is a pagan; therefore the prodigal is a pagan.

246 This is the central theme of Tertullian's treatise *De testimonio animae*. See, also, *Apol.* 17.4–6; *Ad Scap.* 2.1; *Adv. Marc.* 1.18, 4.25; *De resur. mort.* 2; *De spec.* 2. The subject has been studied by L. Fuetscher, 'Die natürliche Gotteserkenntnis bei Tertullian,' ZKT 51 (1927) 1–34, 217–51.

247 1 Cor. 1.21.

248 *Longe a domino factus*; cf. E. Löfstedt, *Zur Sprache Tertullians* (Lund 1920) 94 f. for parallels in Hilary and Augustine. *Iactus* is an emendation of Oehler's, adopted by Dekkers, De Labriolle and others.

249 The prodigal is taken as a type of those pagans who are hungry for the truth but who seek it where it is not to be found, that is, in the wisdom of the world. Thelwall refers to Amos 8.11. It is true that the prophet speaks of those who will be 'starving for the word of God' but he is thinking of Israel and not the pagan world.

250 An allusion to the Gadarene swine; cf. Matt. 8.28–32; Mark 5.9–13; Luke 8.30–33.

251 For *compos* meaning *competens* or *sufficiens* see Hoppe II 81 f. Those who are 'working for God' (the 'servants in his father's house' of the parable) are the Christians who have the heavenly food of true doctrine as well as the nourishment of the Eucharist.

252 The effect of original sin is a loss of heavenly gifts (described as constituting a *status*; cf. above, *De pud.* note 136 for the meaning of this word) for Adam and the whole human family. These gifts and this *status* are recovered for the Christian through his reception of the sacrament of Baptism. This brief sentence supposes a clear understanding of basic theses in the theological treatises on Original Sin, Soteriology, Justification and Baptism. Related passages in Tertullian have been studied by K. Rahner, 'Sünde als Gnadenverlust in der frühkirchlichen Literatur,' ZKT 60 (1936) 491–507.

253 See, above, *De pud.* note 237 and references there. Tertullian asserts that the ring which the prodigal received (Luke 15.22) was one which was given to him for the first time. Therefore it must be understood as the seal of Baptism and cannot be thought of as having reference to *paenitentia secunda*.—*Interrogatus* is an allusion to the examination on faith which was, and still is, a part of the solemn rite of Baptism; cf. F. Dölger's note on *De bap.* 2.1, 'Die Eingliederung des Taufsymbols in den Taufvollzug nach den Schriften Tertullians,' AC

4 (1934) 141, and other literature listed by Refoulé-Drouzy, *op. cit.* 38–40.

²⁵⁴ *Opimitate dominici corporis vescitur, eucharistia scilicet.* This is an important statement of Tertullian's belief in the real presence of Christ's body in the Eucharist. Other references in his writings to the Eucharist as food may be seen in D'Alès I 355–70. On the contrast between *eucharistiam sumere* and *eucharistiam facere,* cf. F. Dölger, 'Öl der Eucharistie,' AC 2 (1930) 186 f. For the literature on this whole subject, see Quasten, *op. cit.* 2.336.

²⁵⁵ Esser, in a note to Kellner's translation, denies the causal sense of *quod* in this sentence. If it is taken as a relative, as he suggests, we might translate, 'He was a prodigal from the beginning, something the Christian is not—from the beginning.'

²⁵⁶ Reading, with Rauschen, *in hunc solum.*

²⁵⁷ Both pagans and Jews know of Christian Baptism; but not even the Jews, whom we might expect to be better informed than pagans on Christian practices, know about the existence of *paenitentia secunda.* Therefore when the Jews complain of our Lord's kindness to publicans and sinners, they cannot be complaining about a pardon granted to the sinner after exomologesis, since this is a Christian mystery of which they have no knowledge.—Tertullian speaks of a *secunda restitutio* and D'Alès III 213 concludes from this that the word has a twofold application, first to a restitution in Baptism and second to a restitution in exomologesis. However, the antithesis between *prima vocatio* and *secunda restitutio* suggests that Tertullian simply wishes to say that the *paenitentia prima* is a *vocatio* and the *paenitentia secunda* is a *restitutio.*

²⁵⁸ The word *paenitentia* is used here, quite clearly, for an ecclesiastical penance terminated by a forgiveness of sins *coram Deo.* Tertullian's language here, as elsewhere in the *De pudicitia,* implies that he is responding to definite arguments employed by his adversaries.

²⁵⁹ The *peccata aequalia* are those of murder and apostasy; cf. above, chapter 5. This is one of the passages regularly cited to prove that adultery and fornication were not forgiven by the orthodox Church *before* this time (*servari inconcessibilia*) and that other capital sins were still unforgiven *at* this time. The sentence is analyzed in Galtier I 206 f.; D'Alès III 199 f.; Motry, *op. cit.* 85 f., 94 f.

²⁶⁰ Therefore the Catholic party should not try to find an argument in the parable for the forgiveness of adultery and fornication through *paenitentia secunda,* since this is not a question with which the parable is concerned.

²⁶¹ Martyrdom is 'another Baptism' (below 22.10), a 'Baptism of blood' and a 'second regeneration' (*Scorp.* 6); cf. F. Dölger's discussion

of *De bap.* 16, 'Tertullian über die Bluttaufe,' AC 2 (1930) 117–41;
D'Alès I 329 f.; and the literature cited by Refoulé–Drouzy, *op. cit.* 89 f.

[262] Literally, 'A transgression in interpretation is no less serious than
one in behaviour (*conversatione*).'

[263] The exact meaning of this sentence remains uncertain. The translation given here is based on the reading *in ethnicos non disserendi*,
suggested by Reifferscheid–Wissowa. Tertullian's opponents, by a
forced exegesis (7.23; 9.1), have argued that the parables must *not* be
interpreted of the pagans. It is the yoke of this forced exegesis which
has now been thrown off by the arguments developed in the preceding
chapters. For other interpretations, cf. D'Alès III 183 and the lengthy
note in Kellner–Esser, *ad loc.*

[264] The arguments from here to the end of the paragraph are those
which Tertullian attributes to his Catholic adversaries, though he, too,
asserts in many places that the sins of pagans are committed in blindness
and ignorance; cf. F. Dölger, 'Die Sünde in Blindheit und Unwissenheit,' AC 2 (1930) 222.

[265] Those who are ignorant of God and His law are not without
guilt, but it is a lesser guilt and one which the natural faculties of man
alone must bear; cf. above, *De paen.* note 70. It is not compounded by
the added culpability which comes from sinning against the light of
faith. Hence pagans have less need of penitence than Christians, since
their fault is less serious in the sight of God.

[266] *Ubi et culpa sapit et gratia.* The word *gratia* is used here simply to
designate the complexus of favors which God showed the sinner in his
first justification. It has not the technical sense which attaches to it in
theology today.

[267] It is the burden of this very difficult chapter to show that God's
promise of pardon to repentant sinners is more appropriate to pagans
than it is to Christians. After proposing the arguments of his opponents,
Tertullian begins his rebuttal in the paragraph which immediately
follows.

[268] That is, for the reason just mentioned. The question is rhetorical.
Did Jonas attempt to escape the duty of preaching to the Ninivites
(Jonas 1.2) because he thought penance unnecessary for them, since
they had sinned in ignorance?

[269] Cf. Jonas 4.2.

[270] Catholics feel, Tertullian argues, that the preaching of penance is
not intended for pagans since they sin in ignorance. Yet the prophet's
life was put in danger (Jonas 1.4 f.) just so that penance might be
preached to pagans such as these. The danger to which he was
exposed in preaching penance to pagans shows how important penance

is for them. Dekkers, with earlier editors, reads this sentence as a question.

[271] *Passus est exemplum dominicae passionis* may mean 'he suffered as' or 'he was constituted a type of the Lord's passion.' The perils which Jonas endured culminated in the salvation of the Ninivites, just as the passion of Christ culminated in the salvation of all men, even the pagans. Jonas would have been lost at sea were it not for the fact that he was a type of Christ who, after His death and burial, arose from the dead on the third day; cf. Matt. 12.39–41.

[272] Cf. Matt. 3.3 ; Mark 1.2 f.; Luke 1.76 ; 3.3–5.

[273] Luke 3.12–14.

[274] Matt. 11.21; Luke 10.13. In the Vulgate, miracles are quite regularly called *virtutes*. Tertullian follows this usage here and in numerous other passages; cf. *Apol.* 18.5 ; *De praesc. haer.* 13. In *De an.* 34.2 he speaks of Simon Magus' magical power as *virtus*, and in *De praesc. haer.* 44 refers to *virtutes* performed by heretics; see, also, cc. 20, 29 and 30 of the same work.

[275] Those who sin 'by nature' sin blindly; those who sin against the light of faith sin by their own deliberate choice.

[276] That is, pardon; cf. *De pud.* 3.3 and *passim.*

[277] The meaning of this sentence is complicated by its heavy irony. No doubt God will pardon Christians more readily than pagans, because Christians are less deserving of pardon! Of course He is not willing that pardon which was wasted on His children should be given to outsiders, for this would mean that He offers salvation to the Gentiles after it is rejected by the Jews!

[278] The Christian who sins prefers spiritual death to that life which he received through the *paenitentia prima* of Baptism. If God prefers that such a man do penance and be saved by *paenitentia secunda* rather than that he suffer the penalty of spiritual death for his sins, then when we sin after Baptism we merit, because our sin leads to repentance, which is pleasing to God. For the Scripture text, cf. Ezech. 18.23 ; 33.11. The paragraph illustrates Tertullian's fondness for the *reductio ad absurdum.*

[279] There are references to rope-walkers and rope-dancers in Terence, *Hecyra, Prologue* 4; Suetonius, *Galba* 6; Arnobius, *Adv. nat.* 2.38. Juvenal 3.77 has *schoenobates*, and Augustine, *Enarr. in Psalmos* 39.9, *funiambulus.* For further details, cf. TLL 6.1546. Compare, also, Origen, *Contra Celsum* 3.69 and references there to the Stoic fondness for this illustration given by H. Chadwick, *Origen. Contra Celsum* (Cambridge 1953) 174.—Tertullian's adversary wishes to lead an upright life, but in the matter of sex morality he is like a man walking

on a tightrope. He wavers from one side to the other, pulled in one direction by the flesh, in another by the spirit; drawn one way by his desires, another by the demands of the faith. And yet, if he believes what he says, there is no reason why he should watch his step so carefully, since even if he should fall, a second penance will help him to rise again.

²⁸⁰ For the causal sense of *dum*, cf. Hoppe I 79.

²⁸¹ *Eris iterum de moecho christianus.* His Catholic opponent believes that the effect of *paenitentia secunda* will be a restoration of the *status* first obtained by *paenitentia prima*; cf. Teeuwen II 415. Tertullian, on the contrary, believed as a Montanist that after a man committed adultery he could never again be a Christian. It is interesting to contrast this with *Apol.* 2.17, where he says that one of the faithful who has apostatized may be *iterum Christianus*, in spite of his sin.—The text of this whole passage is unsatisfactory and there is no uniformity among commentators in its interpretation. Thörnell, *op. cit.* I.69–72, is of the opinion that the 'funambulist' is Tertullian himself and that the passage contains an imaginary attack which is made by the Catholics on Tertullian's own position. He believes that such expressions as *tenuissimum filum disciplinae, carnem spiritu librans, oculum metu temperans* apply much more easily to the Montanist than to the Catholic discipline, and he considers that the sentence: *Haec tu mihi benignissime dei interpres* proves that the words of the whole preceding paragraph must be thought of, not as Tertullian's, but as those of his Catholic opponent. Rauschen places the final sentence of the paragraph in quotation marks, as a statement which Tertullian puts in the mouth of the indulgent *dei interpres*. Neither of these interpretations, however, is acceptable or necessary. It is much more natural to take the whole passage as a direct attack which Tertullian makes upon his opponent. He begins with a description of Catholic inconsistency and vacillation in moral matters. As he presses his attack, he begins to feel that the extreme laxity of the Sensualist system contains its own refutation, and he ends with a statement of what is, actually, the Catholic position. Thus the words *Haec tu mihi* etc. (this is what you *would* say) refer not to the whole preceding paragraph, but to the substance of its conclusion, beginning with *Deus bonus est*.

²⁸² The *Pastor Hermae.* Tertullian refers to *Mand.* 4.1, where the Shepherd permits *paenitentia secunda* to wives who have committed adultery; compare below, 20.2, *pastore moechorum*. The most detailed studies of the penitential discipline in *Pastor Hermae* are those of D'Alès III 52–113 and Poschmann I 134–205. In the light of the present passage it is difficult to see how F. Funk, *Kirchengeschichtliche Abhandlungen und*

Untersuchungen (Paderborn 1897–1907) 1.171, can speak of the teaching of the *Pastor Hermae* on penance as being more rigorous than that of the Montanists.

283 *Divino instrumento meruisset incidi.* These words show the existence of a definite scriptural canon at this time. On the canon which Tertullian received, cf. D'Alès I 223–30. For the meaning of *instrumentum*, 'canon,' see Hoppe II 50 f.—It is well known that in some circles the *Pastor Hermae* was considered a divinely inspired work and placed on a level with Sacred Scripture itself; cf. Irenaeus, *Adv. haer.* 4.20; Origen, *Comm. in Rom.* 10.31; Pseudo-Cyprian, *Adv. aleat.* 2. The author of the *Muratorian Fragment* states that the work should be read privately by individual Christians but that it must not be read publicly in the churches. Tertullian's reference to it in *De orat.* 16 as *scriptura* is respectful, but does not prove that during his ante-Montanist period he considered it canonical, since he uses the same word to describe it in the present passage.

284 This is one of the earliest references in Christian literature to the holding of church councils, and Tertullian is the first writer to use the word *concilium* in describing such assemblages; cf. also, *De ieiun.* 13. It is significant that one of the first questions with which the councils of the Church had to deal was the problem of determining which books belonged to the sacred canon of Scripture and which were false and apocryphal.

285 *A qua et alias initiaris.* This is rather cryptic. Tertullian appears to identify the *Pastor Hermae*, the 'shepherd of adulterers' (below 20.2) and the 'shepherd' painted on the chalice used in the Eucharistic service (above 7.1). The use of such a chalice, Tertullian says, will lead to both drunkenness and sexual debauchery, since the very chalice itself holds forth a promise of pardon for sins.—On the meaning of the word *sacramentum*, i.e. the sacrament of the Eucharist, in this context, cf. E. De Backer, *Sacramentum. Le mot et l'idée représentée par lui dans les œuvres de Tertullien* (Louvain 1911) 60.—Rigault's conjecture, *moechiae asilum* (οἶστρον) for *moechiae asylum*, has not been widely received.

286 There is nothing in the chalice which appeals more to the Catholic than the promise of a *paenitentia secunda*, symbolized by the restoration of the lost sheep there depicted. For the metaphorical use of *bibere* and *ebibere* in Tertullian, cf. Hoppe I 181.

287 The correct reading is *qui (pastor)*, not *quae (scriptura) non potest frangi*; cf. G. Esser, *Der Adressat der De pudicitia und der Verfasser des römischen Bussedikts* (Bonn 1914) 13 f. This suggests that the chalice which Tertullian has in mind was made of glass and that the shepherd pictured there was broken when the glass was broken; see above, *De pud.* note 174. Thus the weakness of the 'shepherd of adulterers' is contrasted with the strength of the true Shepherd, Christ; cf. D'Alès III 184 and references in H. Leclercq's article, 'Calice,' DACL 2.1589. For the evidence of early Christian iconography on the subject of penitence and mercy, see E. Bourque, *Histoire de la pénitence-sacrement* (Quebec 1947) 265 f.—On *lavacrum paenitentiae*, John's baptism, as distinguished from the *intinctio dominica*, or Baptism of the Lord, cf. F. Dölger, 'Zu *dominica sollemnia* bei Tertullianus,' AC 6 (1940) 111, and compare above, *De paen.* notes 24, 192.

[288] Matt. 3.8 f.

[289] *Sic et nos loquitur*, an emendation of Rauschen's for *sic et nos sequitur*.

[290] Cf. above, 10.6.

[291] Tertullian interprets the New Testament text, 'Bring forth fruits proper to penance,' as referring to a change of life which is the fruit of penance. But he himself has stated in other places that the fruit of penance is pardon for sin. He explains the apparent inconsistency by saying that the discontinuance of sin leads to pardon and that this reform is necessary if pardon is to be the fruit of penance; compare *De paen.* 6, *passim*. External penance for sin, or exomologesis, is not effective, even in case of sins where ecclesiastical pardon is possible, if it is not preceded by internal penance, or conversion.

[292] Literally, 'as far as the Gospel is concerned,' or 'in what concerns the Gospel.' Tertullian's study of the New Testament begins in chapter 7 with a discussion of the meaning of the parables. As far as the evidence of the Gospels is concerned, this much of his investigation is now complete.

[293] Matt. 26.6–13; Luke 7.37–50.

[294] John 4.26. Tertullian nowhere alludes to the famous *pericope de adultera* in John 8.1–11, and the omission furnishes a rather good argument from silence that the passage was not found in the Gospel texts with which he and his adversaries were familiar. Throughout the *De pudicitia* he is answering arguments used by his opponents (*nihil ex hoc adversariis confertur*; cf. Quasten, *op. cit.* 2.334) and it is difficult to believe that either he or they would have neglected to comment on so pertinent an example of the mercy of Christ if it had been known to them. The authenticity of the passage has been much discussed by commentators; see, for example, the literature cited by M. Lagrange, *Évangile selon saint Jean* (3rd ed. Paris 1927) 221–26. The pericope appears in MSS of the West before it does in those of the East, possibly because of the greater importance of the penitential controversies in the

Western than in the Eastern churches. Eusebius, however, suggests (*Hist. eccl.* 3.39) that it was known to Papias from the *Gospel of the Hebrews*, and it is cited in the 3rd century *Didascalia*, chapter 7; cf. R. Connolly, *Didascalia apostolorum* (Oxford 1929) lxxi. The first Fathers of the West who use it are St. Pacian, *Epist.* 2.31 and St. Ambrose, *Epist.* 1.26.

295 An allusion to the so-called Messianic secret. On the reasons for Christ's silence see L. de Grandmaison, *Jesus Christ. His Person*; *His Message*; *His Credentials* (tr. from the French by B. Whelan, New York 1934) 2.17-22.

296 Even if the sinners whom Christ forgave had been Christians, this would not prove that the Church has the power which Catholics claim, for, enlightened by the revelations of the Paraclete, we are now able to say that the power to pardon serious sin is a personal power of Christ's and not one which He has communicated to His Church; cf. above, 3.4-6 and below, 21.2.—The translation follows the reading *etiam si*. For the numerous variants, *et si iam, ac si iam, et suam, ut suam, ac si etiam, tamquam*, see De Labriolle, *op. cit.* lii.

297 Rauschen incorrectly supposes that this refers to the power of the Church to forgive sins. Tertullian is thinking, rather, of the direct forgiveness of sin by the divine power which Christ exercised while He was on earth and which He is still able to exercise in heaven; cf. Esser's note to Kellner, *ad loc.*

298 Tertullian argues that even if Christ had forgiven Christians, this would not prove that the Church, also, has the right to do so, since, as he has just stated, this is a power which belongs to Him alone. Actually, however, the sinners referred to in the Gospel narrative were not Christians, as will be shown at once, and the fact that pardon was granted to non-Christians can not be used to prove that it may be granted to Christians also.

299 This subject was treated in chapter 6 of the present treatise.

300 The *ordo fidei* is the divine dispensation or disposition of things contained in, prescribed by and known through the Christian faith.

301 That is to say, the Christian Church began its existence only after the ascension of Christ into heaven. Only then did it begin to be a perfect society, with authority exercised in the name of Christ and with members who could be recognized and designated as Christians. For the view that the Church had its origin on Calvary, *ex latere Christi dormientis in cruce*, cf. *De an.* 43.10. This view was extremely popular throughout the patristic (Waszink, *op. cit.* 469) and medieval periods, and it has not been abandoned today. Patristic teaching on the subject of the Church's origin may be summed up in the following formulae:

The Church began *remote* and *radicaliter* with the Incarnation itself (*Natalis capitis, natalis est corporis*; Leo M., *Sermo* 26.2); it began *proxime* and *meritorie* on the cross; *formaliter* and *effective* it began after Christ's resurrection. For a detailed treatment of the modern controversy which has arisen in connection with this question, cf. T. Zapelena, *De ecclesia Christi* (Rome 1946) 1.86–138.

[302] Since it was only after Christ's ascension that there were Christians in the world, and since it was only after the new revelation of the Paraclete to the prophets of Montanism that the discipline was inaugurated which excludes Christians from pardon for serious sins (*ipsius disciplinae* of the text), it makes no difference what examples of forgiveness we find in the New Testament narrative before this time. They can not be precedents which apply under the new dispensation of sanctity revealed by the Holy Spirit.—The meaning of *ante spiritum sanctum de coelo repraesentatum* may be seen from parallels given in D'Alès I 358; cf. above, note 155.

[303] Cf. John 14.16.—For Tertullian's use of *itaque* where *atqui* would logically be expected, cf. Thörnell, *op. cit.* 1.20 ff.

[304] The Montanists, especially such visionaries as Priscilla and Maximilla. Catholics enjoyed the possession of the Holy Spirit because they were members of the Church founded upon the apostles to whom the Holy Spirit was promised. They no longer possess Him, however, 'even in the apostles' when they reject Him by rejecting His revelations through the prophets in the latter days.

[305] The *instrumentum apostolicum* is not exclusively the *Acts of the Apostles* (Pamelius, quoted by Migne) but it includes all of the New Testament except the four Gospels (the *instrumentum evangelicum*; *Adv. Marc.* 4.3) and certain books which Tertullian thought were not written by the apostles, notably the *Epistle to the Hebrews* (below 20.2). For this division see Rönsch, *op. cit.* 49 f. Tertullian begins his study of the apostolic teaching with the *Acts of the Apostles* and continues it for nine long chapters, through the epistles of St. Paul and St. John, ending with a sneer in 21.5, *Exhibe igitur et nunc mihi, apostolice, prophetica exempla*.

[306] This is another instance of Tertullian's use of the word *paenitentia* in the sense in which modern theologians speak of the sacrament of Penance. It is clear (1) that he refers to the external penitential discipline terminated by ecclesiastical absolution and not merely to penance as a virtue, (2) that the *paenitentia secunda* of exomologesis and not the *paenitentia prima* of Baptism is in question, (3) that the effect of ecclesiastical penance is more than an external reconciliation with the Church, but that it is a removal of the stain of sin itself; cf. Teeuwen II 417.

[307] It is impossible to recover the exact wording and sense of this sentence. The translation is based on De Labriolle's conjecture: *Nos in apostolis quoque, veteris legis forma soluta, cernimus moechiae, quanta sit, demonstrationem.* Alternative readings and interpretations may be found in Esser's note to Kellner, *ad loc.*

[308] This is the so-called Apostolic Decree of the Council of Jerusalem, Acts 15.29; see, also, Acts 15.20 and 21.25. Tertullian's argument that the Decree proves, on apostolic authority, the irremissibility of apostasy (idolatry), murder and adultery is invalid for the following reasons: (1) it is based on an uncertain reading of the text; (2) it cannot be proved that the allusions to idols and blood in the text referred originally to the sins of idolatry and murder as these sins were understood later in the canonical triad; (3) the special prohibition of certain sins by the apostles would not prove that such sins, if committed, were irremissible by the Church.

It may be noted here that two distinct views of the Apostolic Decree developed in the early Church. According to the Eastern tradition of the text, the Apostolic Decree was a mere dietary regulation, to which was added a prohibition of fornication. The inclusion of this moral offense in a disciplinary decree seems inconsistent to some scholars, and Bentley (quoted by Watkins, *op. cit.* 1.18) suggested that the reading should be πορκεία, 'pork,' instead of πορνεία! In the Western Church the Decree was generally viewed as a solemn prohibition of the three capital sins. This view is stressed by Tertullian in the present passage of the *De pudicitia*; cf., also, Pacian, *Parain. ad paenit.* 4 and Cyprian, *Ad Quirinum* 3.119. Further evidence of the Western tradition may be found in the text of the *Codex Bezae*; in Irenaeus, *Adv. haer.* 3.12.14; Augustine, *Contra Faustum* 32.13; Jerome, *In Gal.* 5.2; Fulgentius, *De fide* 9; Ambrosiaster, *In Gal.* 2.2. G. Resch, *Das Aposteldekret nach seiner ausserkanonischen Textgestalt untersucht* (TU 28.3, Leipzig 1905) is of the opinion that the original form of the Decree was that favored in the West; for the opposite view, cf. H. Coppieters, 'Le Decret des Apôtres,' RB 16 (1907) 34-58, 218-39 and K. Six, *Das Aposteldekret. Seine Entstehung und Geltung in den ersten vier Jahrhunderten* (Innsbruck 1912). This whole problem is well synopsized by D'Alès III 200-04 and Doronzo, *op. cit.* 4.347-53. It is interesting that when Tertullian uses Acts 15.29 in *De monog.* 5 and *Apol.* 9.13 he clearly thinks of it as a dietary regulation.—For *observare vos*, meaning *abstinere*, see Rauschen's note *ad loc.* The same editor's citation of *De an.* 15.2 for the meaning of *vectare* is confusing, since the word there has an entirely different sense from that which it bears in the present passage; cf. Waszink, *op. cit.* 223. This final phrase, *vectante vos spiritu sancto*, is not in the Vulgate and has no counterpart in the Greek text.

[309] This is not the sequence found in the Apostolic Decree itself (Acts 15.29) nor in the reference to it in Acts 21.25. In both these passages πορνεία is mentioned in the last place. Acts 15.20, however, has *a contaminationibus simulacrorum et fornicatione et suffocatis et sanguine*.

[310] The words *multo magis humani intellegemus* show that although Tertullian prefers his own explanation of the text, he recognizes that another is possible. The arbitrary nature of his exegesis of the Apostolic Decree is well treated by G. Esser, *Die Bussschriften Tertullians De paenitentia und De pudicitia* (Bonn 1905) 25 f.

[311] *Quae sola in observatione de lege pristina excerpunt*. The words *in observatione* suggest that the special attention devoted to these sins consists in an insistence upon the observance of the law. There is also an echo here of the phrase *a quibus observando vos* in the Scripture text; i.e. the law will be observed by avoiding those actions which are condemned in the Apostolic Decree.

[312] In removing the obligation to observe certain precepts of the Law the apostles may be said to 'remit' these obligations. Tertullian is guilty of an obvious fallacy, however, when he implies that, in insisting upon the fulfillment of the remaining precepts, the apostles make the violation of these precepts irremissible sins.

[313] These three precepts are called *compendia disciplinae* not because Tertullian considers that they contain an epitome of the essentials of the Jewish Law but rather because they represent an abbreviation or curtailment of that Law. Morel, *op. cit.* 30, is of the opinion that *disciplina* in this context refers to an assemblage of laws which are specifically Christian. It would be more correct to say that it refers to the precepts of the Old Law which remain in force under the New. These precepts are, in part, mere matters of external discipline but Tertullian, as has been shown, finds it convenient for his present purpose to identify them with the most serious prescriptions of the moral law.—For references to the use of *compendium* in legal language, cf. Waszink, *op. cit.* 525.

[314] *Compensatio*, etymologically, is a weighing or balancing of some kind. Technically it is what is called, in modern legal language, a 'set-off.' In *Digests* 16.2.1 *compensatio* is defined as *debiti et crediti inter se contributio*, a balancing of accounts through the juridical determination of what must be and what need not be paid. This appears to be the sense which Tertullian attaches to the word in the present passage. God removes many of the obligations of the Old Law but, in return, Christians are bound all the more strictly to observe the major prescriptions which remain. The word *compensatio* is also used to describe the price paid in cancelling a debt. Thus, in Roman jurisprudence, *satisfactio* consisted in the removal of an obligation through *compensatio*.

This notion is present, radically, in the technical meaning of *compensatio* just given, since the price which Christians must pay for God's cancellation of many obligations is a more faithful observance of those laws to which they are still bound. Other instances of Tertullian's use of this word may be seen in *Apol.* 37.10; 50.15; *De paen.* 6; *De orat.* 22; *Adv. Marc.* 4.24 and, a most interesting paragraph, in *Adv. Marc.* 2.20. Further details are given in Beck, *op. cit.* 107–09; Buckland, *op. cit.* 703–07; cf., also, TLL 3.2044–47.

315 When an issue is settled by *compensatio*, the arrangement is legally binding and, in this sense, irrevocable. However, if the terms upon which the settlement was made are violated, then the earlier obligation of the debtor to the creditor must once more be assumed. In the present case God cancels numerous obligations of the Old Law and, in so doing, enters a counterclaim for absolute fidelity in the observance of the three capital precepts which remain. If a Christian violates one of these precepts, he has *de facto* violated the terms upon which *compensatio* was effected and, in consequence, he is no longer free from the other obligations of the Law. There is a possible analogy here with a declaration of bankruptcy. If a man is required by law to pay only a small percentage of what he actually owes, he should be all the more conscientious in paying that percentage since he has been relieved of his more serious obligations. If he fails to meet his lessened obligations, then it would seem only just, at least to Tertullian, that the whole original obligation must again be assumed.

316 The special ingratitude consists in the violation of generous terms spontaneously offered. For a different interpretation of this sentence, based upon the reading *ingratis* (*frustra*), cf. Rauschen's note, *ad loc.* See, also, Esser's comment on Kellner's translation of the whole passage.

317 After the obligations of Christians are determined by the Apostolic Decree, the Holy Spirit will no longer receive what He has abrogated, i.e. the ceremonial observances of the Old Law. At the same time, He will not forgive what He has retained, i.e. the obligation to avoid the three capital sins. The confusion in this sentence is partially due to Tertullian's use of *dimittere* in a twofold sense: (1) to release from an obligation; (2) to forgive the violation of a precept.

318 The *novissimum testamentum* is that of the Paraclete. For *status*, see above, *De pud.*, note 136.

319 *Recitatio* is the technical word for the official reading or proclamation of a will or testament; compare *Apol.* 15.1.

320 *Quorum custodiam elegit*; perhaps this might be translated, 'which He has selected for special restriction.'

321 For Tertullian's peculiar notion that Scripture forbids what it does

not explicitly allow, compare *De cor.* 2: *Prohibetur quod non ultro est permissum.*

[322] *Hinc est quod neque idololatriae neque sanguini pax ab ecclesiis redditur.* This is the most direct statement in the *De pudicitia* that pardon was not granted to sins of idolatry and murder by the ancient Church. Compare the five parallel passages in this treatise: 5.8–15; 6.8 f.; 9.9, 20; 19.15; 22.11. There is some ambiguity in the expression *ab ecclesiis.* It is not certain that Tertullian understands by this *all* Christian churches *everywhere.* Actually the opposite practice is clear from evidence in such writers as Hermas, for the Church of Rome (*Mand.* 4.3.7; *Sim.* 8.2.9; 8.6.6; 9.21.3; 9.26.5; cf. D'Alès III 97–101 and Doronzo, *op. cit.* 1.93 f.); Dionysius, for the Church of Corinth (Eusebius, *Hist eccl.* 4.23.6); Clement for the Church of Alexandria (*Quis dives salv.* 24). It is possible, also, that when Tertullian says that the churches did not pardon these sins he means that they did not do so at the completion of the public penance but deferred absolution until the sinners were on their deathbed. For further details, see the Introduction, pp. 48–51 and literature there listed.—*Hinc,* i.e. because of the Apostolic Decree. Tertullian asserts that the ecclesiastical practice of refusing to pardon sins of murder and apostasy is based on the will of the Paraclete, revealed through the legislation of the apostles.

[323] 1 Cor. 5.1. Such unions were prohibited in Lev. 18.8 and Deut. 22.30.

[324] 1 Cor. 5.5. The difficulty created by Paul's apparent absolution of the incestuous Corinthian is one which will occupy Tertullian's attention through five long chapters, 13 to 17 inc. He contends that the sinner condemned in 1 Cor. 5.1–8 is not to be identified with the sinner pardoned in 2 Cor. 2.5–11. This contention is supported by many, though not by all, modern commentators. Plummer insists that the identification of the two sinners is completely unwarranted and considers that the matter is all but settled by the arguments which Tertullian advances in the present chapter of the *De pudicitia*; A. Plummer, *A Critical and Exegetical Commentary on the Second Epistle of St. Paul to the Corinthians* (Edinburgh 1915, repr. 1951) 54 f. Against this, see J. MacRory, *The Epistles of St. Paul to the Corinthians* (3rd ed. Dublin 1935) 305 f., and D'Alès III 40–42. Patristic exegesis, it may be pointed out, is unanimously opposed to Tertullian on this question; for references to pertinent passages in Origen, Gregory Nazianzen, Isidore of Pelusium, Pacian, Ambrose, Augustine, Gregory the Great, cf. D'Alès I 481.

[325] *Quasi vel ipse postea stilum verterit.* For the reading, cf. Van der

Vliet, *op. cit.* 177 f. Writing on waxen tablets was erased with the bent or flattened top of the *stilus.*

³²⁶ 2 Cor. 2.5–11, with interesting variations from the Vulgate. In verse 7 Tertullian writes: *uti e contrario magis donare et advocare,* where the Greek text reads: ὥστε τοὐναντίον μᾶλλον ὑμᾶς χαρίσασθαι καὶ παρακάλεσαι and the Vulgate: *ita ut e contrario magis donetis et consolemini.* For the accusative with an infinitive after *uti,* in imitation of the Greek construction with ὥστε, cf. Rönsch, *op. cit.* 686 f. and D'Alès I 235.— *Advocare* means to 'act as an advocate for,' hence 'to support' or 'to console.' Tertullian uses the word regularly for the Greek παρακαλεῖν; cf. Rönsch, *op. cit.* 595, 660.—*Donaveritis,* for the Vulgate *donastis,* which according to the Greek ᾧ δέ τι χαρίζεσθε would better be *donatis;* Galtier I 138 f. St. Paul's statement is a general one but, as is pointed out by MacRory, *op. cit.* 308 and Plummer, *op. cit.* 62, the context restricts it to the particular case of the sinner whose pardon is in question. Paul says that if the community shows love and forgiveness to the guilty man, he is ready to do the same. This is one of the arguments used by modern exegetes to prove that the sinner of Second Corinthians is not the incestuous fornicator but rather someone guilty of a personal offense against Paul himself.—For *iniectiones* (Vulgate, *cogitationes*) see Rönsch, *op. cit.* 687 and Waszink, *op. cit.* 407.

³²⁷ Tertullian's first argument is a kind of argument from silence. There is nothing in the passage from Second Corinthians which suggests that St. Paul is granting pardon to the same individual whom he denounced so fiercely in First Corinthians. The condemnation was phrased in most explicit terms; so also (*proinde*) the absolution should be no less circumstantial.

³²⁸ The two preceding sentences are ironical statements by Tertullian himself and not, as Oehler supposes, objections raised by his adversaries. If the incestuous fornicator of First Corinthians is identified with the sinner whom St. Paul pardons in Second Corinthians, then we must suppose that his pardon is less clearly expressed than was his condemnation! This is against our ordinary experience since, as a rule, men would rather give pleasure than offense and, accordingly, they speak out more plainly when they forgive a fault than when they castigate it.

³²⁹ This passage has been much discussed. The translation given here is based on Rauschen's reading *nec aestimaretur* and the interpretation proposed by Esser in his lengthy note to Kellner, *ad loc.* The sentence is taken as a statement of fact: the sin of which there is question in Second Corinthians *is* a lesser sin and it is precisely for this reason that St. Paul does not treat it as he would if it were something as serious as incestuous fornication. For the view that Tertullian is speaking

ironically, 'No doubt there is question here of one of those insignificant pardons . . .' see D'Alès III 185.—The sentences which follow contain an *a pari* or an *a fortiori* argument in an implicit conditional construction. The protasis begins in 13.7 with the words *Tu quidem*, the apodosis in 13.8 with *apostolus vero*. If you, a lax bishop, act with such severity when you grant pardon to the sin of adultery, would the Apostle act with less severity in forgiving the sin of incest? Obviously the lack of solemnity and severity in his forgiveness of the sinner in Second Corinthians proves that it is not a serious crime which he there pardons.

[330] Or, according to the text of the *editio princeps*, favored by Rauschen and Esser, 'You lead the brethren into the church to intercede for the penitent adulterer.' For the grammatical explanation, see Rauschen's note, *ad loc.* Poschmann III 23 argues from this passage that public penance was performed in two stages: first, *in vestibulo ecclesiae* (*De paen.* 7.10), *pro foribus ecclesiae* (*De pud.* 3.5; 5.14) and, second, within the church itself, *in ecclesiam inducens* (*De pud.* 13.7). Following Koch he rejects the reading of the *editio princeps* and insists that it is the sinner himself who is led into the church for this second stage of public penance; cf. Poschmann I 316 f. Grotz, *op. cit.* 366–68, treats this passage at length in developing his thesis that excommunication had no part in ecclesiastical penance before the outbreak of Montanism.

[331] This picture of public penance is substantially identical with that given in *De paen.* 9–11 and *De pud.* 5.14 and 13.7. A new feature is found in the phrase, *omnium vestigia lambentem*, 'pressing the lips to' or 'kissing' (rather than 'licking') the footprints of the faithful. *Lambere* also means to 'fawn upon' or to 'caress' and *vestigia* can mean the soles of the feet, by metonymy, the feet themselves. Thus the words might indicate that the penitents embraced and kissed the feet of the faithful.

[332] The titles *bonus pastor* and *benedictus papa* do not prove that the Catholic opponent whom Tertullian here attacks was the Bishop of Rome. This problem has been treated in the Introduction, pp. 47 f. *Benedictus* was simply a title of respect, here, of course, used ironically, and *papa* was one of the ordinary designations of a bishop. See the discussion of this question in D'Alès III 229 and G. Esser, *Der Addressat* 15 f. On the use of the word *papa* in Christian antiquity and its gradual restriction to the Bishop of Rome, cf. P. De Labriolle, 'Une esquisse de l'histoire du mot *Papa*,' BALAC 1 (1911) 215–20, and H. Leclercq, 'Papa,' DACL 13.1097–1111 and the literature there cited.—The phrase *inque eum hominis exitum* is construed after *contionaris*, though the reading is uncertain and no satisfactory translation can be given. Hoppe I 62 is of the opinion that *contionaris* is to be taken passively, *appellaris*, i.e. 'you are styled good shepherd,' but this seems rather unlikely.

[333] Cf. *De pud.* 7.1–9 and compare Matt. 25.32 f. The *caprae* are Christians who have committed one of the sins which the Montanists consider irremissible. The sentence suggests Matthew Arnold's description of Tertullian: 'He saves the sheep; the goats he doth not save.' It is interesting to note that the Good Shepherd is occasionally represented in early Christian art as caring for goats and kids as well as for sheep. It has been suggested (cf. G. Stokes, 'Novatianism,' DCB 4.56) that such portraits reflect the opposition of orthodox Christians to the Montanist and Novatian heresies. The theory is attractive but it cannot be proved.

[334] *Cum maxime* is an ellipsis for *tum maxime cum* (cf. Waltzing, *op. cit.* 48) and should be translated, 'then especially when . . .' not 'when you are most . . .' The expression occurs repeatedly in Tertullian; cf. *De pud.* 3.1; 15.2; *Apol.* 5.3; *Adv. Marc.* 2.26; other instances are listed in Oehler's note on *De ieiun.* 4.—For the view that the parenthesis beginning *quasi non exinde iam liceat* refers to the fact that public penance could be performed only once, cf. Esser's note to Kellner, *ad loc.*

[335] *Habitum legalem paenitentiae*, according to Oehler's emendation. For a possible interpretation of the traditional reading, *habitum legatum paenitentiae*, see Rigault's note, quoted in Oehler, *ad loc.*—It is clear from this whole passage that exomologesis was performed under the close supervision of the bishop; cf. Galtier I 144 f. Tertullian's Catholic opponents required that works of penance, the equivalent of our contrition, confession and satisfaction, be performed by the sinner, yet they also understood that these were followed by an act of forgiveness granted by the *pastor* and *papa* of the Christian community. This forgiveness is described by such words as *pax, communio, venia, indulgere, donare, ignoscere, reconciliare, restituere, solvere, dispungere, delicta dimittere* etc. Tertullian's language throughout the *De pudicitia* reveals, besides, that his opponents considered this ecclesiastical absolution to be the normal sign of a pardon granted by God. It is the kind of pardon which Paul himself is thought of as granting and one which saves from eternal loss the sheep which has wandered from the fold.

[336] Both *de postero* and *de cetero* refer to the future. Thelwall translates *nihil de postero sit comminatus*, 'uttered no commination on the past,' but this can hardly be right.

[337] These are not to be taken as the words of Tertullian's adversary, as Oehler supposes. The correct explanation is given by Esser in his note to Kellner's translation.

[338] 2 Thess. 3.14 f.

[339] St. Paul says that the sinner in Second Corinthians is to be shown

love, but this would not prove that he was restored to communion with the Church, since, as is clear from Second Thessalonians, it is possible for the brethren to love a sinner and still not communicate with him. This is the treatment which is given to a fornicator. If the sinner in First Corinthians had simply committed fornication we might suppose that he is the sinner referred to in Second Corinthians. Such a man would take his place among the penitents and receive the loving prayers of the faithful but he would not be granted pardon by the Church (*De pud.* 3.5). The sin of incest, however, is among the *monstra* for which not even public penance is permitted (*omni ecclesiae tecto submovemus*; *De pud.* 4.5); such a sinner is removed from the midst of the brethren completely and, *a fortiori*, from their love. Therefore, when St. Paul, in Second Corinthians, speaks of showing love to the sinner he cannot be referring to the incestuous fornicator whom he condemned in First Corinthians.

[340] These are the words of an objection. Tertullian's adversaries assert that there are parallels between 'delivered over to Satan' (1 Cor.) and 'cheated by Satan' (2 Cor.); between 'destruction of the flesh' (1 Cor.) and 'too much grief' (2 Cor.). Thus the language of Second Corinthians suggests that it is the same individual referred to here as in the earlier letter. Moreover, St. Paul's words show that he wishes to avoid the 'loss' of the man *quem proiecerat*, the excessive grief of the man *quem addixerat*. Tertullian devotes the following paragraphs of the chapter to answering this difficulty, explaining in great detail what he takes to be the correct meaning of the words 'deliver over to Satan for the destruction of the flesh.' His argument is *a pari*: since these words have no reference to public penance followed by pardon elsewhere in the writings of St. Paul, they must not be taken to have that meaning in 1 Cor. 5.5. Tertullian's exegesis was favored, at a later date, by the Novatians; it is rejected by St. Ambrose, *De poenitentia* 1.13.

[341] For *satisfacere* compare *De paen.* 5.9; 7.14; 10.2; *De pud.* 9.9, 16; and *satisfactio* in *De paen.* 8.9 and 9.2.

[342] This is a further specification of the Catholic argument derived from the words 'hand over to Satan for the destruction of the flesh.' St. Paul's expression indicates that he sentenced the incestuous Corinthian to that affliction of the flesh which characterizes public penance. In so doing his purpose was to correct the sinner and prepare him for pardon. But if pardon were never granted him by the Church, he would be 'overwhelmed by too much grief' and the Christian community would 'be cheated by Satan.'

[343] 1 Tim. 1.20, Tertullian begins here to answer the preceding objection by examining the meaning of 'deliver over to Satan' in two

other places where St. Paul uses this expression or what seems to be its equivalent, and he shows that in neither of these passages does it mean 'to correct through a public penance followed by pardon.' St. Paul was given an *angel of Satan to buffet him*, but there is no question in his case of correcting one who had sinned. Hymenaeus and Alexander were *handed over to Satan* because they had blasphemed, but blasphemy is a sin for which there is no pardon in this life or the next.

[344] 2 Cor. 12.7.

[345] This is important as evidence that the earliest Christian tradition interpreted St. Paul's *stimulus carnis* as a definite physical malady. Tertullian translates σκόλοψ in two places, here and in *De fuga* 2, as *sudis*. This may mean either a 'stake' such as those used in execution by impalement, or a 'thorn.' Thus the word *sudis* is used metaphorically to indicate either intense physical agony or some sort of suffering which, though sharp, was comparatively less severe. The second sense is preferred by modern commentators; cf. MacRory, *op. cit.* 428. Σκόλοψ is less accurately translated by *stimulus*, the Vulgate version. Quite probably it was the Latin phrase *stimulus carnis* which led later commentators to suppose that St. Paul here complains of temptations against purity. For other theories on the form of suffering which is intended by the metaphor, e.g. epilepsy, ophthalmia, malaria, hysteria etc., cf. Plummer, *op. cit.* 348–51 and the more recent literature listed by J. Collins, 'Bulletin of the New Testament,' TS 15 (1954) 408, and T. Mullins, 'Paul's Thorn in the Flesh,' JBL 76 (1957) 299–303.

[346] One who is 'handed over to Satan' is punished for sin; this is not the case, however, when one is afflicted by 'an agent of Satan.' The biblical meaning of the words 'to hand over to Satan' is explained by W. Lock, *The Pastoral Epistles* (Edinburgh 1936) 19 f. For the meaning of *angelus satanae*, cf. MacRory, *op. cit.* 428. See, too, T. Worden, 'The Remission of Sins,' *Scripture* 9 (1957) 75–78.

[347] 2 Cor. 12.9.

[348] Matt. 12.31. For the exegesis of this text and, in particular, for the nature of the sin of blasphemy in question, see D'Alès III 21–28 and a useful synopsis in D'Alès II 11–13. St. Augustine (*Sermo* 71.5.8) declares that this text is one of the most difficult in the whole of Scripture. In his view, the irremissible sin is the sin of final impenitence; it cannot be forgiven because the sinner does not wish to have it forgiven.

[349] *Terminus*; cf. above, *De pud.* note 70.

[350] *Iam a fide*. Compare *De pud.* 7.12 and instances of *ante* and *post fidem* cited by Teeuwen 1 30, 91 f.—For the relationship of this paragraph to its context in the chapter, cf. above, note 343. The sequence of thought in the whole chapter is extremely difficult to follow; this is

due much more to a lack of order than to a lack of logic in its construction.

³⁵¹ *Naufragos iuxta fidem*; 1 Tim. 1.20. The Vulgate has *circa fidem naufragaverunt*.

³⁵² *Solacium* here means 'help' or 'assistance' rather than 'comfort' or 'consolation;' cf. Waszink, *op. cit.* 150.—The ship as a symbol or image of the Church is found frequently in early Christian literature and art. This developed, no doubt, from the popular idea of life as a voyaging over a troubled sea (cf. Horace, *Carm.* 1.14, 34 and compare Tertullian, *De paen.* 1.3), as well as from such scriptural accounts as the salvation of Noah in the Ark (compare 1 Peter 3.20 and *De bap.* 8) and the various incidents in the life of Christ and the apostles on the sea of Galilee. It has been observed that, architecturally, the early Romanesque churches imitated the form of a ship, with the bishop's throne corresponding to the place occupied by the helmsman and with the priests arranged in rows of *subsellia* nearby, as if they were sailors or oarsmen. This, however, is probably more a *post factum* discovery of Christian piety than a matter of imitative design. Modern languages reflect the identification of ship and church in such words as 'nave,' 'schift,' 'navata,' etc. The symbolism of the Church as a ship is worked out in great detail in an interesting chapter of the *Apostolic Constitutions* (2.57) where the bishop is likened to the captain of a ship, with the priests as his close assistants; the deacons are said to be the sailors and the faithful are the passengers. The author of the article on church symbolism in DCA 1.390, adds that the deaconesses collect the fares, but this is a fanciful embellishment without justification in the text. Illustrations and further details may be seen in H. Leclercq, 'Navire,' DACL 12. 1008–19.

³⁵³ A rather clear statement that in the Montanist discipline the sins of apostasy, murder and adultery were not the only ones regarded as irremissible. It should be noted, however, that the blasphemy of Hymenaeus and Alexander consisted in 'speaking against the Lord' (this is the generic notion of blasphemy) by spreading false religious teaching after they had been baptized in the true faith; cf. Lock, *op. cit.* 20. In this way 'they made shipwreck of the faith.' Thus their sin partook of the nature of apostasy and it may have been regarded as such by Tertullian. Compare the present passage with the reference to blasphemy and its punishment in *De pud.* 7.15.

³⁵⁴ Blasphemers are sunk in false teaching as in a sea of error (*demersos*; *emergunt*). Pagans and heretics are saved from this sea by the reception of Baptism. It is well known that Tertullian, like Cyprian and the Donatists after him, insisted upon the rebaptism of heretics, and his

statement here illustrates this false and dangerous opinion. See, also, *De pud.* 19.5; *De bap.* 15 and the note in Refoulé–Drouzy, *op. cit.* 87.

³⁵⁵ 1 Tim. 1.20. There is nothing in the text corresponding to the word *disciplina* in Tertullian's quotation of the verse.

³⁵⁶ The fact that Hymenaeus and Alexander were excommunicated 'so that they might learn not to blaspheme' might lead us to believe, Tertullian says, that their punishment was medicinal and that they were restored to communion after their correction through the discipline of exomologesis. This is not true, however, since their punishment was intended rather as a warning for others than as a means of salvation for themselves. In *De fuga* 2, written probably some five or ten years before the *De pudicitia*, Tertullian says that the punishment of Phygellus and Hermogenes (2 Tim. 1.5, apparently a mistaken identification with Hymenaeus and Alexander of 1 Tim. 1.20) for blasphemy was inflicted with a view to their own correction.

³⁵⁷ This last sentence ties in the argument of the whole paragraph with Tertullian's effort to answer the original objection posed at the beginning of the chapter. The incestuous man of First Corinthians was not forgiven in Second Corinthians, since he was 'handed over to Satan' as were Hymenaeus and Alexander, i.e. as a warning to the faithful, not so that he might be saved by exomologesis. This is, of course, a completely arbitrary and erroneous interpretation of the text.

³⁵⁸ There can be no question of salvation through public penance in First Corinthians, since, if there were, Paul would have said 'affliction' and not 'destruction' of the flesh.

³⁵⁹ 1 Cor. 5.5. His 'flesh was already lost when Baptism was lost' because, in the matter of rewards and punishments, soul and body are inseparable. Since, as will be shown immediately, the soul of the incestuous fornicator will not be saved on the day of judgement, neither will his body be saved. When he committed the sin which destroyed the grace of Baptism forever, his body as well as his soul was lost forever.

³⁶⁰ *Ipse* in the sense of *idem*; Hoppe I 104.

³⁶¹ The question implies an objection by his adversary that the soul of the incestuous man will be saved by chastisement after death. But this is impossible, Tertullian says, since (1) there is no punishment of the soul apart from the body (cf. *Apol.* 48.4 and often in other treatises) and (2) when the soul is reunited with the body at the last judgement there will be no longer any possibility of its salvation through chastisement. The only alternative is to suppose that the separated soul, after punishment in the next life, will be saved for eternity apart from the body. But this is to deny the resurrection of the flesh. Tertullian chooses

to ignore the possibility, clearly recognized in *De an.* 58, that the soul
may suffer chastisement *after* death and *before* its reunion with the body
on the day of judgement. It is not clear, however, that in this passage of
the *De anima* Tertullian is thinking of chastisement for serious crimes.
For Tertullian's peculiar eschatology, especially with reference to the
body-soul relationship in man, cf. D'Alès I 127–33; for his teaching on
purgatory, see Le Saint, *op. cit.* 144–46.

[362] This is an article which Tertullian writes of frequently and at
great length; see, especially, the treatise *De resurrectione mortuorum*.

[363] Just as Hymenaeus and Alexander were 'handed over to Satan'
for the salvation of the faithful and not for their own salvation, so the
incestuous Corinthian was 'handed over to Satan' not for the salvation
of his own soul, but so that the soul of the Church might remain good
and pure and be without sin on the day of judgement.—For Tertullian's
understanding of the words *spiritus* and *anima*, see *De an.* 10–11 and
Waszink's notes on these chapters, *op. cit.* 180–200. There is always
some difference, at least in connotation, between the two words, yet
Tertullian often uses *spiritus*, by metonymy, for *anima*. He appears to
do this in the present passage, and thus we may see here the first
reference in Christian literature to the 'soul of the Church.' The 'soul'
of the Church is to the mystical body of Christ what the human soul
is to the human body, and sin can touch it just as truly as sin can touch
the soul of the individual Christian. It would be a mistake, however,
to push this analogy too far or to suppose that Tertullian had a well-
thought-out theology of the soul of the Church. It is even possible that
he speaks of *spiritus* here in an abstract sense, referring to the 'spirit' of
the Church as we refer today to the spirit of the times or the spirit of
an organization. In the Encyclical *Mystici corporis Christi*, Pius XII
states that the Holy Spirit is the soul of the Mystical Body; *Acta
apostolicae sedis* 35 (1943) 219 f. Until the appearance of this encyclical
the theory that sanctifying grace is the soul of the Mystical Body was
defended by some theologians; cf. E. Mersch, *The Theology of the
Mystical Body* (tr. from the French by C. Vollert. St. Louis–London
1951) 447–49. Tertullian, of course, has nothing here which suggests
either view.

[364] I Cor. 5.5.

[365] I Cor. 5.6; compare Gal. 5.9. The expression was probably
proverbial: 'a little leaven leaveneth the whole mass.' Tertullian has
desipiat, the Vulgate *corrumpit*. The Greek text is ζυμοῖ (leavens),
although the reading δολοῖ (adulterates or spoils) is also found, and it
is probably this word that Tertullian translates. The Jews thought that
fermentation was a kind of corruption and, for this reason, the 'old

leaven' was removed from their homes before the Pasch as a symbol of the removal of sin; cf. Exod. 12.15–20. For the difficulty created by Matt. 13.33, where Christ says that the Kingdom of Heaven is like leaven, cf. J. Vosté, *Parabolae selectae* (2nd ed. Rome 1933) 1.236–48.

[366] 2 Cor. 2.6. The arguments which Tertullian develops in this long chapter to prove that St. Paul did not pardon the incestuous Corinthian may be summed up as follows. (1) The word 'rebuke' which is used in 2 Cor. 2.6 shows that he was dealing there with a lesser offense than the one which he 'condemned' in 1 Cor. 5.4 f. (2) Paul points out many faults of many individuals in his first epistle; the pardon granted in Second Corinthians may have been intended for any one of these offenses rather than for the grave crime of incest. (3) The faithful are told that they should 'mourn' for the fornicator (1 Cor. 5.2); but this proves that he is dead; therefore he cannot be brought back to life again by pardon. (4) The language of 1 Cor. 5.1–8 shows that Paul is concerned with two different offenses, pride and incest; the incest he condemns absolutely and at once, without hope of pardon; the pride he is content to threaten, with a view to its eventual forgiveness. Therefore when he actually does grant pardon in Second Corinthians, we must conclude that it is granted to the sin of pride and not to the sin of incest. (5) The incestuous man was already 'consumed;' therefore there was no reason why he should be 'pardoned lest he be consumed;' 2 Cor. 2.7. (6) Satan already possessed the fornicator; therefore there was no reason why he should be pardoned lest he be lost to the community by the wiles of Satan; 2 Cor. 2.11. (7) The fornicator was condemned by a judicial sentence; the proud man's sentence was held in abeyance. Hence indulgence was possible in the latter case but not in the former, especially since St. Paul was not accustomed to revoke his condemnatory decisions; Gal. 2.18. (8) Paul's love of chastity was so great, and the sin of the incestuous Corinthian was so serious, that it is impossible for us to suppose he could have been so inconsistent as to forgive it after he had once condemned it.

[367] 2 Cor. 2.1–4. *Sensus* is post-Augustan for 'a thought expressed in words.'

[368] *Mancipes*, those who have acquired a proprietary right in something, who have made it 'their own.' Compare *Ad nat.* 1.9, where the demon is called *manceps erroris*; see, also, Beck, *op. cit.* 104, 166; Waltzing, *op. cit.* 87.

[369] 1 Cor. 1.14. The words which introduce this quotation are ambiguous: *Et qualis invidia humilitatis aculeus?* They may indicate that St. Paul speaks the language of humility even when he expresses his

displeasure with the Corinthians, and that his humility is a spur to their own. If this is not the meaning of the words, it is difficult to see why the texts which Tertullian cites stress Paul's own practice of this virtue. The sentence may also be interpreted: 'What sharp humiliation his displeasure makes them feel!' This labors under the difficulty just mentioned, but a reason for its acceptance is given below, note 373.

370 I Cor. 2.2.

371 I Cor. 4.9. Tertullian's use of *velut bestiarios* is interesting. The Vulgate has *tamquam morti destinatos*, for the Greek ὡς ἐπιθανατίους. The usual Greek word for *bestiarius* is θηριομάχης; cf. Rönsch, *op. cit.* 671. The *bestiarii* were either hired performers or condemned criminals. The former were armed for their fight with the beasts; the latter were put out, unarmed and sometimes bound, to be devoured by them. According to Tertullian's understanding of the text, St. Paul pictures the apostles as *bestiarii* and God as the *editor* or exhibitor of the games who has arranged that the apostles have the last place in the day's performances. Cf. *Apol.* 9.5; 42.5, and Friedlander, *op. cit.* 2.56, 62 f.

372 I Cor. 4.13.

373 I Cor. 9.1. The spirit of this text is different from that of the verses just cited and the reason for its inclusion in the paragraph is not apparent. Its use suggests that the alternative interpretation of the sentence quoted above, note 369, may be the correct one. The Corinthians were 'puffed up' (I Cor. 4.18) and Paul's sharp language, rather than his expressions of humility, was intended to deflate them.

374 *De quali contra supercilio pronuntiare compulsus est.* Two interpretations of this sentence are possible. (1) *Supercilium* refers to Paul; *contra* means 'on the other hand,' i.e. in a manner different from the spirit of humility evident in most of the texts just quoted; *de* is added to an ablative of manner (cf. von Hartel, *op. cit.* 4.45–48). (2) *Supercilium* refers to the Corinthians; *contra* means 'on the opposite side' or 'against him.' Kellner translates: 'Wie gross war auf Seite der andern die Überhebung, die ihn nötigte, unumwunden zu erklären.'

375 I Cor. 4.3 f.

376 Cf. I Cor. 9.15.

377 I Cor. 6.3.

378 Cf. I Cor. 4.8.

379 Cf. I Cor. 8.2.

380 *In faciem alicuius impingens.* This may refer to a stroke with the sword mentioned above. *Impingere*, however, is also frequently used with *pugnus* and, possibly, this is the implication here.

381 I Cor. 4.7.

³⁸² 1 Cor. 8.7. For the meaning of *quasi idolothytum*, a reading found in Tertullian's quotation as well as in the Vulgate, see MacRory, *op. cit.* 117 f.

³⁸³ Cf. 1 Cor. 8.12.

³⁸⁴ *Nominatim* may also mean 'he begins to mention names.'

³⁸⁵ Cf. 1 Cor. 9.5. In *De exhort. cast.* 8 and *De monog.* 8 Tertullian asserts that the women whom the apostles had with them were their wives. The Greek text has ἀδελφὴν γυναῖκα and the Vulgate *mulierem sororem*, but Tertullian never includes the qualifying word 'sister' when he quotes this verse.

³⁸⁶ 1 Cor. 9.12.

³⁸⁷ 1 Cor. 10.12.

³⁸⁸ 1 Cor. 11.16.

³⁸⁹ *Tali clausula maledicto detexta*, 'with a closing like this, completed by a curse.'

³⁹⁰ 1 Cor. 16.21. On the formula *Anathema, Maranatha*, see the note by J. T. Robinson, 'Traces of a Liturgical Sequence in 1 Cor. 16.20–24,' JTS 4 n.s. (1953) 38–41.

³⁹¹ 1 Cor. 4.18–21.

³⁹² 1 Cor. 5.1 f. Tertullian writes *auditur in vobis in totum*, for the Greek ὅλως ἀκούεται and the Vulgate *omnino auditur*. *In totum* or, simply, *totum*, is a frequent variant in Tertullian for *omnino*, i.e. 'in all respects,' or 'actually;' cf. Waltzing, *op. cit.* 141.

³⁹³ *In praesidentis officio*. Tertullian's use of *praeses* and *praesidere* with reference to the hierarchy of the Church may be studied in *De cor.* 3, where he says that the Eucharist is received from the hands of the *praesides* alone, and *Ad. ux.* 1.7, where he cites 1 Tim. 3.2 and Titus 1.6 f. in discussing the digamy of 'those who preside.' Compare, also, *Apol.* 39.5 and *De ieiun.* 17. In these four passages the words seem to be used comprehensively of both bishops and priests. In the present passage, however, the context quite clearly shows that the reference is to the bishop alone. Compare Cyprian, *De unitate eccl.* 5: *Episcopi qui in ecclesia praesidemus*. There can be no doubt that Tertullian recognized the existence of a monarchical episcopacy in the Catholic Church. See, for example, *De praesc. haer.* 32 on the apostolic succession of bishops and *De bap.* 17 on the distinction between bishops, priests and deacons.—For the history of the bishop's role in excommunications, cf. Chartier, *op. cit.* 311. We may presume that since it was the function of the bishop to excommunicate, it was his function, also, to restore the sinner to communion at the close of exomologesis.

³⁹⁴ The incestuous man is already spiritually dead and Tertullian would have us believe that St. Paul desires his physical death as well.

The various readings of this passage are discussed by Thörnell, *op. cit.* 3.27–29.

395 *Interim*, that is, after his offense and before his physical death. For the meaning of *quomodo* in this sentence, cf. Hoppe II 113 f.

396 1 Cor. 5.5.

397 *Sacramento benedictionis exauctoraretur*. The verb *exauctorare* is a military term used to describe a soldier's dishonorable discharge from service; cf. *Digests* 3.2.2: *Si eum (militem) exauctoraverit, id est, insignia militaria detraxerit, inter infames efficit*. This suggests that the sacrament of which the sinner is deprived is not the Eucharist, as Doronzo states, *op. cit.* 3.69, but rather the sacrament of Baptism by which he was first signed as a member of the *militia Christi*. Indirectly, of course, deprivation of membership in the Church means deprivation of the Eucharist, but this is not the primary meaning intended in the present passage; cf. De Backer, *op. cit.* 11. For Tertullian's teaching on the possibility of 'losing' Baptism, cf. *De paen.* 5–7. He seems to know nothing of the indelible character impressed by the sacrament, a point emphasized by Augustine at a later date in his conflict with the Donatists.

398 The phrase *castra ecclesiae* continues the military metaphor begun with the words *exauctoraretur* and *sacramento*. As the son of a centurion in the Roman army Tertullian was familiar with technical military language and he employs it regularly in his treatises; cf. Teeuwen I 33, 101–09. It is significant that the citations in the *Digests* which, with good probability, are attributed to our Tertullian appear under the title: *De castrensi peculio*; *Digests* 49.17.

399 The text is uncertain and has been variously emended; cf. Dekkers' *apparatus* and Esser's note to Kellner.—For *intemptatio*, see Hoppe I 122.—On the clausula *qua increpabat quaque damnabat* in the preceding sentence, cf. Löfstedt, *op. cit.* 82.

400 *Res cum sensibus conferam*. This is not perfectly clear, though some help may be found in the distinction between *res* (*status*) and *sensus* given in *De fuga* 4. The *res* is the essence of a thing; *sensus* is our perception or our experience of it; cf. J. Thierry, *Tertullianus. De fuga in persecutione* (Hilversum 1941) 154 f. We can discover who it is to whom the apostle grants pardon if we consider the nature of pride and incest (*res*) and then study the Scripture text in order to see which expressions found there (*sensus*) apply more naturally to the two classes of sins.

401 In studying the sacred text we see that St. Paul *rebukes* one sinner and *condemns* another. Obviously, it is the greater sin, incest, which is condemned; and since it is condemned, it will not be pardoned later.

402 *Videtur*, i.e., in the light of the *sensus* of Scripture.

[403] 2 Cor. 2.7. *Si*, in this and the following sentence, has a causal connotation. 'If it is true, as it is, that ... then it follows that ...'

[404] The distinction between *culpa* and *sententia condemnatus* corresponds to the distinction which is made by ethicians and moralists today between the natural and the positive juridical order.—Tertullian argues that the incestuous man is already 'condemned' and, hence, already 'consumed.' Therefore the sinner who is pardoned in Second Corinthians 'lest he be consumed' cannot be the man guilty of incest.

[405] *Qui non maerere haberet, sed pati quod ante passionem maerere potuisset.* Since the incestuous man is already condemned, he is incapable of salutary grief. He can only suffer a punishment (i.e. hell) which, before its infliction, might have caused him salutary grief, if its anticipation had led him to avoid the sin for which he was condemned. If *quod* is taken in a causal sense and a comma placed after *pati* instead of after *haberet*, we might interpret the sentence as meaning that the incestuous man suffers now because before his suffering he could have had salutary grief and failed to have it.

[406] 2 Cor. 2.11.

[407] *Transacto*, literally, 'finished' or 'done for.'

[408] *Interlocutio*; cf. *Digests* 1.15.3; 44.1.11.

[409] Compare Gal. 2.18.

[410] Actually the language of First Corinthians makes it clear that in this letter Paul was concerned with correcting various faults of various individuals. But even if he had been concerned with no other sin than that of incest, we should still not be justified in concluding that he forgave this sin in his later letter. Rather we should conclude that there was some other individual who had a lesser role in the affair and who, after having been rebuked, was pardoned.—The reading *in causam eius* is preferred to the emendation of Reifferscheid-Wissowa, *in causa eius*; cf. Thörnell, *op. cit.* 1.16.

[411] This is the title which Paul regularly uses in the introductory salutations of his epistles.

[412] 1 Tim. 2.7.

[413] Acts 9.15.

[414] Paul was unwilling that the incestuous man should enjoy the 'profit' of even a temporary immunity from punishment, and it was for this reason that he condemned him immediately, *absens corpore, praesens autem spiritu*; cf. 1 Cor. 5.3. For the construction after *deputare* in the preceding clause, see Hoppe II 23. The whole sentence may be taken as illustrating the comments made on Tertullian's complicated style in the Introduction, pp. 6-8.

[415] Cf. 1 Cor. 5.4. Throughout this chapter Tertullian has stressed

the judicial nature of Paul's action in condemning the incestuous Corinthian. This is evident in such words as *judicare* (14.27) and *judex* (14.25 *bis*); *pronuntiare* (14.28) and *pronuntiatio* (14.25); *sententia* (14.2, 18 *bis*, 22, 27). God ratifies the sentence of condemnation which His representative pronounces; or, rather, Paul's sentence is God's sentence (*domini virtute damnaverat, ne humana sententia videretur*). It may be presumed, *a pari*, that God will also ratify a corresponding sentence of absolution which His representatives pronounce in His name. That He actually does this is stated explicitly by St. Pacian, *Epist.* 1.6: *Quod per sacerdotes suos facit, ipsius potestas est.* Tertullian's language in this chapter has been used to prove the judicial nature of the power of the keys; D'Alès II 8. It should be pointed out, however, that he makes no explicit statement that St. Paul is here exercising the power to forgive and retain sins which the Church exercises in the tribunal of Penance.

⁴¹⁶ Cf. 1 Cor. 5.3.

⁴¹⁷ This appears to be an allusion to the guardian angel of the church of Corinth and not, as we might suppose from the common interpretation of Apoc. 2.1; 2.8 etc., to its bishop; cf. Esser's note to Kellner, *ad loc.* It is difficult to say what suggested the phrase to Tertullian at this point, since there is nothing in the preceding sentence which it parallels.

⁴¹⁸ Cf. 1 Cor. 5.4.

⁴¹⁹ The meaning of this sentence seems to be that if the passages in Second Corinthians (*illius epistolae*) which follow after (*sequentia*) those which have already been treated are read in the light of the condemnatory language (*si ad intemptationem extendas*) which Paul uses in First Corinthians, it will be seen that they, also, are inconsistent with (*nec comparabuntur*) the view that he pardoned in 2 Cor. 2 the incestuous man whom he denounced in 1 Cor. 5.—Tertullian speaks of the 'obliteration' of incest. Even allowing for his habitual exaggeration of expression, this suggests that in the Catholic view which he opposes ecclesiastical absolution was more than the removal of an excommunication but involved, in some way, the destruction or the removal of the sin itself.—The general argument of this and the two following chapters may be stated thus: St. Paul shows himself, throughout his writings, an uncompromising defender of the highest ideals in all that concerns purity of morals. Therefore it is impossible to suppose that he could ever have been so indifferent to these ideals as to pardon a Christian who had been guilty of incest. The argument is first proposed in the closing paragraph of the preceding chapter.

⁴²⁰ There must be no inconsistency between First Corinthians and the *early* chapters of Second Corinthians; neither must there be

inconsistency between First Corinthians and the *later* chapters of Second Corinthians. This appears to be the force of *ne et hic*, although a difficulty is created by the fact that the later passages of Second Corinthians which Tertullian first cites are severe in tone and, hence, more likely to be taken as inconsistent with 2 Cor. 2 than with 1 Cor. 5. Perhaps we should not attempt to discover just which chapters of which epistles Tertullian has in mind when he speaks of inconsistencies. The general sense of the sentence is clear: If the later chapters of Second Corinthians are consistent with the view that Paul forgave the sin of incest—as they are not—then Paul would be guilty of inconsistency—as he is not.

421 *Quale est ut*; cf. Hoppe I 68, 82.

422 *Postliminium*, etymologically, is a 'return behind one's threshold,' 'a return to one's house;' see the explanation in Cicero, *Topica* 8.36. In legal language *postliminium* has reference to a disposition of Roman law which allowed for the restoration to his former *status* of a man who had been captured and enslaved; cf. *Digests* 49.15.5 and Buckland, *op. cit.* 67 f. Both the etymological and legal meanings of the word are clearly evident in its use in the present context. The *limen*, of course, is the *limen ecclesiae* (cf. *De paen.* 7.10; *De pud.* 1.21; 3.5; 4.5) and the captive who is restored to his former rights and privileges within the Church is the sinner who had been enslaved by Satan. For other references in Tertullian to the 'threshold of the Church' and for the significance of this expression in his teaching on penance, see D'Alès III 411–16.

423 *Amputans maculam*, a mixed metaphor, at least latently.

424 2 Cor. 4.1–2.

425 Reading, with Rauschen, *manifesta donaverit*.

426 *Aliquam impudicitiam*; perhaps 'notorious' or 'conspicuous' impurity, by analogy with Tertullian's familiar use of *aliquis* for emphasis in conjunction with the proper names of well-known persons; cf. Hoppe I 105.

427 2 Cor. 6.5 f.

428 2 Cor. 6.14–16. On the use of the word *infidelis* in early Christian Latin, see H. Schmeck, '*Infidelis*. Ein Beitrag zur Wortgeschichte,' VC 5 (1951) 129–47.

429 De Backer, *op. cit.* 60 f., is of the opinion that the word *sacramenta* refers here to the sacrament of the Eucharist exclusively, and that the plural is used because the Eucharist is considered as the sacrament of both the body and the blood of Christ. So, also, in the Greek Fathers, the plural μυστήρια, without further qualification, is often used to designate the Eucharist. The relationship, in Tertullian, between the words *sacramentum* and μυστήριον has been discussed most recently by

C. Mohrmann, 'Sacramentum dans les plus anciens textes chrétiens,' HTR 47 (1954) 141–52.

430 *Viderint idola,* 'it is the responsibility of idols,' or, perhaps, 'it is a matter of idolatry.' In spite of the frequent occurrence of *viderint* in the writings of Tertullian, there is almost always some difficulty in deciding how best to translate it in a given context.

431 To violate the temple of God, (the Church) is to act like a pagan idolater. But it is a violation of the temple of God (the body) to commit a sin of incest. Therefore to commit a sin of incest is to act like a pagan idolater. If such a person is readmitted to communion with the Church, then a sinner who violates the temple of God joins the assembly (*convenit*) of the faithful within the temple of God. This is, Tertullian insists, a *consensus templo dei et idolis.*—On sins of the flesh as violations of the temple of God and their irremissibility precisely as sins committed against God rather than man, cf. D'Alès I 485–87; D'Alès III 209–11; above, *De pud.* note 68.

432 2 Cor. 6.16 f. Tertullian's text of the Old Testament quotations (Lev. 26.12; Ezech. 37.27; Jer. 51.45; Ezech. 20.34, 41; Isa. 52.11) differs considerably from Paul's version as well as from their original form. The shift from second to third person ('dwell among you' and 'I will be their God') is not found either in Paul or the original Old Testament Vulgate texts, although Lev. 26.12 has *inter vos* and *deus vester,* while Ezech. 37.27 has *in eis* and *ero eis deus.*

433 *Hoc quoque evolvis,* i.e. 'you draw from the passages of the Old Testament your conclusions about the temple of God and you do it at the very time etc;' cf. Esser's note to Kellner, *ad loc.*

434 *Immunditiarum gurgiti.* Thus Cicero, *Actio in Verrem* 2.3.9, describes Quintus Apronius as *gurges vitiorum turpitudinumque omnium.*

435 2 Cor. 7.1. This text is cited in *Adv. Marc.* 5.12 in a form which is less consistent with the Greek: *mundemus nos ab inquinamento carnis et sanguinis.*

436 Reading *nunc revocasse* with the earlier editors and Dekkers, rather than *hunc revocasse* with Kroymann and Rauschen.

437 Tertullian employs two legal terms, *praescribere* and *praeiudicare,* to express the thought of this sentence. The sentiments of St. Paul which have just been considered exclude any appeal (*praescribere*) to earlier passages in his letter which might seem to justify the forgiveness of adultery; this refers especially to 2 Cor. 2. They also determine, by an antecedent judgement (*praeiudicare*), that no passages which follow may be understood to allow the pardon of so great a crime; this refers especially to the text which is immediately cited from 2 Cor. 12.—For *praeiudicare* with the dative in legal language, cf. Waszink, *op. cit.* 161.

[438] 2 Cor. 12.21. Tertullian translates ἀσελγείᾳ by *vilitate*; the Vulgate has *impudicitia*. Compare, below, *De pud.* 18.11: *sine macula fornicationis ut sponsa* (the reference is to the Church), *sine probro vilitatis ut emundata.*

[439] Since he would find them *in* the Church, obviously there can be no question of restoring them *to* the Church.

[440] The treatment which Tertullian supposes that St. Paul prescribes for sins of impurity is that which has already been described in earlier chapters of the *De pudicitia*. See, especially, 1.21 and 3.5.

[441] Tertullian returns to his original contention that when St. Paul grants pardon in Second Corinthians, he grants it to someone guilty of a less serious sin than that of incest (cf. 13.6; 14.2). A *reus humanior* is one who has not been guilty of an 'unnatural' crime.—*Ut . . . praesumant* is explicative.—*Citius* is used for *potius*; cf. other examples in TLL 3.1212.

[442] *Qualem et*; cf. Löfstedt, *op. cit.* 28.

[443] *In prima . . . primus dedicavit.* In First Corinthians St. Paul introduced into Christian literature the concept of the Christian as a temple of God. For *dedicare* in the sense of *initiare*, cf. Hoppe I 128. This sense is also found above, *De paen.* 2.3: *Deus . . . in semetipso paenitentiam dedicavit.*

[444] I Cor. 3.16. Other quotations of this verse in Tertullian are listed and discussed by Rönsch, *op. cit.* 359 f. Both the Vulgate and the Greek original have 'the Spirit of God dwells within you,' but Tertullian cites the verse in this form only in *Adv. Marc.* 5.6.

[445] I Cor. 3.17. Tertullian has *vitiaverit . . . vitiabit* for the Greek φθείρει . . . φθερεῖ and the Vulgate *violaverit . . . disperdet.* His version might be translated, 'If anyone corrupt the temple of God, him will God make corrupt.' Cf. H. von Soden, 'Der lateinische Paulustext bei Marcion und Tertullian,' *Festgabe A. Jülicher* (Tübingen 1927) 256.—The *aedituus* was the keeper of a temple (*aedes-tueor*) and a *lex aeditualis*, literally, would be a law for the keeper of a temple. It is the violation of this law which is referred to below, *De pud.* 19.25. Compare *De cultu fem.* 2.1: *Cum omnes templum dei simus, inlato in nos et consecrato spiritu sancto, eius templi aeditua et antistita pudicitia est.* Purity safeguards the temple of God, impurity violates it.

[446] I Cor. 3.18.—For the variants *redintegrabit* and *redintegravit*, cf. Van der Vliet, *op. cit.* 279 and D'Alès III 208. Tertullian argues that since the sin of fornication means the total destruction of the sinner by God, it is impossible that it should ever be forgiven by the Church.— *Omnino* may be read with *quis* rather than with *vitiatur*, although, if it is, one feels that *redintegravit* would be preferable to *redintegrabit*, 'Who in the world has ever etc.?'

[447] 1 Cor. 6.9.

[448] 1 Cor. 6.11.

[449] When Paul teaches so clearly that sins committed *before* Baptism are forgiven by Baptism, he teaches just as clearly (*quanto-tanto*) that if these sins are committed after Baptism, they may not be forgiven at all, since the sacrament of Baptism can not be repeated. Compare *De paen.* 7.10 and *De bap.* 15 for other references to the non-iterability of Baptism, and see the literature listed in Refoulé-Drouzy, *op. cit.* 88.

[450] The quotations which follow are taken, for the most part, from First Corinthians. They are cited very freely and are combined with other texts from Scripture which Tertullian considers confirmatory or explanatory of Paul's teaching. Possibly Tertullian attributes the whole series of verses to St. Paul, following a rhetorical device illustrated in 1 Cor. 6.16. Cf. De Labriolle, *De paenitentia et De pudicitia* lvi. The quotations are all intended to show that sins of impurity are sins against God and, therefore, irremissible.

[451] 1 Cor. 6.13.

[452] Cf. Gen. 1.26 f.

[453] 1 Cor. 6.13.

[454] John 1.14.

[455] 1 Cor. 6.14.

[456] 1 Cor. 6.15.

[457] John 2.19.

[458] 1 Cor. 6.15-18.

[459] The argument is not perfectly clear and the following paraphrase is tentative. If a man has committed fornication and then thinks that his sin can be pardoned, he is caught up in a contradiction. To be pardoned he must 'flee fornication'; but in doing this he dissolves the 'union in one flesh' which was established by his fornication with a harlot. When he left Christ for a harlot, he was guilty of adultery; if, in seeking pardon, he leaves the harlot and returns to Christ, he will again be faithless and again an adulterer (*moechus denuo futurus*). Thus his turning away from fornication is useless, since once the union with a harlot is established, it is indissoluble. The reasoning is fantastic but it is not beyond Tertullian's capacities.

[460] 1 Cor. 6.18. The meaning of these words is uncertain. Opinions of various commentators are given by MacRory, *op. cit.* 83-85.

[461] Cf. 1 Cor. 6.13, 15, 17.

[462] Cf. 1 Cor. 6.19 f. and compare 1 Peter 1.18 f.

[463] *Omnem notitiam ebibere.* For the metaphorical use of *ebibere*, see above, *De pud.* note 286.

[464] *A matrimonii pomo.* The genitive may be appositional, i.e. 'from

the fruit which is marriage,' though it is more likely a kind of posses-
sive, 'from the fruit which belongs to marriage' or 'which is proper to
marriage,' that is to say, the sex pleasure which is found in it. On the
apple as a symbol of love, cf. RE, s.v. *malum*, De Labriolle's note *ad
loc.* and the literature cited in these places. This symbolism may have
led some of the early heretics who denied the legitimacy of marriage
to speak of the forbidden fruit of the garden of Eden as an apple, and to
suppose that the original sin of Adam and Eve was one of sexual
intercourse; cf. Clement of Alexandria, *Stromata* 3.17.

465 I Cor. 7.1–3.

466 Apparently a reference to the *usus infibulandi*, for which see
TLL 6.644 f. and frequent allusions in Juvenal and Martial.

467 *Iam frenandis continentia coniugiis*; cf. Van der Vliet, *op. cit.* 279 f.

468 St. Paul permits marriage in order to prevent fornication, but
if he pardons fornication he encourages a sin which the remedy of
marriage is intended to prevent. And if it is the fear of fornication which
leads to the toleration of marriage, then marriage must no longer be
tolerated when fornication is no longer feared. Finally, if Paul pardons
it, he shows that he has no fear of it. *Timere*, in this passage, has the
pregnant sense of 'guard against.' The inconsistency of which Tertullian
here speaks has already been made a matter of reproach to his opponents
in an early chapter of this treatise; cf. 1.15–18. The present passage
furnishes further evidence that the arguments which Tertullian combats in the *De pudicitia* were not of his own creation but were actually
used by the Catholic party in defending the practice of granting
ecclesiastical absolution to the sins of fornication and adultery.

469 I Cor. 7.6 f. The *usus matrimonii* refers to the 'usage' or 'custom'
of contracting marriage, the institution of marriage, rather than the
exercise of marital rights after marriage is contracted.

470 The text is unsatisfactory. Thörnell, *op. cit.* 3.29–31, in a lengthy
note on this sentence, suggests *Unde autem licita* in place of the more
commonly accepted *Quando autem* (Oehler) and *Adae autem* (Mesnartius). The subject of *sperant* is understood, i.e. Tertullian's opponents,
and *qui* is interrogatory.

471 I Cor. 7.6–9; cf. above, *De pud.* note 32. In his semi-Montanist
and Montanist treatises Tertullian interprets this text as referring to the
fires of hell; see, besides the present passage, *De exhort. cast.* 3 and *De
monog.* 3. D'Alès I 252 says that in the Catholic treatise *Ad ux.* 1.3
Tertullian understands the text as referring to the fires of concupiscence
rather than to the fires of hell. This is a possible interpretation of the
sentence but it cannot be established with certainty.

472 Tertullian means that it is worse to burn in hell for having committed the sin of fornication than it is to burn on earth with the fires of concupiscence.

⁴⁷³ If the sin of fornication is pardoned by the Church, then the concupiscence which incites to it (*concupiscentia eius*) does not lead to the fire of hell (*non urit*).

⁴⁷⁴ Tertullian concludes that the 'fire' referred to in Paul's text is the fire of hell and not the fire of concupiscence since it better accords with the spirit of the Apostle (or 'the spirit of an apostle') to speak of the flames which punish sin than to speak of those which are lighted by the fires of lust. But if St. Paul says that 'it is better to marry than to burn' in the sense that it is better to marry than it is to commit the sin of fornication which is punished in hell, then, in stating that fornication is so punished, he is stating, equivalently, that it is not pardoned by the Church.—For *magis est ut*, cf. Waszink, *op. cit.* 379.

⁴⁷⁵ The sense of this whole difficult passage may best be given in a paraphrase. 'With what fires is it *worse* to burn—those of concupiscence or those of hell? Surely, if fornication is pardoned, as Sensualists teach, then one need not burn with its concupiscence, since one may yield to it and thus escape the fire of desire as well as the fire of hell. Even on your own principles, then, St. Paul must be understood to say that it is better to marry than it is to burn in hell. Besides, it is the duty of an apostle to caution against the fire of hell rather than the fire of desire. But if it is the fire of hell which is to burn those who do not marry but who commit fornication instead, then fornication does not find pardon, since hell awaits it.' For other interpretations of the passage, see Esser's note to Kellner, *ad loc.*

⁴⁷⁶ Cf. 1 Cor. 7.10 f. 'Perseverance in widowhood' is mentioned in the preceding verses. For Tertullian's view that remarriage after the death of a spouse is a violation of the marriage bond, and for his efforts to support this view from St. Paul, cf. *De monog.* 10–13.

⁴⁷⁷ Matt. 5.32. See, above, *De pud.* note 64.

⁴⁷⁸ These remedies are 'perseverance in widowhood' and 'peaceful reconciliation.' When Tertullian says that the reconciliation of an estranged husband or wife is 'a remedy against the recurrence of something which is allowed only once,' he implies that if such a reconciliation is not effected, a second marriage for one or both is inevitable. Thus he appears to ignore the possibility or practicability of what is now called 'imperfect divorce' as an alternative to remarriage or reconciliation, although he treats the subject elsewhere (e.g. *De monog.* 9) and the possibility is expressly mentioned by St. Paul in 1 Cor. 7.11.

⁴⁷⁹ 1 Cor. 7.26–28. Tertullian complicates his sentence by interpolating comments of his own into St. Paul's text.

⁴⁸⁰ *Parcendo permittit*, as in the verses which have just been discussed. Tertullian deals with this question at great length in his treatises on marriage and remarriage; see, especially, *Ad ux.* 1.3; *De exhort. cast.* 3-4; *De monog.* 3, 11, 14.

⁴⁸¹ I Cor. 7.29. Tertullian has *tempus in collecto*; the Greek ὁ καιρὸς συνεσταλμένος ἐστίν; the Vulgate, *tempus breve est*. Συστέλλειν means 'to shorten' or 'to contract.' Cyprian translates the participle by *abbreviatum* or *conlectum*; cf. von Soden, *op. cit.* 270 and Rönsch, *op. cit.* 380.

⁴⁸² I Cor. 7.30 f.

⁴⁸³ Gen. 1.28. Tertullian felt that the world of his day was over-populated and that, for this reason, the precept 'increase and multiply' could no longer be regarded as binding. The sequence of thought in this sentence is not, 'The end of the world is at hand; therefore this precept is no longer necessary;' but, rather, 'This precept is no longer necessary since it has already been fulfilled; therefore the end of the world is at hand.' Compare *De an.* 30.4; *De exhort. cast.* 6; St. Jerome, *Adv. Helvid.* 21.

⁴⁸⁴ I Cor. 7.32 f.

⁴⁸⁵ I Cor. 7.38. The contrast is between *conservatorem* and *erogatorem*. In legal language an *erogator* is one who pays out or distributes money, goods and the like. Tertullian, however, frequently uses *erogare* in the sense of 'to ruin' or 'destroy;' cf. Hoppe I 131, and he may have wished to suggest something of this kind here. There is, of course, no such connotation in St. Paul's μὴ γαμίζων.

⁴⁸⁶ I Cor. 7.39 f.

⁴⁸⁷ I Cor. 7.40.

⁴⁸⁸ The Catholic bishop who publicly proclaims that pardon may be granted to fornication and adultery perverts the teaching of the Holy Spirit as this is revealed in the writings of the Apostle. For the meaning of *recitare* with words like *testimonium*, *testamentum*, *edictum* (compare above, *De pud.* 1.6: *Audio edictum* etc.) see Waltzing, *op. cit.* 35.

⁴⁸⁹ The phrase 'necessity of the flesh' is not found in St. Paul but is used by Tertullian to express a reality with which the Apostle is often concerned.

⁴⁹⁰ The translation follows an emendation proposed by Thörnell, *op. cit.* 1.53 f., *quique* (*et qui = et quomodo*) *culpae blandiatur*?

⁴⁹¹ The union which is blessed is that of legitimate marriage (Gen. 1.28). The union which is cursed is that of adultery, with which Tertullian as a Montanist identified fornication (*De pud.* 4.1) and second marriage (*De monog.* 9). He argues here that St. Paul, in endeavoring to restrain the legitimate unions which are found in first marriage, hopes

to prevent Christians from becoming tolerant of the illegitimate unions which are found in adultery, fornication and second marriage. Since this is Paul's attitude, it is impossible to suppose that he himself could ever have been so tolerant of illicit unions as to grant absolution to a man guilty of incest.

492 He cannot prevent the lesser evil (*macula*) of marriage, but he is at least able to prevent the greater evil (*sordes*) of adultery.

493 *Psychici*; cf. above, *De pud.* note 23.—For the pleonasm *etiam et*, preferred here to the commonly received *iam et*, see Löfstedt, *op. cit.* 38.

494 *Adversus exercitum sententiarum instrumenti totius.* The same complaint is made in *Adv. Prax.* 20: *His tribus capitulis* (Isa. 45.5; John 10.30; 14.9–11) *totum instrumentum utriusque testamenti volunt cedere, cum oporteat secundum plura intellegi pauciora*; *sed proprium hoc est omnium haereticorum* . . . Compare, also, *Adv. Marc.* 4.19; *Adv. Hermog.* 19, 27. Tertullian's theory of exegesis is sound but, unfortunately, his own practice is often inconsistent with it; D'Alès I 242–54.

495 The *acies apostolica* is a wing of the *exercitus sententiarum* mentioned at the close of the preceding chapter. Tertullian's adversary is challenged to oppose his one text to this mighty force. *Provocare*, in legal language, is often the equivalent of *appellare*. If this sense is preferred, the sentence might be translated: 'Make an appeal to the forces of the Apostle;' that is, attempt to win your case by appealing to the writings of St. Paul.

496 *Praetendunt*; compare *Adv. Marc.* 2.6; 3.13; and see Oehler's note, *ad loc.*

497 I Thess. 2.3. *Advocatio* in Tertullian's text is closer to the Greek παράκλησις than is the Vulgate *exhortatio*; cf. Rönsch, *op. cit.* 595, 711.

498 I Thess. 4.3–5. For the translation of ἁγιασμός as *sanctimonia* (Vulgate, *sanctificatio*) see von Soden, *Der lateinische Paulustext bei Marcion und Tertullian* 255.

499 Cf. Gal. 5.19–21.

500 Reading *non delinquere hominem*, rather than *dominum*; De Labriolle, *op. cit.* lix.

501 Rom. 6.1–11, with some minor variations from the Vulgate.

502 That is, 'no one who has been baptized.'

503 Adultery and fornication are forgiven once, when the Christian is buried in and rises from the waters of Baptism. This forgiveness corresponds to the death, burial and resurrection of Christ. If we suppose that those who sin mortally after Baptism can be forgiven a second time, we must also suppose that Christ can die a second time.

504 Cf. Rom. 6.19.

505 Cf. Rom. 7.18.

[506] Compare 2 Cor. 3.6.

[507] Rom. 8.2, freely quoted. For the reading adopted here, cf. Rauschen's note, *ad loc.*

[508] This is not perfectly clear. Perhaps Tertullian says no more than that a certain sinlessness was required of the Jews by the letter of the Mosaic law, whereas the perfection of this sinlessness is required of the Christian, who lives under the new law of the Spirit.

[509] Cf. Rom. 8.3–5.

[510] Rom. 8.6. φρόνημα τῆς σαρκός is translated in the Vulgate as *prudentia carnis*. Tertullian here and in *De res. mort.* 46 has *sensus carnis*. *Sensus* in Tertullian, as also in classical Latin, often means a way of thinking or feeling; cf. *Apol.* 6.9. On *sapere* for φρονεῖν (compare *De exhort. cast.* 10), cf. von Soden, *Das lateinische N.T. in Africa* 286 f.—For the pleonasm *et inimicitiam et in deum* (that is, *in ipsum deum*) see Thörnell, *op. cit.* 2.82 and Löfstedt, *op. cit.* 40.

[511] Rom. 8.8.

[512] Rom. 8.13.

[513] Cf. Eph. 5.12.

[514] When the Apostle speaks of *sensus carnis* and *vita carnis* in this context, he is referring to sins which result from concupiscence of the flesh. He uses such ambiguous phrases as these because of his principle that it is shameful to mention these sins by name. If he were speaking of other works of the flesh, then even the Apostle (i.e. even one who some might suppose would not refer to *any* sin of impurity by name) would not have hesitated to use plain language; cf. above, 17.3. *Et apostolus* is perplexing, and the interpretation given here is subject to correction.

[515] Eph. 2.3. In *Adv. Marc.* 5.17 Tertullian declares that the true tradition of the Church proves that this epistle should be entitled *Ad Ephesios* and not, as Marcion wished, *Ad Laodicenos*; and yet, he adds, these designations are unimportant, *cum ad omnes apostolus scripserit dum ad quosdam*. For the recent literature, see C. L. Mitton, 'The Authorship of the Epistle to the Ephesians,' *Expository Times* 67 (1956) 195–98, and D. Guthrie's note, 'Tertullian and Pseudonymity,' *ibid.* 341 f.

[516] Eph. 4.20 f.—For the reading: *Notans . . . ingratia*, cf. Rauschen's note, *ad loc.*

[517] Eph. 4.28.

[518] The logic of this is not apparent. Possibly Tertullian wishes to say, simply, that Paul does not grant pardon to these sins since they are so filthy that he does not even mention them. For the textual difficulties, cf. Esser's note to Kellner, *ad loc.*

⁵¹⁹ Eph. 4.29.

⁵²⁰ Eph. 5.3, 5 f. Here and in Eph. 2.2, the Vulgate translates ἀπείθεια (classically = disobedience) by *diffidentia*; elsewhere (e.g. Rom. 11.30, 32; Coloss. 3.6; Heb. 4.6, 11) by *incredulitas*, the word which Tertullian uses here and in *Adv. Marc.* 5.17, quoting Eph. 2.2. For the Semiticism 'children of disobedience,' i.e. the Gentiles, originally, and then all who imitate them, see J. Vosté, *Commentarius in Epistulam ad Ephesios* (2nd ed. Rome 1932) 141 f.

⁵²¹ Eph. 5.18. The combination *ebrietates et comessationes* occurs in Rom. 13.13 and Gal. 5.21.

⁵²² Col. 3.5, freely quoted, with 'filthy speech' (v. 8) substituted for *avaritia* in the text. De Labriolle translates: 'Il montre ainsi aux Colossiens ce que tue les membres sur le terre.' This is grammatically possible (*Demonstrat . . . quae mortificent membra* etc.) and it may be the sense which Tertullian intends, but it does not appear to be the meaning intended by St. Paul.

⁵²³ Compare, above, 16.24. Tertullian is often indifferent to and careless of mixed metaphors. Thus he writes here: *obscura manifestis adumbrantur*.

⁵²⁴ Cf. Acts 16.3 and Gal. 5.2–6.

⁵²⁵ In Roman law *addictio* signified a juridical assignment of goods or properties; *Digests* 40.5.4 and 49.14.50. Other uses of the word are given in TLL 1.577 f., though the present passage is not there considered. Tertullian apparently chooses the word in order to suggest that St. Paul looks upon purity as a virtue which is, in a special way, proper to Christians. For *interdictio*, compare *De spec.* 3 (*interdictio spectaculorum*) and 17 (*interdictio impudicitiae*).

⁵²⁶ *Quando veniae tempus cum damnatione concurrat, quam excludit*. It is incorrect to say that when one reprobates sin one *ipso facto* excludes the possibility of its pardon, since pardon is possible just as long as sin is unremitted. It is only when sin is actually forgiven that it is no longer susceptible of forgiveness. Therefore we may not assume that because Paul condemns impurity he also refuses to pardon it. The meaning of *damnatio* in this passage is ambiguous and the interpretation given here is tentative; cf. above, *De pud.* note 77.

⁵²⁷ *Cavere*, in legal language, means 'to stipulate' or 'to decree.'

⁵²⁸ This is the title used in the Septuagint; cf. C. Toy, *The Book of Proverbs* (New York 1899) v f. and 3 f.

⁵²⁹ Prov. 6.32–34. It is surprising that Tertullian does not cite the words which immediately follow: *Nec acquiescet cuiusquam precibus nec suscipiet pro redemptione dona plurima*.

⁵³⁰ Isa. 52.11, quoted in 2 Cor. 6.17.

531 Ps. 1.1. Here and in *Adv. Marc.* 4.42 Tertullian has *cathedra pestilentiae*; in *De spec.* 3 he reads *cathedra pestium* and in *Adv. Marc.* 2.19, *cathedra pestilentium.*

532 Ps. 25 (26) 4–6.

533 The Psalmist, though a single individual, will be able to 'surround' the altar of God as if he were, in himself, a numerous congregation. Tertullian may wish to imply here that the Montanist, although separated from the great body of Christians, is sufficient in himself to constitute a congregation or a church.

534 Ps. 17 (18) 26 f.

535 Ps. 49 (50) 16, 18. On Tertullian's use of *ut quid*, cf. Rauschen's note *ad loc.* and the literature there mentioned.

536 Cf. 1 Cor. 5.9–11.

537 See above, *De pud.* note 254, for references to Tertullian's teaching on the Eucharist as food.

538 1 Cor. 5.6; cf. above 13.26.

539 1 Tim. 5.22, *ne cito imposueris*, in both Tertullian and the Vulgate. This text is commonly interpreted as referring to the imposition of hands in Holy Orders but it is highly probable that St. Paul intended it as a warning against the too easy reconciliation of sinners through ecclesiastical pardon. This is Tertullian's understanding of the text in the present passage, and his interpretation is adopted by St. Pacian, *Parain. ad paenit.* 15 and *Epist.* 3.39. In *De bap.* 18, where the text is cited *ne facile imposueris*, Tertullian applies the words to the forgiveness of sins in the *paenitentia prima* of Baptism. That the imposition of hands was a prominent feature in the reconciliation of sinners is well known. See, for example, Cyprian, *Epist.* 15.1; 16.2; 17.1; 74.1; the *Didascalia* 7.10 (*bis*); Eusebius, *Hist. eccl.* 7.2, where the practice is called παλαιὸν ἔθος. Arguments supporting the view that 1 Tim. 5.22 has reference to the liturgy of penance rather than to that of ordination may be found in P. Galtier, 'La réconciliation des pécheurs dans St. Paul,' RSR 3 (1912) 448–60. See, also, W. Lock, *The Pastoral Epistles* (Edinburgh 1936) 63 f., and the careful study in E. Doronzo, *De ordine* (Milwaukee 1957) 1.525–42.

540 Eph. 5.7 f.

541 Eph. 5.11 f.

542 2 Thess. 3.6, but reading *otiose* where the Vulgate has *inordinate* for the Greek ἀτάκτως.

543 Eph. 5.25–27.

544 Rigault supposes that Tertullian's words are intended to suggest a contrast between the youth and beauty of the Montanist 'church of the Spirit' and the unlovely antiquity of the church of the Sensualists.

This is not impossible, though one hesitates to accept a supposition which implies so definite a repudiation on Tertullian's part of the argument from prescription.

545 *Ex paenitentiae ambitu.* The significance of the word *ambitus* in connection with the performance of public penance may be seen in *De paen.* 11.4 and *De pud.* 5.14. Grotz, *op. cit.* 363, suggests that *pollutis* should be read as an adjective closely modifying *peccatoribus*, and not as a substantive specifying a distinct class of sinners. The sentence might then be translated, '. . . withdrawn from those who have committed especially serious sins of the flesh,' rather than, '. . . withdrawn from sinners, especially from those who have committed sins of the flesh.'

546 Ezech. 33.11, reading *quae vult* (von Hartel, *op. cit.* 1.24) rather than *qua mavult* (Ursinus) or *quae mavult* (Gelenius, Oehler, Rauschen and Dekkers). For the ellipsis of *magis*, cf. Hoppe II 48.—In the words which immediately follow Tertullian attests the importance which his Catholic opponents attached to this verse as justifying their practice of granting pardon to capital sins: *Hoc fundamentum opinionis vestrae*; compare *De pud.* 2.1; 10.8; 18.17; 22.12.

547 Eph. 5.11.

548 1 Cor. 5.11.

549 1 Cor. 3.17.

550 *Omnium focorum cineres. Omnis* is hyperbolic, as often in Tertullian. Other references to the use of ashes in the performance of penance may be seen in *De paen.* 9.4; 11.1 and *De pud.* 5.14.

551 The distinction between 'not receiving' a man who sins after embracing the faith and 'excommunicating' one who sins after admission to communion with the Church is not exactly clear. Perhaps Tertullian means that St. Paul, first of all, forbids the Christian churches to communicate with sinful brethren and, second, that in cases where this prohibition was violated he personally reexcommunicated the sinner who had been unlawfully admitted to fellowship.

552 Reading *peccatores . . . diluendi.* Rauschen suggests *morte . . . diluenda.* Baptism washes away death, once for all, just as Christ died, once for all, to save men from the death of sin. Cf. *De bap.* 2 and *De an.* 50.3, with Waszink's note, *op. cit.* 522.

553 Tertullian's most eloquent statement on the redemptive death of Christ is found in *De fuga* 12; compare, also, *De carne Christi* 5; *De bap.* 11; *De idol.* 5; *De pat.* 3; *Adv. Marc.* 3.8.

554 1 Tim. 1.13. Tertullian wishes to prove that the grace of Christ is efficacious for the salvation of those who sin before Baptism, not for those who sin after it. He illustrates this by St. Paul's statement that he obtained mercy because he sinned before he was enlightened by faith.

The argument involves a typical example of what logicians call the 'fallacy of the consequent.' St. Paul was forgiven because he sinned *before* he was baptized. Therefore if he had sinned *after* he was baptized, he would not have been forgiven. Cf. above, *De paen.* note 26 for other references to Tertullian's views on sins committed in ignorance and spiritual blindness.

555 Ezech. 33.11.

556 This sentence might also be translated: 'It is to save these that Christ has come, and not to save those already acquainted with God . . .'

557 *Sacramentum fidei*; compare 1 Tim. 3.9, *mysterium fidei*. The word *sacramentum* in the present passage is synonymous with *mysterium sacrum* or *res sacra et mysteriosa*. For other instances of this use of the word in Tertullian, cf. De Backer, *op. cit.* 79–82 and the same author's notes in J. De Ghellinck etc., *Pour l'histoire du mot 'Sacramentum'* (Louvain 1924) 133 f. The phrase *fidei sacramentum* occurs, also, in *De pat.* 12; *Adv. Marc.* 1.28; *De an.* 1.4; *De bap.* 13. In none of these passages, however, does it have the same sense as that which is found here. In the first three it is the equivalent of *signaculum fidei*; in the last it preserves the original etymological meaning of *sacrum faciens*.

558 The *paenitentia prima* of Baptism.

559 *Paenitentia post fidem*; the 'other kind of penance' which is not excluded after the *paenitentia prima* of Baptism is the *paenitentia secunda* of exomologesis. This sentence has been much discussed and is of importance not only for what it tells us of Tertullian's Montanist views but also for what it reveals of the Catholic doctrine and practice which he knew and accepted before his break with the Church. He recognizes, clearly, the existence of an ecclesiastical tribunal established for the forgiveness of sins. As a Montanist he did not deny that the Church has a power to forgive sin; rather he restricted this power to what are here called the *peccata leviora*. His Catholic opponents, in refusing to accept this restriction, reassert the position which he himself held before his lapse into Montanism: the tribunal of penance exists for the forgiveness of all sins, *leviora* and *maiora* alike. Tertullian states that forgiveness of sins in the tribunal of penance is granted by the bishop. This is the first explicit reference in Christian literature to the bishop as minister of ecclesiastical absolution. Other early evidence may be found in Doronzo, *De poenitentia* 4.623–36 and Watkins, *op. cit.* 125 f.

It would appear from Tertullian's language in this passage that ecclesiastical absolution meant more than the lifting of an ecclesiastical penalty through the restoration of a sinner to communion with the Church. It also effected a forgiveness of sins which in no way differs from that which God Himself directly grants. Whether it is God who pardons *grave* sin or the bishop who pardons lesser sins in God's name, the proper object of *venia* in both cases is the sin itself. It is always the *extent* of the power to forgive sin, and not its *nature* or *efficacy*, which is the point at issue between Catholics and Montanists. See the very convincing presentation of this argument in Galtier II 29–33.

The *delicta leviora* of this passage are probably identified with the *delicta modica* mentioned above, *De pud.* 1.19 and 13.6. Cf., also, *De pud.* 2.12, 14, 16 and 7.20. If these are venial sins in the sense in which we use the term today, the passage affords evidence that such sins are *materia sufficiens* for the sacrament of Penance; Doronzo, *op. cit.* 1.226. It is quite likely, however, that they include 'lesser' offenses, which were of a serious character but which the Montanists felt could be forgiven by the bishop after exomologesis; cf. Rauschen, *Eucharist and Penance* 227 and above, *De pud.* notes 35, 130, 198. The sentence has been studied by Motry, *op. cit.* 143, 156 and Galtier II 272, 275 in connection with the problem of Tertullian's distinction of sins. Galtier gives special attention to the bearing which the distinction between *peccata leviora* and *maiora* has on the existence of private penance. It is his contention that the *alia species paenitentiae* here referred to was one which did not require the enrollment of the sinner in the ranks of the public penitents and, hence, that it may properly be called 'private penance;' cf. Galtier I 246 and II 272, 275. It seems much more natural, however, as has been noted above, to understand the *prima species paenitentiae* as the *paenitentia prima* of Baptism and the *secunda* or *alia species* as the *paenitentia secunda* of exomologesis.

[560] Apoc. 2.20–22, with a number of verbal variations from the Vulgate. For example: (a) *habere se adversus eum quod* for *habeo adversus te quod*; (b) *paenitentiam iniret* for *paenitentiam ageret*; (c) *nec vult eam inire nomine fornicationis* for *non vult poenitere a fornicatione sua*. The phrase *nomine fornicationis* can mean either that the woman was unwilling to do penance *for her adultery* (i.e. to put an end to her adultery and make reparation for it), and this is the sense of the Greek text; or it can mean that she did not wish to do penance *because of her adultery* (i.e. precisely as one who had committed the sin of adultery). For this causal and limiting sense of *nomine* followed by a genitive, cf. Thörnell, *op. cit.* 1.56–58.—The interpretation of the Apocalypse which Tertullian gives here differs considerably from that in *De paen.* 8.1 ff.

[561] 1 Cor. 15.11.

[562] The unity of doctrine and discipline found in the writings of the apostles results from the fact that they all composed under the inspiration of the same Holy Spirit. To suppose that there can be inconsistencies in their works is to suppose that God can contradict Himself.

For this important reason, Tertullian insists, we must not believe that John allows what Paul forbids.—*Sacramentum* refers to the whole deposit of faith; cf. De Backer, *op. cit.* 39 f.

[563] The translation is based upon a suggestion proposed by Van der Vliet, *op. cit.* 280. The more common reading places *et* before *merito* rather than before *in ecclesiam*: 'For the woman whom he sought to bring into the church secretly and whom he properly urged to the performance of penance was a heretic, one who had undertaken to teach what she learned from the Nicolaites.' For a defense of this reading see D'Alès III 188. In either version the subject of *urgebat ad paenitentiam* is probably the Holy Spirit (or John, speaking for the Holy Spirit) and not, as Thelwall supposes in an interpolation, 'the angel of the church of Thyatira.'—References to the Nicolaites are found in Apoc. 2.6 (letter to the church of Ephesus) and Apoc. 2.15 (letter to the church of Pergamum). Though they are not explicitly mentioned in the message to the church of Thyatira, modern commentators are in agreement with Tertullian that it is this heresy which John has in mind when he speaks of the errors spread by the woman, Jezabel; cf. H. Swete, *The Apocalypse of St. John* (Grand Rapids 1951; repr. from 3rd ed.) 42 f. The limited information furnished by ancient sources on this sect has been gathered by E. Amann in his article, 'Nicolaites,' DTC 11.499–506. For other references to the Nicolaites in Tertullian, cf. *De praesc. haer.* 33 and *Adv. Marc.* 1.29.

[564] Tertullian argues that it is vain to appeal to this passage of the Apocalypse as a proof that adultery may be forgiven by the Church to members of the Church, since there is question here of the *paenitentia prima* of Baptism and not the *paenitentia secunda* of exomologesis. His assertion that the woman, Jezabel, had not yet been baptized in the true faith at the time she began to spread her erroneous opinions is gratuitous and has no support in the text of the Apocalypse.

[565] *Utroque nomine purgatus.* A heretic is just as bad as or even worse than an infidel, but he is cleansed of both his heresy and the infidelity which it supposes when he is baptized in the true faith. The expression *apud nos* would seem to indicate that the practice of rebaptizing heretics was peculiar to the Montanists, but it is not impossible that the words mean here, 'among us Christians.' See, above, *De pud.* note 354.

[566] *Consecutura restitutionem. Restitutio* quite clearly involves an ecclesiastical act of forgiveness, since it is precisely this forgiveness which the Montanists reject and the Catholics allow. Funk, Vacandard and others concede this meaning of the word *restitutio* in the *De pudicitia* but deny it in the *De paenitentia.* That this distinction is unwarranted has been shown convincingly in D'Alès III 161 ff.

⁵⁶⁷ Tertullian contends that the evidence of the Apocalypse does not destroy the Montanist thesis, for the adulterous woman was either: (a) not a member of the true Church and, therefore, she was forgiven by the *paenitentia prima* of Baptism and not the *paenitentia secunda* of exomologesis; or (b) she was a member of the true Church and therefore she was required to do public penance, but was not allowed ecclesiastical absolution. That the Montanists demanded public penance for sins which they refused to forgive has been seen in earlier passages of the *De pudicitia*; see, for example, 1.21; 2.15; 3.1 ff. Such sins were 'irremissible' in that they could be forgiven by God alone; *etsi pacem hic non metit, apud dominum seminat* (3.5); cf. Batiffol, *op. cit.* 83. f.—It should be observed that Tertullian implicitly recognizes here that in the Catholic system ecclesiastical *restitutio* is inseparable from the divine *venia*. The remission of sins which Montanists 'reserve to God alone' is precisely the remission which their Catholic opponents say the Church grants to her sinful subjects; compare, above, 3.3 and 18.17. This, obviously, is an absolution from sin which restores the sinner to friendship with God Himself and not merely to communion with the Church. Tertullian's language reveals the ancient belief of orthodox Christians that to reconcile a sinner with the Church, the living body of Christ, is to reconcile him also with Christ, the head of the mystical body.

⁵⁶⁸ Christians who sin seriously are condemned to eternal punishment (the 'second death') unconditionally, i.e. without the condition expressed or understood, 'unless they do penance and are forgiven by the Church.' One feels that, if their condemnation in the Apocalypse were as absolute as Tertullian asserts, we should have to say that not even God forgives them after mortal sin. For the interpretation of the 'second death' in patristic documents, cf. J. Plumpe, 'Mors secunda,' *Mélanges de Ghellinck* (Gembloux 1951) 387-403.

⁵⁶⁹ Cf. Apoc. 21.8.

⁵⁷⁰ Apoc. 21.7 f.

⁵⁷¹ Apoc. 22.14 f. Tertullian's version of this text (*qui ex praeceptis agunt*) favors the reading οἱ ποιοῦντες τὰς ἐντολάς (Von Soden) rather than οἱ πλυνόντες τὰς στολάς (Nestle, and the Vulgate, *qui lavant stolas suas*).

⁵⁷² I Cor. 5.12. *Enim*, in the sentence immediately preceding this quotation, has the force of a strong affirmation, without causal connotation. This usage is quite common in Tertullian and has been noted before; cf. Diercks, *op. cit.* 165.

⁵⁷³ I John 1.7. Here and elsewhere in his writings Tertullian recognizes but one epistle of St. John, the first; cf. Rönsch, *op. cit.* 544 f. and

571 f. The references to 2 John 7 (*Adv. Marc.* 5.16) and 2 John 10 (*De praesc. haer.* 8) given in Oehler's *Index scripturarum sacrarum* are incorrect.

574 The answer to the preceding rhetorical question is understood: 'No, we should not sin at all times and in every way.' Tertullian suppresses this answer and begins immediately, 'But if not at all times etc.'

575 Cf. 1 John 1.5–7.

576 *Mundos exinde perstare*. See Rauschen's note *ad loc.* for the justification of this reading as against *mundos exinde praestet*.

577 1 John 1.8 f. The two sentences which follow are taken as an objection which Tertullian himself raises. His opponent continues with the words: *Sed aliud in sensu est*. The interpretation, however, is not certain.

578 This is a return to the *ad hominem* argument developed at length in earlier chapters: you are inconsistent in granting pardon to adultery while you refuse to pardon idolatry.—For the meaning of *aut* in this sentence, i.e. *alioquin*, see Thörnell, *op. cit.* 2.29. *At* is an unnecessary emendation of Reifferscheid-Wissowa.

579 1 John 1.10.

580 1 John 2.1 f.

581 *Aliud* can mean either 'a different sense for the passage just quoted' or 'something else,' i.e. 'a new passage with a sense different from that of the passage just quoted.' Esser, in a note to Kellner's translation, argues for the first interpretation, relating the word to *aliud in sensu* of the preceding paragraph, where he understands *sensus* as 'the meaning of the sentence' rather than, simply, 'the sentence' or 'the passage.'—The apparently conflicting texts in 1 John with which Tertullian is here concerned have been discussed at length by P. Galtier, *Aux origines du sacrement de pénitence* (Rome 1951) 69–76.

582 Tertullian's use of *ut* is often troublesome. In the present sentence there seems to be an instance of the *ut explicativus*, described by Thörnell, *op. cit.* 2.72 f.

583 1 John 3.3–5.

584 1 John 3.6–8. The texts which Tertullian cites in this paragraph to prove the sinlessness of Christians have been used by some historians of dogma to show that the early Church was regarded as a society of saints and not a society to make saints. For a refutation of this exegesis, see P. Galtier, 'Le chrétien impeccable,' MSR 6 (1947) 137–54.

585 Cf Col. 2.14.

586 1 John 3.9 f.

587 From this it is clear that Tertullian thinks of the 'children of the

devil' as Christians who, although born of God by Baptism, prove that they are not truly His children by sinning after Baptism; for, as St. John says, 'The children of God cannot sin.' Since these Christians have thus proved by their sin that they are not truly His children, even though they were once born of Him by Baptism, it is impossible that they should ever be restored by penance to that heritage of which they have proved unworthy. They are 'children of the devil' and, therefore, they can never again be 'children of God.'

588 1 John 3.10.

589 Rauschen substitutes *quia* for the traditional reading *qui*. This is uncalled for, as has been shown by Thörnell, *op. cit.* 2.70, in a lengthy note on Tertullian's use of the relative pronoun.

590 Cf. *De pud.* 1.19; 2.15. The words of the preceding objection are given by Thelwall as a direct quotation of Tertullian's Catholic adversaries. This is a possible but not a necessary interpretation.

591 *Delicta cotidianae incursionis quibus omnes simus objecti*. Oehler believes that *incursio* is the actual commission of a sin, not merely the temptation to commit it. This meaning has been adopted by Thelwall, and it must be admitted that it gives a sense which seems more consistent than its alternative with the sentence which immediately follows: *Cui enim non accidet aut irasci* etc.? We might, then, translate: 'There are some sins, committed daily, to which we all are subject.' *Peccata cotidiana*, moreover, are mentioned by a number of later Christian writers; see, for example, St. Ambrose, *De paen.* 2.10.95: *cotidiani nos debet paenitere peccati*; St. Augustine, *Enchiridion* 71: *Delet oratio . . . cotidiana peccata*; and *Sermo* 351 (ML 39.1541): *medicamento cotidianae paenitentiae*, in a passage closely resembling that of the *De pudicitia* presently being considered.

Usually, however, the *peccata cotidianae incursionis* are understood to be sins which trouble or assault men daily (De Labriolle; Kellner), not those which they actually commit daily. They are not sins to which all men are subject or enslaved, but rather those to which all men are regularly tempted and which they sometimes commit; cf. Daly, *op. cit.* 70.735. Tertullian speaks of the attacks of the demons as *incursus* (*Apol.* 37.9; *De an.* 57.4), and this would seem to be the sense of *incursio* also in this context; cf. TLL 7.1090. On the difference between the *peccata cotidiana* of Augustine and the *peccata cotidianae incursionis* of Tertullian, see Galtier II 272 f.

592 Cf. Eph. 4.26.

593 The *peccata cotidianae incursionis* here listed appear to be identified with the *peccata non mortalia* of *De pud.* 7.14–16. This identification, however, remains controversial; see, above, *De pud.* note 198, where the

question is treated in detail. To the literature there cited may be added K. Kirk, *The Vision of God* (2nd ed. London 1932) 515–17, and Motry, *op. cit.* 75–84. It would seem evident from the context that these sins were not 'venial' in our modern sense of the word, since Tertullian says that if they were not pardoned, no one would be saved. Thus the inadvertence of the sinner (*facile, temere*) and other mitigating circumstances (*verecundia, necessitas*) will lessen guilt to the extent that pardon may be granted by the Church, but not to the extent that the sinner will escape eternal punishment if he is unforgiven. Tertullian's severity in judging these cases appears to us today to be extreme and yet, as has been noted above in the commentary on *De pud.* 7.20, it is not impossible that the orthodox Church itself punished such sins as these, or at least some of them, by a temporary excommunication.

Motry, *op. cit.* 137–56, is of the opinion that the contrast which Tertullian makes here between lesser sins and the *peccata exitiosa istis contraria* reveals a concept of mortal and venial sin not essentially different from that in the Church today. His arguments, however, are not convincing. It is clear from the paragraph which follows that the *peccata cotidianae incursionis* are to be identified with the *peccata non ad mortem* of St. John's text, whereas the *peccata contraria istis*, or at least adultery and fornication which alone are mentioned in 19.28, are his *peccata ad mortem*. This seems somewhat inconsistent with the statement that the *peccata cotidianae incursionis* are so serious that no one would be saved if such offenses were irremissible. Where so much is obscure, it is best not to assert too positively that we can find here a distinction between mortal and venial sins which is substantially identical with that which theologians make today. Further discussion of this question may be found in H. Gerigk, *Wesen und Voraussetzungen der Todsünde* (Breslau 1903) 28–30; F. Cavallera, 'La doctrine de la pénitence au III siècle,' BLE 31 (1930) 54 ff.; E. Durkin, *The Theological Distinction of Sin in the Writings of St. Augustine* (Mundelein 1952) 4 f.

[594] In the forgiveness of sins God must always act as the principal cause. Christ is the meritorious cause, and His intercession is externalized through the ministerial action of the Church. When the Church intercedes it is Christ who intercedes (cf. *De paen.* 10.7: *cum illi agunt . . . Christus patrem deprecatur*) and, as Tertullian adds: *Facile impetratur semper quod filius postulat.*

[595] The sins which are here called *graviora* and *exitiosa* are elsewhere referred to as *maiora* (18.18), *maxima* (1.19; 13.6), and *mortalia* (3.13; 19.28; 21.2). They are also called *capitalia* (19.20; 21.14), although it cannot be proved that *mortalia* and *capitalia* are exactly synonymous; cf. above, *De pud.* note 85. In a number of his works, both Catholic and

Montanist, Tertullian gives lists of serious sins which resemble rather closely the list found here in the *De pudicitia*. From his Catholic period we have, for example, in *Apol.* 2.6, 'murder, adultery, injustice (*fraus*), treachery (*perfidia*) and other crimes;' in *De bap.* 4, 'Idolatry, adultery, injustice (*fraus*);' in *De spec.* 3, murder, idolatry, adultery and injustice (*fraus*) are mentioned, with an explicit reference to the condemnation of these sins in the Decalogue. From his Montanist or semi-Montanist writings we may note, besides the present passage of the *De pudicitia*, *De idol.* 1, where idolatry is called the greatest of all crimes and where murder, adultery, fornication and injustice (*fraus*) are closely associated with it. In this same chapter Tertullian states that these sins *mortem afferunt*, that they are *exitiosa* and *devoratoria salutis*, expressions which may help to show that the treatise on idolatry was written after Tertullian's lapse from orthodoxy. In *Adv. Marc.* 4.9 he speaks of *septem maculae capitalium delictorum*: they are *idololatria, blasphemia, homicidium, adulterium, stuprum, falsum testimonium, fraus.*

These lists, evidently, are intended as typical rather than exhaustive and, accordingly, they are not strictly uniform. They contain sins which during both periods of his life he considered grave, but which he calls 'irremissible' only after his lapse into Montanism. They are 'capital' almost in the sense in which moral theologians today speak of the 'seven capital sins,' i.e. they are sources or causes of other sins, and they are sins which are, or which may be, punished by the death of the soul. For the influence of Scripture, especially the Decalogue, on Tertullian's catalogues of capital sins, see Daly, *op. cit.* 70.733. Somewhat similar lists may be found in Pastor Hermae, *Mand.* 8.3.5; Cyprian, *De bono pat.* 14 and Origen, *De orat.* 28.

The expression *si qua alia violatio templi dei* refers to other sins of impurity besides those of fornication and adultery. It does not denote, as Preuschen and Rolffs have supposed, a sin committed against the Christian community; cf. above, *De pud.* note 168. Since sins which violate the temple of God are sins committed against God Himself, obviously their forgiveness can never be within the competence of men. This notion is implicit in Tertullian's Montanist views on the irremissibility of the *peccata capitalia*; cf. above, *De pud.* note 68 and compare below 21.15 for other allusions to 'sins committed against God' as contrasted with those committed against men. This question has been treated at length by D'Alès I 274 f. and 485-87. In the present list, as elsewhere in Tertullian's enumeration of serious sins, *fraus* means 'injustice.' It is defined in *De idol.* 1 as 'taking away what belongs to another or refusing another his due.' On the meaning of *negatio* and *blasphemia*, see above, *De pud.* note 192 and Motry, *op. cit.* 133.

596 *Ultra*='no longer,' i.e. after Baptism; contrast *De paen.* 10.6. Since Christ will not intercede with His Father for such sinners, the Church may not grant them pardon. Here, again, Tertullian's language reveals the traditional belief that Christ and the Church are one in their effective intercession for sinners.

597 Since his sins after Baptism prove that he is a child of Satan, he can have no communion with the saints, who are the children of God.

598 1 John 5.16. This text is also quoted in *De pud.* 2.14.

599 Cf. Jer. 7.16; 11.14; 14.11. These passages were cited by Tertullian in an earlier chapter of the *De pudicitia* (2.4-6). The words *meminerat et ipse* signify that John, also, had the texts of Jeremias in mind when he wrote of the *peccatum ad mortem*.

600 Cf. 1 John 5.17 f.

601 When the Church grants pardon for sins after the performance of exomologesis, it does this in union with Christ through an effective supplication of God the Father. To say that the Church is not permitted to make supplication for a sin is tantamount to saying that the sin cannot be forgiven by the Church. Therefore, to say that the Church *can* make supplication for a sin is tantamount to saying that the sin can be forgiven by the Church. This forgiveness is, at least in part, an objective effect of the Church's *supplicatio*. It is a sacramental effect in that it is produced *ex opere operato* when the Church's intercession is a part of the whole process of exomologesis, terminated by episcopal absolution (above, 18.18).

602 The general sense of this passage is fairly plain, but the text is difficult and there is considerable diversity among the editors on its details. The translation follows, in part, the *editio princeps*, with certain modifications suggested by Esser in his lengthy note to Kellner, *ad loc.* Esser reads: *Disciplinam igitur apostolorum propria quidem instrumenta determinant principaliter* . . . This preserves an antithesis with a number of elements in the following sentence: *quidem* with *tamen*, *principaliter* with *ex redundantia* and *de proximo iure*, *apostolorum propria instrumenta* with *comitis apostolorum testimonium*. The *propria instrumenta apostolorum* are the writings of the apostles themselves, as distinguished from other related compositions of the apostolic period; cf. Rönsch, *op. cit.* 555-72. For the term *instrumenta apostolica* and its equivalents, see *De res. mort.* 39; *De praesc. haer.* 36; *Adv. Prax.* 15 and, above, *De pud.* 12.1, with note 305.—*Sanctitatis antistitem* is a conjecture of Gelenius; compare *De monog.* 8 and other instances listed by Rönsch, *op. cit.* 632.

603 Tertullian speaks of the apostles as *magistri* and recognizes their teaching authority as absolute. In *De praescriptione haereticorum* he treats at length of the *vivum magisterium* established by Christ and of its descent to the successors of the apostles in the Church. See, especially, chapters 23–27, 32, 35–37.

[604] Tertullian is the first writer who represents Barnabas as the author of the *Epistle to the Hebrews*. This tradition is mentioned, also, by St. Jerome (*De viris illust.* 5; *Epist.* 129.3), Philastrius (*De haer.* 89) and Gregory of Elvira (*Tractatus Origenis* 18); cf. P. Batiffol, 'L'attribution de l'Épître aux Hébreux à saint Barnabé,' RB 8 (1899) 278–83. For the view that St. Luke or St. Clement of Rome was the author of the letter, see the patristic evidence gathered by C. Spicq, *L'Épître aux Hébreux* (Paris 1952) 1.198 f. Apollos is suggested by F. Lo Bue, 'The Historical Background of the Epistle to the Hebrews,' JBL 75 (1956) 52–57. The most complete statement in Christian antiquity on this subject is that of Origen, preserved by Eusebius, *Hist. eccl.* 6.25. Origen gives it as his opinion that the ideas of the epistle are Paul's, 'but the language and composition belong to someone who recalled the Apostle's teaching and, as it were, made notes of what his master said.' Compare the response of the Biblical Commission, DB 2178. Many scholars today favor the authorship of Barnabas, though some, at least, are willing to accept the conclusion of Origen: 'Who actually composed the letter, God alone knows.'

[605] *Auctorare* is a legal word signifying that one becomes security for another or gives a pledge for another as his bondsman; *Digests* 26. 8.4; 27.6.9. For Tertullian, see also *Ad Scap.* 1; *De cor.* 2; *Ad nat.* 1.18; *Ad mart.* 5.

[606] 1 Cor. 9.6. In the preceding verse St. Paul says that 'the other apostles, the brethren of the Lord and Peter, have with them a woman, a sister.' Tertullian, apparently, understands Paul to ask, 'Have not Barnabas and I also the right to do this?'—implying that they have the right but that they do not exercise it. Thus Barnabas would be associated with Paul in an act of renunciation which Tertullian describes by the ambiguous word *abstinentia* but which he probably intends us to understand as abstinence from marriage. In *De exhort. cast.* 8 he interprets the preceding verse, 1 Cor. 9.5, as referring to the marriage 'of the other apostles,' though he finds it necessary to reject this interpretation in *De monog.* 8.—The Greek text of 1 Cor. 9.6 is best taken as meaning: 'Is it only Barnabas and I who have not the right to abstain from manual labor (μὴ ἐργάζεσθαι)?' The other apostles, because of their ministry, have the right to be supported without manual labor, and Paul wishes to make it plain that he and Barnabas also had this right, even though they did not excercise it. The Vulgate version is *potestatem hoc operandi.* Tertullian writes: *Aut ego solus et Barnabas non habemus operandi potestatem?*

607 The *Pastor Hermae*, called in an earlier chapter (10.12) *scriptura quae sola moechos amat*. Tertullian is the first Christian Latin writer to use the word 'apocryphal' as a designation of non-canonical or spurious books of the New Testament; compare *De res. mort.* 63; *De an.* 2 and, above, 10.12. The original meaning of the word is 'hidden' or 'occult' and the contents of the *Pastor Hermae* suggest that this may have been the sense primarily intended by Tertullian when he described the treatise as apocryphal. The history of this word and its definition by early ecclesiastical writers is given in E. Mangenot's article, 'Apocryphes,' DTC 1. 1498–1500; see, also, TLL 2.242 f.

608 Heb. 6.1, though reading *ab initiis* for *inchoationis sermonem* and *opera mortuorum* (see Hoppe I 19 on the genitive used in place of an adjective) for *opera mortua* of the Vulgate. Tertullian interprets the text to mean that Christians 'lay a foundation of penitence' when they turn away from sin (*opera mortua*) and receive Baptism. This must be done once for all, and therefore a *paenitentia secunda* is impossible. This conclusion is not justified by the text. Actually it is not the performance of second penance which is forbidden there, but rather the commission of sins after Baptism, which would make a second penance necessary. Tertullian's error is in the false assumption that because the sins which would make a *paenitentia secunda* necessary are not permitted, therefore the penitence itself is not permitted.

609 Heb. 6.4–8. Historically this has been one of the most controversial passages in the *Epistle to the Hebrews* and its interpretation is still a matter of dispute among commentators. Verses 4–6, in particular, appear to vindicate the Montanist and Novatian thesis on the irremissibility of serious sins committed after Baptism, as well as the view of modern writers who contend that the early Church refused to pardon grave sins committed by her members. Analysis of the text and context, however, reveals that these conclusions are unwarranted. It is quite probable that the author wishes to say that it is impossible, at least humanly speaking, for those who sin after Baptism to recover the same spirit of repentance, the same docility to grace and determination to lead a good life which characterized their first turning away from sin and turning towards God. For this interpretation, see Spicq, *op. cit.* 2.153 f. and the lengthy *excursus* in 2.167–78. The importance of this passage in the history of penitential theology, along with a solution of the difficulty which it presents, are discussed in Galtier I 169–73.—Tertullian's reading *occidente iam aevo* has no justification in the Greek δυνάμεις τε μέλλοντος αἰῶνος. Perhaps, in line with his own strong convictions about the proximity of the *parousia*, he wishes the author of the letter to suggest, in passing, that one reason why repentance will be impossible is that the end of the world is at hand.

⁶¹⁰ *Figuras eius iam in ipsa veritate servabat.* The ancient Law prefigured the discipline revealed at length in the truth of the New Testament. Barnabas, in his epistle, preserved in actuality the discipline prefigured by those passages of the Old Testament which are about to be quoted.

⁶¹¹ Lev. 13.12–14.

⁶¹² The old sins of the flesh and the new purity of the Christian life, corresponding to the old leprous growth and the new skin which replaces it.

⁶¹³ *In vetustatem* depends upon *revixerit*; the subject is *aliquid ex illa (vetustate)*.

⁶¹⁴ Literally, 'the oneness of the new color,' i.e. the whiteness of baptismal innocence. The point of the argument is clear, although the primitive pathology which it supposes is distractingly vague. If a leper is covered over completely by a growth which is perfectly white, he is clean. But if, thereafter, some sign of the old flesh underneath again appears, he is defiled. So the Christian, made clean by Baptism, is pure. If, thereafter, the old sin of adultery is again committed, he is defiled. It is an assumption of Tertullian's that the leprosy mentioned in Lev. 13.14 is incurable and, therefore, 'no longer purified by the priest (*nec expiari iam a sacerdote*).' No such statement is made in the sacred text.

⁶¹⁵ A paraphrase of Lev. 14.36–42.

⁶¹⁶ Apoc. 6.4, 8. Tertullian finds it interesting and significant that just as the dangerous contaminations of leprosy are described as red and green, so also the destructive forces of bloody war and death, symbolized by the horsemen of the Apocalypse, are pictured as mounted on red and green horses. Green is the color of morbidity and death, red is the color of blood. Thus the passions, also, are described as 'deadly and bloody' because they bring death and destruction to the soul. For χλωρός Tertullian has *viridis*, the Vulgate *pallidus*.

⁶¹⁷ Cf. Matt. 3.9. For the ellipsis of *filios*, see Hoppe II 44. Tertullian's extraordinary imagination and fertility are well illustrated in this paragraph, although distortions result from his efforts to fit his thesis into figures not meant for it.

⁶¹⁸ *Habilis deo.*

⁶¹⁹ Cf. Lev. 14.44 f.

⁶²⁰ Reading *sacerdotis*, with a reference to Christ, 'the High Priest of the Father (20.10)' as well as to the priest who acts for Him in the administration of Baptism; Thörnell, *op. cit.* 1.3 f. The *et* is explicative.

⁶²¹ 1 Cor. 5.5. This text was treated at length in chapter 13.

622 Cf. Lev. 19.20–22. Death was the punishment demanded in case of adultery, but a slave who was espoused and not yet married, because not yet freed for marriage by her master, did not incur the guilt or punishment of adultery if she had intercourse with another man. This law is explained by P. Heinisch, *Das Buch Leviticus* (Bonn 1935) 90.

623 Scripture shows that sin committed by a slave who is espoused but not yet married is forgiven. If, however, the slave obtains freedom and then commits adultery after marriage, the crime is punished by death. In this same way, Tertullian concludes, a pagan who is a slave of sin though pledged to Christ (*cui servabatur*) will be forgiven if he sins. He will not be forgiven, however, if he sins after he has been made free by Christ and united to Him in the Church.

624 It is correct penitential discipline which the apostles understand (Kellner-Esser), not just the Old Testament figures which foreshadow it (Thelwall; De Labriolle). This discipline, or disciplinary teaching, is the 'doctrine' of the apostles which is at once distinguished from their 'power.'—*Si* is causal, equivalently *si quidem* (εἴγε, εἴπερ). 'If the apostles understood (as they did) . . . then (as a result) they were . . .'

625 *Decurrere in gradum* is another metaphor derived from the language of the arena (cf. above 6.1 and compare *Adv. Marc.* 1.7 and *De an.* 26.1). *Gradus* is the ground taken by a combatant; *decurrere in gradum* may mean either 'to take up a position' or, possibly, 'to attack the position' held by an adversary. The first sense seems preferable here. The point in his argument which Tertullian has now come to is this: there is a distinction which must be made between the doctrine of the apostles and their power. He will take his stand on the ground which this distinction affords and defend his thesis from this position.

626 The significance of the distinction between *disciplina* and *potestas* is discussed in D'Alès III 193 f. and Poschmann I 341. There is a useful synopsis of the whole difficult chapter in D'Alès I 483 f. It should be noted that Tertullian equates *doctrina* and *disciplina*. The *doctrine-discipline* of the apostles is the moral teaching which they received from God; this they have handed on to their successors. The *power* of the apostles is a charismatic gift granted them by the Spirit for their own personal ministry; this they do not hand on to their successors. The point of the chapter is to reject the pretensions of the Catholic bishops who, because they have received the *doctrine* of the apostles, claim their *potestas* also, particularly and pertinently the power to forgive sins which, they assert, was granted to Peter and transmitted by him to the Church. Tertullian insists that the power to forgive sins belongs to God alone. If He communicates it to men in some limited degree, it is a special gift of the Spirit which does not belong to the episcopal office as such (cf. below, 21.16 f). The tone of the chapter is strongly Montanistic. For some of the inconsistencies within the chapter itself and with other parts of the *De pudicitia*, see Poschmann I 314 f. and Daly, *op. cit.* 73.166 f.

[627] F. Dölger is of the opinion that *adsignare* in this sentence means 'to strengthen' or 'to confirm;' cf. 'Das Niedersitzen nach dem Gebet,' AC 5 (1936) 119. It seems better, however, in the context, to take it as meaning 'set a seal upon' or 'mark in a special way.' The power of the Spirit, which is a thing apart (see the following note), marks out the *charismatici* in the Church and sets them apart from other Christians by reason of the special, distinctive gifts which they have received from the Spirit.

[628] *Seorsum quid potestas spiritus*; *spiritus autem deus*; cf. Esser's note to Kellner, *ad loc. Autem* is used for *enim*; see Stolz-Schmalz, *Lateinische Grammatik* (5th ed. Munich 1928) 668, and Thörnell, *op. cit.* 1.20 ff. on the *syllogismus abbreviatus vel confusus* in Tertullian. Possibly there is an allusion here to John 4.24, *Spiritus est deus*, quoted in *De orat.* 28 as *Deus enim spiritus est.*

[629] Cf. Eph. 5.11, and the explanation of the text given above, *De pud.* 18.10, 13. This verse is cited to show what the *doctrine-discipline* is which God has taught the apostles; it lays down a norm or commandment which the Church must observe in dealing with sinners. The text which is next quoted has to do with *power*, the power to forgive sins. This is *seorsum quid*, a 'thing apart' because it belongs to God alone.

[630] Mark 2.7; Luke 5.21. The Novatians regularly appealed to this text in their attacks on the Church's claim of a power to forgive sins; see, for example, Ambrose, *De paen.* 1.2 and Pacian, *Epist.* 1.6.

[631] Reading *quae in ipsum* (Gelenius; Dekkers), though *quod in ipsum* is given in the *editio princeps* and is preferred by Rauschen. The reading *mortalia, quae in ipsum* etc. may mean either, 'mortal sins which are committed against God,' with the implication that there are other mortal sins which are not of this nature; or, better, 'mortal sins, that is to say, those which are committed against God and His temple.' In this second version sins are mortal precisely *because* they are committed against God and His temple, i.e. man's body.

[632] Cf. Matt. 18.22. Such personal offenses are forgiven personally, without any ecclesiastical intervention whatever. Thus the non-mortal sins of which there is question in this sentence are probably not to be identified with the *peccata levia* mentioned elsewhere in the *De pudicitia*.

[633] Tertullian says it is not proved that the apostles actually did forgive mortal sins. If, however, they had forgiven them, it would have

been because God committed to them a personal power to do so. Therefore such a power, being personal, would not have descended to the successors of the apostles in the episcopal office.

634 *Nam et*; Thörnell, *op. cit.* 2.87–90.

635 Cf. Acts. 9.36–43, the restoration of Tabitha through the prayer of St. Peter, and Acts 20.9–12, the restoration of Eutychus by St. Paul.

636 Cf. Acts 3.1–11; 5.13–16; compare Matt. 10.1; Mark 6.7; Luke 9.1 f.

637 Acts 5.1–6.

638 Acts 13.8–12.

639 The logic is elusive but Tertullian seems to mean this: The apostles received all of their powers from Christ; therefore whatever we read that the apostles do, Christ also can do, since the servant is not greater than the master and can do nothing which the master cannot do. In curing disease and in raising the dead they performed miracles by divine power; so, also, in inflicting the punishments of death and blindness they reveal powers which are divine. This proves that Christ, too, could have inflicted these punishments, if He had so desired. For the use of *ut*, see above, *De pud.* note 582. It is taken here as explicative, though the notion of result is also present.

640 Again, the sequence of thought is not perfectly clear and a paraphrase must be attempted. The apostles received special power from God in their dealings with sinners and they proved their right to this power by their punishment of Ananias and Elymas. If they had also forgiven sins, they would have done this, too, because of the special power which they received from God. We see something similar in the case of the prophets. They, too, by their severity in dealing with sinners proved that they acted as God's representatives. Hence their severity may be taken as proof that they also were divinely authorized to forgive sins. This appears to be an allusion to the story of Nathan and David (his sin was one of 'murder and adultery joined with it') in 2 Kings 12.1–14.

641 Some historians of dogma have thought that the title *apostolice*, taken in conjunction with the expressions *episcopus episcoporum . . . pontifex maximus* (1.6) and *benedictus papa* (13.7) proves that Tertullian's adversary in the *De pudicitia* was the Bishop of Rome. The argument is not conclusive and has often been refuted; see, for example, G. Bardy, 'L'édit d'Agrippinus,' RSR 4 (1924) 1–25. In all three of these passages Tertullian is speaking ironically; cf. above, *De pud.* notes 14, 332. There is an interesting parallel to the present sentence in *De carne Christi* 2, where Tertullian challenges Marcion: *Exhibe auctoritatem. Si propheta es,* *praenuntia aliquid*; *si apostolicus, cum apostolis senti.* Compare, also, *De praesc. haer.* 30: *Probent se novos apostolos esse.*

[642] On Tertullian's use of the word *disciplina* as a synonym for *doctrina*, see Morel, *op. cit.* 26 f.

[643] *Indulgere* is used absolutely, but since Tertullian says elsewhere (e.g. *De pud.* 18.18) that the bishops have power to pardon lesser sins, we must suppose that he is thinking here of *peccata capitalia* exclusively. For his use of *praesidere* with reference to episcopal authority, see above, *De pud.* note 393.

[644] This statement must be used with caution as proof that Tertullian, even as a Montanist, recognized the existence of an ecclesiastical power to forgive serious sins. This power, he will say, belongs only to the 'spiritual' and it is a power which not even they are permitted to use!

[645] The Montanists accepted the oracles of their 'new prophets' as a source of revelation equal in authority to Sacred Scripture; cf. Bardenhewer, *op. cit.* 1.381–83. Nineteen of these oracles are quoted by early Christian writers; they have been collected and studied in detail by De Labriolle, *La crise montaniste* 34–105. The fact that Tertullian appeals to a 'new' prophecy to support his contention that grave sins may not be forgiven by the Church would seem to indicate that the doctrine which he defends was not received in the Church before this prophecy; compare, above, 1.10–13.

[646] The text of the oracle is discussed by De Labriolle, *op. cit.* 56–60; see, also, 447 f. The phrases *ceteros temperare* and *cum plurium malo* which occur in the context favor the reading *alii* rather than *alia delinquant*. Moreover, when Montanists refused absolution to sinners they intended this more as a salutary warning to others than as a means of preventing the sinners themselves from committing other, different sins. That the early Montanists recognized some power in the Church to grant forgiveness of sins may be seen from a remark of Apollonius, quoted in Eusebius, *Hist. eccl.* 5.18, on the practice of certain prophets and martyrs in the Montanist church.—The subject of *faciam* is the Holy Spirit, speaking through the Montanist prophet. There is a hint, in the future tense, that the practice of refusing absolution is not one which was followed in the past. No significance attaches to the apparent contrast between Church and Spirit; for Tertullian the Church *is* the Spirit (21.16). It is not impossible, however, that the *non faciam* is a statement of what the prophet's own policy will be. He recognizes that he is empowered to forgive sins but, on his own authority and by his own decision, he refuses to do so. Such an interpretation removes some of the inconsistency in the chapter; see, below, note 667.

647 *Temperare* is 'to arrange' or 'to place in a certain state or condition;' see Hoppe II 108 for this use of the word in the present passage. —*Eversor* is taken as a title of Satan, the deceitful and destructive spirit who imitates the Spirit of truth.

648 The point which Tertullian makes here is this: If we suppose that it is the spirit of falsehood who utters this oracle, disguising himself as the Spirit of truth, the prophecy will still reflect the mind of the true Spirit, just as any copy reflects the original. *Adfectare* is used elsewhere by Tertullian to describe the efforts of Satan to imitate God; compare *Ad ux.* 1.7 and *De exhort. cast.* 13.

649 Taking *ecclesiae* as a dative, 'for your Church,' i.e. for the Church conceived as authoritative precisely because hierarchical. If *ecclesiae* is read as a genitive, we would translate: 'How are you (i.e. a bishop without charismatic power) entitled to claim this right of the church (i.e. the church of the spiritual)?' For the arguments favoring the first interpretation, cf. Galtier II 147–49 and Poschmann I 344.

650 Matt. 16.18 f., omitting the clause *et portae inferi non praevalebunt adversus eam*, and reading *dedi* for *dabo*. The text is also cited in *Scorpiace* 10 and *De praesc. haer.* 22; it is alluded to in *De monog.* 8 and, more ambiguously, in *Adv. Marc.* 4.13. As far as can be ascertained, this is the first evidence in Christian literature that Catholics appealed to this text as proof that the Church had received from Christ a power to forgive sins; cf. Poschmann I 334 f. On the early exegesis of the text, see the series of articles by H. Bruders, 'Mat. 16.19; 18.18 and Jo. 20.22 f. in frühchristlicher Auslegung,' ZKT 34 (1910) 659–77; 35 (1911) 79–111, 292–346, 466–81, 690–713.

651 The words *ad omnem ecclesiam Petri propinquam* have provoked much discussion and there is still disagreement among scholars as to their exact meaning. They are of interest not only because of their bearing on the controversy over the authorship of the *edictum peremptorium*, quoted in *De pud.* 1.6, but also because of their possible import in the controversy over the origin of the Roman primacy. The interpretation given here seems to be most consistent with (1) the meaning of the crucial words in the passage as far as this can be determined from a study of their use elsewhere in Tertullian, (2) the grammar of the passage and (3) the situation of the passage in its context.

The expression *ad te, id est, ad omnem ecclesiam* reveals the identification, in the Catholic system, of ecclesiastical and episcopal power. Logically the words *id est* do not show that the power of the keys passes to every church through its bishop; rather they indicate that the bishop whom Tertullian attacks supposes that the power has come to him because it has come to every church which is akin to Peter. It is as though he said: 'I believe that the power of the keys has come to me because I believe that it has come to every church etc.'—*Omnem* does not mean 'the whole Church' but has its distributive sense of 'each and every;' this use is quite frequent in the *De pudicitia* and could be easily illustrated by many examples; see, above, note 81 and compare Irenaeus, *Adv. haer.* 3.3.2: *necesse est omnem convenire ecclesiam.*—*Propinquam* does not denote geographical proximity but rather a spiritual relationship to the apostle Peter engendered by the seed of doctrine and possessed by all of the churches which have descended from him. For this concept of the spiritual relationship between the apostles and the churches which have descended from them, see *De praesc. haer.*, where we find such expressions as *semina doctrinae*; *suboles apostolicarum ecclesiarum* (c. 20) and *consanguinitas doctrinae*; *traduces apostolici seminis* (c. 32); compare, also, *Apol.* 16: *Nos christiani . . . judaicae religionis propinqui* and *De carne Christi* 1, where Tertullian says that those who deny the resurrection of the flesh are *Sadducaeorum propinqui*.

We conclude, then, that the bishop who makes the claim which Tertullian rejects as presumptuous is a bishop who presides over one of the many churches which have a spiritual relationship with the apostle Peter because of the faith which they have received from him. Which church this is Tertullian does not state explicitly, but it could be Carthage just as easily as it could be Rome; and, in fact, the use of the word *omnem* is more difficult to explain if we suppose that it is Rome. Rauschen's statement, *Eucharist and Penance* 177 that *De pud.* 21 'flatly contradicts' the view that the author of the *edictum peremptorium* is the Bishop of Carthage must be dismissed as dogmatism or, more charitably, may be regarded as a conclusion based on an incomplete appraisal.

Harnack, as has been remarked earlier (*De pud.*, note 16), sees in this edict an *ex cathedra* papal pronouncement, the first which we possess in its original verbal form. The present passage of the *De pudicitia* creates a difficulty against this position which he resolves by emending the text to read: *ad romanam ecclesiam Petri propinquam*; A. Harnack, 'Ecclesia Petri propinqua. Zur Geschichte der Anfänge des Primats des römischen Bishofs,' *Sitzungsberichte der Preussischen Academie der Wissenschaften* 18 (1927) 148 f. This emendation is arbitrary, tendentious and unconvincing, but not absolutely impossible. For a masterly discussion of the whole question, see Galtier II 149–66. To the literature cited by Galtier may be added later studies listed by Quasten, *op. cit.* 2.314 f.

Erich Caspar has argued that the doctrine of the Roman primacy, in as far as it is derived from Matt. 16.18 f., is of African origin; E. Caspar, *Primatus Petri. Eine philologisch-historische Untersuchung über die Ursprünge der Primatslehre* (Weimar 1927). There is nothing in the present passage to support this contention. Even if Callistus or Zephyrinus issued the *edictum peremptorium* and justified it by an appeal to Matt. 16.18 f., we would still be able to say no more than this: the first evidence furnished by Christian antiquity that a bishop of Rome claimed to be the successor of St. Peter in possessing the power of the keys is found in a writer of the African church. Thus the African church, or more correctly, an enemy of the African church, testifies to a Roman belief; it is not the African church itself which introduces the belief into the stream of Christian tradition.

[652] A somewhat different opinion is expressed in *Scorpiace* 10, written probably about five years earlier, during the period of Tertullian's semi-Montanism: *Nam etsi adhuc clausum putas coelum, memento claves eius hic dominum Petro et per eum ecclesiae reliquisse . . .* It should be noted, however, that the keys of the kingdom referred to in this passage of *Scorpiace* are not possessed *ex officio* by the bishops but belong, rather, to those members of the Church who have been put to the torture and who have confessed the faith.—The view that the power of the keys was personal to the apostles and not transmitted to their successors in the ecclesiastical hierarchy was revived by Abelard and condemned in the Council of Sens; cf. DB 379. It is interesting that Tertullian's opponent appears to have based his claim on Christ's *promise* to Peter of the power of the keys (Matt. 16.19)—though, as has been noticed, Tertullian reads *dedi* for *dabo*—rather than on the power of binding and loosing granted to the other disciples (Matt 18.18). This is probably because he was bishop of a church which had descended in the apostolic line from St. Peter rather than from one of the other apostles. Matt. 18.18 is not quoted in any of the extant treatises of Tertullian.

[653] Tertullian changes Christ's metaphor when he substitutes *in ipso* and *per ipsum* for *super hanc petram*. According to this new interpretation, Peter, acting as Christ's minister, is a *founder* of the Church; he is not its *foundation*. It is through his apostolic activity that he exercises the power of binding and loosing conferred upon him by Christ, and through this apostolic activity he establishes the Church and leads men into the kingdom of heaven. In the sentences which follow Tertullian insists that the power to bind and loose which Peter used in establishing the Church was exercised in a ministry of preaching, teaching, baptizing and wonder-working; it was not exercised by forgiving the sins of the faithful.

[654] The key which Peter first used to open the gates of heaven was his preaching of salvation through Christ; after this, he used his power again when he baptized the men who had just heard his words.

655 Cf. Acts, 2.22.

656 Van der Vliet, *op. cit.* 281, wishes to read *in Cornelii baptismo* for *in Christi baptismo*, with a reference to Acts 10. This, however, cannot be right. Tertullian is thinking, rather, of Acts 2.41, where we read that the men who had just heard Peter preach received Baptism. The 'Baptism of Christ' is not the Baptism which Christ received but the one which He instituted.

657 *Quo* means 'in the Baptism of Christ' (Kellner-Esser), not 'in heaven' (Thelwall and De Labriolle). Sins 'not loosed in the way of true salvation' are those which are not forgiven through the *prima paenitentia* of Baptism. Modern Catholic theologians reject Tertullian's notion that there is an exercise of the power of the keys in the granting or refusing of Baptism. The act by which one is made a subject of the Church can not itself be a juridical act on the part of the Church; cf. Boyer, *op. cit.* 34-29.

658 Cf. Acts 15.10 f.

659 The preceding two paragraphs furnish an illustration of one of Tertullian's favorite methods of argumentation. He insists that an opponent's conclusion rests on a false premise, and then shows that even if the premise were true, it would still not justify the conclusion. Thus, in the present instance, he states that the power of the keys which Peter received belonged to him personally and did not descend to his successors. He then argues that even if it had descended to them, it would not justify their forgiveness of serious post-baptismal sins, since this is not a power which Peter himself exercised when he used the keys of the kingdom.

660 This, possibly, is an allusion to John 20.23: 'Whose sins you shall retain, they are retained;' compare, above, *De pud.* 12.9. Modern theologians stress the parallelism between (1) the power to loose (Matt. 16.19; 18.18) and the power to forgive (John 20.23), and (2) between the power to bind and the power to retain, referred to in the same passages; Galtier I 96-110.

661 When Peter is told to forgive sins, it is specified that these are sins committed against himself (Matt. 18.22); they are not sins committed against God. Therefore, although he may have a power to retain the serious sins of the faithful, he does not have the power to forgive them. The implication is that what Scripture does not assert, it denies; for this principle see *De monog.* 4; *De cor.* 2; *De pud.* 12.10. Scripture asserts that lesser sins may be forgiven; therefore it denies that serious sins may be!

662 *Et quidem tuam* contrasts the hierarchical Church with the church of the Spirit; for other interpretations of this much disputed passage, see Poschmann I 343 and Galtier II 149.—*Secundum* is taken to mean 'in

the second place after . . .' There is much to be said, however, for Esser's view (cf. his note to Kellner *ad loc.*) that it means 'as in the case of.' This power will belong to the 'spiritual' *secundum personam Petri*, that is to say, it will be a personal power of 'the spiritual' just as it was a personal power of St. Peter himself. It will belong to those who are other prophets and apostles, who possess the Spirit of the earlier prophets and apostles and manifest the Spirit by the external wonders which they perform. The radical error of this whole chapter is found in the Montanist concept of Church authority which Tertullian here expounds. It is worth recalling that there is not a trace of any such notions as these in the orthodox treatise *De paenitentia*.

[663] On the identification of the Church and the Spirit in Montanist ecclesiology, see De Labriolle, *La crise montaniste* 447. This identity is apparent, also, in such expressions as: *Ecclesia potest donare, sed non faciam* (cf. above, *De pud.* note 646) and *Ecclesia potest donare* (21.7) . . . *spiritus veritatis potest indulgere sed non vult* (21.8). This is in sharp contrast with *De paen.* 10.6, where Tertullian states emphatically that the Church is Christ.

[664] Tertullian is the first Latin writer to use the word *trinitas* as a technical theological term; see, also, *Adv. Prax.* 2–4. For other early writers, cf. A. Blaise–H. Chirat, *Dictionnaire latin-français des auteurs chrétiens* (Strasbourg 1954) 829. The present formula, *trinitas unius divinitatis, pater et filius et spiritus sanctus* is an admirably succinct and perfectly orthodox description of the central Christian mystery. It is not quite clear, however, in just what sense we are to understand that this trinity is 'in the Spirit.' The expression is ambiguous, though it may be that *spiritus* is intended to mean simply God, as in John 4.24, *spiritus est deus* and, possibly, above 21.1, *Spiritus autem deus*. For bibliographies on Tertullian's trinitarian teaching, cf. Quasten, *op. cit.* 2.286, 327.

[665] Cf. Matt. 18.20. The Holy Spirit, that is to say, God manifesting Himself in the world through His spiritual operations, is the bond of union in that church which is had when two or three are gathered in the name of the Lord. Tertullian has just said that 'the church is the Spirit,' and that there are three persons in the Spirit, Father, Son and Holy Ghost. It is peculiarly appropriate, therefore, that the church should be found on earth whenever there are three persons united in the Spirit. This thought occurs repeatedly in Tertullian; see, for example, *De exhort. cast.* 7; *De fuga* 14; *De bap.* 6.

[666] In this sentence, also, *omnis* has a distributive rather than a collective sense; it should not be translated 'the whole number of those who share this faith' (De Labriolle) but, rather, 'each and every

number,' i.e. 'any number of persons you please (even though only two or three) of those who etc.'—*Censeri* means 'to be what it is reckoned to be,' not, 'to be thought of as if it were;' cf. Evans, *op. cit.* 214–16. The sentence might also be translated '. . . comes into existence as a church (*censetur*='to be regarded as present or existing'; cf. Waszink, *op. cit.* 282) because of (*ab*= 'by the will of' or 'by reason of the statement of') its founder and sanctifier.'—Tertullian probably thinks of the Holy Spirit as both the founder and the sanctifier of the Church. He is its *auctor* because He unites its members into a congregation; He is its *consecrator* because He sanctifies its members through His indwelling presence. This is, of course, the church of the Spirit. In his pre-Montanist days Tertullian taught quite clearly that the Church, a visible, magisterial and hierarchical organization, was founded by Christ through the apostles; see, especially, *De praesc. haer.* 20–21.

[667] It must not be supposed that Tertullian is thinking here of two distinct churches, with the Montanist church conceived as a congregation organically separated from the hierarchical Church. Rather, within the external church of the bishops there is an amorphous, internal church of the Spirit. The bishops, as successors of the apostles, are authorized to teach; this is the function of the hierarchical church. Those members of the church who are endowed with charismatic gifts, whether they be priests or laymen, have power to forgive sins; this is a function of the church of the Spirit. Thus Montanism, in divorcing the power to sanctify from the power to teach, introduces a dichotomy into the Church which subverts all effective ecclesiastical government, breeds heresy and schism, and gives over to enthusiasts one of the most important responsibilities of the episcopal order.

To a great extent the inconsistencies of the present chapter result from the two conceptions of the church which Tertullian here sets in such sharp contrast. The church of the Spirit will pardon sins which bishops can not pardon. These must be the *peccata graviora*, since Tertullian says earlier that bishops do pardon lesser sins (18.18). But the *peccata graviora* will not be forgiven by the Spirit, *ne et alii delinquant* and *cum malo plurium* (21.7 f.). Thus there is a power which is conferred on the spiritual in the church and which they will use (21.17) but it is one which the Spirit does not wish them to use (21.7 f.). So, also, the power which St. Peter has to bind and loose is a power which has nothing to do with the forgiving of sins (21.14); this power not to forgive sins, which belongs to Peter personally and after him to the church of the Spirit (21.16) is a power by which the church of the Spirit does forgive sins (21.17)!

The principle that one must possess the Holy Spirit in order to sanctify others persisted in Africa through the Donatist heresy. It is found, also, at a later period, in the Oriental Church where, for many centuries, the power to forgive sins was regarded as a prerogative of monks rather than of bishops and priests, because it was felt that monks alone possessed the holiness required for conferring the Holy Spirit in the sacrament of penance; cf. K. Holl, *Enthusiasmus und Bussgewalt beim griechischen Mönchtum* (Leipzig 1898). A somewhat similar view is expressed by Origen (*De oratione* 28; *Hom. in Matt.* 12.14) and a few other early writers; but see Doronzo, *op. cit.* 4.600–42. For the influence of Tertullian on the development of Donatism, cf. W. Frend, *The Donatist Church* (Oxford 1952) 118–24.

[668] The power to forgive sins in the internal forum belongs to God alone. In insisting that the power to forgive sins as God Himself forgives them does not belong to the bishops, Tertullian implies that it is precisely this power which his opponents claimed for the hierarchical Church. His statement thus gives indirect evidence that at this time the orthodox Church believed: (1) that the minister of ecclesiastical absolution was the bishop or priest, or better, perhaps, the bishop *as* priest; (2) that the effect of absolution was not merely the reconciliation of the sinner to the Church by the removal of an excommunication, but also the reconciliation of the sinner to God Himself by the forgiveness of sin as God Himself forgives it. Catholics and Montanists agreed that the effect of absolution is a forgiveness of sins which is possible to God alone. The only point at issue between them here is this: who has been empowered to grant this absolution in His name?

[669] A power to forgive sins which the bishop himself does not have he confers upon the martyrs of his (i.e. the hierarchical) Church! Tertullian does not deny this power to Montanist martyrs, but he would insist that if they forgive sins, they do so because they possess the Spirit and not because they have suffered for the faith; see the reference to Apollonius, above, note 646. The special privileges of the martyrs in assisting penitents are mentioned, also, in the account of the persecution at Lyons (Eusebius, *Hist. eccl.* 5.1.45 f.; 5.2.5–7) and in the letter of Dionysius of Alexandria to Fabius (Eusebius, *Hist. eccl.* 6.42). In the introductory chapter of his orthodox treatise *Ad martyras* Tertullian writes: *Pacem quidam in ecclesia non habentes a martyribus in carcere exorare consueverunt.* His tone is respectful and it is evident that the practice to which he refers is a custom of some standing. It is well known that in Africa, at the time of the Decian persecution, the usage alluded to in these passages degenerated into a serious abuse, in which the so-called *libelli pacis* were granted indiscriminately to sinners, without any reference whatever to the episcopal power to bind and loose.

There are a number of expressions in the final chapter of the *De pudicitia* which seem to indicate that in Africa, at the time Tertullian wrote, the orthodox Church considered that martyrs had a power to forgive sins which was not essentially different from that of the bishop himself. We read, for example, that the bishop confers upon martyrs the very same power to forgive sins which he claims for himself (22.1). Sinners seek peace from the martyrs and, after their appeal, they return to the Church as communicants (22.2). Thus martyrs do what is reserved to God alone (22.3), and their intervention effects a release from the death of sin (22.4). In imitation of Christ (22.5) and because they believe that Christ is in them (22.6) they grant absolution from sin. Since Tertullian objects to all of these claims, the supposition is that they represent the belief of his Catholic opponents.

In the light of this evidence and that which is synopsized in the preceding paragraph of the present note, some scholars have insisted that the power to forgive sins was first exercised in the Church by martyrs, and that only at a relatively late date was it regarded as an exclusively episcopal and sacerdotal prerogative. Against this opinion the following considerations may be listed. (1) There is no evidence outside the African church that martyrs ever attempted to restore sinners to communion independently of the bishop. Within the African church abuses existed at the time of the Decian persecution and they may have existed, to some extent, before it. There is no mention of the intervention of the martyrs after this persecution. (2) The role of the martyrs was that of privileged intercessors. Thus they helped to create the conditions necessary for the reconciliation of the sinner by adding their merits to the penance which he himself performed in the course of exomologesis. It is this concept which remains in the doctrine of a *thesaurus meritorum* upon which the Church draws in granting indulgences; cf. B. Poschmann, II 83. We may suppose that the *cari dei*, referred to in *De paen.* 9.4, were, first of all, members of the Church who had suffered for the faith. Cyprian, it is quite plain, regarded the *libelli pacis* as simple petitions presented to the bishop asking for the reinstatement of a sinner, and he declares that in the past, also, martyrs did no more than this in the forgiveness of sins. In one of his letters (*Epist.* 15.4) he objects: *Audio enim quibusdam sic libellos fieri ut dicatur, 'communicet ille cum suis,' quod numquam omnino a martyribus factum est.* Numerous statements to this same effect may be found scattered throughout his correspondence. It is significant that in *Epist.* 21.3 the expression *peccata dimittere* is used in referring to the intervention of the martyrs, when it is perfectly clear from the letter which follows (*Epist.* 22.2) that in this case the 'remission of sins' and the 'granting of peace' were effective only *exposita causa apud episcopum et facta exomo-logesi*. Quite probably 'forgiveness of sins by the martyrs' means no more than this in the present chapter of the *De pudicitia*. (3) It is unlikely that so strong a bishop as the author of the *edictum peremptorium* would have allowed the martyrs of his church to restore sinners to communion independently of his own final decision in the matter. Rolffs, *op. cit.* 114–16, has suggested that the complete formula of the edict may have been phrased thus: *Ego et moechiae et fornicationis delicta paenitentia functis dimitto . . . si veniam a martyre acceperint*. This is an unnecessary amplification of the terms of the edict, but it represents what may well have been the course pursued in the Church at this time. (4) Poschmann argues that the martyrs could have had no authoritative, ecclesiastical power to forgive sins, since this power was exercised primarily and formally in restoring a sinner to communion with the Church. Such a power, in the very nature of things, must be exercised by the supreme authority within a church, i.e. by the bishop who imposed the ex-communication originally and whose decision must remain in force until such time as he himself lifts the ecclesiastical penalty which he himself imposed. Thus the theory which attributes to the martyrs a direct power to forgive sins overlooks completely the distinction which was made in Christian antiquity between divine and ecclesiastical forgiveness. The argument is developed in detail in Poschmann I 270–83. (5) Finally, we must not neglect the possibility that Tertullian's language in this chapter represents an effort to bring Catholic doctrine into disrepute by portraying the power of the martyrs as greater than it actually was. He is attacking what he considers laxness in the Church and it may well be that for controversial reasons he gives a distorted picture of his opponents' practice. Even the most casual reader of Tertullian's treatises knows that in the interest of what he regards as a good cause, he is not above calumny or, at least, caricature. Detailed studies of this question may be found in D'Alès I 350–55; D'Alès III 244–51; Galtier I 134–49; Doronzo, *op. cit.* 4.665–84.

[670] *Ex consensione*. The readings *ex confessione* and *ex concessione* have also been suggested. In *De ieiun.* 12 Tertullian writes even more scathingly of the luxuries enjoyed *ex facultate custodiae liberae* by the Catholic martyr Pristinus.

[671] The practice of paying a fee to the jailer for the privilege of visiting the martyrs is mentioned, also, in the *Passio S. Pionii* 12 and in the pagan Lucian of Samosata's satire *De morte Peregrini* 2. For a vivid description of the prisons in which the martyrs were detained before their trial and execution, or at the pleasure of the magistrates, see P.

Allard, *Ten Lectures on the Martyrs* (tr. from the 2nd French ed. by L. Cappadelta, New York 1907) 219–32.

[672] *Violantur viri ac feminae in tenebris* etc. Tertullian's first objection to the martyrs' claim that they have a power to forgive sins is based upon his belief that this claim is a cause of scandal in the Church since the martyrs themselves are not free from sin. The darkness of the dungeons in which they were kept is repeatedly stressed by the martyrs. We know, too, that the sexes were not separated in Roman prisons. These circumstances lead to Tertullian's vicious charge that serious sins of impurity were committed there.

[673] This sentence has been interpreted to mean that certain sinners had themselves condemned to the mines so that after a period of punishment there they might, as martyrs, be restored to communion with the Church. These sinners, Tertullian would then say, need to be sentenced to the mines a second time in order to make reparation for the offenses which they committed there at the time of their first condemnation; D'Alès I 351. It seems better, however, to take the sentence as a parallel to the one which immediately precedes. Some sinners have recourse to the martyrs in prison; others go to those who have been sentenced to the mines. In neither case, however, is this recourse efficacious since the persons to whom they have recourse are themselves 'in danger of losing their peace with the Church.'—Esser, *Der Adressat der Schrift De pudicitia* 23–26, argues that the reference to mines in this passage is more easily understood of the church of Carthage than the church of Rome, since there were no mines in the vicinity of Rome and many in the vicinity of Carthage. This would furnish confirmatory proof that Tertullian's opponent in the *De pudicitia* was bishop of an African see and not the bishop of Rome.

[674] No certain explanation can be given of the meaning of this sentence. The following paraphrase, however, seems to contain its essential thought and most important implications: There is no efficacy in having recourse to men who still live on earth, even though they be imprisoned for the faith. They are themselves sinners (*non sine culpa*) and they are subject to the various degrading miseries and necessities of this life. As long as men live they must seek the favor of others by petty bribery; they need the care of physicians to preserve their life and health; they are under constant pressure from creditors to pay their debts. Such servitude is inconsistent with the glory which comes of martyrdom. Therefore a man is not truly a martyr until he has actually been put to death—and then, of course, he cannot grant absolution from sin! It may be observed, in this connection, that in Christian antiquity a theoretical distinction was made between confessors

(ὁμόλογοι) and martyrs (μάρτυρες). The former suffered persecution for the faith; the latter died for it; cf. Eusebius, *Hist. eccl.* 5.2, in the account of the persecution at Lyons. The distinction was not always observed in practice, although Tertullian seems to hint at it here; compare, also, *De cor.* 2 and *Scorp.* 6. There is a good discussion of this question of terminology in H. Leclercq, 'Martyr,' DACL 10.2360–66.

Various other suggestions have been proposed in an effort to throw light on this passage. They are all subject to serious objections, and in the interest of brevity they are listed here without comment. (1) Rigault, rather diffidently, conjectures *damnatis* for *dinariis*, *moecho* for *medico* and *fornicatori* for *foeneratori*. (2) Oehler reads the words, *Quis enim in terra et in carne sine culpa*, as a question which Tertullian puts in the mouth of his opponent. This question he answers with one of his own: How can anyone be a martyr for you while he is yet on earth, you who supplicate him with pennies, trying to buy the medicine of pardon which he sells at an exorbitant price? Thus *saeculi incola* refers to the martyr, while the expressions which follow refer to the Christian who seeks pardon at his hands. (3) Esser, in a note to Kellner *ad loc.*, sees an allusion to the parable of the unmerciful servant, Matt. 18.23–35. (4) H. Lea, *A History of Confession and Indulgences* (Philadelphia 1896) 3.5 f., interprets the passage to mean that certain men had themselves imprisoned in order that they might profit by selling *libelli pacis* to adulterers and other sinners. This would be an early instance of traffic in indulgences. (5) D'Alès I 352 punctuates with question marks after *incola*, *supplex* and *foeneratori*. The *supplex denariis* is the man who has used money in order to secure an easy imprisonment.

⁶⁷⁵ Tertullian has said that a man is incapable of forgiving sins while he is in prison; now he adds that this is beyond his power at the very moment of martyrdom itself. For *librato*, see Hoppe II 100. The methods of execution mentioned in this paragraph are described more fully by Allard, *op. cit.* 283.

⁶⁷⁶ *Patibulum* (from *patere*), strictly speaking, a forked yoke. In executions, this was fastened to the *stipes* or *palus* to form a cross. Hence, by metonymy, *patibulum* is often used for *crux*. See the article *patibulum* in RE 18.2167–69. The Vulgate has the word ten times in the Old Testament, never in the New.

⁶⁷⁷ *Leone concesso*. Tertullian repeatedly speaks of this form of martyrdom. Christians exposed to the beasts were usually placed on an elevated platform so that they might be seen more easily by the spectators. Upon this platform was a stake (*in stipite*) to which the martyr, stripped naked, was fastened by the hands. Numerous illustrations have come down to us from early Christian art which represent

men and women in this attitude; cf. Allard, *op. cit.* 271 for further references.

⁶⁷⁸ For the text, see Borleffs II 78. In death by burning it was customary to nail the victim to a pillar by his hands; cf. *Martyrium S. Polycarpi* 14; *Passio S. Pionii* 21. Not infrequently, under the Empire, judicial punishments were combined with quasi-theatrical exhibitions or pageants, the victims suffering in the character of some well-known historical or mythological figure. Thus Tertullian (*Apol.* 15.5) says that he himself had seen, in the amphitheatre, representations of the castrating of Atys and the burning of Hercules. It has been suggested that the words here, *in axe iam incendio adstructo*, refer to the punishment of a martyr who dies representing Ixion tortured on the wheel; cf. J. B. Lightfoot, *The Apostolic Fathers: St. Clement of Rome* (London 1890) 2.32, and H. Leclercq, 'Actes des martyrs,' DACL 1.434. One hesitates, however, to accept the suggestion, since it hardly seems likely that so specialized a form of cruelty would be mentioned in the sort of general list that Tertullian is giving here. Moreover, in the present passage, *axis* is almost certainly for *assis* (cf. *asser, assula*) a 'board' or 'plank,' not *axis*, the 'axle' of a wheel. Compare *Apol.* 50.3, where there is an allusion to the nickname *semiaxii* which was given to the Christians because of the stake to which they were fastened for burning.

⁶⁷⁹ *Damnare sine excusatione* is to condemn without hope of release or pardon, hence to condemn as irremissible. *Excusatio* can also mean 'a reason for excusing,' i.e. 'They are condemned and God does not recognize any plea in extenuation of their guilt.' This sense is possible here but it seems less apt in the context.—*Quod sciam* is used ironically in speaking of something about which the author has no doubts; cf. below 22.10.

⁶⁸⁰ Cf. 1 Cor. 15.32 and, for *interitum carnis*, 1 Cor. 5.5. Even though St. Paul had already suffered for the faith, he did not feel that this entitled him to grant pardon to the incestuous Corinthian. *Denique* denotes that something is being added to the argument by way of illustration or corroboration.

⁶⁸¹ This 'cost' or 'price' seems to refer to the suffering which the martyr has endured, although there is at least a suggestion that he has obtained pardon because of the merit of Christ's passion; compare 1 Cor. 6.20; 7.23 and 1 Peter 1.19.

⁶⁸² Cf. Luke 23.43. *Liberavit latronem* might also be translated, 'He gave absolution to a thief.' For *nam et* see Thörnell, *op. cit.* 2.87–92.

⁶⁸³ Compare 1 Peter 3.18. This statement of the purpose of the Incarnation is found frequently in Tertullian. For the literature dealing with his doctrine of the Redemption, cf. Quasten, *op. cit.* 2.328.

684 An allusion to the parable of the wise and foolish virgins, Matt. 25.1-13, especially verse 9. The merit acquired by a sinner who suffers for the faith is needed to ensure his own entrance into the kingdom of heaven; it is not sufficient to secure another's salvation also.—For the meaning of *facula*, cf. TLL 6.144 f.

685 Christ is known, first of all, by His sinlessness. He is known, secondly, by His ability to read the secrets of hearts. Only if the martyr is like Him in these two respects will he be able to forgive sins. *Probare Christum*, literally, is 'to test for Christ,' i.e. 'to test whether one be Christ,' or 'to test for the presence of Christ.'

686 Tertullian may be speaking here for Montanist martyrs, who, if they were also prophets, were thought to have the gift of cardiognosis among their *charismata*; compare *Adv. Marc.* 5.8; *De an.* 9.4; 15.4; and see Waszink, *op. cit.* 169.—The question of Christ's inhabitation in the martyr, and its bearing on the power of forgiving sins may be further studied in De Labriolle, *La crise montaniste* 451; Poschmann I 281; Galtier II 37; M. Viller, 'Les martyrs et l'Esprit,' RSR 14 (1924) 544-51; F. Dölger, 'Christophoros als Ehrentitel für Märtyrer und Heilige,' AC 4 (1934) 74 f.

687 Matt. 9.4-6, freely quoted. Compare Mark 2.1-12 and Luke 5.17-26.

688 You presume that the martyrdom of another will wipe out your own sin. But this is an absurdity, for the very fact that you go to a martyr proves that you recognize the necessity of a baptism of blood to atone for sin. Baptism, however, by its very nature is something personal. Therefore when you acknowledge the necessity of martyrdom (second Baptism) to wash away your sins, you acknowledge, at the same time, that this martyrdom must be your own. Cf. A. D'Alès 'Tertullianea. De pudicitia 22.9 f.' RSR 26 (1936) 366 f. for further details on the meaning of this obscure and elliptical passage.

689 The pleonastic use of *et* is well explained by Thörnell, *op. cit.* 2.78, in defending the reading of the *editio princeps* against suggested variants. There is here, apparently, a combination of two propositions: *Et martyrium erit baptisma* and *Martyrium aliud erit baptisma*.—For the concept of martyrdom as a second Baptism, compare *Apol.* 50.15; *Ad mart.* 1; *Scorp.* 6; *De bap.* 16; *De pat.* 13; *De an.* 55.5; *De res. mort.* 43, 52; cf. D'Alès I 329 f., 419-33. This idea is constantly stressed by other early Christian writers, from Ignatius of Antioch (*Epist. ad Rom.* 2-6) on. The subject may be studied further in H. Lennerz, *De sacramento baptismi* (2nd ed. Rome 1948) 109-25 and W. Hellmans, *Wertschätzung des Martyriums als eines Rechtfertigungsmittels in der altchristlichen Kirche bis zum Anfang des 4 Jahrhunderts* (Breslau 1912).

690 Cf. Luke 12.50. The words *et aliud* are additions of Tertullian to the text. The Vulgate, following the Greek closely, has: *Baptismo autem habeo baptizari.*

691 John 19.34; compare *De bap.* 16, and see F. Dölger, 'Tertullian über die Bluttaufe,' AC 2 (1930) 117–41, especially 124 f. and 134.— *Paratura* is a coinage of Tertullian's for *materia,* i.e. *id quod paratum est.*

692 Since it is impossible for me to wash away another's sins by receiving the *lavacrum aquae* for him, neither is it possible for me to free him from his sins by receiving the *lavacrum sanguinis* in his stead. If I were able to receive second Baptism for another, there is no reason why I should not be able to receive first Baptism for him also. This sentence throws light on the rather obscure statement in 22.9; cf. note 688.

693 *Ingeram usque in finem*; see Rauschen's note *ad loc.* for the reading and interpretation adopted here.

694 Tertullian has used this *a fortiori, ad hominem* argument repeatedly in the *De pudicitia*; see, above, 5.8, 15; 6.7 f.; 9.20; 12.5, 11; 19.15. Here he wishes to say that if the Catholic martyrs can forgive adulterers, they can forgive the other *peccata capitalia* also. For the use of the word *subvenire* in the patristic literature on penance, see Galtier II 98 and D'Alès III 330.

695 It will be recalled that in Christian antiquity apostasy and idolatry were closely identified; cf. above, *De pud.* note 68.

696 For Tertullian's use of *ceterum,* see Hoppe I 108 f. It is taken here as the equivalent of *alioquin* rather than *sed,* although neither of these meanings fits perfectly.—Tertullian has dropped the question of the martyrs' power to forgive sins, and from here to the end of the chapter he concentrates his attention once more on the old charge of his opponents' inconsistency. If they are going to appeal to Ezechiel, they ought to recognize that his words apply more easily to apostates than they do to adulterers. Other allusions to the text (Ezech. 33.11) are found in *De pud.* 2.1; 10.8; 18.12–17.

697 The opposition is between *subando* and *dimicando.* Compare *De monog.* 15, where the same thought is developed in almost identical language.

698 *Revocare,* used also in *De paen.* 5.1 and *De pud.* 7.6; 15.9. In this context the word seems to suggest restoration to life as well as restoration to the Church; for the former meaning, cf. Waszink, *op. cit.* 412.

699 *Paenitentia miserabilior*; compare *De pud.* 5.15: *Miserabiliores paenitentias reliquisti.*

700 *Quam voluntarius an quam invitus.* This reading is confirmed by the *Codex Ottobonianus*; cf. Borleffs II 78.

701 The translation follows Rauschen's emendation, *quod libet.* The

Ottobonianus has *quolibet*, the reading given by Gelenius. Other variants are: *quo libet* (Mesnartius, Reifferscheid-Wissowa, Preuschen, Dekkers) and *quodlibet* (Pamelius and Oehler).

[702] *Carnificis*, not *carnificii*; cf. Hoppe II 68.

[703] Literally, 'since they wished to have been victorious.' For the meaning of *invidiosus*, see Rauschen's note *ad loc.*

[704] *Non vincendo cesserunt. Cessare* is 'to fail' or 'to fall short.' They did not really lose; they simply failed to win! This seems to be a distinction without a difference, but Tertullian wishes to stress the fact that they had engaged in an honest struggle and yielded only because they were unable to persevere to the end. One loses with honor if, after a generous effort, one merely fails to carry off the prize.

[705] *Piaculariter negaverunt*. Their apostasy is pardonable because, before yielding, they suffered for the faith, and their sufferings constitute a kind of antecedent expiation for their sin. *Dimittetur* refers to ecclesiastical absolution; *denuo* indicates that it is granted a second time, i.e. after their sins were first pardoned in Baptism. Tertullian speaks here as if he were actually willing, even as a Montanist, to allow the Church's forgiveness to the sin of apostasy. He denies it above, *De pud.* 19.25, where *idololatria* and *negatio* are listed among the irremissible sins.— The word *piacularis* (*piare*= to appease or propitiate) has had a long and interesting history in theology. It is used technically today to describe the suffering (*satispassio*) of Purgatory. *Piaculum* in *Apol.* 8.3 denotes a serious crime, i.e. a crime requiring ceremonial expiation. This, perhaps, has led lexicographers to misapprehend the meaning of *piaculariter* in the present passage. Harper's *Latin Dictionary* translates, 'sinfully,' and Blaise-Chirat, *Dictionnaire des auteurs chrétiens* has 'd'une manière indigne, criminelle,' but this pejorative sense is quite incorrect. For the reading *peculiariter negaverunt*, see Oehler's note *ad loc.*

[706] Cf. Matt. 26.41. This plea may be made by a man who has apostatized after torture; it may not be made by an adulterer. Compare *De monog.* 14-17, where Tertullian is much exercised over the argument that second marriage is permitted because 'the flesh is weak.'

[707] Cf. *De monog.* 16. The abrupt ending of the treatise appears to indicate that the text has not come down to us completely. Kroymann, however, is of the opinion that the closing words sum up effectively and artistically Tertullian's whole case against his opponents; cf. *Quaestiones Tertullianeae criticae* (Innsbruck 1893) 95.

INDEXES

INDEXES

1. OLD AND NEW TESTAMENT

Genesis

1.26 f.	259
1.28	262
1.28 f.	141
2.7	145, 216
2.17	164, 205
3.6	215
3.9–11	187
3.17–19	187
19.33–35	214
25.21–25	224
38.15–18	214

Exodus

4.22	224
12.15–20	250
14	186
20.5	198
20.13	210
20.14	209
34.6	198
34.14	198

Leviticus

13.12–14	279
14.36–42	279
14.44 f.	279
18.8	241
19.20–22	280
26.12	257

Numbers

18.22	205
25.9	214
25.18	214

Deuteronomy

4.24	198
5.9	198
5.17	210
6.15	198
22.30	241

Deuteronomy—*contd.*

23.19	226
32.2	158
32.39	198

Joshua

24.19	198

2 Kings

12.1–14	282
12.13	214

3 Kings

8.33	149
21.27–29	214

2 Paralipomenon

6.24	149
7.14	149

Tobias

4.11	159

Job

5.18	198

Psalms

1.1	266
1.2	213
1.3	150
2.12	140
17.26 f.	266
18.8	214
25.46	266
49.16, 18	266
85.15	198
96.3	199
102.8	198
110.4	198
111.4	198
144.8	198
145.8	135

Proverbs 106

5.22	184
6.32–34	265
15.27	140, 159
16.6	159

Wisdom

1.12	164
13.1–9	154

Ecclesiasticus

1.27	140
5.7	140

Isaias

1.2	224
5.18	183 f.
6.9	224
40.15	150
42.14	198
43.18	213
45.5	263
45.7	198
52.11	257, 265
62.5	194

Jeremias

3.1–14, 20	194
4.3	213
7.16	198, 276
8.4	169
11.14	198, 276
14.11	276
14.11 f.	198
19.11	150
31.19	149
51.45	257

Ezechiel

18.21–23	148
18.23	198, 232
20.34	257

301

Ezechiel—*contd.*		Matthew—*contd.*		Luke—*contd.*	
27.37	257	5.32	199, 207, 261	3.3	140
33.11	148, 198, 232,	6.14	199	3.3–5	232
	267, 268, 297	6.16	183	3.7 f.	159
34.2–4	220	7.1	198	3.12–14	232
		7.2	199	5.17–26	296
Daniel		7.6	162	5.21	281
2.35	150	7.26	161	5.22	205
4.24	159	8.28–32	229	6.36	198
4.29–33	186	9.4–6	296	6.37	198
		9.12	228	7.36–50	155, 235
Osee		9.13	169, 198	8.30–33	229
1.2	214	9.15	194	9.1 f.	282
2	194	10.1	282	9.31 f.	228
3.1	214	10.26	160	9.62	213
·6.6	169, 198	10.28	140, 199	10.13	232
13.3	150	11.13	213	12.40	297
		11.21	232	13.3	159
Joel		12.7	169, 198	15.1	227
2.12	149	12.31	246	15.4–7	169, 217
2.13	198	12.39–41	232	15.7	218
		13.33	250	15.8–10	169, 218
Amos		16.18 f.	284 ff.	15.10	169
5.10	224	16.19	131, 202, 287	15.11–32	170, 224
8.11	229	18.11	228	15.21	170
		18.15–18	131	15.22	229
Jonas		18.18	202, 286, 287	15.23	228
1.2	231	18.20	177, 288	15.29	224
1.4 f.	231	18.21–35	155, 223	16.16	213
4.2	231	18.22	281, 287	16.22	187
		18.33–35	294	18.20	210
Micheas		19.9	199, 207	19.10	228
6.6–8	198	21.13	194	19.46	194
		22.11–14	228	22.61	143
Nahum		24.12	191	23.43	295
1.2	198	25.9	296		
		25.32 f.	244	John	
Matthew		26.6–13	235	1.1–10	139
3.2	142	26.41	298	1.3	137
3.3	232			1.14	215, 259
3.8 f.	235	Mark		2.19	259
3.9	279	1.2 f.	232	3.5	216
3.10	150	2.1–12	296	3.29	194
3.12	150	2.7	205, 281	4.24	281, 288
5.7	198	5.9–13	229	4.26	235
5.9	198, 212	6.7	282	5.14	140
5.15	147	10.19	210	8.1–11	235 f.
5.17	147, 213	11.17	194	10.30	263
5.21	214			11.41	178
5.27 f.	214	Luke		14.9–11	263
5.28	147	1.76	232	14.16	237

John—*contd.*		1 Corinthians		1 Corinthians—*contd.*	
19.34	297	1.14	250	8.2	251
20.19–23	131	1.21	229	8.7	252
20.23	202, 287	2.2	251	8.12	252
		2.14	194	9.1	251
		3.16	258	9.5	252
Acts		3.17	258, 267	9.6	277
2.22	287	3.18	258	9.12	252
2.41	287	4.3 f.	251	9.15	251
3.1–11	282	4.7	251	10.12	252
5.1–6	282	4.8	251	11.16	252
5.13–16	282	4.9	251	11.31 f.	159
9.5	177	4.13	251	12.4–11	177
9.15	254	4.18	251	12.26	177
9.36–43	282	4.18–21	252	12.27	216
10	287	5.1	241, 252	13.11	195
10.34	212	5.1–8	241, 250	13.26	266
11.3	227	5.2	250	15	216
13.8–12	282	5.3	254, 255	15.11	269
15.10 f.	287	5.4	254, 255	15.32	295
15.20	238 f.	5.4 f.	250	16.13, 18	199
15.29	210, 238 f.	5.5	199, 241, 245, 248,	16.21	252
16.3	265		249, 253, 279, 295		
19.2–6	141	5.6	249, 266	2 Corinthians	
20.9–12	282	5.9–11	266	1.22	152
21.25	238	5.11	267	2	255
		5.12	199, 271	2.1–4	250
		6.1	199	2.5–11	241 f.
Romans		6.3	164, 251	2.6	250
1.19 f.	154	6.9	259	2.7	250, 254
2.1	198	6.11	259	2.11	250, 254
2.11	212	6.13	259	3.6	263
3.20	213	6.14	259	4.1 f.	256
3.31	214	6.15	216, 259	5.1	145
6.1–11	263	6.15 ff.	194, 259	6.5	256
6.2 ff.	164	6.16	259	6.14–16	256
6.3–5	160	6.18	259	6.16 f.	257
6.19	263	6.19	216	6.17	265
7.12	214	6.19 f.	259	7.1	257
7.18	263	6.20	295	7.10	159
8.2	263	7.1–3	260	11.2	194
8.3–5	264	7.6–9	260	12.7	246
8.8	264	7.9	196	12.9	246
8.13	264	7.10	260	12.21	199, 258
9.4	224	7.23	295		
9.10–13	224	7.26–28	261	Galatians	
9.21	150	7.29	262	1.14	196
11.30, 32	265	7.30 f.	262	2.12	227
13.9	210	7.32	262	2.16	213
13.13	265	7.38	262	2.18	250, 254
14.4	198	7.39 f.	262	3.27	216

Galatians—*contd.*

5.9	249
5.12	196
5.19–21	263
5.21	265
5.26	265
6.7	198

Ephesians

1.13	152
2.2	265
2.3	264
2.5	164
4.3	177
4.12	216
4.20 f.	264
4.26	273
4.28	264
4.29	265
4.30	152
4.32	198
5.3, 5	265
5.7 f.	266
5.8–14	142
5.11	267, 281
5.11 f.	266
5.12	264
5.18	265
5.23–33	194
5.25–27	266
5.26	216
5.30	216

Philippians

3.13	213

Colossians

1.24	177 f.
2.12	160
2.14	272
2.21	178
3.5	265
3.6	265
3.13	198

1 Thessalonians

2.3	263
4.3	199
4.3–5	263

2 Thessalonians

2.10	191
2.15	196
3.6	266
3.14 f.	244

1 Timothy

1.13	267
1.19	149
1.20	245, 248
2.7	254
3.2	252
3.9	268
4.10	198
5.4	211
5.22	163, 266

2 Timothy

1.5	248
3.1–5	191

Titus

1.6 f.	252
3.5	216

Hebrews

4.6, 11	265
6.1	278
6.4–8	278
6.6	152, 228

James

5.11	198

1 Peter

1.17	212
1.18 f.	216, 259
1.19	295

1 Peter—*contd.*

3.18	295
3.20	247
3.21	155

1 John

1.1	178
1.5	160
1.5–7	272
1.7	271
1.8	272
1.10	272
2.1 f.	272
3.3–5	272
3.6–8	272
3.9	152
3.9 f.	272
3.10	273
5.16	148, 203, 205, 276
5.17	276
5.18	152

Apocalypse

2.1	255
2.4	168
2.6	270
2.7	168
2.8	255
2.15	169, 270
2.20 f.	169
2.20–22	269
2.21	199
3.2	169
3.17	169
6.4, 8	279
12.11	216
17.5	194
19.2	199
20.6, 14	164
20.14	205
21.7	271
21.8	271
22.14	216, 271

2. AUTHORS

Aalders, G., 147
Adam, K., 48, 174, 177, 210
d'Alès, A., 128, 131, 137, 140, 141, 142, 144, 147, 152, 155, 158, 161, 164, 167, 171, 173, 182, 184, 190, 193, 200, 203, 209, 214, 216, 225, 227, 230, 241, 243, 255, 257, 270, 280, 292, 296
Allard, P., 196, 293
Amann, E., 270
Ambrose, 241
  Epist. 1.26: 236; *De paen.* 1.2: 281; 1.13: 245; 2.10: 273
Ambrosiaster, 238
Anciaux, P., 149, 170
Aristotle, 135, 138, 145, 185, 191
Arnobius, 232
Arnold, Matthew, 244
Augar, F., 196
Augustine, 140, 152, 229, 241, 253
  Quaest. in Hept. 3.20: 143; *Contra Faustum Man.* 22.27: 144; 32.13: 238; *De civitate dei* 20.16: 185; *Enarr. in Psalmos* 39.9: 232; *Enchiridion* 71: 273; *Sermo* 71.5: 246; 351: 273

Backer, E. de, 234, 253, 256, 268, 270
Bardenhewer, O., 134, 157, 283
Bardy, G., 282
Basil, *In Hex. Hom.* 8: 185
Batiffol, P., 156, 161, 200, 222, 277
Beck, A., 195, 198, 207, 240, 250
Bévenot, M., 131
Bingham, J., 161
Blaise, A., 133
Bonaventure, St., 175
Bonsirven, J., 199
Borleffs, J., 13, 128, 139, 141, 142, 144, 147, 149, 150, 154, 157, 159, 160, 162, 164, 168, 169, 174, 182, 183, 185, 186
Botte, B., 190
Bourque, E., 235
Boyer, C., 148, 287
Brooke, A., 203

Bruders, H., 202, 284
Bruns, C., 193
Buckland, W., 153, 159, 192, 195, 217, 240, 256

Cappadelta, L., 196
Caspar, E., 285 f.
Cavallera, F., 274
Chadwick, H., 232
Charles, R. H., 187
Chartier, C., 166, 220, 252
Chirat, H., 133
Chrysostom, *De statuis* 15.1: 140; *Hom.* 10 *in Matt.* 3.5: 153; *Hom.* 31 *in Rom.* 5: 185
Cicero, 149, 185, 256, 257
Clement of Alexandria, 4, 51, 165, 176
  Paed. 2.10: 211; *Stromata* 3.17: 260; 4.24: 165; 7.12: 140; *Quis dives salv.* 24: 241
Clement of Rome, 277, 295
Coebergh, C., 195
Collins, J., 246
Commodianus, 173
Connolly, R., 236
Coppieters, H., 238
Cyprian, 4, 51, 131, 165, 169, 199, 203, 247
  De lapsis 16: 172; 29: 181; 35: 173; *De unitate eccl.* 5: 252; *De op. et eleem.* 2: 165; 14: 143; *De bono pat.* 14: 275; *Ad Quirinum* 3.119: 238; *Epist.* 4.3: 172; 15.1: 266; 16.2: 172, 266; 17.1: 266; 29: 157; 43.3: 181; 55.17: 203, 210; 55.21: 190; 74.1: 266
Cyril of Jerusalem, *Catech.* 1.5: 153; 3.11: 216

Daly, C., 131, 148, 179, 190, 191, 197, 222
Daniélou, J., 162
Davis, H., 146
De Faye, E., 156
Dekkers, E., 52, 133, 161, 172, 191, 196, 198, 211, 212, 216, 253, 281
De Lisle Shortt, C., 145, 151

Deneffe, A., 156
Diekamp, F., 156, 213
Diercks, G., 133, 142, 271
Dio Cassius, 185
Dionysius of Alexandria, 51, 290
Dionysius of Corinth, 4, 241
Dirksen, A., 140
Dix, G., 157
Dodgson, C., 13, 136, 146, 160, 175
Dölger, F., 136, 142, 144, 151, 152, 153, 157, 160, 162, 176, 192, 205, 211, 229, 230 f., 235, 281, 296, 297
Doronzo, E., 141, 146, 151, 153, 158, 173, 204, 214, 241, 266, 269, 290, 292
Duchesne, L., 132
Dürig, W., 143, 163
Durkin, E., 274

Edmonds, H., 173
Englebrecht, A., 210
Esser, G., 52, 132, 170, 197, 206, 215, 234, 239, 253, 276, 288
Eusebius, 236, 241, 266, 277, 283, 290, 294
Evans, E., 137, 194, 289
Evodius, 176

Flesseman-Van Leer, E., 225
Freese, J., 219
Frend, W., 290
Friedlander, L., 219, 251
Fruetsaert, E., 182
Fuetscher, L., 154, 229
Fulgentius, 238
Funk, F., 132, 233 f.

Gagneius, J., 190
Galtier, P., 48, 51, 128, 131, 141, 142, 149, 152, 156, 163, 165, 167, 169, 172, 173, 175, 176, 179, 182, 186, 190, 193, 197, 201 f., 203, 204, 206, 221 f., 230, 242, 244, 266, 272, 273, 278, 284, 285, 287, 292, 296
Gelenius, W., 216, 281, 298
Gerigk, H., 274
Gerlo, A., 183
Ghellinck, J. de, 268
Girard, P., 193
Glover, T., 217
Gonzalez Rivas, S., 163
Grandmaison, L. de, 236

Gregory of Elvira, 277
Gregory the Great, 241
    Hom. in 1 Reg. 5.11: 140; Dial. 4.42: 185
Gregory Nazianzen, 241
Gregory Thaumaturgus, 165
Grotz, J., 166, 197, 202, 219, 223, 243, 267
Guthrie, D., 264

Haguenin, M., 215
Harnack, A., 12, 132, 133, 183, 193, 199, 285
Hartel, W. von, 192, 195, 225, 251
Hefele, C., 209
Heffening, W., 138
Heinisch, P., 280
Hellmans, W., 296
Hemmer, H., 52
Higgins, A., 169
Highet, G., 191
Hilary, 226, 229
Hippolytus, 4
    Apost. trad. 19: 157; 20: 152; 20, 21: 160; 21: 162; 21.9: 154; Philosop. 9.12: 48
Holl, K., 290
Holmes, P., 139
Hoppe, H., 128, 135, 141, 158, 172, 175, 187, 195, 196, 197, 201, 212, 214, 215, 217, 220, 234, 253, 254, 262, 284, 294, 297
Horace, 158, 247
Hübscher, I., 141

Ignatius of Antioch, 216, 296
Irenaeus, 4
    Adv. haer. 1.13.5: 172; 2.27: 226; 3.3.2: 285; 3.12.14: 238; 4.20: 234
Isidore of Pelusium, 205
Isidore of Seville, Etymol. 1.23: 194; 6.19.76: 171; 6.19.79: 174; 10.159: 208; 19.31: 183

Jerome, 226
    De viris illust. 5: 277; In Gal. 2.2: 238; Adv. Helvid. 21: 262; Adv. Jovin. 1.7: 196; Adv. Lucif. 4.11: 212; Adv. Pelag. 3.6: 212; Adv. Rufin. 3.14: 213; Epist. 21.3: 226; 43.3: 219; 54.7: 175; 58.10: 8; 77.4:

Jerome—*contd.*
  183; 107.2: 186; 108: 174; 123.4:
  211; 129.3: 277; 130.9: 149
Josephus, 226
Joyce, G., 202, 222
Jungmann, J., 172, 173
Junius, F., 185
Justin, *Apol. prima* 61: 152; *Dial. cum Tryph.* 86: 216
Juvenal, 191, 194, 211, 232, 260

Karpp, H., 141
Kellner, H., 13, 52, 134, 136, 137, 146,
  174, 195, 207, 215
Kelly, J., 178
Keseling, P., 191
Kirk, K., 274
Kissane, E., 184
Koch, H., 165, 215
Köhne, J., 208
Kroymann, A., 185, 200, 214, 298

Labriolle, P. de, 13, 52, 134, 136, 146,
  156, 183, 187, 193, 194, 206, 225,
  259, 265, 283, 288, 296
Lactantius, 8
Lagrange, M., 235
Latko, E., 131
Lea, H. C., 294
Leclercq, H., 165, 178, 188, 217, 235,
  243, 247, 294
Lejay, P., 52
Lennerz, H., 296
Leo the Great, *Serm. de Quad.* 5.3: 153;
  Sermo 26.2: 237
Lercher, L., 156
Le Saint, W., 157, 249
Lightfoot, J. B., 295
Livy, 225
Lo Bue, F., 277
Lock, W., 246, 266
Löfstedt, E., 229, 253, 258, 263, 264
Lovejoy, A., 191
Lucian of Samosata, 292
Lucretius, 147

MacRory, J., 241
Mangenot, E., 278
Magnus, L., 219
Martial, 194, 260
McComb, S., 136
Mead, G., 151, 172

Mersch, E., 178, 249
Mesnartius, M., 190, 197
Minucius Felix, *Octavius* 25.11: 211;
  35.3: 185; 37.11 f.: 219
Mitchell, W., 162
Mitton, C. L., 264
Mohrmann, C., 13, 134, 136, 147, 161,
  162, 169, 174, 188, 257
Monceaux, P., 12, 132, 133
Morel, V., 143, 163, 173, 196, 213, 239,
  283
Morgan, J., 141, 160
Morinus, J., 132
Mortimer, R., 168, 190, 195, 202, 204,
  214, 222
Motry, H., 144, 197, 201, 205, 209, 222,
  230, 274
Mullins, T., 246

Nerney, D., 167
Nisters, B., 148, 157
Noeldechen, E., 12, 133, 190
Noldin, H., 207
Norden, E., 132, 191, 196
Novatian, 189, 191

Oehler, F., 13, 52, 149, 158, 174, 177,
  183, 213, 244, 272
Origen, 4, 131, 162, 176, 241, 277
  Contra Celsum 3.69: 232; *Comm.
  in Rom.* 10.31: 234; *Hom. in Luc.* 21:
  152; *Hom. in Matt.* 12.14: 290; *De
  orat.* 28: 275, 290
Otten, B., 148
Ovid, 158

Pacian, 133, 163, 241
  Parain. ad paen. 4: 238; 8: 176; 8,
  9: 176; 9: 186; 10: 171; 11: 185; 12:
  169; 15: 163; *Epist.* 1.5: 163, 164,
  168; 1.6: 255, 281; 2.31: 236; 3.19:
  266; 3.39: 163
Palmer, P., 175
Palmieri, D., 190
Pamelius, J., 169, 186, 189, 195, 226
Papias, 236
Pastor Hermae, 4, 44, 51, 82, 115, 131,
  156, 165, 278
  Mand. 4.1: 233; 4.3: 165, 241;
  8.3: 275; *Sim.* 8.2: 241; 8.6.3.: 152;
  8.6.6: 241; 9.21.3: 241; 9.26.5: 241

Paulinus of Nola, 186
Pauw, F. de, 137
Petavius, D., 132
Peter Lombard, 149
Petronius, 178
Philastrius, 277
Pius XII, 249
Plato, 149
Plautus, 147, 194, 219
Pliny, 155, 185
Plummer, A., 241
Plumpe, J., 212, 271
Pohlmann, H., 141
Polycarp, 140
Poschmann, B., 3, 48, 51, 128, 131, 132, 153, 162, 164, 167, 171, 173, 175, 176, 181, 190, 200, 202, 203, 209, 210, 222, 243, 280, 284, 287, 291, 292, 296
Prat, F., 160
Preuschen, E., 13, 52, 174, 193, 275
Pseudo-Cyprian, 234
Puniet, P. de, 158

Quaquarelli, A., 148
Quasten, J., 131, 132, 138, 157, 190, 203, 215, 225, 230, 285, 288, 295
Quintilian, 214

Rahner, K., 131, 153, 173, 175, 182, 193, 197, 221, 229
Rauch, G., 145
Rauschen, G., 13, 52, 133, 159, 163, 182, 190, 192, 193, 195, 196, 198, 200, 203, 206, 207, 210, 222, 238, 266
Reding, M., 131
Redlich, E., 131
Refoulé, R., 160, 227, 230, 231, 248, 259
Reid, J., 183
Reifferscheid, A., 52, 231, 254
Resch, G., 238
Rhenan, B., 150
Richard, M., 185
Rigault, N., 155, 160, 174, 215, 216, 294
Rimml, R., 140
Rivière, J., 155
Roberts, R., 141, 215
Robinson, J. T., 252
Rolffs, E., 167, 275, 292

Rönsch, H., 198, 215, 237, 242, 251, 258, 262, 263, 271, 276
Rufinus, 226

Salvian, 219
Sandys, J., 183
Scaliger, J., 185
Schmeck, H., 256
Schmitt, A., 207
Schneider, C., 174
Scholte, W., 214
Schwartz, E., 153
Scribonius Largus, 183
Seneca, 149
Sirmundus, 131
Six, K., 238
Soden, H. von, 199, 258, 262, 263, 264
Soranus, 211
Spartianus, Aelius, 226
Spicq, C., 277
Stelzenberger, J., 192
Stier, J., 154
Stirnimann, J., 153
Stokes, G., 244
Stufler, J., 153, 170, 190, 204, 206
Suarez, F., 149 f., 175, 182
Suetonius, 194, 214, 232
Sulpicius Severus, 174
Swete, H., 170, 194

Teeuwen, St. W. J., 128, 133, 140, 149, 152, 153, 157, 162, 163, 164, 172, 173, 184, 197, 198, 205, 233, 237, 246
Terence, 232
Tertullian, *for subject analysis see entry in General Index*
    Ad martyras 1: 143, 290, 296; 5: 277; *Ad nationes* 1.1: 137; 1.5: 152; 1.9: 250; 1.10: 151; 1.15: 211; 1.16: 194; 1.17: 151; 1.18: 217, 277; 2.8: 154; *Apologeticum* 1.2: 139; 1.4: 195; 2.6: 275; 2.15: 175; 2.17: 233; 2.18: 154; 3.1: 219; 5.2: 175; 5.3: 244; 6.4: 152; 6.9: 264; 8.3: 298; 9.5: 251; 9.6–8: 211; 9.9: 151; 9.13: 238; 9.16–20: 191; 11.5: 137; 15.1: 240; 15.5: 295; 15.7: 211; 16: 285; 16.4: 139; 17.4: 154; 17.4–6: 229; 18: 138; 18.2, 5: 141; 18.5: 232; 21.5: 224; 21.10: 215; 21.15 f.: 225; 21.17: 215; 23.3: 208; 23.4: 196; 25.2: 196;

Tertullian—*contd.*

28.3 : 151; 32.1 : 139; 32.2 : 151; 34.1 :
144; 35.5 : 189; 36.4 : 147; 37.9 :
273; 37.10 : 240; 38.3 : 218; 38.4 :
219; 39.1 : 177; 39.4 : 172, 202, 214;
40.2 : 192; 40.7 : 135; 40.15 : 173, 178;
42.5 : 251; 45.3 : 176; 46 : 138;
47.12 : 185; 47.13 : 187; 48.4 : 248;
48.14 : 185; 50.3 : 295; 50.12 : 189;
50.15 : 159, 240, 296; *De test.
animae* 2 : 154; 3 : 142, 214, 216; *De
praesc. haer.* 2 : 185; 3.14 : 157; 7 :
138; 8 : 272; 9 : 138; 13 : 232; 16 :
147; 20 : 232; 20, 21 : 289; 22 : 284;
29 : 232; 30 : 202, 232, 283; 32 : 252;
36 : 276; 36.3 : 144; 37 : 215; 38 :
226; 39 : 224; 40 : 154; 41 : 157; 52 :
187; *De spectaculis* : 157; 2 : 176, 229;
3 : 265, 266, 275; 16–19 : 219; 17 :
211, 265; 22 : 171; *De oratione* : 157;
5 : 139; 7 : 171; 16 : 234; 19 : 228;
20 : 186; 22 : 152, 240; 23 : 156; 28 :
281; *De baptismo* : 157; 1 : 157, 227;
1.1 : 142; 2 : 138, 267; 2.1 : 229; 3 :
227; 4 : 227, 275; 5 : 154, 160, 227;
6 : 177, 288; 8 : 247; 9 : 154, 216,
227; 10–12 : 142, 185; 11 : 267; 12 :
227; 13 : 156, 161, 268; 15 : 215, 248,
259; 16 : 231, 296, 297; 17 : 252; 18 :
161, 162, 266; 20 : 152, 154, 157, 161,
186; *De patientia* 3 : 267; 5 : 154; 7 :
163; 12 : 169, 268; 13 : 156, 186, 296;
15 : 171; *De cultu fem.* : 157; 1 : 154;
1.1 : 152, 156; 1.8 : 183; 1.9 : 219; 2 :
189; 2.1 : 258; 2.6 : 159; 2.8 : 171;
Ad uxorem 1.2 : 214, 226; 1.3 : 196,
260, 262; 1.4 : 185; 1.7 : 252, 284;
1.8 : 143; 2.2 : 199, 226; 2.2, 8 : 208;
2.8 : 178; *Adv. Hermog.* 3 : 144; 8 :
138; 19 : 263; 27 : 263; *Adv.
Marcionem* 1.7 : 280; 1.10 : 154; 1.13 :
138; 1.18 : 229; 1.22 : 138; 1.23 :
137; 1.24 : 135; 1.27 : 185, 219;
1.28 : 152, 268; 2.2 : 138, 187;
2.3–4 : 144; 2.5–10 : 143; 2.6 : 263;
2.10 : 187; 2.13 : 198; 2.16 : 183;
2.17 : 162, 210; 2.19 : 266; 2.20 : 240;
2.24 : 137, 139, 143, 171; 2.25 : 187;
2.26 : 151, 244; 3.8 : 267; 3.13 : 263;
3.18 : 178; 3.23 : 224; 3.24 : 185;
4.3 : 237; 4.4 : 200; 4.9 : 210, 275;

Tertullian—*contd.*

4.10 : 152, 198; 4.13 : 284; 4.19 : 263;
4.24 : 240; 4.25 : 229; 4.34 : 185, 199;
4.42 : 266; 5.6 : 258; 5.8 : 296; 5.12 :
187, 194, 257, 264; 5.15 : 198; 5.16 :
272; 5.17 : 155, 265; *De pallio* 4 :
183; *Adv. Valent.* 4 : 220; *De anima*
1.2 : 138; 1.4 : 268; 2 : 278; 2.6 : 183;
3.1 : 138; 3–4 : 145; 5–8 : 145; 6.7 :
177; 6.8 : 145; 7.55–58 : 184; 9 :
145; 9.4 : 144, 296; 10–11 : 249;
12.1 : 135, 150, 227; 12.3 : 135; 12.4 :
135; 12.6 : 135; 14.4 : 145; 15.2 :
238; 15.4 : 145, 147, 296; 16 : 137;
19 : 216; 20.2 : 229; 21.6 : 143; 25 :
183, 211; 25.5 : 208; 26.1 : 280;
26.2 : 224; 27 : 216; 30.4 : 262; 32 :
145; 34.2 : 232; 34.4 : 194; 35.2 : 226;
38.2 : 215; 38.4–6 : 145; 39.4 : 215;
40 : 216; 40.1 : 142, 215; 40.4 : 147;
41 : 216; 41.4 : 142, 216; 41.14 : 142;
43.10 : 236; 47.2 : 154; 50.3 : 267;
55 : 187; 55.5 : 296; 57.4 : 273;
57.12 : 178; 58 : 249; 58.6 : 147; *De
carne Christi* 1 : 285; 2 : 282; 5 : 225,
267; 12 : 196; 14 : 198; 18 : 215; 20 :
183; 23 : 152; *De res. mort.* 2 : 229;
3 : 137, 138, 154; 4 : 177; 6 : 144; 9 :
198; 14–16 : 144; 15 : 147; 16 : 145;
17 : 185; 26 : 187; 34 : 200; 37 : 215;
39 : 152, 276; 40 : 144; 41 : 145; 43 :
296; 46 : 145; 47 : 198; 52 : 296; 63 :
215, 278; *De exhort. cast.* 2 : 143, 186,
229; 3 : 196, 260; 3–4 : 262; 5 : 194;
6 : 207, 214, 262; 7 : 288; 8 : 252,
277; 9 : 147; 10 : 264; 12 : 211; 13 :
186, 284; *De corona* 2 : 157, 241, 277,
287, 294; 3 : 144, 154, 200, 252; 5 :
177; 6 : 154; 11 : 151; *Scorpiace* 2 :
154; 4 : 213; 6 : 145, 230, 294, 296;
10 : 192, 284, 286; *De idolol.* 1 : 275;
2 : 147; 5 : 267; 11 : 151; 13–23 :
219; 15 : 217; 20 : 151; *Ad Scapulam*
1 : 277; 2 : 151; 2.1 : 229; *De fuga* 2 :
246, 248; 4 : 253; 9 : 158; 12 : 185,
267; 14 : 144, 288; *Adv. Praxean* 1 :
154; 2–4 : 288; 5 : 215; 5–7 : 137;
15 : 215, 276; 20 : 263; 26 : 215; *De
virg. vel.* 1 : 196, 225; 5 : 152; 12 :
159; 14 : 194, 211; *De monogamia*
52; 2 : 225; 3 : 196, 260, 262; 4 :

Tertullian—*contd.*
210, 287; 4–14: 209; 5: 194, 238;
6: 214; 8: 252, 276, 277, 284; 9:
207, 260, 262; 10: 147; 10–13: 260;
11: 194, 208, 262; 14: 143, 262;
14–17: 298; 15: 208, 297; 16: 211,
298; *De ieiunio* 3: 156, 214, 216; 4:
244; 6: 198; 9: 184; 10: 184; 12:
292; 13: 192, 234; 15: 144; 17: 252;
Adv. Iudaeos 1: 200, 224; 2: 154; 7:
225; 8: 216; 10: 216; 13: 224; *De
censu animae*: 145; *De paradiso*: 188
Thelwall, S., 13, 52, 136, 137, 143, 146,
159, 189, 195
Theodotion, 186
Thierry, J., 253
Thomas Aquinas, 149, 151
Thörnell, G., 137, 143, 161, 171, 198,
210, 223, 233, 237, 253, 254, 264, 272,
279, 296
Tixeront, J., 160, 173
Toy, C., 265

Umberg, J., 190
Ursinus, F., 196, 200

Van der Vliet, J., 176, 185, 192, 225,
226, 241 f., 258, 270, 287
Vergil, 185
Vigilius, 210
Viller, M., 296
Vincent of Lerins, 132
Virieux-Reymond, A., 147
Vollert, C., 249
Vosté, J., 250, 265

Walker, A., 187
Waltzing, J., 137, 143, 148, 151,
175, 197, 199, 207, 219, 244, 250,
252, 262
Waszink, J., 132, 138, 141, 142, 144,
154, 158, 176, 183, 184, 201, 208,
215, 216, 225, 228, 238, 261, 296
Watkins, O., 131, 172, 238
Whelan, B., 236
Wilhelm-Hooijbergh, A. E., 144
Wirth, K., 143
Wissowa, G., 52, 231, 254
Worden, T., 246

Zapelena, T., 237

3. LATIN AND GREEK WORDS

abrumpere, 220
absolutio paenitentiae, 172
absolvere, 133, 180
abstinentia, 277
abstinere, 238
acies apostolica, 263
actio paenitentiae, 172
acus, 183
addictio, 265
adfectare, 284
adgeniculari, 174
adhibere paenitentiam, 133
adimplere paenitentiam, 133
administrare, 171
adsignare, 281
adsistere, 211
adsumere paenitentiam, 133
adulari, 158
adulter, 159
adulterium, 61, 199, 275

advocare, 242
advocatio, 263
aedituus, 258
aemulus, 154
ἀγαθῇ τύχῃ, 194
ἁγιασμός, 263
alia species paenitentiae, 269
alioquin, 272, 297
aliquis, 256
ambitus, 267
amplexari paenitentiam, 133
angelus satanae, 246
anima, 135, 249
animus, 135, 150
ante fidem, 246
ἀπείθεια, 265
aphesis, 164
apostolicus, 282
appellare, 263
apud nos, 270

artes curiositatis, 219
ἀσέλγεια, 258
asser, 295
assis, 295
assula, 295
ἀτάκτως, 266
auctorare, 277
auctor (ecclesiae), 289
auctor generis, 229
audientes, 157, 161, 163
auditores, 157, 161
aut, 272
autem, 281
avaritia, 265
axis, 295

benedictus papa, 243, 282
bestiarius, 251
bibere, 234
bisulcum, 183
blasphemia, 275
bonum factum, 194
bonus pastor, 243

cadere, 147
candidatus, 183
capessere paenitentiam, 133
capitalis, 205
capra, 244
cari dei, 174, 291
carnifices obstetrices, 211
castigatio, 201, 221
castitas, 189
castra ecclesiae, 253
cathedra pestilentiae, 266
causa, 200
cavere, 265
censeri, 289
censura, 191, 202
certum quia impossibile, 138
cessare, 298
ceterum, 297
charismata, 296
χλωρός, 279
citius, 258
clausula, 224, 252
clibanus ignis, 184
cogere paenitentiam, 133
commeatus, 158
comminus, 147
communicare, 205

communio, 133, 181, 244
compassio, 205
compendia disciplinae, 239
compendium, 239
compensatio, 133, 159, 239 f.
competentes, 161
compos, 229
concilium, 214, 234
condicio, 203, 204
confessio, 170, 173
conscientia, 148
consecrator, 289
contrectabilis, 178
contrectare, 178
conversio, 152
correptio, 202
credibile quia ineptum, 138
crux, 294
culpa condemnatus, 254
cum maxime, 244
cuneus, 210
curatio, 133
custodia libera, 292

damnatio, 201, 265
dativus finalis, 141
de, 212, 251
de cetero, 244
dedicare, 258
delicta cotidianae incursionis, 273
delicta leviora, 269
delicta maxima, 196 f.
delicta media, 197
delicta modica, 196 f., 269
delictum, 143
denarius, 220
denique, 295
dentifricium, 183
denuo, 298
de postero, 244
deputare, 254
deversari, 139
dictamnum, 185
diffidentia, 265
dimittere, 202, 240, 244, 298
disciplina, 143, 163, 173, 191, 196, 206,
    213, 239, 248, 280 f., 283
dispungere, 133, 201, 244
docere, 199
doctrina, 280, 283
dolor, 152

dominicus, 143 f.
dominus, 144
donare, 244
dos, 141
dum, 207, 233

ebibere, 234, 259
ecclesiam Petri propinquam, 284 ff.
edictum, 262
edictum peremptorium, 192
editio princeps, 190, 194, 216, 243, 276, 296
editor, 251
electi, 161
elogium, 207
emendare, 133
emendatio, 133
enim, 142, 151, 199, 271
episcopus episcoporum, 192, 282
erogare, 262
erogator, 262
et, 296
etiam et, 263
eucharistiam facere, 230
eucharistiam sumere, 230
eversor, 284
exauctorare, 253
exceptio, 153
excludere, 225
excusatio, 295
exempla caelestia, 213
exhortatio, 263
existimatio, 179
exitus, 200 f.
ἐξομολογεῖσθαι, 171 f.
exomologesis, 4, 162
exorare, 205
expiatio, 133
expungere, 133, 175, 201
extra ecclesiam datus, 220 ff.
extra ecclesiam nulla salus, 204
extranei, 139

facula, 296
falsum testimonium, 275
fasces, 183
fides, 149, 160, 161, 163, 207
fimus, 216
flentes, 209
fornicatio, 147, 199
fraus, 275

fructus paenitentiae, 210
funes peccatorum, 184, 194
fungi paenitentia, 133, 162, 193, 194
funiambulus, 232
furnus ignis, 184

gehenna, 184
genus, 228
gradus, 280
gratia, 151, 231

hiemantes, 209
hirundo, 185
homicidium, 275

ianua, 133
ianua ignoscentiae, 165, 173, 180 f., 209
iasis, 133
idololatria, 275, 298
ignoscentia, 133, 164 f.
ignoscere, 244
impingere, 219, 251
impositio paenitentiae, 172
impudicitia, 189, 258
includere paenitentiam, 133, 159
incredulitas, 265
incursio, 273
incursus, 273
indulgentia, 133
indulgere, 244, 283
infectus, 159
infida paenitentia, 159
infidelis, 256
ingerere, 220
ingratia, 139
iniectiones, 242
inquit, 148, 227
inrogare, 139
instrumentum, 171, 234
instrumentum apostolicum, 237, 276
instrumentum evangelicum, 237
intemptatio, 253
interdictio, 265
interim, 253
interitus carnis, 295
interlocutio, 254
interrogatus, 229
intinctio dominica, 235
in totum, 252
invadere paenitentiam, 133
invidiosus, 298

ipse, 220, 248
itaque, 237
iudex, 255
iudicare, 145, 255
iugulatio, 208

lambere, 243
λάτρις, 208
latrocinium, 208
lavacrum aquae, 297
lavacrum paenitentiae, 235
lavacrum sanguinis, 297
leno, 189
leo, 189
lex aeditualis, 258
libelli pacis, 290
libidinum virus, 215
librare, 294
limen ecclesiae, 165, 197, 205, 208, 256
limus, 216
locus paenitentiae, 165
λόγος, 137, 215
λόγος ἐνδιάθετος, 216
λόγος προφορικός, 216
lusus, 219

macula, 263
magis est ut, 261
magistri, 276
maliloquium, 176
malum, 260
mancipes, 250
μάρτυρες, 294
matrimonium, 147
mederi, 133
melius est nubere quam uri, 196
mens, 227
merx, 133
μετάνοια, 171
metanoia, 140 f., 149, 164
metus, 171
metus integer, 159, 162
militia Christi, 253
ministerium, 171
minutiloquium, 177
miserabiliores paenitentiae, 297
modestia, 189
moechia, 199
monstra, 245
mortalis, 205
moveri, 135

mox, 141
mulier soror, 252
multa, 139
mundare, 133
μυστήρια, 256
mutatio mentis, 133
mysterium fidei, 268

nam, 295
nam et, 282
natura, 191
necessitas, 274
negatio, 275, 298
nomen, 196
nominatim, 252
nomine fornicationis, 269
notae, 160, 186
novissimum testamentum, 240
novitioli, 157
nubere, 208
nummus, 159
nupta, 207

oblatio, 228
oblitteratio, 133
observare, 238
obsignatio fidei, 161
oculare, 223
offensa, 136
offensio, 136
officium paenitentiae, 212
omnino, 252
omnis, 203, 207, 267, 285, 288
ὁμόλογοι, 294
opera, 213
ordo, 218
ordo fidei, 236
otiose, 266

pacifici, 198
paenitentia, 132 f., 135, 141, 145 f.,
    149 f., 152, 154, 160, 171, 184,
    186, 193, 194, 206, 230, 237
paenitentia miserabilior, 297
paenitentia prima, 10, 44, 133, 148,
    153, 162, 163, 168, 180, 182, 186,
    218, 227, 230, 232, 233, 237, 268,
    270, 271, 287
paenitentia secunda, 10, 11, 44 f., 51,
    133, 148, 153, 163, 164, 165 ff., 168,
    170, 171 f., 179 ff., 182, 186, 218,

paenitentia secunda—*contd.*
228, 230, 232, 233, 237, 268, 270, 271, 278
palam absolvi, 179
pallidus, 279
palus, 294
papa, 243
παράκλησις, 263
paratura, 297
παροιμίαι, 106
passio animi, 135 f.
passiones, 135
pastor, 244
pastor moechorum, 233
patefacere, 165
patibulum, 294
pax, 133, 166, 181, 198, 244
pax divina, 206
pax humana, 206
peccata aequalia, 230
peccata capitalia, 12, 44, 46, 164, 169, 197, 201, 205, 213, 221, 274, 283, 297
peccata cotidiana, 273 f.
peccata cotidianae incursionis, 46, 197, 220 f.
peccata exitiosa, 46, 197, 274
peccata gravia, 46, 190, 197, 204
peccata graviora, 274, 289
peccata inconcessibilia, 197
peccata irremissibilia, 180, 190, 201
peccata levia, 190, 281
peccata leviora, 46, 197, 221, 268, 269
peccata maiora, 46, 197, 269, 274
peccata maxima, 46, 274
peccata mediocria, 46, 197, 220 ff.
peccata modica, 46, 197
peccata mortalia, 46, 197, 201, 205, 274
peccata remissibilia, 221
peccatum, 143
peccatum ad mortem, 148, 203, 205, 274, 276
penes nos, 208
perfidia, 275
pericope de adultera, 235 f.
periculum, 175
personae acceptatio, 212
Petri propinquam, 284 ff.
φρονεῖν, 264
piacularis, 298
piaculariter, 298
piaculum, 298

planca, 133
planca salutis, 149, 168, 182, 186
plane, 212, 224
poena, 139, 201 f.
poena ecclesiastica, 181
pontifex maximus, 192 f., 282
πορκεία, 238
πορνεία, 199, 207, 239
post, 197
post fidem, 246
postliminium, 256
potestas, 280 f.
praecepta caelestia, 213
praeiudicare, 257
praeiudicium, 195
praescribere, 217, 257
praescriptio, 195
praeses, 252
praesidere, 252, 283
prima lex, 209
prima vocatio, 230
princeps generis, 229
principalia delicta, 210
probare, 296
probitas, 189
pronuntiare, 255
pronuntiatio, 255
propinquus, 285
propria instrumenta apostolorum, 276
prostitutio, 199
provocare, 198, 263
prudentia carnis, 264
psychicus, 194, 263
pudicitia, 189, 191
pugnus, 251
pulsatio, 165, 180 f.
purgare, 133

quale est ut, 217, 256
quomodo, 253

racha, 214
ratio, 137 f., 138 f., 215 f.
reaedificatio, 133
reatus culpae et poenae, 204
recipere in ecclesiam, 133
recitare, 262
recitatio, 240
reconciliare, 244
reconciliatio, 133
reddere in ecclesiam, 133

redigere in ecclesiam, 133
redintegratio, 133
reductio ad absurdum, 232
reformatio, 133
refrigeria, 184
regula fidei, 225
regula veritatis, 225 f.
remedium, 133
remissa, 165
remissio, 165
repastinare, 183
repraesentare, 147, 214
res, 137, 253
resignare, 152, 215
respicere, 143
restituere, 180, 244
restitutio, 133, 270
retinere, 202
retro, 195
reviviscere, 133
revocare, 133, 297
risiloquium, 176

sacramenta, 256
sacramentum, 234, 253, 256 f., 270
sacramentum fidei, 268
sacramentum militiae, 160
sacrificium, 228
saeculi incola, 294
saeculum, 141
salus, 133
salutificator (salvator), 198
sanare, 133
sanctificatio, 263
sanctimonia, 263
sapere, 135, 264
satisfacere, 245
satisfactio, 133, 239 f., 245
satispassio, 298
scalptus, 159
schoenobates, 232
scriptura, 234
secunda lex, 209
secunda restitutio, 230
secundum, 287 f.
sedere, 212
semel, 152, 157
semiaxii, 295
sensus, 250, 253, 264, 272
sensus carnis, 264
sententia, 136 f., 141, 195, 200, 255

sententia condemnatus, 254
sentire, 135
sermo, 215
sermo caro factus est, 215
servus Christi, 163
si, 254, 280
si forte, 177
signaculum fidei, 268
signare, 152
simpliciter, 226
sinus Abrahae, 187
σκόλοψ, 246
sobrietas, 189
solacium, 247
solvere, 244
sordes, 263
species, 217
spectacula, 219
spes, 163
spiritus, 249, 288
spoliati, 228
spurciloquium, 177
stagnum ignis, 184
stare, 192
status, 63, 65, 85, 213, 229, 240, 253,
    256
stilus, 242
stimulus carnis, 246
stipes, 294
stuprum, 61, 147, 199, 275
subvenire, 297
sudis, 246
suggestus, 210
supercilium, 251
super hanc petram, 286
supplex denariis, 294
supplicia, 139, 184
suscipere paenitentiam, 133
συστέλλειν, 262
syllogismus abbreviatus, 281

tabula post naufragium, 149 f.
temperare, 284
tenus, 135
terminus, 200, 246
testamentum, 262
testimonium, 262
thesaurus, 137
thesaurus ecclesiae, 175, 291
thesaurus ignis, 184
θηριομάχης, 251

timere, 260
tinctus, 159
titulus, 194, 195
trinitas, 288
turpiloquium, 177

ultra, 276
usus matrimonii, 260
uterque, 146
ut explicitivus, 272, 282
utor, 208
ut quid, 266

vacare, 196
vectare, 238
venia, 133, 194, 201, 210, 244, 269, 271

venia episcopi, 182
verbum, 137, 139, 215
verecundia, 189, 274
veritas paenitentiae, 159
versus, 159
vestibulum, 165, 208 f.
vestigia, 243
viderit, viderint, 143, 191, 257
vidua, 207
vilitas, 258
viridis, 279
virtutes, 232
vitium originis, 214 f.
vivum magisterium, 276

zelotes, 198

4. GENERAL INDEX

Abelard, 286

abortion, 211; *see* infanticide

Abraham, 16, 81, 117

absolution, 11; terms for, 133; effected by exomologesis, 32, 175 f.; as a public act, 33, 43, 180, 193 f.; as an ecclesiastical act, 175 f., 179 ff.; not granted by God alone, 179 ff.; by a condemnation to penance, 175; effect of, 244, *see* forgiveness; in external and internal forum, 170, 193 f., 201, 204, 244, 268; of capital sins, 164, 203 f., *see* capital sins

accounts, balancing of, 239

Achab, 66

Acta Petri, 51

actors, 74, 225

Adam, 15, 37, 67, 78, 184, 186 f., 214 f., 228 f.

adulteress, as potential poisoner, 211

adultery, nature of, 19, 60, 61, 147, 207; a capital sin, 62 ff., 114, 164, 200, 275; associated with murder and apostasy, 63, 66, 77, 84 f., 124, 200, 210 ff., 297; forgiven by Catholics, 42, 54, 56, 60 f., 65 f., 82, 85 f., 110, 169, 193 ff., 210 ff., 230, 233, 262, 297; not forgiven by Montanists, 42 ff., 48 ff., 54, 56 f., 65 f., 82, 85 f., 110, 114, 195, 197 f., 210 ff., 218, 230, 233, 238, 262; arguments given to prove it irremissible, 56, 71 ff., 84, 85 f., 98, 105, 106 ff., 116 f., 209 f., 217, 230, 263, 270

advocate, 242

Aetna, 185

Africa, 48, 161, 190, 214, 215, 285 f., 290

Agamemnon, 211

Agrippinus of Carthage, 48

Alexander, 88 f., 246 f.

allegory, 225, 226

Alleluja, 151

altar, swearing by, 151

amendment, purpose of, 146

amphitheatre, 213, 219, 295

Ananias, 119, 121, 282

anathema maranatha, 92, 252

Ancyra, Council of, 209

Andromache, 74, 225

angel, of the churches, 109 f.; of church at Corinth, 255

angel of Satan, 246

anger, 71, 114

apocrypha, 82, 115, 234, 278

Apollonius, 283, 290

Apollos, 277

apostasy, 45, 71, 114, 164, 200, 203, 212, 214, 233, 238, *see* idolatry; more pardonable than adultery, 5, 65, 124 f., 297 f.; *see* capital sins

apostles, 83 ff., 110, 115, 121, 123, 251, 277; had wives, 252; personal powers of, 280 f.; teaching authority, 225 f., 276 f.; distinction between their doctrine and power, 118, 280 f.; and pardon of capital sins, 119, 238 f., 281 f.; miracles of, 282; spiritual fathers of the churches, 285

Apostolic Ordinance, 210, 238

Apostolic Constitutions, 247

apostolic succession, 252

apple, as symbol of love, 260

apple of marriage, 100, 259

arena, 280

argument *ad hominem*, 272, 297; from silence, 242

Ark, 247

ascension of Christ, 83, 216, 236, 237

ashes, 31, 34, 64, 86, 108, 173 f.

association of adultery, idolatry and murder, 63, 64, 66, 77, 84 f., 107, 124, 200, 210 ff., 297

athletics, 71, 219

Atys, 295

author of *edictum peremptorium*, 47 f., 87, 102, 119, 192 f., 243, 282 f., 284 ff., 293

authority in the Church, 288

Babylon, 36

bankruptcy, 240

banquets, 71
baptism, 16, 54, 67 f., 76, 82, 89, 108, 149, 215, 253; as a seal, 26, 77, 152, 161, 228, 229; for those who have ceased from sin, 26; the 'symbol of death,' 25, 160; as burial and resurrection, 263; symbolized by wound in Christ's side, 124; dispositions for, 161; Satan renounced in, 154; abuse of, 24 ff., 160, 162; loss of, 253; of water and of blood, 124; of blood, 230, 296; *in re* and *in voto*, 161; sins committed after, 70, 84, 103, 111, *passim*

as penitence, 133, 148, 152 f., 163, *see paenitentia prima*; closes door of forgiveness, 29; second not permitted, 99, 259; efficacy of, 36, 113, 142, 155, 161, 216, 229, 247; as the *prima tabula salutis*, 150; gate of the kingdom of heaven, 121; and the forgiveness of sins, 25, 180; and the Holy Spirit, 141, 227; instituted by Christ, 287; as sacrament, 227, 253; of Jesus and John contrasted, 141 f., 185, 235

confession before reception, 173; by immersion, 160; conferred at Easter, 153; minister of, 25, 118; second marriage not permitted after, 57; received by pagans and heretics, 110; rebaptism of heretics, 247 f.
Barnabas, 45, 115, 277
baths, 34
beasts, exposure to, 251, 294
bestiality, 209
biblical numbers, 226
bind and loose, power to, 120 f., 286 f.
bishop(s), successors of apostles, 280 f.; as presiding officer, 252; teaching authority, 119, 280 f.; and power of keys, 286; Montanist concept of, 289 f.; claim of apostolic power to forgive sins, 280 f.; role in excommunication, 252; as minister of penance, 290; supervises exomologesis, 172 f., 244; grants pardon for sin, 5, 45, 87, 109, 119 ff., 175, 193, 243, 268, 283
'bishop of bishops,' 54
bishop of Rome, 243, 282 f.

blasphemy, 71, 77, 88 f., 114, 219, 246, 247
blood of Christ, 100, 111, 124
body of Christ, 228, *see* Eucharist
bonds of martyrs, 122
brachylogy, 8, 197
branding of soldiers, 160
broom in parable of drachma, 75

Caius, 91
Callistus, 48, 51, 286
Calvary, contrasted with garden of Eden, 216; origin of Church on, 236
candidates, conduct of, 71, 183
canonical triad, 210
canon of Scripture, 82, 234
canons of faith, 110; of discipline, 110
capital sins, 6, 12, 46 ff., 56 f., 79, 85, 114, 119, 121, 164, 169, 200, 203, 210, 212, 213, 220, 230, 238, 241, 274 f., 297, *see* adultery, apostasy, murder, *peccata mortalia, exitiosa, maxima, maiora, graviora, irremissibilia, capitalia*, etc.
captives, restoration of, 256
cardiognosis, 296
caricature, 292
Carthage, 48, 166, 192, 285, 293
catalogues of capital sins, 275
Catechism of Council of Trent, 149
catechumens, 157 f., 161, 163; penitence of, 24 ff., 152 f.
Catholic party, pardons murder and apostasy, 203; pardons sins of impurity, 260, *see* absolution, adultery, pardon, forgiveness; inconsistency of, 212, 260, *see* Sensualists
causality of ecclesiastical absolution, 181 f., *see* forgiveness
celandine, 36, 185
chalice, 68, 82, 217, 234
character, impressed in Baptism, 253, *see* Baptism as a seal
chariot races, 71, 219
charismatic gifts, 280 f., 289
charity, 65
chastisement, refusal of, 71
chastity, 42, 55, 65; violation of during persecutions, 189
children 'of disobedience,' 265; of Satan, 272 f.

Christ, as Saviour, 198; the Good Shepherd, 69, 169, 234; the second Adam, 216; the hope of the world, 225; baptism of, 216; His sinlessness, 296; as High Priest, 279; author of Church discipline, 67; miracles of, 81, 215 f.; reads secrets of the heart, 123, 296; as physician, 77; examples of His mercy, 83; communicates with sinners, 68, with heathen 75; forgives sins, 124, 236; body of, 228, 256; present in Eucharist, 299, *see* Eucharist; flesh of, 67; blood of, 100, 110, 124, 256; grants power of keys, 286; personal powers not communicated to the Church, 236; passion and death of, 83, 103, 109, 123, 228, 267, 295; satisfies for sin, 110, 112, 122; meritorious cause of forgiveness of sins, 274; resurrection, 216; ascension, 83, 216; resurrection and ascension in relation to Baptism, 263; intercession of, 33, 114, 175

Christian, vocation of, 79; as temple of God, 258, *see* temple; sinlessness required of, 162; and swearing, 151; has one expectation with Israel, 74; in parable of prodigal son, 73 ff., 218; concept of penitence, 15, 80

Christian religion, 109

Church, founder of, 122; founded by Christ, 289; origin from side of Christ, 236; founded by Holy Spirit, 289; founded by St. Peter, 286; descends from the apostles, 285; beginning of its existence, 236 f.; sanctified by Holy Spirit, 289; the temple of God, 257; God's house, 72; a society of saints, 194, 272; purity of, 54, 108; a virgin, 54, 108; the bride of Christ, 54, 194; the Lord's flock, 69; as mother, 64, 212; and temple of Jerusalem, 194; relation to the Synagogue, 224; Christ's body, 33, 42, 177 f., 249; soul of, 249; as ship, 89, 247; Councils of, 82, 234

hierarchy of, 252, 284, 287; shepherds of, 220; relationship to St. Peter, 120 f.; authority in, 288; her teaching as rule of faith, 225 f.;

Church—*contd.*
Montanist concept of, 121 f.; defiled by promulgation of *edictum peremptorium*, 54; consists of three persons, 122, 288; of Sensualists, 121; internal and external, 289; of the Spirit, 121, 266, 287 f.; in parable of the drachma, 70

determines canon of Scripture, 82, 115, 234; her liturgical service, 228; controls Christian marriage, 208; confession to, 172; as place of penance, 29, 32, 72, 86, 108, 165, *see limen*, *vestibulum*; reconciliation to through penance, 166; intercedes for sinners, 175; her authority to forgive sins, 4, 45, 60, 72, 119 ff., 236; grants absolution for sins, 179 ff., 199, 201 f., 203 f., 207, *see* absolution, forgiveness, ecclesiastical penance, bishop, exomologesis, etc.; and forgiveness of capital sins, 131 f., *see* capital sins; forgives and retains sin, 175; pardons murder and apostasy, 203, *see* murder and apostasy; forgives sins of impurity, 54, 108, 297, *see* adultery; pardons all sins after exomologesis, 268

Church Orders, 4

circumcision, 55, 106

clandestine marriage, 208

classification of sins, 47, 59 f., 61, 72, 114, 164, *see* sins, distinction of, and *passim*

Codex Bezae, 238

Codex Ottobonianus, 13, 135, 137, 139, 140, 164, 185, 186, 190, 211, 216, 297

Codex Trecensis, 13, 135, 137, 141, 157, 159, 164, 168, 170

cognition, 147

coins, 159

collusion, in custody of martyrs, 122

commandments, 17, 210, *see* Decalogue

commerce, 114

communion, ambiguity in word, 166, 205; abstention from, 201; with the Church, 61, 87, 97, 170; restoration to, 96, 98, 110, 122, 124, 169, 181 f., 245, 248, 292

communion of saints, 32 ff., 61, 175, 177 f.

compensation, 85
composite nature of man, 18, 144, 248
concupiscence, 66, 101, 215, 260 f., 264
condemnation, punishment after, 59
condignity, in merit, 159
confession, 4, 31, 153, 170, 171, 172 f., 176, 182, 184, 244
confessors, 174, 293 f.
Confirmation, sacrament of, 142
conscience, 144
consequent, fallacy of, 268
continence, 56, 100, 115
contract of marriage, 57
contrition, 167, 182, 244; perfect, 149, 161
conversion, 15, 133, 149, 152, 159
cooperation in sin, 71
Corinth, church of, 255
Corinthians, First and Second contrasted, 90 ff., 94 ff., 242 ff., 250 ff., 255 f.
correction, of lesser sins, 72; pardon after, 59, 88
cosmetics, 34
Councils of Church, 82, 234
counterfeit coin, 24, 159
creation, 14, 137
Crete, 185
crimes excluded from public penance, 43, 62, 209, 220
Crispus, 91
cross, used in martyrdom, 122; of Christ, 67, 216
crucifixion of Christ, 228
cursing, 114

daily duties, as occasions of sin, 114
date, of De paenitentia, 12; of De pudicitia, 51 f.
David, 66, 282
deaconess, 247
deacons, 247, 252
deadly sins, see sins, distinction of
death, the punishment of sin, 15, 205; inflicted for adultery, 280; reconciliation at time of, 51, 167, 203, 241; on green horse, 117
debauchery, in pagan worship, 211
debt, cancellation of, 59, 201, 239 f.
Decalogue, 43, 62 f., 209, 275
Decius, persecution of, 290

demons, 78, 273
deposit of faith, 270
Destroyer, the, 120
'destruction of the flesh,' 87 ff., see I Cor. 5.5
devil, 22, 28 f., 77, 113, 125; apes spirit of truth, 120
dialectics, attack on, 138
dice, 219
Dicte, Mount, 185
Didascalia, 4, 236, 266
dietary regulations, 238
digamy, 57, 252
Digests, 155, 192, 217, 239, 253, 254, 256, 265, 277
disease, as type of sin, 176
dittany, 36, 185
dittography, 216
divorce, 101, 261
Docetism, 225
doctrine of apostles, 118
doctrine, unity of, 269
Donatists, 247 f., 253, 289 f.
door of forgiveness, 29
doors of Church, 61, see limen
drachma, 30, 70 ff., 218 f., 220
drunkenness, 82, 105

eagle, 36, 186
earache, 88
ecclesiastical penance, 148, 163, 172, 176, 220 ff., 243, 298; before 250 A.D., 131; effect of, 4, 203 f., 255, 268; reconciles sinners to God, 204, 230, 237, 290; see pardon, absolution, second penance, exomologesis, excommunication, public penance, etc; judicial nature of, 214
economy of faith, 83
Eden, 187; contrasted with Calvary, 216
edict, granting pardon to adultery, 42, 47, 54, 87, 192 ff.; see author of edictum peremptorium
education, 53 f.
effect of absolution, 6, 11, 255; terms for, 133, 244; see forgiveness, pardon, absolution
effects of sin, 76
effeminate, the, 98
Egypt, 36

elder son, in parable of prodigal, 73
elections, 183
Elymas, 119, 282
emotions, 135 f.
emperor, swearing by, 151
Ephesians, 29; authorship of epistle to, 264
Ephesus, 123
epilepsy, 246
episcopal powers, 284, see bishop
Esau, 224
eschatology, 184, 249
eternal punishment, exomologesis saves from, 35 f., 244
ethics, synthesis of, 144
Eucharist, 78, 107, 147, 166, 170, 180, 228, 230, 234, 252, 253, 256 f., 266
Eutychus, 282
Evangelium Nicodemi, 187
examination, on faith before Baptism, 229
excommunication, 57, 62, 71 f., 87, 89, 92, 97, 106, 108 f., 111, 115, 162, 165 ff., 181, 193, 194, 197, 202, 219 f., 220 ff., 252, 274, 290, 292
executioner, ingenuities of, 125
execution, methods of, 294
exegesis of Scripture, 75, 79, 102, 106, 226, 263
Exhortatio de paenitentia, 169
exomologesis, 4, 133, 171 f.; description of, 31 f., 64, 86 f., 108, 178, 212, 243; instrument of penitence, 36, 186; terminated by ecclesiastical absolution, 179 ff., 193 f.; supervised by bishop, 244; role of martyrs, 291; allowed but once, 167; necessity of, 170, 172, 182, 184, 212; effect of, 4 f., 32 f., 34 ff., 142, 165 ff., 179 ff., 184, 186, 203, 228, 233, 268, 276; reconciles sinner to God, 168, see forgiveness; remits eternal punishment, 32, 36; obtains pardon for all sins, 178 f.; cancels punishment of sin, 175; restores graces lost by sin, 228, 233; as satisfaction for sin, 227, see satisfaction; without ecclesiastical absolution, 197 f., 209; see public penance
extenuating circumstances in sin, 114, 125, 219, 274

external penance, 31, 163 f., 165 ff., 186; necessary for post-baptismal sins, 170; terminated by ecclesiastical absolution, 179 ff.; see exomologesis

Fabiola, 183
Fabius, 290
faith, 78, 83, 109, 110, 116, 156, 161, 224, 236
fasting, 32, 34, 41, 201
fatted calf, 228
fear of God, 15, 26 f., 54, 70, 133, 140, 162
festivals of pagans, 71, 219
fig leaves, 67, 215
final impenitence, 246
fingernails, 34, 183
fire, of hell, 35, 54, 101, 111, 184 f.; of concupiscence, 101; used in martyrdom, 123
First Corinthians, spirit of, 90 ff.
flesh, integrity of, 55; sanctified by Christ, 68; resurrection of, 90, 248; necessity of, 102, 262; weakness of, 104 f., 125, 298; mortification of, 183; sins of, 207; 'destruction of,' 245, 295
food, Eucharist as, 230, 266
forbidden fruit, 216, 260
forgiveness of sins, terms used to describe, 133, 244; in early Church, 4, 164; before 250 A.D., 131; through baptism, 25, 142, see baptism; through exomologesis, 142, *passim*, see exomologesis; granted by Church, 193 f., 200, 276; through communion of saints, 175; and power of the keys, 284, 286; and power of martyrs, 122 ff., 290 ff.; effects of, 166 f.; mediately and immediately, 181; of idolatry and murder, see idolatry and murder; described as commercial transaction, 158 f., 201; cancels debt of punishment, 175; in internal and external forum, 179 ff., 204, 206, 244, 255, 268 f., 271; in internal forum, 204, 290; of adultery by the Church, 195, 196, 297, see adultery; of capital sins, 48 ff., 131 f., 164, 169, 213, see capital sins; committed against man, 119; com-

forgiveness of sins—*contd.*
mitted after exomologesis, 167 f.;
granted by God alone, 200; refused
to adultery by Montanists, 71, 106 ff.,
230, *see* adultery; by 'the spiritual,'
283, 289 f.
form of penance, 59 f., 87, 109, 200,
204
fornication, 43, 54, 61, 62, 95, 111, 114,
189, 207, 216, 245, *see* adultery
foundation of Church, 286
founder of Church, 122, 286, 289
fountains, 64
fowls, 34
free will, 143
friendship of God, restored by absolution, 271; *see* forgiveness of sins in
internal forum
'fruits proper to penance,' 235
funambulist, 81
furlough, 158

Gadarene swine, 229
gambling, 219
games, 171
garment, grace as, 228
garments, patched with purple, 73,
224; of penance, 32
Gentiles, 81
genuflection, 178
gestures, in relation to meaning, 225
gladiators, 71, 213
glass, used in chalices, 217, 234
Gnostics, 156
goats, 87, 244
God, natural knowledge of, 78; known
through creatures, 22, 154; Stoic
concept of, 138; a spirit, 281; a
trinity, 121; attributes of, 137; His
breath, 145; His goodness, 17, 57,
144; omnipotence, 19; omniscience,
19; justice, 43, 57; judges men's
actions, 17; His law, 144; His
mercy, 15, 28, 30 f., 42, 81; His
repentance, 15, 141; fatherhood of,
30 f., 78, 114; children of, 113 f.,
273; cooperates through grace, 143;
His house, the church, 70; the just,
His temple, 98, 114, 200, 281; alone
forgives in internal forum, 290;
ratifies Church's sentence, 204, 255;

God—*contd.*
the principal cause of forgiveness,
274; forgives all sins, 60, 109, 148;
forgives 'irremissible' sins, 271
good shepherd, 30, 68 ff., 82, 169, 217,
244
good thief, 123
Gospel of the Hebrews, 236
gospels, swearing by, 151
grace, 15, 21, 80, 141, 143, 228; as
soul's vesture, 77 f.; actual and
habitual, 151 f.
green, as color of death, 279
guardian angel, of church at Corinth,
255
guilt, relative in apostasy and adultery,
124 f.

habit, in relation to sin, 114
hair, neglected in penance, 183
hair pins, 34, 183
hands, imposition of, 107, 163, 266, *see*
I Tim. 5.22
harmony, of apostolic teaching, 110
headache, 88
heart, in relation to soul, 145; secrets
of, 123
heathens, forgiveness of, 80; in parable
of the prodigal, 75 ff.
heaven, 54, 67, 187 f.; eternity of, 76
Hebrews, Epistle to, 115, 237; authorship of, 277
Hecuba, 225
hell, 35, 54, 67, 111, 140, 184, 185, 260 f.
helmsman, bishop as, 247
Hercules, 295
heresy, confused with infidelity, 110,
270
heretics, 74, 102, 110, 232
Hermogenes, 248
hierarchical Church, 122, 252, 287 f.,
see bishop
Holy Orders, 266
Holy Spirit, 85, 109, 118; indwelling
of, 16, 142; descent of, 83; possession
of, 237; and Baptism, 68, 141;
cloaks the just, 77; lost by sin, 76 f.;
soul of the Mystical Body, 249;
inspires writings of the apostles,
269 f.; consistency of, 109; founder
of the Church, 289; sanctifies the

Holy Spirit—*contd.*
  Church, 289; Church of, 122, 283, 287 f.; *see* Paraclete
hope, of Israel and Christianity compared, 225
horsemen of the Apocalypse, 117, 279
house of prostitution, 54, 194
house, purification from leprosy, 117 f.
humanity, virtue of, 65
humility, 250 f.
Hymenaeus, 88 f., 246 f.
hysteria, 246

iconography, early Christian relating to penance, 235
idolatry, 43, 48 ff., 62 ff., 71, 77, 84, 85, 112, 114, 124, 151, 169, 210, 219, 241, 275, 297, *see* apostasy, capital sins
ignorance, in relation to sin, 44, 80 f., 109, 142, 231 ff., 267
image of God, 99, 141, 200
immersion, in Baptism, 160
imperfect divorce, 261
imposition of hands, 107, 163, 266, *see* 1 Tim. 5.22
impurity, various sins of, 207; a violation of God's temple, 200, 258 f., 275; Church pardons, 54, 108, *passim*; Montanists refuse to pardon, 259, *passim*; *see* adultery
incarnation, purpose of, 123, 295; swearing by, 151
incest, 66, 87, 199, 253
incestuous Corinthian, 44, 85 ff., 241 ff.; not pardoned by St. Paul, 90 ff., 123, 250 ff.
inconstancy, defense of, 55
incontinence, 56
indulgences, 175
indwelling of Christ, in martyr, 296
infanticide, 64, 208, 211
infibulation, 260
infidelity, 270
infidels, salvation of, 217 ff.
ingratitude, 81
injustice, sin of, 114, 275
inspiration, of apostolic writings, 269 f.
intercession of Christ, 33, 114, 274, 276; of clergy, 174 f.; of martyrs, 291; of the faithful, 32, 64, 86, 178
internal sins, 19, 66, 147

irremissible sins, 246, *see* sins, distinction of
Isaias, 106
Israel, 74; bride of Yahweh, 194
Ixion, 295

Jacob, 224
jailers, fees paid to, 292
jealousy, 71
Jerusalem, Council of, 44, 84, 210, 238
Jesus, baptism of, 142, 185, *see* baptism
Jews, 15, 70, 73 ff., 76, 81, 218, 227
Jezabel, 110, 270
John the Baptist, 16, 80, 82, 141, 185, 216
John the Evangelist, epistles of, 271 f.; on remissible and irremissible sins, 114, 272, *see* 1 John 5.16
Jonas, a type of Christ, 80, 232
Juda, 66
Judaism, 104
Judea, 76
judgement on fornication, 58
judicial, process, justice in, 125; sentence of St. Paul, 93, 255; nature of ecclesiastical penance, 214
jurisdiction, not exercised in baptism, 287
justice, 65
justification, 229

keys, power of, 255, 284 ff., 287; of the kingdom, 45, 120
kingdom, of God, 45, 98; of heaven, 250
kissing of feet, 243

Laodiceans, 30; Epistle to, 264
lamp, in parable of drachma, 72; oil for, 123; of God's word, 70
Last Judgement, 184
law, spirit and letter, 104; Old and New compared, 209; Tertullian's knowledge of, 132, *see* Tertullian, legal language
laxness of Sensualists, 56
laymen, in Church, 289 f.
leaven, 90, 107, 249 f.
legislation, by Edict, 193
Lent, 153
lepers, 116

leprosy, type of sin, 117, 279
Leviticus, legislation of, 116
lictors, 183
lie, 114
light, in relation to sin, 112, see
  ignorance
lion, 36, 122, 186
literal sense of Scripture, 75, 226
liturgy of penance, 172, 266; see
  exomologesis
Livius Andronicus, 225
Lord's prayer, 199
'lost,' two senses of word, 71 f.
lost sheep, 30, 68 ff., 218 f.
Lot, 66
love, 87
Lucullus, 76, 226
Luke, Tertullian's gospel of, 169
Lyons, 290, 294

Madian, daughters of, 67
Magdalene, 83, 175
magic, 71, 219
magistrates, 171, 183, 219
majority, errs in matters of belief, 195
malaria, 246
man, unity in composition, 145;
  brotherhood of, 228; the image of
  God, 99; as temple of God, 98, 117
mankind, world as house of, 70; God's
  flock, 69; sins of, 15
Marcion, 135, 202, 264, 282
Marcionites, 169
Mariology, 215
marriage, blessed by God, 102, 262;
  the pleasure proper to, 260; Paul's
  attitude to, 100; 'better' than
  burning, 101, 196, 260 f.; repetition
  of, 56, 83, 101, see second marriage,
  remarriage; clandestine, 62;
  Church's jurisdiction, 208; of apostles, 277
Martin of Tours, 174
martyrdom, 79, 159; forms of, 123,
  295; another baptism, 124, 230,
  296 f.; second, 122
Martyrium Polycarpii, 140, 295
martyrs, distinguished from confessors,
  293 f.; sins committed by, 293; their
  role in forgiveness, 6, 45, 122 ff.,
  174, 290 ff.

Mary, virginity of, 67
Mass, as sacrifice, 228; celebrated on
  Sunday, 144; assistance at, 228
masturbation, 209
Maximilla, 237
medicinal punishment, 248
medicine, 34; Tertullian's knowledge
  of, 132, 183
mercy, 65, 81, 124, 203; parables of,
  169 ff., 217 ff.
merit, 17, 25, 81, 143, 159 f.
Messianic secret, 236
metonymy, 184, 227
midwives, 64
military language, 253
mines, 122, 293
minister, of penance, 290, see bishop
ministry of St. Peter, 286 f.
miracles, 232; of apostles, 119, 282; of
  St. Peter, 121; of Christ, 81, 123,
  215; prove power to forgive sins,
  124
Mithridates, 226
mixed metaphors, 256, 265
modesty, 189
monarchical episcopacy, 252
money-lenders, 122
monks, and power to absolve from sin,
  290
Montanism, 5, 12, 41, 46 f., 50, 52,
  148, 191, 203, 236, 244; prophets of,
  120, 296; martyrs of, 283, 296;
  concept of the Church, 122, 177,
  266, 287 f.; on episcopal powers,
  280 f.; teaching on second marriage,
  197; views on second penance, 202,
  204, 205, 221 f., 233, 268, 271, 275,
  278, 283, passim; and irremissible
  sins, 247, see adultery, capital sins
morality, determinants of, 191
moral law, 17, 144
mortal sins, 60, 115, 119, 203, 205, 213,
  281, see sins, distinction of
mortification, 34
Moses, 218
Muratorian Fragment, 234
murder, 43, 45, 48 ff., 61, 63 ff., 66, 84,
  85, 111, 114, 124, 200, 203, 210, 214,
  238, 241, 275, 297, see capital sins
mysteries, 138
mystery of faith, 109

mystical body of Christ, 33, 42, 177 f., 249
Mystici corporis Christi, 249

Naboth, 66
Nabuchadonezzer, 184
Natalius, 4
Nathan, 282
natural juridical order, 254
nature, 53 f.; as norm, 191
nave, 247
Neocaesarea, Council of, 178
neologisms, 8, 176
New Law, 66, 83, 104, 213, 239
Nicaea, Council of, 178
nicknames, given Christians, 295
Nicolaites, 110, 270
Ninivites, 80, 231
Noah, 247
Novatians, 203, 244, 245, 278, 281
numbers, in interpretation of Scripture, 75

oath, of God, 21, 151
oaths, attitude of Christians to, 151
obedience, 21, 150
obligation, divine law as foundation of, 144
office seekers, 35
Old Law, in relation to New, 84, 104, 213, 217, 239, 279; and condemnation of adultery, 62 ff.
ophthalmia, 246
oracles, of Montanists, 283
Orange, Second Council of, 143
ordination, rite of, 163, 266
original sin, 15, 37, 78, 141, 142, 155, 186, 214 f., 229, 260
Osee, 66
overpopulation of world, 262
oxymoron, 161

pagan(s), confused with heretics, 110; and Christian sinners, 68 ff.; 73 ff.; Jews avoid at table, 76; and ritual of Baptism, 160; and penance, 80; festivals, 219
pageants, executions combined with, 295
pantomime, 225

parables, 30 ff., 68 ff., 217, 223; theory of interpretation, 72 f., 75 f., 225; symbolism in, 77; tendentious interpretations of, 224
Paraclete, 83, 197; disgraced by digamists, 57; new revelations of, 41, 45, 120, 226, 236, 237, 240
paradise, 15, 37, 184, 187 f.
pardon, words used to describe, 132; effected by exomologesis, 178 f., 268 f.; granted to all sins, 20, 30 ff., 178 f.; purchased by penance, 17; the fruit of penance, 60, 82, 110, 210; and capital sins, 79, 89; granted sins against man, 121; granted by Church to all capital sins, 203; granted by Church to adultery, 54, 108, 297; not granted murder and apostasy, 212, 214, 230, 241, 297 f.; refused by Montanists, 60, 85; granted in next life, 61; allowed for lesser sins, 114; not granted by hierarchical Church, 122; not to be granted sins against God, 121; granted by God alone, 111, 123; granted by church of the Spirit, 122; *see* absolution, exomologesis, adultery, apostasy, murder, capital sins
parents, reverence for, 62
parousia, proximity of, 53, 191, 278 f.
Pasch, 250
passion of Christ, 83, 295
passions, 279
Passio SS. Perpet. et Fel., 157
Passio S. Pionii, 292, 295
Pastor Hermae, 4, 44, 51, 81, 115, 131, 156, 165, 278; regarded as inspired, 234
pathology, primitive ideas of, 279
patriarchs, polygamy of, 214
Paul, character of, 95; his severity, 91 ff.; a founder of churches, 95; his thorn, 88, 246; works miracles, 282; his personal purity, 98; attitude to marriage, 100 ff.; consistency of, 96, 102 ff.; refuses pardon to impurity, 85 ff., 90 ff., 95 ff., 105 f., 123, 241 ff., 263; excommunicates fornicators, 107; exceptions to his general practice, 106
Paula, 174

peace, with Church, 122, 198, *see* pardon, communion, forgiveness

pen, Paul chastises with, 92

penance, meaning of term, 132 f., 135; as virtue, 151, 158; early history of, 3; and mercy of God, 109; of heretics and infidels, 110; of pagans and Christians, 80; and excommunication, 292, *see* excommunication; necessity of, 59, 81, 111, 146, 158, *passim*; first and second, *see paenitentia prima, paenitentia secunda*; with and without pardon, 59; before and after Baptism, 109, 153; forms of, 109; baptism of, 141; personal and ecclesiastical, 161 f.; internal and external, 235; without pardon, 97; without ecclesiastical absolution, 204; sacrament of, 148 f., 181, 237, 276; second allowed but once, 163; proportioned by bishop to offense committed, 173; performed in church, 108, 165, *see* exomologesis; words used to describe effect of, 133; efficacious for all sins, 268; a remedy for sin, 80; fruit of, 81, 235; restores grace, 152; followed by ecclesiastical pardon, 108, 230, *see* absolution, forgiveness, pardon, penitence, public penance, ecclesiastical penance, private penance

penitence, definition of, 132, 135, 230; concept of, 139, 140 f., 146, *see* penance; as satisfaction for sin, 155 f., *see* satisfaction; of Adam, 187 f.; required of both body and soul, 18; merit of, 15; perseverance in, 25; obligation of, 82; of catechumens, 24 ff.; of the baptized, 27 ff.; before and after Baptism, 163; not exclusively internal, 163; ritual of, 133, *see* exomologesis, ecclesiastical penance; through excommunication, 223, *see* excommunication; includes ecclesiastical absolution, 194; prostituted by leniency, 59; excluded through severity, 59; and capital sins, 79, *see* capital sins; most deserving of pity, 65, 124 f.

pennies, 122

peremptory edict, nature of, 192

Pergamos, 30

persecution, flight during, 41

personal powers, of St. Peter, 120 f., 286, 288; of the apostles, 118 f.

Pescennius Niger, 226

Peter, St., 45, 119, 120 f., 277, 280, 282, 286 ff.; churches 'akin' to, 284 ff.; as 'founder' of Church, 286

petitions, made to martyrs, 122

Pharisees, 68, 75, 78

Pharaoh, 184

philosophers, attacks on, 138

philosophy, Tertullian's knowledge of, 132; strictures on, 138

Phygellus, 248

physicians, 122, 176; disease concealed from, 32

piety, 65

pillar, used in martyrdom, 122

plagues of Egypt, 36

planks of salvation, 36, 149 f., 168, 182, 186

platform, used in martyrdom, 294 f.

Platonism, 145

Plautian, 12

pledge, violation of, 114

poisoners, 64, 211

politicians, 12, 34

polygamy, 67, 214

Pompey, 76, 226

Pontifex Maximus, 54

pope, *ex cathedra* pronouncement of, 285

positive juridical order, 254

power of apostles, 118

power of keys, judicial nature of, 255; not exercised in Baptism, 287; personal to apostles, 286

prayer, 32, 58 f., 64

prescription, rule of, 226

president, of Christian community, 92, 119, 252, *see* bishop

presumption, of catechumens, 24 ff.

pride, 71

priest(s), 252; as physicians, 176; purifies leprosy, 116 ff.; role in Baptism, 118, 279; role in exomologesis, 32, 86, 174, 176; Montanists deny power to forgive sins, 122

primacy, of Roman church, 284 ff.
Priscilla, 237
prison, 122, 292
Pristinus, 292
private penance, 5, 193 f., 197, 201 f., 204, 220 ff., 269
prodigal son, 30, 72 ff., 170, 180, 224, 228
promised land, 74
prophets, function of, 141; powers of, 282; preach repentance, 15, 70, 218; power to forgive sins, 121; pardoned murder and adultery, 119; of Montanism, 41, 83, 120, 237, 283
propitiation, 298
prostitutes, 66, 83, 194
prostitution of Christian women, 189, 196
prostrations, in penance, 31, 64, 86, 108, 178
Psalms, 107
publicans, 68, 76, 78, 80
public office, 71, 183
public penance, 4, 31; sins subject to, 46; stages of, 165, 243; of women, 183; Church's role in, 184, see Church; as sacrament, 181 f.; as exomologesis, 172, 205, see exomologesis; distinguished from private penance, 201 f.; for private sins, 172 f., 176; for greater and lesser sins, 200; duration of, 173; its difficulty, 32; shame in, 32, 176; terminated by ecclesiastical absolution, 179 ff., see absolution; reconciles sinner to God, 186, see forgiveness; Montanist concept of, 43; as 'destruction of the flesh,' 245; not followed by pardon, 271
public penitents, enrollment with, 269
punishment, combined with theatrical pageants, 295
punishments, inflicted by apostles, 119
purgatory, 249, 298
purity, encomium on, 53; virtue of, 189; proper to Christians, 265; of Christian women, 55; according to Old and New Law, 65; endangered by the edictum peremptorium, 54; in relation to modesty, 189

questions, in ritual of Baptism, 78
quintuplets, 145
Quintus Apronius, 257

Rabbinic Literature, and capital sins, 210
real presence, of Christ in Eucharist, 230; see Eucharist
reason, as guide, 14; various senses of the word, 137 ff.
rebaptism, 247 f., 270
Rebecca, 74, 224
reconciliation to God, 166 f., 179 ff., 206, 268 f., 271, see pardon, forgiveness
redemption, 100, 109, 111, 123, 228, 267, 295
relapse into sin, 22 f.
remarriage, 262, see second marriage
remissible sins, see sins, distinction of
remission and retention, 85
repentance, meaning of term, 14, 132 f., 135; object of, 16 f.; its necessity, 21, 23, 141; its efficacy, 16, 20, 21, 24, 159, see paenitentia, conversion, penance, penitence; the pagan concept, 14 f.; the Christian concept, 15 ff.
restoration, of baptismal graces lost by sin, 233; see exomologesis, effects of
resurrection, of Christ, 216; of the flesh, 90, 145; of body and soul, 18
retention of sins, 59, 175, 202, 287
revelation, 83; through Montanist oracles, 283, see Paraclete
rigorism, in African churches, 190
ring, 77 f., 228, 229
ritual of penance, 133, 172, see exomologesis; includes imposition of hands, 107, 163, 266
Romanesque churches, 247
Roman Pontiff, 192
Rome, 161, 293; primacy of church, 284 ff.
rope of contention, 59
rope walkers, 232
rule of faith, 75, 225 f.

Sabbath, 62
sackcloth, 31, 34, 64, 86, 173 f., 183

sacrament(s), 77, 82, 96; of Baptism, 227, see baptism; of Eucharist, 234, 256, see Eucharist; of Penance, 148 f., 181, 237, 276; sacrament of Penance, necessity of, 204, see exomologesis; deprivation of, 253; valid and fruitful reception of, 162

sacred groves, 64

sacrifice, Eucharist as, 77, 228

sacrilege, 115

sailors, deacons compared to, 247

salvation, the fruit of penance, 15, 24, 34, 36, passim; see exomologesis, penance, forgiveness

Samaritan woman, 83

sanctions, 54

sanctify, 65

Sardians, 30

Satan, 'handed over to,' 87 ff., 245 f.; slavery to, 256; renounced in Baptism, 154, 162; imitates God, 284

satisfaction, 6, 23, 29, 31, 32, 77, 88, 133, 145, 155 f., 158 f., 160, 168, 170, 171, 173, 176, 182, 183, 227, 244

'savior,' as title of Christ, 198

scales, 76

scars, of martyrs, 125

schisms, 91

'schub,' meaning of, 149

Scripture, canon of, 82, 234; norms for interpreting, 72 f., 75 f., 106, 226, see exegesis, types, typology; the appeal to, 57 f., 106 ff., 200, 212, 284, passim; abuse of, 59, 102; a guardian of discipline, 115; secondary authorities in, 115; its apparent contradictions, 59; inspiration of, 110, 269

seal, of Baptism, 26, 77 f., 152, 161, 228, 229

Second Corinthians, subject of, 93 ff.

second Baptism, 297

'second death,' 111, 271

second marriage, 41, 57, 101, 197, 206, 261, 262

second martyrdom, 122

second penance, before 250 A.D., 131; remits sin coram Deo, 168, see pardon, forgiveness; nature of, see exomologesis; see paenitentia secunda

second regeneration, 230

secret marriage, 62

Sens, Council of, 286

Sensualists, 55, 81, 102, 106, 121, 194 f., 233; inconsistent policy in forgiving capital sins, 63, 64 f., 79, 112, 124, 212, 297

Septuagint, 184, 198, 210, 213, 224, 265

sermon form, in Tertullian's compositions, 9, 133

'set-off,' 239

seven capital sins, 275

sex, unnatural use of, 62

sexual intercourse, extramarital, 61 f.

Shakespeare, 225

shame, role in penitence, 32 f., 61, 176

sheep, 244

shepherd, represented on chalice, 234

Shepherd of Hermas, 4, 44, 51, 82, 115, 234

ship, symbol of Baptism, 149; symbol of Church, 89, 247

shipwreck, 36, 247; see planca salutis

Sidon, 81

signet ring, 228

Simon Magus, 232

sin(s), definition of, 17, 144; effects of, 33, 76 f.; an injury done to God, 183; as loss of grace, 152; as disease, 80, 176; leprosy, a type of, 116; the cause of death, 203, 205, 211, see mortal sin; as opus mortis, 164; involves contraction of debt, 155 f., see forgiveness, as commercial transaction; daily attack of, 114; committed knowingly and willingly, 80; examples of, 71; extenuating circumstances, 114, 125, 219, 274

distinction of, 6, 46 ff., 190, 196 f., 201, 206 f., 220 ff., 268 f., 274 f.; spiritual and corporeal, 18, 146; of thought and deed, 18; internal and external, 19, 66, 146 f., 208; greater and lesser, 56, 72, 86, 98, 109, 114, 190, 197; against God and against man, 58, 119, 121, 199 f., 257, 275, 281, 287; remissible and irremissible, 43, 45 ff., 59 f., 72, 89, 99, 109, 114, 115, 123, 148, 178 f., 190, 197, 201, 203, 210, 238, 278, 298; material and formal, 146; of thought and desire, 147; mortal and venial, 115, 197, 201, 222, 269, 273 f.; of pagans and Christians, 231 ff.; capital, list of, sin(s)—*contd.*

275, *see* capital sins, *peccata capitalia*; committed in ignorance, 22, 40, 72, 80, *see* ignorance; committed against God's temple, 114, 119; 'unto death,' 114 f., *see* 1 John 5.16; of compulsion, 114; committed against the body, 99 f.; after Baptism, 111

forgiveness of, 3, 29, 159, *see* absolution, forgiveness, pardon; effaced by Christ, 113; Christ dies for, 109, 111; forgiven by Christ, 124; Church's power to forgive, *see* Church; forgiven by church of the Spirit, 122; forgiven by bishop, 244, *see* bishop; not pardoned by martyrs, 122 ff.; not pardoned by hierarchical Church, 122; sorrow for, 133, *see* contrition; satisfaction for, *see* satisfaction; martyrs accused of, 293; of Adam, 15, *see* original sin; *see peccata aequalia, peccata gravia, peccata leviora, peccata mortalia,* etc.

sinners, remain members of the Church, 72; slaves of Satan, 155; corrected by Church, 201 f.; separated from the Church, *see* excommunication

slaves, 25, 160

slave girls, intercourse with, 118, 280

slavery, of sin, 77, 256

sodomites, 98

soldiers, 25, 80, 160, 253

Solomon, Proverbs of, 106

songs, interpreted by actors, 74

Sophists, 196

sorcerers, 64

sorites, 229

sorrow, for sins, 133

soul, nature of, 145; unity of, 135; united with body, 18, 144, 248; condition before Baptism, 142; of the Church, 249

speech, impurity in, 105

spelling, of *paenitentia*, 133

sperm, 68

spiritual relationship, of apostles with their churches, 285

stag, 36

stages of public penance, 243

stake, burning at, 123; martyrs nailed to, 294 f.; used in impalement, 246

Stoics, 138, 145, 147, 217, 218, 232

striking another, 114

substance, in relation to property, 138

Sunday, 144

swallow, 36

swallow-wort (celandine), 185

swearing, 114

swine, 77 f., 229

sword, 122

symbolism, in parables, 77; of Baptism, in blood and water, 124; in church architecture, 247; of leaven, 249 f.

'symbol of death,' 160

Sympronian, 163

synagogue, supplanted by Church, 224

synecdoche, 171 f., 194

Tabitha, 282

talent, weight of, 72, 223

Tatian, 187

taxation, of Jews, 226

teaching authority, of bishops, 119

tears, of penitents, 32, 64, 80, 183

teeth, care of, 183

temple, of God, 115, 194; of Jerusalem, 194; of Holy Spirit, 216; violation of, 257

temple of God, the just man as, 98, 114, 200, 281

temples of gods, 64

temporary excommunication, 108, 274

temptations, 28; daily, 114, 273

Tertullian,

character of, 148, 195; his voluntarism, 148; exaggerated asceticism, 41 f.; self-depreciation, 37, 160, 186; his learning, 7, 132; knowledge of Scripture, 42; knowledge of medicine, 132, 183; supposed anti-intellectualism, 138; position as catechist, 157; as preacher, 133; influenced by Stoicism, 217, 218; priesthood uncertain, 157; lapse into Montanism, 41, 52; cause of his defection, 157; inconsistency of, 42, 46, 55, 169, 179, 281, 288 f.; innovations as Montanist, 46, 50 f., 169, 179, 195, 283

his style, 6 ff., 191, 214, 279; his obscurity, 132, 158, 254, 261, 264, 293, 296; irony, 23, 26, 34, 54, 56,

Tertullian—*contd.*
81, 87, 119, 123, 192, 232, 242, 282;
use of military language, 253; legal
language, 139, 159, 175, 195, 198,
207, 217, 239, 250, 256, 262, 277;
attitude in controversy, 223, 292;
method of argumentation, 287;
fallacies in argument, 239, 259, 268,
278; arbitrary exegesis, 42, 239,
240 f., 248, 287, *passim*; word play,
137, 189, 216

changing attitude to capital sins,
178 f., 195, *see* above, inconsistency
of, and innovations as Montanist; on
ecclesiastical penance, 4 ff., 131,
passim; theory of exegesis, 263; his
primitive eschatology, 184 f., 249;
Mariology, 215; Montanist ecclesiology, 288 ff.; influence on St. Pacian,
163

purpose of treatise *De paenitentia*,
9; outline of contents, 9 ff.; theological importance, 3; principal problems of treatise, 11; its date, 12;
allows pardon to capital sins, 169,
179; contains no reference to
irremissible sins, 201; addressed to,
163

purpose of treatise *De pudicitia*, 42;
title of the work, 189; its character,
41; severity of, 197; outline of
contents, 42 ff.; principal problems
of the treatise, 46 ff.; date of composition, 51 f.; its occasion, 42;
contrasted with the *De paenitentia*, 5,
169, 190, 227, 212; the question of
innovation, 190; refuses pardon to
peccata capitalia, 169, 179, *passim*;
answers arguments used by opponents, 235; adversary in, 218, 282, *see*
author of the *edictum peremptorium*
testament, last will and, 85
Testaments, relation of Old and New,
209
theatre, 64, 71, 211, 219, 295
'thorn of the flesh,' 88, 246
threshold of Church, 62, 256, *see limen*
Thyatirenes, 30, 110, 270
titles, of Tertullian's treatises, 135
toll, exacted of Jews, 76
tooth powder, 34

torture, in martyrdom, 124 f.
tradition, 225 f.
traducianism, 215, 216
treachery, as capital sin, 275
Trent, Council of, 149
Trinity, 121, 288
truth, permanent law of, 65
types, in Scripture, 73 ff., 80, 116, 118,
194, 280; of Christ's cross, 216
typology, danger in, 74, 76
Tyre, 81
Tyrium, 183

unclean spirits, 77
unnatural vice, 43, 62, 209
Uriah, 66

Valentinus, 202, 226
venial sins, *see* sins, distinction of
vestibule, of church, 29, 165, 209
Vesuvius, 12, 185
virginity, of Mary, 215
virgins, wise and foolish, 296
visions, 154
visiting of martyrs, 292 f.
Vita Adae et Evae, 187
volcanoes, 35, 184
Vulgate, 198, 210, 212, 213, 216, 232,
238, 242, 246, 269, 297

water, from Christ's side, 124; sancti-
fication of, 216
wheel, torture on, 295
widowhood, 101, 261
widows, 86, 102, 207
will, freedom of, 143; its role in sin, 19,
125
wine, 34
Wisdom, identified with the *Verbum*,
138 f.
wives, of apostles, 252
woman, taken in adultery, 235 f.
women, penance of, 183; defilement of,
55
wood, used in chalices, 217
Word of God, 67
word play, 137, 189, 216
world, overpopulation of, 262; end of,
139, *see* parousia

xerophagies, 198

Zephyrinus, 48, 286

ANCIENT CHRISTIAN WRITERS

THE WORKS OF THE FATHERS IN TRANSLATION

Edited by

J. QUASTEN, S.T.D., and J. C. PLUMPE, PH.D.

1. THE EPISTLES OF ST. CLEMENT OF ROME AND ST. IGNATIUS OF ANTIOCH. Trans. by JAMES A. KLEIST, S.J., PH.D. Pages x + 162. 1946.
2. ST. AUGUSTINE, THE FIRST CATECHETICAL INSTRUCTION. Trans. by JOSEPH P. CHRISTOPHER, PH.D. Pages vi + 176. 1946.
3. ST. AUGUSTINE, FAITH, HOPE, AND CHARITY. Trans. by LOUIS A. ARAND, S.S., S.T.D. Pages vi + 165. 1947.
4. JULIANUS POMPERIUS, THE CONTEMPLATIVE LIFE. Trans. by SR. MARY JOSEPHINE SUELZER, PH.D. Pages vi + 220. 1947.
5. ST. AUGUSTINE, THE LORD'S SERMON ON THE MOUNT. Trans. by JOHN J. JEPSON, S.S., PH.D. Pages vi + 227. 1948.
6. THE DIDACHE, THE EPISTLE OF BARNABAS, THE EPISTLES AND THE MARTYRDOM OF ST. POLYCARP, THE FRAGMENTS OF PAPIAS, THE EPISTLE TO DIOGNETUS. Trans. by JAMES A. KLEIST, S.J., PH.D. Pages vi + 235. 1948.
7. ARNOBIUS, THE CASE AGAINST THE PAGANS, Vol. 1. Trans. by GEORGE E. McCRACKEN, PH.D. Pages vi + 372. 1949.
8. ARNOBIUS, THE CASE AGAINST THE PAGANS, Vol. 2. Trans. by GEORGE E. McCRACKEN, PH.D. Pages vi + 287. 1949.
9. ST. AUGUSTINE, THE GREATNESS OF THE SOUL, THE TEACHER. Trans. by JOSEPH M. COLLERAN, C.SS.R., PH.D. Pages vi + 255. 1950.
10. ST. ATHANASIUS, THE LIFE OF SAINT ANTONY. Trans. by ROBERT T. MEYERS, PH.D. Pages vi + 155. 1950.
11. ST. GREGORY THE GREAT, PASTORAL CARE. Trans. by HENRY DAVIS, S.J., B.A. Pages vi + 281. 1950.
12. ST. AUGUSTINE, AGAINST THE ACADEMICS. Trans. by JOHN J. O'MEARA, D.PHIL. Pages vi + 213. 1950.
13. TERTULLIAN, TREATISE ON MARRIAGE AND REMARRIAGE: TO HIS WIFE, AN EXHORTATION TO CHASTITY, MONOGAMY. Trans. by WILLIAM P. LE SAINT, S.J., S.T.D. Pages viii + 194. 1951.
14. ST. PROSPER OF AQUITAINE, THE CALL OF ALL NATIONS. Trans. by P. DE LETTER, S.J., S.T.D. Pages vi + 234. 1952.
15. ST. AUGUSTINE, SERMONS FOR CHRISTMAS AND EPIPHANY. Trans. by THOMAS C. LAWLER. Pages vi + 249. 1952.
16. ST. IRENAEUS, PROOF OF THE APOSTOLIC PREACHING. Trans. by JOSEPH P. SMITH, S.J. Pages viii + 233. 1952.
17. THE WORKS OF ST. PATRICK, ST. SECUNDINUS, HYMN ON ST. PATRICK. Trans. by LUDWIG BIELER, PH.D. Pages vi + 121. 1953.
18. ST. GREGORY OF NYSSA, THE LORD'S PRAYER, THE BEATITUDES. Trans. by HILDA C. GRAEF. Pages vi + 210. 1954.
19. ORIGEN, PRAYER, EXHORTATION TO MARTYRDOM. Trans. by JOHN J. O'MEARA, D.PHIL. Pages viii + 253. 1954.
20. RUFINUS, A COMMENTARY ON THE APOSTLES' CREED. Trans. by J. N. D. KELLY, D.D. Pages viii + 166. 1955.

[P.T.O.

21. ST. MAXIMUS THE CONFESSOR, THE ASCETIC LIFE, THE FOUR CEN-
TURIES ON CHARITY. Trans. by POLYCARP SHERWOOD, O.S.B., S.T.D.
Pages viii + 285. 1955.

22. ST. AUGUSTINE, THE PROBLEM OF FREE CHOICE. Trans. by DOM MARK
PONTIFEX. Pages vi + 291. 1955.

23. ATHENAGORAS, EMBASSY FOR THE CHRISTIANS, THE RESURREC-
TION OF THE DEAD. Trans. by JOSEPH H. CREHAN, S.J. Pages vi + 193. 1956.

24. TERTULLIAN, TREATISE AGAINST HERMOGENES. Trans. by J. H.
WASZINK. Pages vi + 178. 1956.

25. ST. CYPRIAN, THE LAPSED, THE UNITY OF THE CATHOLIC CHURCH.
Trans. by MAURICE BÉVENOT, S.J. Pages vi + 133. 1957.

26. ORIGEN, THE SONG OF SONGS: COMMENTARY AND HOMILIES.
Trans. by R. P. LAWSON. Pages vi + 385. 1957.

27. ST. METHODIUS, THE SYMPOSIUM, A TREATISE ON CHASTITY.
Trans. 1958. by HERBERT MUSURILLO S.J., D.Phil. (Oxon). Pages vi + 249. 1958.

28. TERTULLIAN, TREATISES ON PENANCE. Trans. by WILLIAM P. LE SAINT,
S.J., S.T.D. Pages vi + 330. 1959.

Reserve books taken out
overnight are due in the
library by 8:30 the next
morning.